Sweet Celebrations

The Art of Decorating Beautiful Cakes

SYLVIA WEINSTOCK with Kate Manchester

PHOTOGRAPHS BY ZEVA OELBAUM,
BEN WEINSTOCK, AND SARAH MERIENS

ILLUSTRATIONS BY MICHELE HICKEY

SIMON & SCHUSTER

SIMON & SCHUSTER
Rockefeller Center
1230 Avenue of the Americas
New York, NY 10020

Designed by Katy Riegel

Manufactured in the United States of America

1   3   5   7   9   10   8   6   4   2

Library of Congress Cataloging-in-Publication Data
Weinstock, Sylvia.
     Sweet celebrations : the art of decorating beautiful
cakes / Sylvia Weinstock, with Kate Manchester ;
photographs by Zeva Oelbaum, Ben Weinstock, and Sarah
     Meriens
          p.   cm.
Includes index.
     1. Cake decorating.   2. Cake.   3. Icing, Cake.
I. Manchester, Kate.   II. Title.
TX771.2.W45   1999
641.8'653—dc21   99–41805
                                                                              CIP
                 ISBN 0-684-84675-6

Acknowledgments

The output of my small shop is the result of a team effort. Although at the beginning everything was done solely by me and my husband, Ben, we now have a conglomeration of talent, with team members having their areas of expertise. There is an amazing lack of ego in this shop; everyone is focused on creating the best possible cakes. This results in discussion and inquiry among my artisans, who consult with each other in their concern for the perfection of the finished product. For my success and the creation of our cakes and this book, I express my thanks to my team: Bonnie Altholz, Anne Michele Andrews, Yolanda Anthony, Tina Eng Caban, Richard Harris, Michele Hickey, Lynn Lorenz, Cyleen Peters, Vilna Peters, Julie Quiles, Nora Soriano, and Ben.

The teamwork ethic is based on mutual respect for each other, and for the beautiful cakes they are dedicated to produce. This team has designed and produced many unique and exquisite cakes, each one as delicious to eat as it is beautiful to look at. Our cakes, large and small, are truly works of art. In this book I hope to show you how to create masterpieces of your own!

A tiered cake combines basketweave with sugar-dough flower garlands.

Contents

A sweet beehive.

Preface

I will show you how to make beautiful cakes that people will "ooh" and "aahh" over. It takes practice and artistic skills to create many of the cake designs I will share with you. You will need some special tools, time, and patience, but the results will be spectacular.

I have been in business for over twenty years. In that time I have, with the assistance of my able staff, created some wonderful cakes. When I first started creating specialty cakes, I worked by myself while my children were at school and my husband worked. Not only was it a real expression of love for the people for whom I was baking, but I got the added satisfaction of accolades from others. And that is essentially why you want to do your own cakes; not only do they show that you care, but you have taken the time to create a gorgeous presentation that you will never find in a bakery. Some of our cakes are so beautiful that they are placed on the table in lieu of flowers!

For the most part, I never remember what I ate for dinner or lunch on any given day, but I do remember a spectacular dessert. A cake that you spend time creating, not just a dessert but the centerpiece of the party, is unique. I think that's why I love doing specialty cakes so much. I hope you will, too.

"There is hardly anything in the world that some man cannot make a little worse and sell a little cheaper, and those people who consider price only are this man's lawful prey."

—John Ruskin

Cascades of bright flowers against white frosting.

Introduction

When we married in 1949, Ben and I were both students. He had returned to college from World War II in the Pacific, and I was working on getting a teaching degree. We were too poor to have a wedding reception and we didn't even have a wedding cake. I graduated and became an elementary school teacher, learning domestic skills while working full-time to support my husband through law school. When Ben became a lawyer, we moved to suburban Long Island, where Ben opened a law office. Although I taught in the local school district, I increasingly cherished the relief and relaxation that homemaking brought after the stress of days in the classroom. I found myself becoming more proficient as a cook and a baker, and such skills served me well when my daughter Ellen was born, followed thereafter by Amy and Janet.

As our daughters grew, Ben, who was an avid skier, taught the girls to ski with him. We found ourselves migrating almost every winter weekend to the Catskill Mountains where Ben and our daughters enjoyed their sport at

Hunter Mountain Ski Area. My birthday is in January, and as a surprise for one birthday, Ben bought me a fetching, fashionable ski outfit, skis, poles, boots, gloves, and a booklet of tickets for ten ski lessons with a professional instructor. With great trepidation (and Ben tagging along), I accompanied the instructor to the small slope where I was supposed to learn to ski. It looked like a precipitous mountain to me. With great courage, I turned to my husband, asserted myself, and said "Ben, I'm wise to you! You have a new cutie somewhere and you're just trying to kill me." I kicked off the skis, threw away the poles, and hiked down the slope to the lodge, where I spent the rest of the day while Ben and the girls skied. The next day, while they skied, I remained in our little house, cooking and baking, and my family relished the goodies lavished on them as the result of my not being a skier.

Because Hunter Mountain is the best ski area within a

Edible gold leaf was used to gild this elaborate cake.

reasonable distance of New York City, it is very popular with city ski enthusiasts. Among them are a substantial number of chefs from some of the city's best restaurants and hotels. When the kitchens close on Saturday night, these chefs drive up to Hunter, catch a few hours of sleep, and are on the slopes early on Sunday. Ben got to know many of the chefs on the ski slopes. One day I asked Ben to inquire of the chefs whether they could recommend how and where I could learn to advance from a good home cook and baker; I wanted to become a professional pastry chef. As luck would have it, one day on the mountain Ben asked André Soltner (then the chef/owner of Lutèce, one of New York's premier restaurants) where I could study to become a professional pastry chef. André told Ben that living in the village of Hunter was retired chef George Keller, who had worked in some of New York's best restaurants. George, with his wife Lisa, was operating a modest guest house in their home. André suggested that we approach him to see if he would take me on as a pupil.

Neither Ben nor I knew the Kellers, and our introduction to them was almost comical. Having learned of the location of the Kellers' guest house, Ben took me to meet them one morning. Ben knocked on the door, and it was opened by a short, rotund gentleman who spoke with a French accent. Ben said, "Monsieur Keller?" George said, "Oui." Ben said, "Professor, I want you to meet your pupil," pulling me forward from where I was hanging back in embarrassment. George said, "I do not want zee pupil!" Just about that time Lisa Keller came to the door and she and I began talking together while Ben continued to spar with George verbally about the benefits of taking me on as a pupil. Lisa Keller and I quickly took a liking to each other and soon it was three against one. His protestations that he could not get "zee butter, zee eggs, flour, shortening" were quickly fended off by our promises to bring all the needed materials with us from the city. Finally, with Lisa's and our persuasion, George agreed to take me on as a pupil.

Thereafter, when Ben and our girls went to ski, they would drop me off at the Kellers' guest house where I worked in the kitchen all day with George and Lisa. When Ben and the girls came off the mountain, they picked me up and took me home. George was a wonderful, talented teacher. I learned quickly from him, but because my daughters were always figure-conscious, they ate few of the goodies I was creating. I found an outlet for my productivity by supplying five restaurants in the Hunter/Windham area with desserts every weekend while my family enjoyed the skiing.

Sadly, I must report that wonderful George Keller passed away a few years ago. Lisa Keller and I remain the best of friends, and when Ben skis at Hunter Mountain these days, I visit with Lisa.

Time flew by and our three daughters completed college. They all obtained challenging jobs in New York, leaving Ben and me rattling around in our then too big house in suburbia. At that time, I was diagnosed with breast cancer, underwent a mastectomy, and was put on a course of chemotherapy, which required me to travel to New York City three times a week for treatment. The chemicals made me sick and nauseous, and I lost my hair. One funny aspect of the ailment and treatment was the assortment of glamorous and often comical wigs that Ben and my friends bought for me. I wore them, sometimes changing color and style several times during any given social occasion.

Ben found it depressing to see me traveling to the city for treatments and feeling sick and weak from the chemicals. He had been practicing law for twenty-eight years and suggested that it was time to retire and follow our daughters to the city. It was convenient for my medication, and we would also have the added benefit of seeing the girls more often. In 1980, Ben sold his law practice, we sold our house, and we moved into New York City.

Once there, I again got the benefit of Ben's relationships with chefs, because a number of them allowed me to come into their kitchens to work (without pay) with their pastry chefs to polish my culinary skills. It was not play, and I worked many long hours in pretty hot kitchens with some wonderful masters of the pastry arts. I am and will be forever grateful for everything they taught me.

By that time I was an accomplished baker, and at a social evening, I ran into an old friend, William Greenberg Jr., who owned four bake shops in Manhattan. He told me that he was frequently approached by customers who wanted grand, romantic, floral wedding cakes, but that he didn't do that sort of thing so he had to turn them down. William said that if I would learn to do such cakes he would refer them to me. Beyond that, he said that until I established an inspected, licensed facility in which to produce such cakes, I could use his premises after hours. Excited by the prospect, I enlisted William's help in finding a teacher from whom I could learn to make the sugar flowers with which to decorate cakes. (I would not and could not use real flowers to decorate, because many are poisonous and most flowers are fumigated and sprayed with insecticides.) With William's help, we found Betty Van Norstrand, who had magic hands. Betty created exquisite sugar-dough flowers, and she agreed to teach me the requisite skills.

Most cake decorators use icing, pastry tubes or bags, and a decorator tip to create icing flowers, as I did in my early years. This method simulates petals but they are too thick, and have no resemblance to real flowers. Sugar-dough flowers however, can be made botanically correct, with petals as thin as and the exact shape of real flowers. (Often they cannot be distinguished from real flowers.) With sugar-dough flowers, the cake can be exquisitely decorated and yet be completely edible, decorations and all. In order to make my flowers botanically correct, I would go to the florist and buy one single bloom of whatever flower I wanted to create. I'd take it home, study it, and then take it apart petal by petal to note the configuration and shape of each petal. On assembling each of my sugar-dough blossoms I created a flower almost indistinguishable from the real thing.

My real introduction as a professional creator of exquisite cakes came when my daughter Amy asked me to make a wedding cake for her friend who had a small takeout food shop on the West Side. Ben and I delivered her cake on Saturday afternoon; it was scheduled to be placed in the cooler for her Sunday wedding. The bride-to-be was so taken with her flower-laden cake that she put it in the display window of her shop. As luck would have it, one of the people passing by the shop was Lauren Berdy, who was chef for society caterer Donald Bruce White. Lauren came into the store and asked where the cake came from, and she and Donald started ordering several cakes every weekend. People who attended their catered receptions began to inquire about the cakes, and soon my cakes were showing up in some of New York's finest hotels. When the hotel banquet managers saw the cakes, they began to order directly from me, and my business literally blossomed.

I have had the good fortune of continuous help and support from my husband, Ben. Beyond his long, successful law practice, he is a carpenter, plumber, auto mechanic, cabinet maker, electrician, photographer, machinist, cake architect, tennis player, and skier. My cakes, however huge, never collapse, and it is Ben's design that is responsible. He also has the intuitive ability to recognize and highlight the innate talents of coworkers. A prime example of this is one of my mainstays, a young man named Richard Harris, who Ben says is so capable that he can do everything, thus freeing Ben for more tennis and skiing! With the help of Ben and Richard in planning and creating structural support, my cakes have been successfully flown, fully decorated, all over the world from Japan to Saudi Arabia and all points in between. My only restriction in air-shipping cakes is that there must be a nonstop flight from New York to the destination.

My business is a custom shop that has no walk-in customers; we create only cakes that have been ordered in advance. Customers come to our office, where they view pages of cake photographs to determine the style of cake they prefer. I always seek client input because the occasion for which they are ordering a cake is so important and personal to them. This way they get exactly what

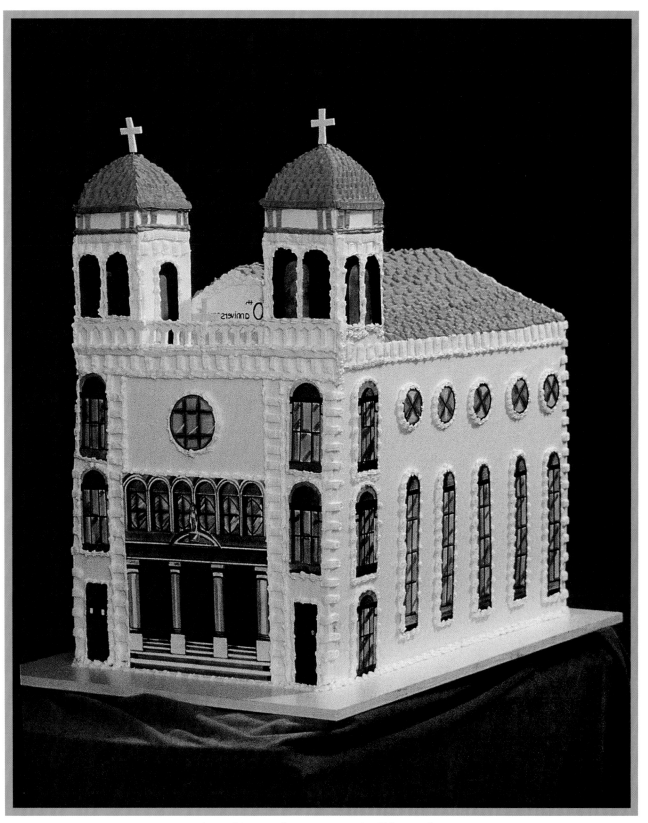

An architecturally accurate and edible creation.

A fantasy of white feathers and flowers.

they picture, whether it is a color or type of flower, or even the reproduction in sugar or marzipan of an object, pet, or person they want to feature. Although the majority of our cake orders are for weddings, we regularly create cakes for corporate functions and occasions, reproducing logos, letterheads, themes, buildings, or whatever else the customer wants and needs for a planned reception.

My personal rule that I do not duplicate cakes has had some exceptions, primarily for TV soap operas. When I have been asked to supply bridal cakes for such shows, we have had to make duplicates, because often a scene including the cake will be shot over a period of several days, or even weeks. In order to preserve the continuity of a scene (which in its final form may take only a few minutes of TV time), the cake must appear to be unchanged.

One memorable incident in one of the soaps involved a woman with a murderous grudge against the bride. During the ceremony, she sneaks into the reception room where the cake is on display. The villainous character plants a bomb in the cake, intending that it explode and kill the bride and groom when they made the ceremonial cutting of the cake. Because the explosion had to have exactly the dramatic effect intended, the studio ordered *nine* identical cakes. They blew up six of the cakes to make sure the scene was precisely as they wanted it. Then the script called for the cake not to explode when the bride cut it, but after the reception, killing a guest who threw himself over the fiancé to protect her. I phoned the prop man to complain that the death of the fiancé cheated me of *their* potential wedding cake order!

Another interesting TV cake incident involved an older man from Texas who was about to be married to a beautiful young woman. In the script, he insisted that he wanted a "Texas-size cake." The outside prop man described his problem, and we devised a creation that consisted of three segments, the first of which was a three-tier cake with columns between the tiers. In the taped scene, this cake was presented to Mr. Texas, who rejected it as not being a "Texas-size cake." We then placed the next segment beneath the first three-tier section so that the cake was five tiers high. This, of course, was also rejected by Mr. Texas in the scene as not being a "Texas-size cake." We then placed the third segment beneath the first two, so that the cake was eight tiers high and stood about six feet above the table, with the cake top almost nine feet above the floor. His comment was, "Now *that's* a Texas-size cake."

Even though my shop is small, the complexities of business life require technical know-how and record-keeping. I have the good fortune to employ the talents of my daughter, Janet Reilly, an MBA refugee from the corporate world. Working in the shop allows Janet more time with her two small children while they are young, and she still keeps her fingers on the intricacies of business practices by helping her mother wend her way through the computer world. Janet has benefited from the more-than-able assistance of her alter ego, Maryanne Lyden, upon whom we are both greatly dependent.

I also enjoy the benefit of the business of my daughter Ellen Weldon, who is the best and most talented calligrapher in the world. She creates exquisite invitations, announcements, scrolls, place cards, menus, and personal stationery. She works in every script and style. Her taste is legendary and her knowledge of the socially correct way to do things is outstanding. I always refer my cake customers to Ellen, and she in turn refers her customers to me.

As absurd as it may seem, I have to thank a talkative New York city taxi driver who engaged me in a conversation about my business. He asked me what I did, and I told him I baked specialty cakes. He asked if I ever needed help, because he had a niece who had just come to New York to live. Because he was so friendly, I gave him my card, telling him to have his niece call me. She didn't telephone, but instead showed up at my office a few days later, and has been working in our shop for fifteen years now! Vilna Peters has magic fingers, and after I taught her how to make flowers, she became an important cog in the wheel of my business. She has great taste, the flowers she makes are botanically correct, and the cakes she decorates are beautiful. I think Vilna and I will grow old together, although I have a head start on her! I believe that if you're a good teacher, your students should surpass you, and everyone who works in this shop has proved that.

I am particularly grateful to a real artist, Michele Hickey, who did the illustrations for this book and with whom it is my pleasure to work on a day-to-day basis. She has real talent and ability, and with her golden hands she crafts enchanting figurines out of marzipan and sugar dough. Her many creations adorn my cakes, and her decorator's eye is unsurpassed. Working with her has been a real blessing to me.

Another gem with whom it has been my pleasure to work with is Ann Michele Andrews. Ann has great food integrity and knowledge, coupled with tireless dedication to creating a product that is as beautiful to taste as it is to look at. She is a tireless worker whose smiling countenance is an inspiration at the end of a long and tiring day's work.

One thing that contributes to my ability to establish rapport with people is an outgrowth of my bout with breast cancer in 1980. Although I still carry the scars of my mastectomy, I was and still am philosophical about my encounter with cancer. I believe too many women become aware of possible problems and then hide from them in the hope that they will disappear. That attitude can be fatal, and I try to do everything I can to awaken women to that fact. I am a regular contributor to breast cancer research, and as a survivor for almost twenty years, I still get calls from my wonderful oncologist, Ezra Greenspan, M.D., who asks me to do a lot of verbal hand-holding for some of his frightened patients. My experience reinforced my positive outlook on life, and I try my best to help others.

Basic Guidance

EQUIPMENT

Folllowing are listed items that you will need to get started. Some are very simple, and you may already have them on hand; some you can order through the mail or find in a well-stocked kitchen store. The standing electric mixer is a wonderful investment; it proves its worth when you have a buttercream that needs to be beaten for twenty-five minutes or more, because it frees you to do other things. Most mixers come with one $4\frac{1}{2}$-quart bowl, but I strongly suggest that you get yourself two bowls. The standing mixer is something you cannot live without. I would also not be without a turntable. Once your cake is baked, you will use the turntable for every subsequent step, from slicing and trimming to filling, icing, and decorating; it will cut your decorating time in half. It's another key piece of equipment that will make these cakes infinitely easier, and I don't recommend doing a cake without one.

Standing electric mixer with dough hook and
  whip attachments
Two 4½-quart beater mixing bowls
Handheld electric mixer
Set of graduated mixing bowls
Citrus zester
Wire whisks
Measuring spoons
Sifter
14-inch serrated knife
Turntable
Small offset spatula
Icing blade
Rubber spatulas
Pastry bags and couplings
Set of pastry decorating tips

Vegetable paste colors
Vegetable gel colors
Petal dust or vegetable powder colors
Paint or pastry brushes
Baking parchment or wax paper
6-inch, 8-inch, 10-inch, and 12-inch round and
  square cake cardboards
Plastic drinking straws
12-inch bamboo skewers
Swivel-blade utility knife
Candy thermometer
Baking pans (2 of each size):
  6 × 3-inch round and square
  8 × 3-inch round and square (at least 2)
  10 × 3-inch round and square
  12 × 3-inch round and square

RESOURCE GUIDE

Bridge Kitchenware
214 East 52nd Street
New York, NY 10022
(212) 838-6746

Broadway Panhandler
477 Broome Street
New York, NY 10013
(212) 966-3434

Creative Cutters
561 Edward Avenue, Units 1 & 2
Richmond Hill, Ontario
Canada L4C 9W6
(905) 883-5638

Kerekes Bakery & Restaurant Equipment, Inc.
6103 15th Avenue
Brooklyn, NY 11219
(800) 525-5556
Fax (718) 232-4416

New York Cake and Baking Distributors, Inc.
56 West 22nd Street
New York, NY 10026
(212) 675-2253

Pfeil & Holing
58-15 Northern Boulevard
Woodside, NY 11377
(800) 247-7955

J. B. Prince Company
29 West 38th Street
New York, NY 10018
(212) 302-8611

ABOUT CAKES

One of the reasons for my success is that I take no short-cuts. All of my cakes are made with only the freshest and finest available ingredients. If you want something to be the best, you must start with the best materials available. I believe that people are willing to pay for a quality product, and that is what they get from me. The flowers for a big cake can be made several weeks in advance, but the cakes are never baked, filled, and iced more than one or two days before an event. My customers always get a fresh, tender, and delicious cake. I understand that for the home baker, it may be unreasonable to bake, fill, and decorate cakes in just two days, but I don't recommend baking the cake more than three days prior to an event. Some layer cakes have a better shelf life than others. A carrot cake, nut cake, or chocolate cake can hold several days without noticeable deterioration, but a sponge or yellow cake should be as freshly made as possible.

People often ask what kind of cake mix we use for our cakes. The answer is, of course, that we do not use mixes. All of the cake recipes are classics. I don't use cake mixes

Pretty in pink.

The King and Queen of Hearts preside over Alice's tea party.

because I don't like the taste, and I prefer a cake without preservatives. One also can control the flavor when a cake is baked from scratch. In the end the difference in taste will be noticeable. I haven't created any "new" recipes; all of the cakes in this book are from recipes that I have been using for years, some of which were given to me by George Keller and other pastry professionals who taught me, but most of the time I have no idea where they came from. We have fiddled with them, modified and fine-tuned them, and I am passing them on to you.

The structure of the cake is very important. You will be working with cakes that have tiers and decorations, so the cake must hold up. You cannot put tiers of cake and icing and decorations on a delicate angel food cake; it simply will not hold the weight of fillings and flowers. You can fill your cake with mousse or whipped cream, but you must use a cake that is sturdy enough to hold its shape and the added weight. Over the years I have determined which cakes work best for which structures, and the recipes I give here will work well for all of the cakes I discuss. Remember that the cake is part of the palette of the feast, and that it should not overwhelm the meal but complement it. Certain foods and certain flavors marry well, and I have given suggestions for which washes and fillings go well with each cake.

Read the recipes from beginning to end before starting, have all the equipment and ingredients out and ready, and use this book as a creative guide. Look at the photographs, and then use your imagination to make each cake uniquely yours.

A few very simple tricks will assure a successful cake. First, it's very important to sift the flour. Flour tends to settle and get heavy; sifting will aerate and lighten it and get rid of any lumps, making a lighter cake. I always use the freshest extra-large eggs I can find. Eggs should be cold, because they separate more easily, and butter should always be at room temperature. I always use sweet butter in my cakes; salt is added to butter as a preservative and therefore sweet butter tends to be fresher. Also, I want to be able to control the amount of salt I use in the cake.

Baking is not stovetop cooking. You can be creative with a pot of sauce, but baking is chemistry. There is a balance and a relationship to the proportions of eggs, baking powder, salt, and other ingredients. Measure, do not improvise. You can play with flavoring washes and fillings, you can play with design, but following the recipes exactly will yield the best results.

I recommend that you butter your cake pans and line them with parchment. This ensures that cakes will come out of the pans evenly, not in ragged sections. Buttering the pan(s) will produce nicely browned, moist cakes. Always preheat the oven. Always fill the prepared pans ¾ full. Place the pans in the center of the oven to assure even heat.

Test with a wooden skewer; the cake is done if the skewer emerges dry. The cake in its pan should be removed from the oven and placed on a wire rack to cool. Only when the cake has cooled to room temperature should it be removed from its pan. To remove the cake from its pan, insert a thin knife along the edge of the pan and run it around the cake. Then invert the pan and the cake should slip out. If the cake does not slip out easily, place the pan bottom over very low heat on the stove for a few seconds to warm the butter in the cake just enough to get it to slip out of the pan when the pan is inverted. Once out of the pan, the cake, on a cake cardboard, should again be placed on the wire rack to completely cool so it will be ready to be trimmed and sliced.

Trimming, slicing, filling, icing, and decorating are functions that make a turntable essential. You should also have on hand a supply of various-sized cake cardboards.

As the result of the baking process, cakes usually mound up on top. This mound must be sliced off to get a flat-topped cake that can then be sliced into discs about one-half inch thick that will make up the filled cake. I usually discard the bottom slice that was next to the pan bottom, because it tends to have a browned crust.

With the cooled cake on a cardboard cake board, place on the turntable. Using a long, sharp, serrated knife, mark the cake horizontally at ½-inch intervals. A cake baked in an 8 × 3-inch pan will usually yield three to four segments, depending on which cake you have used—some bake higher than others. Hold the knife against the cake and parallel to the base of the turntable, and turn the turntable while keeping the knife at arm level. As you spin the turntable, apply a subtle but firm inward pressure, allowing the knife to go deeper to cut through the cake; this is the first slice. Now take a long icing spatula and lift the edge of the cake slice slightly. Slide a cardboard cake base under the first (top) slice, and remove. Repeat at the next 1/2-inch mark. Repeat until you have sliced the whole cake. Very often the cake will yield four or even five slices. Use cake cardboard to support your cake slices until you are ready to assemble the cake layers. If you have cake slices left, you can always wrap them tightly, date them, and freeze them for up to one month.

It is important that the cake slices be completely cooled before you attempt to fill them, otherwise the filling will soften, melt, and make a mess, with the slices sliding out of alignment and oozing filling.

Only the first cake layer will remain on a cardboard and will sit on a platter or wooden cake base. Once you have put filling on the first cake slice, use a long spatula to ease the remaining cake slices off their cardboard and onto the filling below

If you are baking the cake ahead of time, after you have trimmed and sliced it you can plastic-wrap the slices on their cardboards and freeze them until you are ready to fill and decorate the cake.

When you are ready to fill the cake, place the first cake disc, on its cardboard, on the turntable. Assuming that you have prepared your filling with the mixer and that it is soft and workable, using a plastic spatula fill a pastry bag that you have equipped with a #789 tip and squeeze out a bead of filling in a close spiral, starting at the outer edge of the cake disc and winding inward to the center. The same principle applies to a square cake, where the spiral has square corners. When you have covered the cake disc with a spiral of filling, smooth and level the filling using a larger metal spatula so that it is even, and then place the next cake disc on top and repeat the process until the entire cake is filled. Don't apply filling on top of the uppermost slice, because that is where icing will be applied.

Using your large metal spatula, holding it vertically against the side of the cake as you rotate it on the turntable, you can smooth out any filling that may squeeze out between the cake disc slices. The filled cake should be refrigerated to chill and harden the filling so that the cake discs will not slide out of alignment.

It is preferable to do a crumb coat before the final icing (see box below).

When you are ready to begin icing, fill a clean pastry bag with buttercream icing and attach a #789 icing tip. Place the cake on the turntable and apply the icing to the stacked cake, icing the sides of the cake first, then the top. Smooth the icing with a blade or an icing spatula. Remember that the icing should be at room temper-

CRUMB COATING

As the first step for icing, I always apply a crumb coat to the cake. Using a pastry bag filled with icing and equipped with a wide basketweave tip, I apply a thin layer of icing to the sides and top of the filled cake and smooth it out with a large metal spatula, so that it seals the cake and keeps crumbs from surfacing in the final icing. The crumb-coated cake should be refrigerated to cool and harden the crumb coat. Once the crumb coat has hardened, return the cake to the turntable and apply the final coat of icing.

ature. If it is too cold, it will be very difficult to spread; too warm and it could slide off the cake. Do not be discouraged; practice is the name of the game.

In various sections of this book, I have defined and given formulas for the various ingredients and terms to which I have already referred and which I may mention hereafter in giving hints about formulas for icings, fillings, washes, and other ingredients for wonderful cakes. Please make reference to all parts of this book so that all aspects of making wonderful cakes are clear to you.

My listing of equipment and ingredients for each cake may seem repetitive, but it is intended to make it easier for you to assemble the tools you need.

An architectural fantasy and its support structure.

You can get incredible detail with buttercream and sugar dough.

Basic Cake Recipes

Classic Yellow Cake

The name says it all. This is the only yellow cake recipe you will ever need. Many people don't like chocolate or nuts, but everybody loves this buttery cake.

EQUIPMENT

Measuring cups
Measuring spoons
Flour sifter
Standing electric mixer
One set beaters
Two 4¹/₂-quart mixing bowls
Two small bowls
Rubber spatula
Parchment
Two 8 × 3-inch baking pans or one 12 × 3-inch round or square pan

INGREDIENTS

2¹/₄ cups sifted cake flour
2 teaspoons baking powder
¹/₂ teaspoon salt
¹/₂ pound (2 sticks) sweet butter, at room temperature
2 cups sugar
4 large egg yolks
2 teaspoons vanilla
1 cup sour cream
4 large egg whites

1. Preheat the oven to 350 degrees. Butter and line the baking pans with parchment.
2. Sift together the flour, baking powder, and salt. Set aside.
3. Cream the butter in a large bowl with an electric mixer until fluffy and light in color, about 2 minutes on medium speed. Add the sugar and continue to mix until fluffy and light.
4. Add the egg yolks, one at a time, being sure each is well incorporated before adding the next one. Add the vanilla.
5. Reduce the mixer speed to low and add the dry ingredients alternately with the sour cream, beginning and ending with the flour. Be sure the mixture is completely blended after each addition. Scrape the sides of the bowl, and beat for 1 minute.

6. In a separate bowl, with clean beaters, beat the egg whites to soft peaks. Gently fold the whipped egg whites into the batter with a rubber spatula.

7. Pour the batter into the prepared pans and smooth with a rubber spatula. Bake in the preheated oven, 60 minutes for the 12-inch square pan, or 45 to 50 minutes for the 8-inch pan. The top of the cake should be nicely browned. Test for doneness with a skewer or a toothpick—the tester should come out dry and clean.

SUGGESTED WASH FLAVORS (page 38)
Raspberry
Strawberry
Lemon
Orange

SUGGESTED FILLINGS:
Raspberry (or strawberry) Buttercream Filling (page 33)
Lemon or Orange Buttercream Filling (page 33)
Mocha Buttercream Filling (page 33)
Chocolate Mousse Filling (page 35)

Lady Baltimore White Cake

A delicious and beautiful white cake.

EQUIPMENT

Measuring cups
Measuring spoons
Flour sifter
Standing electric mixer
Two 4¹/₂-quart mixing bowls
One small bowl
Rubber spatulas
Parchment
Two 8 × 3-inch baking pans or one 12 × 3-inch round or square pan

INGREDIENTS

³/₄ cup (1 ¹/₂ sticks) unsalted butter
2 cups sugar
3 cups sifted cake flour
3 tablespoons baking powder
¹/₂ teaspoon salt
¹/₂ cup milk
1 teaspoon vanilla
6 large egg whites

1. Preheat the oven to 350 degrees. Butter and line the baking pans with parchment.
2. Place the butter and sugar in a large standing mixer bowl and beat at medium speed until light and fluffy.
3. Sift the dry ingredients together; set aside.
4. Combine ¹/₂ cup water, the milk, and vanilla. Add to the sugar and butter mixture alternately with the flour mixture, beating until smooth after each addition.
5. In the second 4¹/₂-quart mixing bowl, using a clean whisk attachment, beat the egg whites on high until soft peaks form.
6. Using a large rubber spatula, fold the whipped egg whites into the batter. Stop as soon as the mixture is incorporated.
7. Pour the batter into the prepared pans and place the pans in the center of the oven. Bake for 30 to 40 minutes in an 8-inch pan, or 40 to 50 minutes in a 12-inch pan. The top of the cake should be nicely browned on top and a toothpick inserted in the center comes out clean.

SUGGESTED WASH FLAVORS *(page 38)*

Orange
Lemon
Raspberry or strawberry
Hazelnut

SUGGESTED FILLINGS:

Orange Buttercream Filling (page 33)
Raspberry (or strawberry) Buttercream Filling (page 33)
Mocha Buttercream Filling (page 33)
Chocolate Mousse Filling (page 35)

Spice Cake

Try this lovely, light, tasty cake. I would use it for a wedding cake, perhaps for a summer luncheon wedding. It is versatile, and if you fill it with a delicious lemon-lime filling or an apricot praline cream, you will have a winner!

EQUIPMENT

Flour sifter

Measuring cups

Measuring spoons

Standing electric mixer

Two 4¹/₂-quart mixing bowls

Wire whisk

One small bowl

Rubber spatula

Parchment

Two 8 × 3-inch baking pans or one 12 × 3-inch
    round or square pan

INGREDIENTS

2¹/₂ cups sifted cake flour

¹/₂ tablespoon unsweetened cocoa powder

¹/₄ teaspoon baking soda

1 teaspoon baking powder

¹/₂ teaspoon cloves

¹/₂ teaspoon allspice

1 teaspoon cinnamon

3 large eggs

1 cup milk

¹/₄ pound (1 stick) unsalted butter

2 cups sugar

1. Preheat the oven to 325 degrees. Butter the pans and line them with parchment.

2. Sift the flour, cocoa, baking soda, baking powder, and spices into a large mixing bowl. In a small bowl, combine the eggs and the milk.

3. In the bowl of a standing mixer, cream the butter and sugar until light and fluffy.

4. Add ¹/₃ of the dry ingredients to the butter mixture, then ¹/₃ of the egg mixture, and mix on low speed until completely incorporated. Continue adding the dry and wet ingredients alternately, mixing until the batter is smooth and lump-free.

5. Pour the batter into the prepared pans and place the pans in the center of the oven. Bake for 40 to 50 minutes in an 8-inch pan, or 50 to 60 minutes in a 12-inch pan, or until the sides of the cake pull away from the pan and a toothpick inserted in the center comes out clean.

SUGGESTED WASH FLAVORS (page 38)

Raspberry

Strawberry

Orange

Apricot

SUGGESTED FILLINGS:

Raspberry (or strawberry) Buttercream Filling (page 33)

Orange Buttercream Filling (page 33)

Mocha Buttercream Filling (page 33)

Chocolate Mousse Filling (page 35)

Chocolate Fudge Cake

This is delicious, and will stay wonderfully fresh and moist for up to 6 days. The key to this cake is the double hit of chocolate, a cocoa-powder fudge, and additional melted chocolate. This cake will bake at 300 degrees for a long time—it is dense and requires a slower oven. Make sure the fudge mixture is at room temperature before you add it to the rest of the recipe.

EQUIPMENT

Measuring cups
Measuring spoons
Flour sifter
One 4½-quart mixing bowl
Beater attachment
Wire whisk
Small saucepan
One small bowl
Rubber spatula
Parchment
Two 8 × 3-inch baking pans or one 12 × 3-inch
    round or square pan

INGREDIENTS

¼ cup vanilla
⅔ cup water
¾ cup unsweetened cocoa powder
1 pound sweet butter, at room temperature
2⅓ cups sugar
12 large eggs
11½ ounces unsweetened chocolate, melted
2½ cups cake flour
1 tablespoon baking soda

1. Preheat the oven to 300 degrees. Butter the baking pans and line them with parchment.
2. In a small saucepan, bring the water to a boil. Pour the boiling water into a bowl and add the cocoa powder and the vanilla, whisking vigorously until the mixture is smooth and no lumps remain. Set aside and let mixture cool to room temperature.
3. In a standing mixer, cream the butter on medium speed for 3 minutes. Add sugar and mix for another 3 minutes, or until the batter is light in color and fluffy. Add the eggs, one at a time. Stop the mixer and scrape down the sides with a rubber spatula.
4. Add the melted chocolate and mix on medium speed for 1 minute, until all the chocolate is incorporated.
5. Sift the flour and baking soda together. Reduce the mixer speed to low, and alternate adding the flour and the cocoa mixtures. Pour into the prepared pans.
6. Bake an 8-inch cake for 60 to 70 minutes at 300 degrees; a 12-inch cake may take two hours. This cake is dense and bakes more evenly in a slow oven. Test for doneness with a skewer inserted in the center of the cake—it should come out clean.

(continued)

SUGGESTED WASH FLAVORS (page 38)
Raspberry
Strawberry
Orange
Hazelnut
Coffee

SUGGESTED FILLINGS:
Raspberry (or Strawberry) Buttercream Filling
  (page 33)
Orange Buttercream Filling (page 33)
Basic Buttercream Filling (page 31)
Mocha Buttercream Filling (page 33)
Chocolate Mousse Filling (page 35)

Carrot Cake

For a carrot cake, I wouldn't ever stray too far from a cream cheese buttercream filling. If I add nuts to the cake, very often I will use a nutty liqueur to flavor the wash, but an orange-flavored liqueur works well too. You can also add raisins or dried cranberries or cherries to the cake, or consider walnuts or pistachios.

EQUIPMENT
Measuring cups
Measuring spoons
Flour sifter
Standing electric mixer
Food processor with a grating attachment or
   hand grater
Two 4½-quart mixing bowls
One small bowl
Rubber spatula
Parchment
Two 8 × 3-inch baking pans or one 12 × 3-inch
   round or square pan

INGREDIENTS
2¼ cups sugar
4⅔ cups sifted cake flour
1½ teaspoons baking powder
1½ teaspoons baking soda
½ teaspoon salt
2 teaspoons cinnamon
1 teaspoon ginger
⅛ teaspoon allspice
1¾ cups vegetable oil
6 large eggs
3 cups grated carrots (grate as if for cole slaw)

1. Preheat the oven to 350 degrees. Butter the baking pans and line them with parchment.
2. Combine the sugar, flour, baking powder, baking

soda, salt, and spices in the bowl of a standing mixer. Set on low speed and slowly pour the vegetable oil into the dry ingredients. After all the oil is added and blended in, add the eggs, one at a time. When the eggs are fully incorporated, add the carrots and continue to blend just until they are evenly mixed into the batter. Stop the mixer and scrape down the sides with a rubber spatula, then continue to beat on low for another 30 seconds.

3. Pour the batter into the prepared pans and place the pans in the center of the oven. Bake for 40 to 50 minutes in an 8-inch pan, or 50 to 60 minutes in a 12-inch pan, or until the sides of the cake pull away from the pan and a toothpick inserted in the center comes out clean.

SUGGESTED WASH FLAVORS (page 38)
Orange
Hazelnut
Coffee

SUGGESTED FILLINGS:
Orange Cream Cheese Buttercream Filling (page 33)
Cream Cheese Buttercream Filling (page 32)

Almond Cake

Almond flour can be made by grinding skinned almonds in a food processor. The trick (as always when grinding nuts for flour) is to watch carefully and stop processing when the nuts are ground to a fine flour texture but before they turn to paste. See the Hazelnut Cake recipe (page 24) for tips on folding wet ingredients into dry ingredients.

EQUIPMENT
Food processor
Measuring cups
Measuring spoons
Two 4^{1}/$_{2}$-quart mixing bowls
Beater attachment
Whip attachment
One medium bowl
Rubber spatula
Parchment
Two 8 × 3-inch baking pans or one 12 × 3-inch
   round or square pan

INGREDIENTS
10 large egg yolks
1^{3}/$_{4}$ cups sugar
2^{1}/$_{2}$ tablespoons almond extract
5 cups sliced, skinned almonds, ground to make 4
   cups almond flour
^{1}/$_{3}$ cup sifted cake flour
10 large egg whites

1. Preheat the oven to 350 degrees. Butter the baking pans and line them with parchment.
2. In a large standing mixer bowl, combine the egg yolks, 1¼ cups of the sugar (reserve ½ cup of sugar for egg whites), and almond extract. Using the beater attachment, mix on medium until the pale yellow ribbon stage, about ten minutes.
3. Sift the cake flour, then fold the almond flour into the flour with a rubber spatula. Reduce the mixer speed to low and add one-third of the flour mixture into the yolk mixture. Add the next third and incorporate well before adding the rest.
4. In another standing mixer bowl using the whip attachment, whip the egg whites on high until they begin to foam. Add ½ cup sugar and beat on high until soft peaks form.
5. Using a large rubber spatula, fold a quarter of the whipped egg whites into the yolk mixture. Gently fold in with the spatula, then add the rest of the whites and fold in. Stop as soon as the mixture is incorporated.
6. Pour the batter into the prepared pans and place the pans in the center of the oven. Bake for 40 minutes, or until the cake is nicely browned on top and a toothpick inserted in the center comes out clean. As this cake cools, it will shrink in the pans.

SUGGESTED WASH FLAVORS (page 38)
Orange
Hazelnut

SUGGESTED FILLINGS:
Mocha Buttercream Filling (page 33)
Chocolate Mousse Filling (page 35)

Hazelnut Cake

For this cake you will need hazelnut flour, which is nothing more than skinned hazelnuts ground in the food processor. Be careful not to overprocess the hazelnuts or you will have hazelnut butter.

Here the dry ingredients are folded into the beaten yolks; then this mixture is folded into the beaten egg whites. You will need a large rubber spatula and a large mixing bowl. To fold one ingredient into another, hold the spatula against the side of the bowl and push it down into the center of the bowl and up one side. Rotate the bowl and repeat this motion, rotating and repeating until your ingredients are combined. When folding the dry ingredients into the egg yolks, be careful not to overmix; you want to retain the airiness of the eggs. The mixture will not be smooth at first.

EQUIPMENT

Food processor
Measuring cups
Measuring spoons
Standing electric mixer
Two 4¹/₂-quart mixing bowls
Wire whisk
One medium bowl
Rubber spatulas
Parchment
Two 8 × 3-inch baking pans or one 12 × 3-inch
   round or square pan

INGREDIENTS

10 large egg yolks
1³/₄ cups sugar
5 tablespoons vanilla extract
2¹/₂ tablespoons almond extract
¹/₃ cup sifted cake flour
¹/₃ cup unsweetened cocoa powder
8 cups whole skinned hazelnuts to make 4 cups
   hazelnut flour
10 large egg whites

1. Preheat the oven to 350 degrees. Butter the baking pans and line them with parchment.
2. Beat the egg yolks in the large bowl of an electric mixer until they reach the pale yellow ribbon stage. Add 1¹/₄ cups of the sugar and the vanilla and almond extracts and beat on high until light and airy. Set aside.
3. Combine the cake flour, cocoa, and hazelnut flour and mix with a rubber spatula. Using the rubber spatula, fold ¹/₃ of the dry ingredients into the yolk mixture, folding gently until just incorporated. Repeat with the remaining dry ingredients, adding ¹/₃ at a time.

4. In another large mixing bowl, with clean beaters, beat the egg whites on medium speed. Just as they start to get foamy, add the remaining ¹/₂ cup sugar in a slow stream. Beat the whites until stiff peaks form. When the beaters are removed, you should have peaks that stand straight up.
5. With a rubber spatula, gently fold about 2 cups of egg whites into the yolk and flour mixture just enough to lighten the batter. Working quickly, fold in the remainder of the whites.
6. Pour the mixture into the prepared pans and bake for 45 to 50 minutes, or until the cake is springy to the touch and brown on top.

SUGGESTED WASH FLAVORS (page 38)
Orange
Hazelnut

SUGGESTED FILLINGS:
Mocha Buttercream Filling (page 33)
Chocolate Mousse Filling (page 35)

Roses and ribbons.

Icings, Fillings, and Washes

Most cake decorators ice their cakes using rolled fondant. An inexpensive commercial icing, it is a thick sugar and glycerin mixture. I don't like it, don't want to eat it, and would never serve it to guests in my home. It doesn't taste as wonderful as a delicious buttercream, and is much harder to swallow, let alone digest. It also produces a cake surface difficult to cut and serve. Rolled fondant cannot be refrigerated, since sugar and moisture do not marry well. Cakes covered with fondant cannot be filled with delicious mousses, buttercreams, or whipped cream.

I use a classic buttercream for icing and filling my cakes. The recipes are very similar, except that only egg whites are used in the icing, and egg yolks in the filling (to produce a richer taste).

Basic Buttercream Icing

MAKES ABOUT 12 CUPS

This recipe yields more than enough to ice and decorate most cakes, but for cakes that use lots of different colors, you will need this amount. Leftover buttercream can be frozen in an airtight container for up to three months, although in my shop I prefer to use everything fresh. Be sure to label and date the container. The containers should be absolutely airtight so that the creams don't pick up any odors from the freezer or other foods. To defrost, remove from the freezer and leave at room temperature for 2 hours, then return the buttercream to the refrigerator until you are ready to use it. (Whenever the buttercream has been chilled for any length of time, it will be necessary to whip it again to bring it to the right consistency for icing or piping.) Don't be alarmed if the buttercream breaks when you rewhip. Just keep whipping until the icing is smooth again. This may take as long as 20 minutes.

If you choose to color your buttercream, I suggest using vegetable paste colors, which may be ordered through one of the companies listed in the Resource Guide. Be sure to use a clear vanilla if you want a pure white icing; otherwise the brown in the vanilla will give the icing a slightly yellowish tinge.

When we deliver our cakes to the caterer several hours in advance of an event, we have sealed them in new, clean corrugated boxes. We request that the boxed cake sit in a wine cooler or a clean refrigerator, not placed near the garlic or marinating shrimp! Cake buttercream should taste sweet, creamy, and pure—without a trace of onions or fish.

Once you try this buttercream icing, you will never use a commercial icing again. The trick is to be sure to boil the sugar

A creative use of tinted buttercream.

and water until the proper temperature is attained, and then add it very slow to the beaten egg whites. If it is added too fast, the icing will be grainy, not smooth and satiny. Do not pour the hot sugar directly into the center of the bowl, but add slowly near the edge of the bowl.

As a rule, I like to keep the buttercream icing simply flavored so as not to detract from or compete with the taste of the cake and the filling. We use this version, or chocolate, to ice all our cakes.

EQUIPMENT
Measuring cups
Measuring spoons
Medium saucepan
Wooden spoon
Pastry brush
Candy thermometer
Standing electric mixer with whisk attachment
4½-quart mixing bowl

INGREDIENTS
3½ cups sugar
13 large egg whites
3 pounds (12 sticks) unsalted butter, at room temperature, cut into half sticks
6 tablespoons clear vanilla extract

1. In a medium saucepan, combine the sugar and ¾ cup water, mixing with a wooden spoon until the sugar is mostly dissolved. Place the pan on the stove, and use a clean pastry brush to paint the area just above the water line with water. Turn the burner on to medium and heat, watching the sugar mixture to be sure it does not carmelize or burn. Lay a candy thermometer in the pan and simmer the sugar-water mixture without stirring until the thermometer reaches 240 degrees (soft-ball stage); this will take about 5 to 7 minutes.

> About the sugar and water: This mixture should be at the soft-ball stage—240°F.—when it goes into the egg whites. This means you must start to whip the egg whites *before* the sugar reaches the soft-ball stage. If you're not sure, or have trouble reading the thermometer, remove a teaspoon of the sugar mixture with a metal spoon and drop it into a measuring cup of cold water. Using your fingers, reach into the water and try to gather up the mixture; you should be able to form a soft ball with it.

2. As the sugar nears the required temperature, place the egg whites in the large bowl of an electric mixer. Using the wire whisk attachment, beat the egg whites at medium speed until they turn from opaque to white and begin to hold soft peaks. They should be at least double in volume in about 3 to 5 minutes. Do not overbeat.

> Overbeating causes egg whites to lose their sheen and become dry.

3. Turn the mixer on high and very carefully and slowly pour the hot sugar mixture in a very thin stream near the edge of the bowl and into the stiffly beaten egg whites. Beat for 20 to 35 minutes on medium to high speed. The egg whites will lose some of their volume and the mixture should resemble a very thick meringue. The outside of the bowl should be moderately warm to touch.

4. At this point, reduce the speed to medium or low and add the room temperature butter pieces, one at a time. The mixture will break and begin to look like cot-

tage cheese, but don't worry. Keep the mixer running, continue adding butter, and let the mixer whip the buttercream until it begins to get smooth again; this could take up to 10 minutes. Once the mixture is smooth, add the vanilla and beat for 5 minutes more. The buttercream is now ready to be colored or chilled. (If the buttercream is too soft, chill for 10 minutes and then whip again. If this doesn't work, cream 4 tablespoons of chilled butter, and then gently whip the creamed butter into the buttercream, 1 tablespoon at a time. Beat until the buttercream is smooth and there are no lumps.)

Chocolate Buttercream Icing

---

¹/₂ cup strong coffee

³/₄ cup unsweetened cocoa powder

4 to 6 cups Basic Buttercream Icing (page 28)

---

1. Pour the coffee and the cocoa into a medium mixing bowl and stir or whisk together until there are no lumps.

2. Blend 1 cup of the buttercream into the cocoa mixture and whisk or stir to blend, then add the cocoa mixture to the remaining buttercream and blend thoroughly until no streaks remain.

Basic Buttercream Filling

The directions for making filling are very similar to those for making icing. The difference is that one uses the egg yolks instead of whites. The heat from the hot sugar mixture will ensure that the eggs will be fully cooked. But be careful to pour the hot liquid in a very thin stream down the side of the bowl or near the edge to avoid getting scrambled eggs. If this happens, there is no recourse but to throw out the filling and begin again.

EQUIPMENT
Measuring cups
Measuring spoons
Medium saucepan
Pastry brush
Candy thermometer
Rubber spatula
Standing electric mixer with whisk attachment
4$^{1}/_{2}$-quart mixing bowl

INGREDIENTS
1 egg
5 egg yolks
2 cups sugar
6 sticks unsalted butter at room temperature, cut into $^{1}/_{2}$ sticks
6 tablespoons vanilla extract or $^{1}/_{3}$ to $^{1}/_{2}$ cup flavored liqueur of choice

1. Place the egg and yolks in the large bowl of an electric mixer. Using the wire whisk attachment, beat at medium speed until the mixture turns from orange yellow to pale yellow. Continue whisking while you proceed with Step 2.
2. In a medium saucepan, mix the sugar and $^{1}/_{3}$ cup water with a wooden spoon until the sugar is mostly dissolved. Place the pan on the stove and use a clean pastry brush to paint the area just above the water line with water. Turn the heat on to medium, and watch the sugar mixture, being sure that it doesn't caramelize or burn. Lay a candy thermometer in the pan and simmer the sugar-water mixture until the thermometer reaches 240 degrees (soft-ball stage); this will take about 5 to 7 minutes.
3. With the mixer still running on medium speed, very carefully and slowly pour the hot sugar mixture in a very thin stream down the side of the bowl (near the edge) and into the yolks. (Do not pour the hot sugar all at once directly into the middle of the eggs.) Beat for 12 to 15 minutes on medium speed, or until the outside of the bowl is moderately warm to touch.

4. Add the butter pieces, one at a time. The mixture may break and begin to look like cottage cheese, but don't worry. Keep the mixer running, continue adding butter, and let the mixer whip the buttercream until it begins to get smooth again. This could take up to 10 minutes. Once the mixture is smooth, add the vanilla or other flavorings and beat for 3 minutes more. (If the filling is too soft, chill for 10 minutes before you fill your cake. If the filling is still too loose, cream 4 tablespoons of chilled butter and then gently whip the creamed butter into the filling, 1 tablespoon at a time.) The filling may be stored in an airtight container in the refrigerator for up to 5 days.

Flavored Buttercream Fillings

Flavorings for buttercream fillings should be added at the end, at the same time the butter is added. Be adventurous; don't be afraid to use your imagination and experiment with tastes—the flavoring will make the cake uniquely yours.

CREAM CHEESE BUTTERCREAM FILLING

2 cups (1 pound) cream cheese, at room temperature

6 cups Basic Buttercream Filling (page 31), at room temperature

Combine the softened cream cheese and the buttercream filling in the bowl of a standing mixer and beat for 3 minutes on medium speed, or until no lumps remain.

CHOCOLATE BUTTERCREAM FILLING

1/2 cup strong coffee
3/4 unsweetened cocoa powder
1/4 cup Grand Marnier, dark rum, or raspberry or hazelnut liqueur

4 to 6 cups Basic Buttercream Icing (page 28) or Basic Buttercream Filling (page 31)

1. Pour the coffee and the cocoa into a medium mixing bowl and stir or whisk together until there are no lumps. Add the flavoring and whisk until the mixture is completely incorporated.

2. Stir 1 cup of the buttercream filling into the cocoa mixture and whisk or stir to blend; then add the cocoa mixture to the remaining buttercream filling and blend until thoroughly mixed and no streaks remain.

MOCHA BUTTERCREAM FILLING

4 to 6 cups Basic Buttercream Filling (page 31)
2 ounces bittersweet chocolate, melted and
  cooled to room temperature

1½ teaspoons instant espresso
2 tablespoons coffee liqueur

Blend ½ cup of the buttercream filling into the melted chocolate. Stir in the espresso powder, and then add the mixture to the remaining buttercream filling. Using a standing electric mixer, whip briefly on medium-low speed to combine. Blend in the liqueur and mix for 1 minute.

ORANGE BUTTERCREAM FILLING

2 tablespoons freshly grated orange zest

1 teaspoon freshly grated lemon zest
2 tablespoons orange-flavored liqueur

1. Add the orange and the lemon zests to the buttercream in Step 4 of the master buttercream filling recipe (page 32).

2. Blend in the liqueur. For stronger flavor, add more orange zest after the liqueur has been added.

LEMON BUTTERCREAM FILLING

4 teaspoons freshly grated lemon zest

2 tablespoons orange-flavored liqueur
Juice of three lemons

Add the lemon zest to the buttercream in Step 4 of the master buttercream filling recipe (page 32). Blend the liqueur and the lemon juice into 1 cup of the buttercream filling; then add to the remaining filling. Whip briefly on medium-low speed to combine.

RASPBERRY BUTTERCREAM FILLING

4 to 6 cups Basic Buttercream Filling (page 31)
2 cups frozen raspberries (or strawberries for
  strawberry buttercream filling)

¼ cup raspberry-flavored syrup or framboise liqueur
  (or strawberry-flavored syrup for strawberry buttercream filling)

Defrost the raspberries so that they are loose. Squeeze out as much excess liquid as possible and add the raspberry pulp to the buttercream. Add the syrup or liqueur and mix well. It's all right if the buttercream is lumpy.

I frequently grate lemon, lime, or orange zest, mix with a little sugar, and freeze in a small container. This way I can spoon out a little at a time when I need it.

A fantasy island.

Chocolate Mousse Filling

MAKES 8 CUPS

This makes a delicious filling, but it can also be eaten by itself. The recipe requires that you prepare several ingredients ahead of time. You will have better luck if you whip the cream, dissolve the gelatin, and whip the egg whites before proceeding with the recipe.

Never boil gelatin: you'll kill the binding action. Always dissolve it in warm water until it is clear and no grains show.

EQUIPMENT
Measuring cups
Measuring spoons
Double boiler
Small saucepan
Standing electric mixer with whisk attachment
Two 4 1/2-quart mixing bowls
Small mixing bowl
Wire whisk
Rubber spatula
Large mixing bowl of ice

INGREDIENTS
1 pound semisweet or bittersweet chocolate
1 stick (1/4 pound) butter
1 quart heavy cream
2 tablespoons powdered gelatin
7 egg yolks
3 egg whites
1/4 cup sugar

1. Melt the chocolate and butter together in a double boiler set over gently simmering water. When the mixture has melted, remove it and set aside to cool to room temperature.

2. Pour all but 1 cup of the heavy cream into the bowl of a standing mixer with the whisk attachment. Whip the cream to soft peaks, but do not overwhip. Refrigerate the whipped cream, covered. Dissolve the gelatin according to the package directions.

3. Pour the remaining 1 cup heavy cream into a small saucepan and bring to a simmer over low heat.

4. In a separate bowl, whisk the egg yolks together. Use a measuring cup to dip out 1/4 cup of the hot cream, and pour it slowly into the yolks, whisking rapidly. Now pour the yolk mixture in a thin stream into the remaining cream, whisking rapidly as you pour. Pour in the dissolved gelatin, keeping the heat at low, and whisk constantly until the blend begins to thicken,

about 2 minutes. Do not let it simmer or boil. Remove from the heat, set the pan on top of the bowl of ice, and continue to whisk until the mixture is cool and thick.

5. Pour the mixture into the cooled chocolate and stir until incorporated. (If the chocolate breaks, or gets grainy, beat with an electric or immersion blender, and add 3 tablespoons cold heavy cream.) Beat for 2 minutes, or until the mixture is silky and shiny.

6. Whip the egg whites and sugar, using clean beaters, in the large bowl of a standing mixer to form stiff peaks. Working quickly, fold in the chocolate mixture. Fold in the chilled whipped cream. Refrigerate for at least 3 hours before using.

Royal Icing

MAKES ABOUT 2 CUPS

Even though I prefer using buttercream, there are certain applications for which royal icing works very well. It is traditionally used on fruitcakes, and never refrigerated. The English used it as the topping for a wedding cake that was saved and eaten at the birth of the first child. Royal icing dries quickly, and is very stable when kept at room temperature. It is difficult and messy to cut and slice a cake iced in royal icing, because the icing hardens and will crack when you cut it. However, as soon as you put it in the refrigerator, it melts and loses its integrity. If you want to fill a fresh cake with a mousse or a whipped cream filling, you will need to refrigerate that cake before or after you serve it. This is why I don't usually ice my cakes in royal icing.

However, because royal icing is very firm and holds up well for decorating, we like to use it with a template to create lace patterns, lattice, or letters that will be dried and put on the cake later. (Lace may be made by placing a piece of wax paper over a piece of lace and just piping Royal Icing to follow the pattern. If you are using Royal Icing to decorate, the pattern should be made ahead, dried, and placed on the cake just before serving.)

EQUIPMENT
Standing electric mixer with whisk attachment
4½-quart mixing bowl
Small mixing bowl
Wire whisk
Rubber spatula
Plastic container and lid for storage

INGREDIENTS
2 tablespoons meringue powder, available through baking suppliers (see Resource Guide, page 10)
¼ cup warm water
1 tablespoon lemon juice
¼ teaspoon salt
3 cups confectioners' sugar

Red piping on gold icing is a stunning effect.

1. Combine the meringue powder, water, lemon juice, and salt in the bowl of a standing electric mixer. Beat on high speed just until soft peaks begin to form.
2. Transfer about 1 cup of the meringue mixture to a small bowl and combine it with ½ cup of the confectioners' sugar. Whisk together for about 30 seconds until well combined, then fold into the meringue mixture using a rubber spatula.

3. Add the remaining confectioners' sugar to the meringue, about 1 cup at a time, and beat on low speed until all the sugar is incorporated and the frosting is thick.
4. Store at room temperature in a sealed plastic container for up to 1 week. Royal icing may be rewhipped before using. Royal icing hardens very quickly at room temperature, so work with small amounts and keep the remainder covered when not in use.

Washes: Simple Syrup

Once the cake layers are baked and trimmed, I like to add a bit more flavor and moisture by brushing all of the layers with a wash before applying the filling. A wash is a simple sugar syrup made of equal parts sugar and water, which is boiled until the sugar is completely dissolved. To this simple syrup we add all kinds of flavorings, as long as they are compatible with the cake and filling. Feel free to add orange-flavored liqueur, brandy, or rum to the wash. Taste to see if the flavor is to your liking. Save some coffee from the morning pot to create a coffee-flavored wash, or add coffee liqueur.

Brush the wash on with a pastry brush, or spray it on the cake using a small plastic spray pump bottle. We use a 3-inch brush of natural fibers, available in kitchen supply stores or through the stores listed in the Resource Guide (page 10).

This basic recipe will be enough to cover one cake. The rule of thumb for flavoring the syrup is to add ¼ cup liqueur or extract to the basic mixture. Again, taste as you go. Don't be afraid to be bold, and use your imagination.

1 cup water	1 cup sugar

1. In a medium saucepan combine the sugar and water. Turn the heat to medium, bring to a boil, and remove from the heat as soon as the sugar is dissolved.

2. Add ¼ cup of one or more of the following to make a flavored wash:

Vanilla extract
Almond extract
Lemon juice
Coffee
Orange liqueur

Hazelnut liqueur
Chocolate liqueur
Coffee liqueur
Raspberry liqueur

Working with Sugar Dough

Sugar dough, also known as sugar paste or gum paste, is what we use to make flowers, ruffles, drapes, ribbons, and figurines of people and animals. It is completely edible and will keep indefinitely if it is sealed, wrapped, and stored in a cool, dry place. You can make sugar dough, but I suggest you buy it through the mail. It comes in 1- or 2-pound packages, and depending on the thickness you can usually get 6 pansy-sized flowers out of $\frac{1}{2}$ cup.

I never recommend fresh flowers on a cake. Most are sprayed with insecticides or fumigated, either while growing or when they're imported. Also many flowers, such as lily of the valley, are poisonous. If certain flowers are in contact with the cake, poisons may be introduced. Whether you're feeding two or two thousand, you must be sure that everything you're serving is edible, because many people will eat the flowers!

Flowers made from sugar dough are preferable to fresh flowers. If you want to adorn your cake with an abundance of flowers, it is a good idea to start making them well in advance of your cake, so that when it is time to decorate, they are ready to use.

Nosegays of sugar-dough roses are accurate in every detail.

It's always a good idea to have on hand a real flower as a model, or at least a picture of the flower you wish to design. When I first started making flowers, I would go to the florist, buy the flower, and then take it apart petal by petal so that I could make each petal in sugar dough. Working with a real flower gives a reference for the shape of the petals, how thin they should be, the nuances of color and detail, how each petal is attached to another. Try to get the petals as thin as you possibly can, so the finished flowers look real. Practice will help you to avoid a heavy, doughy-looking bloom.

If you love flowers, this will fulfill you. You can make flowers on rainy days when you have nothing to do, or after dinner at night while you are sitting in front of the television. Assemble a flower-making kit as you would a sewing kit, and keep it in your pantry so that you will have all your tools ready. Keep a box stocked with paste colors, powdered dusting colors, small paintbrushes, dowels and skewers, a couple of flower catalogs, florist wire and florist tape, ball tools, clear plastic wrap, a rolling pin, vegetable shortening, leaf and petal cutters, and a utility knife. When I first started making sugar dough flowers, I became a scavenger. I saved egg cartons, apple trays, empty boxes, you name it. I began to look at everyday things and think, "What could I use that for?" Use your imagination. You don't have to run out and buy everything.

COLORING

Sugar dough can be colored using vegetable color dyes that come in paste or gel form. Since the colors are so concentrated, you need only a tiny amount. I usually use a dab on the end of a toothpick, add it to a piece of sugar dough, and then knead it in with my hands as if kneading bread. It's better to use too little at first; you can always add more.

Certain very intense colors, like red or black, will tend to break down the sugar in the dough, so the deeper the colors, the less stable the dough will be. If you intend to make flowers or decorations using these intense colors, it may be better to make them only a few days prior to use, as they may not keep as well.

There are no strict rules or formulas when it comes to mixing colors. Experiment on a piece of white paper, using toothpick dabs of color. When you are satisfied with the colors, apply the same mix to the sugar dough or icing, again using toothpick drops of color.

HANDLING SUGAR DOUGH

Sugar dough should be worked at room temperature so it is pliable and easy to handle. Everyone's hands are different, and the temperature of your hands will affect the dough. I remember trying to teach some women to roll and stretch the dough, and watching it melt in their hands. Whether it was nerves or tension, I'll never know, but cool hands are best. It is critically important to keep the dough covered with plastic wrap at all times when you are not using it, as it will dry in a matter of minutes. Once you have finished rolling out the dough, cover it with plastic wrap and remove only the piece you will be working with. Keep any unused portions in sealed plastic bags.

Always keep a container of vegetable shortening on hand when working with sugar dough; any solid vegetable shortening will do. You will use it to coat your hands, the surface on which you roll out the dough, and the rolling pin, to keep the dough from sticking. While working with the dough, you will also need to coat your fingertips and hands with shortening from time to time. (Do not use too much shortening; just a light coating will do.) If the dough should begin to get a little dry or hard, add a few drops of corn syrup or water and work it in with your fingers to remoisten it. If it is too soft and doesn't hold its shape or falls apart, coat your hands with cornstarch and work it into the dough. Add a little more if needed. Cornstarch is also used to coat the edges of any cutters you will be using so that the dough doesn't stick to the edges.

To get sugar dough to the thinness desired for flower petals, you will need a level hard-surface board on which to roll out the dough, preferably of plate glass or clear plastic, approximately 10 by 14 inches, beneath which you can put a cloth with a patterned print of some kind. When the sugar dough is thin enough, you should be able to see the pattern through the dough. If the patterned cloth is moistened, it will help to keep the glass or plastic board from sliding around as you roll out the sugar dough. I recommend using a round plastic rod about 1¼ inches in diameter, 10 inches long, as the rolling pin.

Many of the flowers can be started by taking a marble-sized piece of the dough and rolling it, then flattening it with your fingers to shape the petal. You can, however, use a template or metal gum paste cutters to cut petals or certain shapes. When using a template, trace the shape you want on a piece of tracing paper, lay the trac-

ing under a piece of plastic wrap or a clear plastic board, and just roll the dough over the template and cut when you can see the shapes through the dough. We use a swivel blade utility knife to cut dough patterns, but using metal cutters is by far the easiest method. There are hundreds of cutters available from cake and baker supply houses; I have listed several suppliers in the Resource Guide (page 10).

Working with sugar dough takes patience. The more you handle it, the more you will begin to feel at ease with it. Experiment with its limits, roll it out and see how thin you can make it, and use your fingers to see where it breaks and tears. Once you have a feel for it and you learn a few basic techniques, you will begin to see that the range of possibilities is limitless in terms of what you can create with it.

Swags of flowers on a tiered cake.

STORING FLOWERS

Once the flowers are dry, they will keep for months in sealed plastic storage containers. Stack the flowers carefully, because they are delicate and they do break. I save and use sheets of bubble wrap between the layers. If you are going to place the dried sugar dough flowers on the cake and refrigerate it, you must be sure that you have a box big enough to enclose the decorated cake. The moisture in the refrigerator will wilt and ruin the flowers, so it is imperative that they be enclosed in a box. If your refrigerator is too small to hold the decorated, boxed cake, I suggest that you add the flowers just before presentation and serving.

EQUIPMENT

Swivel blade utility knife: like the hobby type of utility knife you may already have in the house, only this one has a swivel blade that makes cutting curves easier. A regular utility knife will do, but a flexible blade is preferable.

Palette knife: a small kitchen knife will do, but a palette knife has a thinner, more pliable blade that works well for picking up thin pieces of dough

Offset spatula: used like a palette knife

Smooth-surfaced 10 × 14-inch plate glass or clear plastic cutting board: a surface on which to roll out dough

Plastic or wood rolling pin: to roll out the dough

Petal or leaf cutters: to cut petals of flowers and leaves

Leaf and petal veiners: rubber leaf with lines and veins used to put veins in leaves and flowers to make them look more lifelike

Florist wire: for the stems of all flowers, and also used to stick ribbons into the cake

Florist tape: use to bunch sprays of flowers together and to wrap bare wires (it's not a good idea to stick bare wire into the cake; always wrap first)

Vegetable shortening: to coat fingers, hands, work surfaces

Vegetable gel or paste colors: to color sugar dough and icing

Vegetable powder or petal dust colors: to dust finished flowers to give them nuance and true color

Small paintbrushes or makeup brushes: the right size and softness to apply vegetable powder or petal dust colors to delicate flowers

Nontoxic magic markers: to give fine detail to finished flowers

Nontoxic paints: to paint the flowers

Small scissors: cuticle scissors are the right size to make cuts in dough

Foam egg crate or cardboard egg container: to drape petals and to hold flowers to dry

Foam plastic block: handy for drying flowers or when decorating

Coat hanger: to hang flowers upside down to dry; a pasta drying rack also works well

Ball or balling tool: to roll petal edges out paper-thin into your palm

Petal cutters or template: to cut petals or a calyx; the rounded ends of some pastry tips can also be used as a cutter

Chopstick: great for doing ruffles (the chopstick should be enameled; smooth, raw wood tends to splinter or stick to dough)

Toothpicks: can be used as stems for some flowers

Bamboo skewer: for ruffling

Pastry crimper: for making seam marks in ribbons, and cutting gum paste

Pillars support tiers crowned with an explosion of flowers.

Basic Flower Instructions

The following instructions are for the most basic flowers. These can be bunched together with florist tape to crate a spray, or combined with roses or other colorful flowers. All of the following flowers use the same basic technique, but consult a photograph before you begin, as some of the petals are round, while some are pointed. Color the sugar dough appropriately before you begin.

Spray Flowers

(PHLOX, HYDRANGEA, STEPHANOTIS, LILAC, ORANGE BLOSSOMS)

EQUIPMENT

Vegetable shortening

Vegetable paste colors

Scissors

Bamboo skewer

Florist wire (4 inches long)

Florist tape

Foam-plastic block

Coat hanger

Paintbrush

Vegetable powder or petal dust colors

Nontoxic Magic Markers

1. Coat your fingers and hands with a film of vegetable shortening. Start with a small ball of sugar dough, about the size of a marble. Place the dough in the palm of one hand, and with your other hand roll it and shape it into a teardrop shape.

2. Holding the smaller, bottom end of the teardrop between the thumb and index finger of one hand, use scissors to make 4 cuts straight down into the fatter end of the teardrop, cutting only about ¾ of the way.

3. Holding the smaller, bottom end of the teardrop in the thumb and index finger of one hand, start to flatten each cut piece with the thumb and index finger of the other hand, using a pinch-and-pull motion (think of rubbing your thumb and index finger against each other but in opposite directions). As you work, flatten each piece of dough outward onto your index finger to form a petal. With a bamboo skewer, flatten each petal gently against your index finger, ruffling the edges when necessary, depending on the type of flower you are doing. (When making hy-drangeas, for example, you will pinch each petal very lightly at the base to give a slight pleat to each petal.)

4. After the flower is formed, stick a piece of florist wire into its base for a stem. With your thumb and index finger, round the bottom of the flower so that it is smoothly attached to the wire. (You may want to pinch off a piece of dough if there is too much.) Stick the stem into the foam-plastic block, or hang upside down on a coat hanger and allow to dry.

5. After the flowers have dried, add details and color. Dust the outer edges of each flower with a complementary color. (For example, if the dough is lavender, you may want to dust the edges with purple powder color to give the flower a more realistic look.) Use nontoxic Magic Markers to paint in any dots or lines that the real flower would have.

6. Finally, bunch the flowers together 3 or 4 at a time, and wrap the group of wires with florist tape to secure.

Pansy

EQUIPMENT

Toothpicks

Foam plastic block

Nontoxic markers

1/2 cup sugar dough colored for pansies

Vegetable shortening

Vegetable paste colors

Florist tape

Skewer or chopstick

Egg carton

Scissors

Egg white

COLORING: Start with white, yellow, pale purple, or deep purple dough. Use a brown marker to make the lines in the center of the pansy, and a darker powder dye to accent the edges and center of the petals. Some pansies have contrasting inner and outer petals, like a deep rust color on the outer petals and yellow on the interior petals. Look carefully at a real pansy or a good photograph, and choose the colors you wish to use.

1. Coat your hands with a thin coating of vegetable shortening. Start with a piece of dough the size of a large pea. Roll around between your palms and form a teardrop shape.

2. Holding the smaller, bottom end of the teardrop between the thumb and index finger of one hand, use scissors to cut the teardrop in half, cutting only three-quarters of the way to the bottom.

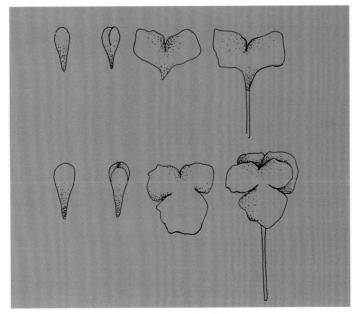

Making a sugar-dough pansy.

3. Begin to pull out the first petal, rubbing the dough with your thumb and pressing it out with your forefinger, making the edges of each petal slightly square instead of completely round. Using a bamboo skewer or chopstick, lay the petal on your forefinger and thin it out even further by rolling the skewer back and forth over the surface and edges to create a very subtle ruffle. Repeat with the second petal.

4. Once this part is done, insert a toothpick into the bottom of the petals and stick the toothpick into the foam-plastic block to dry for about $1/2$ hour. (You can continue to make more pansies to this point before you proceed with the next step.)

5. Take a marble-size piece of dough and roll to form a teardrop shape. Holding the bottom end of the teardrop between thumb and forefinger, use scissors to make 3 evenly spaced cuts in the fatter part of the teardrop, cutting only about three-quarters of the way.

6. Flatten one petal with your thumb and forefinger, then use the skewer to flatten and ruffle. Repeat with the second petal. Pull the third petal outward with your thumb and forefinger, making this the largest petal. Use the skewer to further flatten and ruffle the petal. Attach the three petals to the front of the two petals with a dab of egg white.

7. When they are completely dry, finish coloring the flowers.

Iris

The basis of the iris is the pansy. To make an iris, make 3 pansies, then add 3 long separate petals; wrapped together, these make one iris. The leaves of the iris are the same shape as the center petals, but much longer. Make your life really easy and buy an iris cutter. Iris come in many colors; you'll have a field day with a mixed palette. Color the dough in your favorite shades and add the details with markers when they dry.

EQUIPMENT

Gel food colors—lavender, purple or blue, leaf green
$1/2$ cup sugar dough colored for iris blossoms
$1/2$ cup green sugar dough for leaves
Vegetable shortening
Small scissors
Tiger lily cutter, $2^{1}/2$ inches × $3/4$-inch

Skewer or chopstick
Leaf veiner
Styrofoam block
Florist wire (6 to 8 inches long)
Florist tape
Foam egg crate
Vegetable powder or petal dust colors
Nontoxic markers

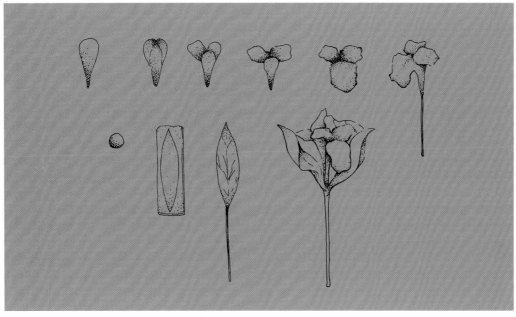

Making a sugar-dough iris.

TO MAKE THE PETALS:

1. Rub your hands with a thin coating of vegetable shortening. Start with a marble-sized piece of dough. Roll it around between your palms to form a teardrop shape.

2. Holding the smaller, bottom end of the teardrop between the thumb and index finger of one hand, use scissors to make 3 evenly spaced cuts into the middle of the fatter part of the teardrop, cutting only about ¾ of the way.

3. Begin to pull out the first petal, rubbing the dough with your thumb and pressing it outward onto your forefinger, making the edges of the petal slightly square instead of completely round. Using a bamboo skewer or chopstick, lay the petal on your forefinger and thin it out even further by rolling the skewer back and forth over the surface and edges to create a very subtle ruffle. Repeat with the second petal.

4. Pull the third petal outward with your thumb and forefinger, making this the largest of the three petals. Use a skewer to further flatten and ruffle the petal.

5. Once this part is done, insert a piece of wire into the bottom of the iris and stick the wire into the Styrofoam block to dry for about 30 minutes.

6. Repeat steps 1 through 5 twice more, to make 3 pansies.

7. Roll out a marble-sized piece of dough flat. Using a 2¼ × ¾-inch tiger lily cutter, cut three iris petals from the dough. Apply each petal to a leaf veiner.

8. Take a piece of wire, holding it so it points to the ground. Attach one end of one of the veined petals to the end of the wire that is pointing downward, squeezing it around the wire. Press the sides of the petal slightly toward one another, and lay the petal in an egg crate to dry. Repeat with the other two veined petals.

9. Once all of the shapes are dry, group the three tiger lily petals together; now add the three pansies, grouping them around the outside of the tiger lily (iris) petals. Keep the center petals up slightly higher than the outside (pansy) petals. Secure with florist tape. Bend pansy petal downward.

10. Finish dusting and coloring the flowers.

TO MAKE THE LEAVES:

1. Use your eye to determine the length and shape to cut out.
2. Roll out about ½ cup green sugar dough about 8 to 12 inches long by about 5 inches wide.
3. Cut 4 pieces of dough about 8 inches by about ½ inch, making sure that one end of the leaves is tapered to a point (the pointed end of the leaf will be the top.)
4. Attach each of the leaves to a length of wire and lay it on a foam egg crate to dry. If you want one or two of the leaves to drape or curl, gently bend them to the desired shape and let them dry on the egg crate.
5. Attach to the iris blossoms with florist wire when they are dry.

Violet

Violets are very similar to the basic flower spray. They are simply a small two-petal flower attached to another larger two-petal flower. Violets are made in two stages; the smaller petals must be partially to fully dry before you attach the larger petals. You could make all the two-petal flowers on one day, and then make the larger petals and attach them on another day. Use violet food color to color the dough, and add details later with nontoxic markers.

EQUIPMENT
Vegetable shortening
Vegetable paste colors
Scissors
Bamboo skewer
Florist wire

Florist tape
Foam-plastic block
Egg carton
One egg white
Nontoxic Magic Marker
Vegetable powder or petal dust colors

1. Coat your fingers and hands with a film of vegetable shortening. Take a small ball of sugar paste about the size of a large pea (smaller than a marble). Place the dough in the palm of one hand, and with the other hand roll and shape it into a teardrop.
2. Holding the smaller bottom end of the teardrop between the thumb and index finger of one hand, use scissors to make one cut straight down into the middle of the fatter end of the teardrop, cutting only about ¾ of the way.
3. Start to flatten each cut piece with the thumb and index finger of your other hand, smoothing outward onto your index finger to form two small petals. Using a bamboo skewer, flatten each petal gently against your index finger, ruffling the edges slightly.
4. Once the flower has been formed, insert a piece of

florist wire into its base. With your thumb and index finger, round the bottom of the flower so that it is smoothly attached to the wire. (You may want to pinch off a piece of dough if there is too much.) Stick the wire into the foam-plastic block.

5. Take another slightly larger pea-sized piece of dough and repeat the rolling process to form a small teardrop. Holding the smaller bottom end of the teardrop between the thumb and index finger of one hand, use scissors to make one cut straight down into the middle of the fattest end of the teardrop, cutting only about ¾ of the way.

6. Repeat Step 3, making these two petals almost twice the size of the first two, flattening, and gently ruffling them to give them life.

7. Using a toothpick, dab a bit of egg white on the base of the dried smaller petals. Attach the larger petals to the smaller, pressing them into the base of the flower where it attaches to the wire.

8. Once the flowers have dried, add details and color using a nontoxic marker and dusting with powder colors to get the proper look.

Calla Lily

This is a very simple two-piece flower, very easy to make but with a dramatic visual impact. The classic calla is white, but calla lilies now come in some very exciting colors like lime green or deep burgundy. The colors can be bold or soft, depending on the look you want to achieve. Always use yellow sugar dough for the stamen, but use your imagination with the color of the petals. You can also group larger and smaller calla lilies together, either in one color or a mix of colors. These directions will give you a 3-inch flower, which I consider a large lily. (To create smaller flowers, start with a smaller stamen.) Use a 3-inch rose petal cutter to cut the petals, or cut the dough yourself, using a swivel blade utility knife.

EQUIPMENT

Vegetable paste colors
4-inch length of florist wire
Florist tape
Yellow sugar dough for stamen
White sugar dough for petal

Vegetable shortening
Swivel blade utility knife or 3-inch rose petal
   cutter
Palette knife
Chopstick

1. Coat your hands with a thin film of vegetable shortening. To make the stamen, color a grape-sized piece of sugar dough pale yellow. Roll between your hands to a cigar shape about 2 inches long. Insert 1 inch of a 4-inch length of florist wire into the stamen, letting the wire protrude about 3 inches to form the stem. Lay on a flat surface to dry.

2. Roll out a grape-sized piece of the white sugar dough

on a flat surface. Cut out a 3-inch-wide by 4-inch-long teardrop-shaped piece of dough to form the petal.

3. Lay the dough in the palm of one hand, with the point of the teardrop pointing up toward your fingertips. Use a chopstick to flatten the edges of the petal, rolling the chopstick around the entire edge of the petal. Place the stamen in the center of the petal, with the wire end pointing at your wrist.

4. Fold one side of the petal over the top of the stamen, then roll the other side over it. Press both sides at the base where the wire sticks out, to seal.

5. Hold the lily upright, stick a finger in the center to open the flower, and place upright in a small glass or cup to dry. (Do not lay flat to dry or your flower will collapse and flatten out.)

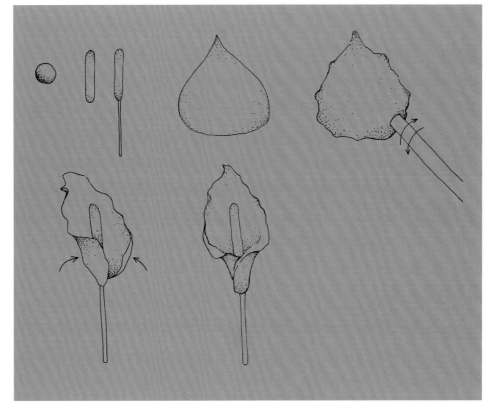

Making a sugar-dough calla lily.

Roses

When making roses, always start by making a number of buds first. (The color of the bud dough should be half a shade darker than the petals.) After the buds have dried for at least an hour, you can begin to make petals and attach. Making a larger rose may take up to three days. You can only affix three or four petals at a time, then you must wait several hours for the petals to dry before you can add more petals. (Don't worry about how many petals; you decide when your creation looks like a rose and pleases you.) The petals can be very soft and open, tight and closed, or a combination of both; be as free with them as nature is. Look at a real rose and note how the petals overlap; that is how you will attach your petals to the bud. You can buy rose petal cutters, which often come in kits of two or three cutters, as well as a calyx cutter. If you choose, you can create your own template and cut out petals and calyx with a swivel blade utility knife.

Experiment with colors. Roses come in many shades—there's even a new brown rose on the market. Your sugar roses will last longer than the real thing, and will generate excitement when people see how real they look.

EQUIPMENT

Vegetable shortening

Vegetable paste colors

Rose petal cutter or template

Calyx cutter or template

Swivel blade utility knife

Ball tool or chopstick

Florist wire

Green florist tape

Egg white

Egg carton

Coat hanger

Skewer or chopstick

TO MAKE THE BUDS:

1. Rub your hands with a thin coating of vegetable shortening. Roll a marble-sized piece of dough around between your palms to form a teardrop shape.
2. Begin to flatten the smaller part of the teardrop into a round petal about the size of a dime.
3. Lay the petal on the forefinger of one hand and take the bottom ball of the dough between the thumb and forefinger of your other hand. Gently roll the bottom of the bud against the finger holding the petal, curling the petal around inside itself to form the center bud.
4. Impale on florist wire and hang upside down to dry.

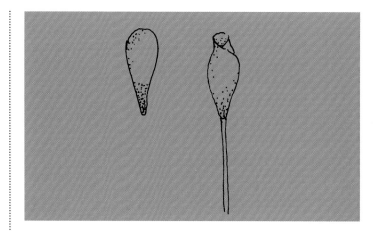

TO MAKE THE PETALS:

1. Roll out a 6-inch square sheet of dough. The dough should be very thin, almost transparent.
2. Using a teardrop petal cutter or a teardrop template, cut out as many petals as you can; remove one and cover the rest as you work.
3. Place the petal in the palm of one hand and, using the ball tool (or a chopstick) with your other hand, begin to roll it around the petal, ruffling the edges slightly as you go.
4. Gently place the rose petal over a mound of an inverted egg crate. Let the petal rest for about 5 minutes before you attach it to the bud. Continue making petals and place each one on the egg crate.
5. To attach your petals, dab a little drop of egg white onto the base of a bud, gently press the base of the petal onto the base of the bud, and wrap the petal gently around the bud. Very carefully curl the outer edge of the petal.
6. Attach each petal to the base of the bud in the same way, slightly overlapping them as you work. Add petals until you are satisfied with effect.

TO MAKE A CALYX:

Applying a calyx to the bottom of rosebuds and roses will cover a multitude of sins. It will finish and tidy the roses and add a touch of green. Add green paste color to the dough before you begin.

1. Roll out a thin layer of green sugar dough. Cut as many calyxes as you will need.
2. Lift the calyx with a palette knife, and holding the rose upside down by the florist wire, pierce the center of the calyx with the end of the wire and slide the calyx down the wire with your fingers until it meets the bottom of the rose. Gently press the calyx to the rose. Hang the finished rose upside down to dry the calyx. When the calyx is dry, wrap the wire with florist tape.

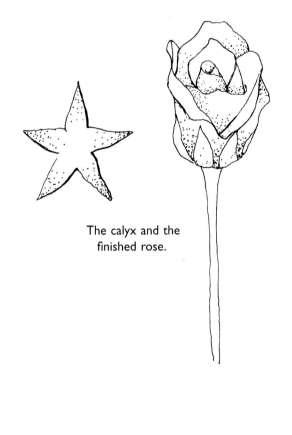

The calyx and the finished rose.

Individual rose petals and the heart of the rose.

Additional Decorations

Ribbons

1. Roll out 1 cup of sugar dough so that it is about 10 inches long and 6 to 8 inches wide. Working with the long edge of the dough, use a ruler as a guide to mark and cut out a 10 × 1-inch length of ribbon. (Do not lift the ribbon yet.) Move the ruler over and repeat, marking and cutting at least six 1-inch-wide ribbons. Using a knife, slice a straight line across the top and bottom of the ribbons so that they are now all the same length and have straight ends.

2. Lay a 10-inch length of clear plastic wrap on top of the sugar-dough ribbons. Using a pastry crimper, gently trace a light seam along the edges of each ribbon, about $1/8''$ from the edge, being careful to use a gentle touch so that you don't cut through the ribbon.

3. Cut an inverted V from what will be the bottom of the first ribbon, then lift the ribbon. Place it on the cake surface. You can then ripple the ribbon so it appears to drape down and curl against the cake, using your fingers to lift the ribbon away from the cake in places. Where the ribbon touches the cake, press gently against the ribbon so that it adheres to the cake, using a dab of buttercream if necessary to hold it.

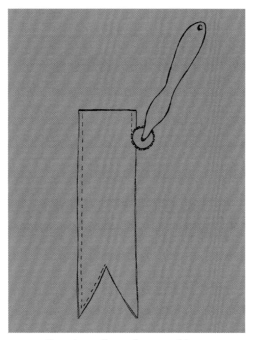

Creating a "seam" on a ribbon.

1. Roll out sugar dough and cut it into 1 × 4-inch strips. Using a pastry crimper and a ruler, gently trace a light seam along both edges of the strips about ¹/₈ inch in from each edge. Use a light touch so that the crimper doesn't cut through the strip. Cover the strips with plastic wrap.

2. Raise the plastic wrap and remove one of the strips. Cut a pointed notch in one end and with the crimper add seams along the notch. Place the strip on a surface to dry. While it is still flexible, you can cause it to curve and/or bulge slightly like a ribbon.

3. Remove a strip from under the plastic wrap and loop it (crimped seams to the outside), squeezing and attaching together the two ends. Place the loop on an edge on a surface to dry. To keep the loop open, you can stuff tissue inside.

4. Make additional notched ends and loops with which to make bows.

5. To make a center knot for the bow, cut a 1 × 2-inch piece from a strip (with crimper seams impressed) and roll it over your pinkie so that the ends overlap. Squeeze the ends together so that they attach together, then place the "knot" on its edge on a surface to dry. It is not necessary to keep the knot of the bow open, but if you wish you can stuff a little tissue in to keep it open.

6. The bows can be affixed to the cake by putting a dab of buttercream on the back side and pressing the loops and ends against the buttercream icing of the cake. A dab of Royal Icing on the back of the knot loop will affix it to the loops and ends of the bow.

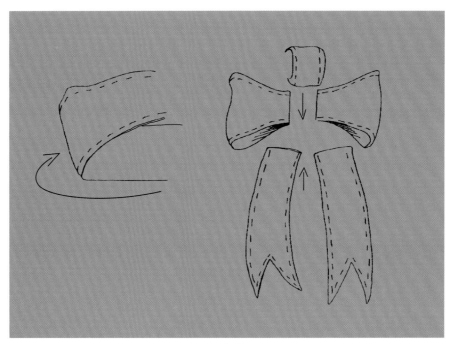

A simple bow.

L o o p   B o w s

Try mixing colors in loop bows. A bouquet of rainbow-colored or sherbet-colored loops is exciting and festive. You will need a large surface area (at least 36 square inches) to make ribbons; a large table or counter works well.

1. Spread a clean work surface with vegetable shortening. Prepare a rolling pin with a thin coating of shortening, and roll out 1 cup of sugar dough so that it is about 10 inches long and 6 to 8 inches wide. Working with the long edge of the sugar dough, use a ruler as your guide to mark and cut out a 10 × ½-inch length of ribbon. (Do not lift the ribbon yet.) Move the ruler and repeat, marking and cutting at least twelve ½-inch-wide ribbons. Using a knife, slice in a straight line across the top and bottom of the ribbons so that they are now all the same length and have straight ends.

2. Place a 10-inch length of clear plastic wrap on top of the sugar-dough ribbons; it is not necessary to cover the dough completely. Using a pastry crimper, gently trace a light seam about ⅛ inch from each edge of the ribbon, being careful to use a light touch so that you don't cut through the ribbon.

3. Raise the plastic wrap so that you can lift up one ribbon. (Cover the rest of the sugar-dough ribbons with plastic wrap.) Hold a 6-inch length of wire vertically in one hand, straight out in front of you. With your other hand, pick up one end of the ribbon and attach it to the bottom end of the wire. Then grasp the free hanging end of ribbon and loop it up to meet and attach to the other end of the ribbon so that the two ends meet, and squeeze the two ends so that they attach to each other securely to the ends of the wire. Lay the ribbon in an 8 × 12 flat sheet pan on its side, so that one edge of the ribbon is resting on the pan and the other edge is exposed to the air. Gently shape the loop so that it is rounded and curved, and let dry. Continue making loops with your sugar dough. Try to keep all the ribbons the same shape; it will make bunching them together easier. Set aside any remaining sugar dough, covered with plastic wrap.

4. Once your ribbons are completely dry, you can bunch them as for a nosegay. Start with one ribbon and add ribbons one at a time to assemble a "bouquet" of ten to twenty ribbons. Now, using florist tape, and starting at the top of the wire where the ribbons meet, begin to wrap the wires with the tape. Wrap the tape around and around the wire until you reach the middle. At the midway point, take a good look at the ribbon bouquet. If there are any bows that need to be repositioned, pulled up, or pushed down, make adjustments now. Be gentle and careful; the ribbon is very brittle and will break easily. Pull or push the ribbons into place using the wire. If you do break one, pull the broken loop out of the bunch from the top and just add a loop from your extras, wrapping the tape around to secure it to the group. Once your adjustments are made, continue wrapping the wires to the ends. To allow the nosegay to dry, stick the wires into a foam-plastic block so that the loops are in the air.

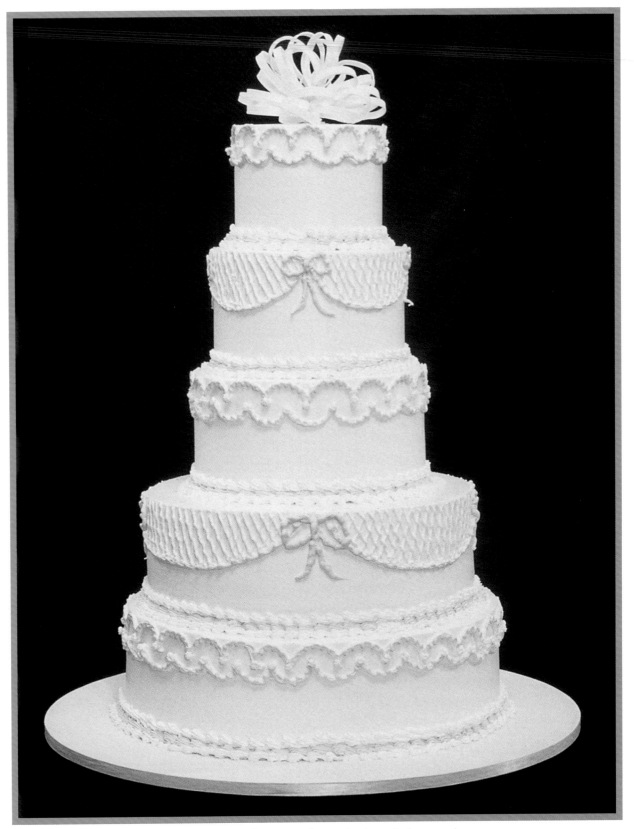

White-on-white frosting makes a simple and elegant cake.

Piping Techniques

There is a certain skill to piping, but this is a skill that can be acquired through practice. Piping is a two-hand job: one hand holds and squeezes the bag while two or three fingers of the other hand guide. Remember, a steady, even pressure on the bag is all that is necessary to squeeze the icing out. Squeezing too hard will give the piping a heavy look, while too little pressure will result in broken lines.

I always recommend practicing piping on a plate or a piece of parchment before starting on the cake itself.' Even the most experienced decorators in my shop always pipe their patterns and designs on a clean surface before they ever put a pastry bag to a cake. This practice will give you a sense of the pattern you plan to pipe; you will feel just how much pressure is necessary to get the proper amount of icing out of the bag. You will gain confidence very quickly by practicing for 5 to 10 minutes first. You can then scrape up the icing with a clean butter knife and put it right back in the bag.

Once the cake has been iced, decide on the type of decorative piping to use. Choose any style you want, but be sure to have plenty of extra buttercream and at least two clean pastry bags to start. When coloring buttercream icing with vegetable dyes, always start with the tiniest amount possible. If using liquid food colors, always start with one drop. If using vegetable powder or paste dye, dip the end of a toothpick into the dye and add this small amount to the buttercream icing. Blend the color into the buttercream with a wooden spoon, mixing until the color is uniform and there are no streaks of white left. If the color is too dark, add a cupful of white buttercream icing to lighten the color. If you want a deeper shade of your chosen color, add another drop of color. Mix the buttercream icing completely after each addition, adding icing or color until you achieve your desired color. You may choose to dye the buttercream a color different from the frosting. (See the chapter called Icings, Fillings, and Washes.) The buttercream should be slightly chilled so that it flows out of the bag smoothly. Buttercream for piping should be colder than buttercream used to ice a cake, but not too cold or it will not pipe smoothly; you will have to force or push it out of the bag and it will break up as you try to work. If it is too warm, patterns will not hold, so remove it from the bag, chill it for 20 minutes or so, then rewhip it before putting it back in the bag. Experiment on a plate or piece of wax paper before you begin.

You can make a pastry bag using a piece of parchment, but you will still need the coupling and tips. I like to use Ateco polyurethane bags; you can also purchase the couplings and a kit with a variety of pastry tips. Remove the nut from the coupling and push the coupling to the bottom of the pastry bag so that the first two or three threads are showing. (If it doesn't fit, you may have to cut about 1/2 inch from the bottom of the bag.) With the coupling in the bag, you can then attach your tip and screw on the nut to keep the whole thing in place.

Holding the pastry bag close to the tip loosely with one hand, fold down the top like a cuff over your hand. Using a plastic spatula, scoop about 2 cups of buttercream into the bag. Pull the folded part of the bag up and over the buttercream and, holding the bag from the top with two hands, give it two good downward shakes. This will settle the icing, and eliminate some of the air. Now twist the top to close the wide, open end. Using one hand to guide the tip, squeeze out some buttercream with your other hand onto a plate or a piece of parchment or wax paper to release any excess air. You are now ready to begin.

Basketweave

You will need two bags and two tips for this technique, a #6 tip for the vertical strokes and a #48 tip for the horizontal strokes. A #6 tip has a plain hole opening, while the #48 tip is flat on one side and serrated on the other.

1. Start with the pastry bag with the #6 tip. Squeeze the pastry bag with one hand and guide with your other hand, keeping your guiding hand close to the tip. Working top to bottom, place a vertical line on one side of your cake. Take the second bag, starting at the top of your cake, and about 1 inch from the

vertical line, make a series of horizontal lines across the vertical line, continuing the stroke about 1 inch beyond. Your horizontal line will be about 2 inches long and will lie over the vertical line. Leave a space as wide as the #48 tip between your horizontal lines, and continue making identical horizontal lines up the cake until you have reached the top edge.

2. Using the bag with the #6 tip, and starting at one end of your horizontal lines, make a second vertical line. By making this second vertical line, you will hide the ends of your horizontal lines.

3. Using the bag with the #48 tip, starting at the first vertical line, fill in the alternating empty spaces with horizontal strokes, and carrying them across and 1 inch beyond the second vertical line.

4. Repeat this process around the perimeter of the cake.

NOTE: You may find it helpful to mark the places of the vertical lines with dots of buttercream before you begin piping the whole cake. By doing so you will be better able to keep your horizontal lines uniform in length.

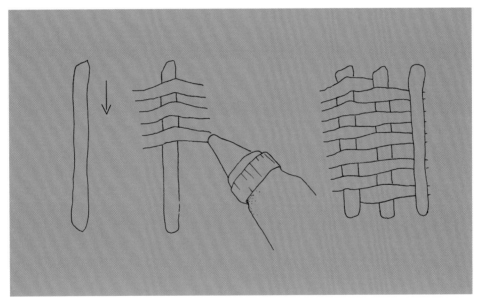
Creating a classic basketweave pattern.

Nantucket Weave

This is another type of basket weave. You will need one pastry bag, and you can use any number of tips for this method. I like to use a #6 plain tip, but you could also use a #14 star tip.

1. Pipe a vertical line the height of your cake.
2. With the same tip, starting at the top edge of your cake, and about 1 inch to the left of the vertical line, make a horizontal line across the vertical line, continuing the stroke about 1 inch beyond. Leave a gap as wide as the #6 tip between your first horizontal line and the next horizontal line. Continue making identical horizontal lines down the cake until you have reached the bottom edge.
3. Now pipe a second vertical line, covering the ends of one set of the horizontal lines.
4. Start at the top edge of the cake. Begin to fill in the gaps between the horizontal lines with new horizontal lines that start at the first vertical line, and run across and over the second vertical line and 1 inch beyond. There will be new gaps between your horizontal lines where they cross the second vertical line. Repeat this process to cover your cake.

Cornelli

This is an elaborate technique for covering a cake. It looks beautiful, almost like a lace pattern, when piped on over an icing in a contrasting color. It will take a fair amount of time and patience to cover a cake in this beautiful pattern, but it is well worth the effort. Remember that the movement of the bag comes from your shoulder and elbow, not your hand. There are no straight edges and no straight lines. Practice this technique on a plate or wax paper before you attempt this pattern on a cake.

Use a #2, #3, or #4 round tip. Exert a gentle pressure on the pastry bag and move in one continuous motion so that the line is unbroken and never overlaps or touches another line. Practice using the illustrated pattern (you can enlarge the figure about 25 percent if you want to use it as a template). Cover the cake evenly with this pattern: avoid leaving large spaces or "holes."

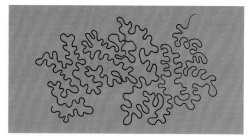

A sample Cornelli pattern.

Dotted Swiss, Pearls, Writing

Using a #2 round tip, which has a small plain opening, you can dot the cake with small pearls. This tip is also good for writing on top of the cake; you will probably want to dye the buttercream a different color for writing.

To make dots, hold the tip at the surface of the cake. Gently squeeze a drop of buttercream and pull straight away, being careful not to pull the bag away on an angle. Repeat this squeeze-and-pull action, taking care to place the dots at equal intervals. You can also create a pattern by placing three small dots close together in groups, all over the cake. Practice squeezing dots on a plate before you dot the cake.

To write on a cake, you must first practice. Cut two pieces of wax paper so they match the dimensions of the surface of your cake. Mark one piece of wax paper accurately to represent where there will be objects, such as sugar flowers or figures. You will be left with the writing surface. Using a pencil and your best handwriting, write your message on the paper. Place the second piece of wax paper over the first. Trace over the message using a full pastry bag and the #2 round tip. Continue practicing and retracing until you are comfortable with your writing. To conserve icing, you can scrape the icing from the wax paper with a knife and put it back in the bag before you write on the cake.

Leaves

Remember, color counts with leaves. Try to color your icing so that your green really looks like the color of leaves.

With a #67 or #70 tip, use a downward or a diagonal stroke, easing up on the icing at the end of the stroke so that the leaf will be wider and fatter on the top and narrower and thinner on the bottom. Practice leaves on a plate until you are comfortable with the technique. Scrape the icing back into the bag when you are done.

Dragging Pearl Border

We use the dragging pearl border on many of our cakes. Sometimes we vary it by exaggerating the drag or looping it like an "m" or a "u." You can double, triple, or quadruple a border by placing borders side by side, on top of, or in between other borders—use your imagination and be creative. Use different sizes of round tips (#2, #3, #4, or #6 round) to do this; star tips work well too.

Holding the bag on a diagonal, squeeze and release the bag at regular intervals using an up-and-down motion, moving around the base of the cake to create a pearl or snail-like effect. Work smoothly and rhythmically, being careful to keep the pattern connected and evenly arranged.

The looping **m** is a lowercase **m**, with a loop on the downstroke or the bottom of the design. Use a continuous up-and-down motion to create a continuous **m** with uniform loops. The same technique is used to create a looped **u**, but in reverse — the loop is on the upstroke. Practice the designs on a plate before you begin on the cake.

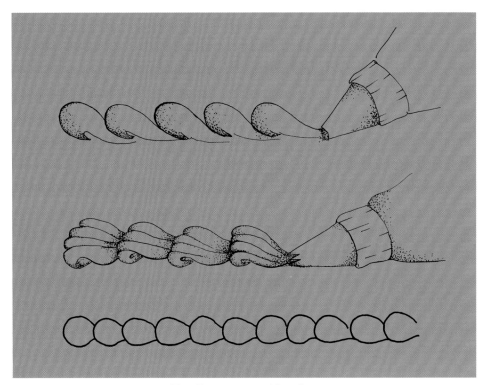

Top: Dragging pearl border.
Middle: Dragging pearl border using star tip.
Bottom: Dragging pearl loops.

Lily of the Valley

Using a lily of the valley tip, squeeze out a tiny bit of buttercream, dot the cake, and pull up. The trick here is to release a little buttercream ahead of time, then dot and pull up, dot and pull up. You can add lily of the valley decorations to stems, and layer them on top and beside one another. Remember that the lower bells are full, tapering to buds at the top of the stem. Practice the technique on a plate first.

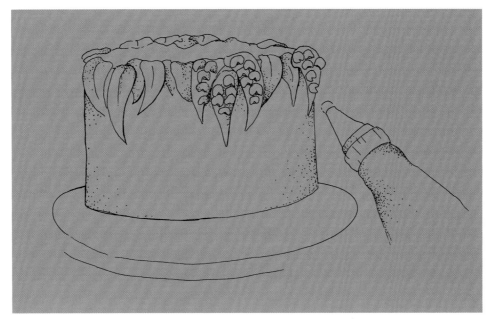

Adding lilies of the valley to the leaves.

Swags

You can use a variety of tips to create swags. If you use a plain hole tip like a #6 or #8, you will want to layer swag upon swag to get fullness. Or use a #32 ribbon tip to give a wide, full swag in one stroke, depending on how you want the cake to look.

1. Start by measuring the beginning and end point of your swag, marking the points by dotting the icing with a toothpick. Now mark the middle low point of the swag, which will be centered between the beginning and end points, about 2 inches below. Connect the three dots in one smooth, curved, even stroke. Once you have piped the first swag, then mark the rest of the swags with the toothpick before you continue.

Piping a swag.

Specialty Cakes

One of the great rewards of my business is the fact that, to an extent, I get to participate in people's happy occasions and celebrations. At the same time it is my responsibility to treat each customer to the most beautiful, most delicious cake that their money can buy, a cake that is truly a reflection of their style and taste.

When I interview a customer, I try to get to know something about him or her so that I can personalize the cake. So often people feel anxious about planning the details of a very special occasion, and I want to engage them in the process so they feel more comfortable about their own party. I try to learn their likes and dislikes, so we'll talk about their food and restaurant preferences. We talk about clothes, their families, their fantasies about the party and the cake, and what foods will be served at the party. We talk about the room in which the event will take place, the flowers that will be used to decorate it, and the ceiling height. All of these details are important elements that will become the basis for the design of the cake.

All of the cakes in this book require a generous commitment of time and patience. For simplicity and guidance for the home baker, I have given all the cakes a level of difficulty rating of 1, 2, or 3. You will want to know what you are getting into before you begin.

Cakes with a level 1 rating can be undertaken by those with very little decorating experience. Cakes with a 2 rating require significantly greater time and focus, and more skilled hands with flowers or icing. Cakes with a rating of 3 should be attempted by serious bakers and decorators. These cakes require the greatest skill level when it comes to icing and decorating, as well as more planning and time. Don't be intimidated, however; skill is learned and comes from practice. Piping can be practiced on a plate or wax paper before you pipe the cake; to conserve icing just scrape it back into the bag when you feel ready to begin on the cake. And remember that you can improvise—use my designs as a guide to create your own. Flower making should be done weeks in advance of your cake. Don't wait until the week of your cake project to begin making flowers. If you are organized, have all the necessary equipment and ingredients, and have given yourself plenty of time to complete a cake, your cake will be a work of art!

Antique White Tiered Wedding Cake

SERVES 60 TO 75

Some brides are lucky enough to inherit their mother's or grandmother's wedding dress. Some have only the ornament from the top of Mom's or Grandma's wedding cake. Either way, this can be a perfect basic design for a meaningful, sentimental, antique wedding cake. If the cloth of the gown is available, chances are it is lacy and/or embroidered. The same patterns can be replicated on the icing of the cake. The floral decorations most appropriate are nosegays of small flowers placed where the patterns dictate.

If you have the cake's top ornament, a little touch-up work should restore this treasure. It will be a lovely crown to place atop the bride's antique wedding cake.

LEVEL OF DIFFICULTY: 3

TIMING: Flowers may be made and stored from 2 to 6 months in advance, and the cakes baked up to 2 days ahead, with filling and icing added then. Assembly and bordering may be done 1 to 2 days ahead if you have enough refrigerator space to accommodate the cake. Decorations should be added to the cake the day of the event; this will not take more than an hour.

HINTS: Use regular drinking straws as supports for the layers. You will use 1 pastry bag and 2 tips to border this

entire cake; the cakes are round layers. Use real brown vanilla for the icing; this will give it a slight creamy tint (not pure white), which will go well with the off-white flowers. This is a cake with large areas of icing visible, so you want as smooth a finish as you can possibly manage; take your time. I have given basic guidelines for adding flowers, but you will be working by eye and really cannot make mistakes; allow yourself the freedom to place them where you see fit.

This cake may be made with any cake/filling/icing combination. As for colors, you could add a very pale peach or pink tint to the icing and still use the same antique white flowers. Whatever you choose, I suggest that you keep it very pale.

SPECIAL EQUIPMENT
Two 10 × 3-inch round cake pans
Two 8 × 3-inch round pans
Two 6 × 3-inch round pans
Four 10-inch cardboard cake rounds
Four 8-inch cardboard cake rounds
Four 6-inch cardboard cake rounds
Turntable
14-inch serrated knife
Pastry brush
Standing mixer with whisk or paddle attachment
Two 4½-quart mixing bowls
Additional mixing bowls
Two pastry bags

Two sets couplings
  #47 basketweave tip
  #13 star tip
8-ounce drinking glass
Small sable paintbrush for dusting flowers

STRUCTURAL SUPPORT
  14 plastic drinking straws
  14-inch round cake platter or board
3 recipes Hazelnut Cake (page 24)
1 cup Vanilla Wash (page 38)
2 recipes Mocha Buttercream Filling (page 33)
Two recipes Basic Buttercream Icing (page 28)

FLOWERS

30 medium ivory roses

30 small ivory roses

48 ivory rosebuds

48 ivory hydrangea sprays

1/4 teaspoon yellow food color dust

1/4 teaspoon black food color dust

1/2 cup cornstarch

ASSEMBLY:

1. Bake the cakes, let them cool, and unpan them. Slice the bulging top off the cakes so that the top and bottom layers are equally flat. Score each cake horizontally at 1-inch intervals, slice, and reserve 4 slices from the 10-inch layer, 4 slices from the 8-inch layer, and 4 slices from the 6-inch layer. Wrap and freeze any remaining slices.

2. Remove the buttercream filling and icing from the refrigerator and let it come to room temperature.

3. Paint each of the 12 slices with vanilla wash.

4. Set the first 10-inch slice on a cake round and place it on a turntable. Fill the first slice with mocha buttercream filling. Repeat with the next two 10-inch slices, placing the fourth 10-inch slice on top of the cake.

5. Check the cake to be sure the top is level and flat, applying pressure to any spots where it is uneven. Remove any oozing filling with a spatula. Trim the top edge of the cake, removing any excess so the edges are rounded. (Shave off just the smallest amount of cake that you possibly can, just rounding the edge.) Crumb-coat the entire cake with buttercream icing and refrigerate on a cake round for 1 hour (see page 14).

6. Repeat the washing, filling, crumb-coating, and trimming for the 8-inch cake, then the 6-inch cake, refrigerating each after crumb-coating.

7. Remove the 10-inch cake from the refrigerator and ice smoothly. If your edges are not round enough, refrigerate the cake for 20 minutes. After 20 minutes, remove the cake from the refrigerator, and use your hand to gently smooth and round the edges. Repeat with the 8-inch cake, then the 6-inch cake. Refrigerate all the cakes until you are ready to assemble.

8. Remove the 10-inch cake from the refrigerator and set it on the 14-inch platter or cake board, then place on the turntable. Center an 8-inch cake pan on top of the cake and press gently into the icing to leave an outline. Place a straw in the center of the circular outline and thrust it vertically into the cake to the baseboard. Mark the straw at the top of the cake, remove it, and cut it at the mark. Using your cut straw as a guide, mark the other 6 straws in the same place and cut them. (When they are placed into the cake, they should be level with the top of the cake.) Place the first straw back in the center of the cake, and place the other 6 straws at equal intervals just inside the circular outline, thrusting the straws through the cake to the baseboard. Center the 8-inch cake on top of the 10-inch cake so that the 8-inch cake is resting directly on top of the 10-inch cake and the straw supports.

9. Repeat step 8, marking the 8-inch cake with a 6-inch round, marking and cutting 7 straws, and placing the straws in the 8-inch cake. Center the 6-inch cake atop the 8-inch cake.

10. Fill a pastry bag with 2 cups of icing and attach a #47 basketweave tip. Using the flat edge of the tip, do a border around the bottom edge of each cake where it meets the board. The object here is to cover the board. Try to make one complete, seamless line.

11. Fill a pastry bag with 3 cups of icing and attach a #13 star tip. Triple-border around the edge of the cake where it meets the board or platter, first with the dragging pearl, then with a looping U, then with the dragging pearl stroke again. Border all 3 cakes. Refrigerate until ready to add flowers.

12. For the flowers, start by making antique white petal dust: mix ¼ teaspoon yellow food color powder, ¼ teaspoon black food color powder, and up to ½ cup cornstarch. Blend the yellow and black colors in an 8-ounce drinking glass and gradually add the cornstarch until you have an antique white. Experiment by using a sable brush to tint one of your flowers with the dust. Add more cornstarch if necessary, or a toothpick dab of yellow or black. To dust the flowers, dip your brush into the powder mixture and very lightly brush over each flower.

13. Begin with 4 medium roses. Place the roses at equal intervals on the top of the 10-inch cake where it meets the 8-inch cake. Now take 4 more medium roses and place them in between and equidistant from the first four roses.

14. Place a bunch or two of the hydrangeas between each two roses.

15. Place one small rose at the top of each hydrangea, and another at the bottom of each hydrangea.

16. Insert rosebuds between each two medium roses and in any places where there are gaps. You are working by eye now, and you cannot make a mistake, so insert the rosebuds where you think they fit. At this point you may want to add more hydrangeas in any large gaps, and rosebuds in any small gaps.

Another white-on-white cake.

17. Move to the 8-inch cake, and repeat steps 13, 14, 15, and 16.

18. Decorate the 6-inch cake by inserting 4 medium roses into the center of the top of the cake. Place 1 or 2 sprays of hydrangeas snugly between the roses. Next add small roses, about 10 in all. Go back and add more hydrangeas. *Your goal is to cover the top of the cake with flowers.* Insert the last of the rosebuds, maybe 10 in all, into the cake where you see fit.

19. To serve the cake:* Remove the 6-inch cake. Remove the straws and flowers from the 8-inch cake, and cut it for service by making a circular, vertical cut about 2 inches in from the edge—as though you are cutting away the outer 2 inches of cake. You can then slice the cut circle of cake into perfect 1-inch-thick slices. Place a small flower on each of the plates. You will be left with a 4-inch inner section, which you will continue to slice and serve. Repeat this process with the 10-inch cake.

* When it is time to cut and serve the cake, the bride and groom will cut the first piece from an edge of the 10-inch cake. The top 6-inch tier should be removed, boxed, and frozen for the bride and groom to enjoy on their first anniversary.

Baby Block Cake

SERVES 15 TO 20

When I think of a baby, I think of a quilt, blocks, and toys in shades of pastel blues, pinks, yellows, or greens. These soft colors always seem to recall the nursery. This is one of the easiest cakes to make, especially when you use letters or numbers, the baby's name, or the date of birth on the blocks. These blocks also remind me of the baby name bracelets that hospitals place on the baby's wrist. I have three tiny pink ones, one for each of my daughters, and I treasure them. You can string the blocks out like a bracelet, or stack them.

This cake works for a baby shower, but it could also be used for a christening, or a birthday for a baby or a toddler. Taken a step further, the cake could be a symbol for building blocks. Just change the colors and customize the message or logo, and it could be used at a corporate party. Two squares make dice—any gamblers here?

LEVEL OF DIFFICULTY: 1

TIMING: This cake can be baked, filled, and iced in 1 day; or prepared in stages as early as 3 days ahead.

HINTS: This cake is designed with 2 blocks side by side supporting a third block on top. The 3 blocks serve 12 to 15 people; however, you will have enough cake to make a fourth block to fill, ice, and use to serve extra guests or send home with the guest of honor.

This cake is an exception to the "trim first" rule. This time you slice and fill first and trim later. If you choose to make a bracelet, you may want to round the corners slightly, and use all of the blocks instead of just 3.

When you color the buttercream, start with tiny amounts of gel coloring; your objective is to create soft, baby pastels.

When it is time to pipe letters and numbers on the blocks, make sure the cakes are cold. Then if you make a mistake writing, it will be easy to remove the decoration with an offset spatula and begin again. If the cakes are too warm, you risk ruining your smooth icing work.

This cake needs square edges, so the chocolate fudge cake or classic yellow cake would work very well. Fillings should be stable to keep the layers flat; try the orange or basic buttercream filling with the chocolate fudge cake, or chocolate or mocha buttercream filling with the classic yellow cake. If you want to use fresh raspberries with the vanilla or chocolate buttercream filling, I suggest pushing them into the filling to keep the layers even.

SPECIAL EQUIPMENT

Two 8 × 8 × 3-inch square cake pans

Four 8 × 8-inch square cake cardboards

Four 4 × 4-inch square pieces cake cardboard

Turntable

Ruler

Pencil

14-inch serrated knife

Standing electric mixer

Two 4½-quart bowls

Mixing bowls

10-inch icing spatula

Two pastry brushes

4-inch offset spatula

Three #14 pastry bags

Three sets couplings

   #789 icing tip

   #13 star tip

#6 round tip

Icing blade

Damp kitchen towel

STRUCTURAL SUPPORT

One 18-inch round cake board or platter

INGREDIENTS

2 recipes Classic Yellow Cake (page 17)

1 recipe Raspberry Wash (page 38)

1 recipe Basic Buttercream Filling (page 31)

1 cup fresh raspberries (optional)

1 recipe Basic Buttercream Icing (page 28)

Gel food colors to make:

   3 cups baby blue

   3 cups pale pink

   3 cups light yellow

ASSEMBLY:

1. Bake and cool, then trim *only* the tops and bottoms of the cakes, not the sides.

2. Score and slice the layers at ½-inch intervals; you will have 3 to 4 slices from each 8-inch cake. Wrap and freeze any leftover cake.

3. Apply the wash and fill the first 3 slices, pressing fresh raspberries into each layer. Place the fourth layer atop the third, pressing down gently to be sure the top of the cake is level. The cake should be about 4 inches tall. Chill for at least 1 hour.

4. Lay the four 4 × 4-inch cardboard squares on top of the cake with the edges touching, being careful not to overlap.

5. Score the top of the cake with the serrated knife in a cross fashion where the cardboard edges meet.

6. Remove the cardboard pieces and cut the cake from

top to bottom so that you have four 4-inch square blocks to give 4 blocks.

7. Place a cardboard square on top of one block and use the cardboard as your guide to carefully trim the two brown sides of each cake with a serrated knife. Do your best to make the blocks perfectly square. Repeat for the other blocks.

8. With an icing spatula, remove any excess buttercream filling that may have oozed out, and use a dry pastry brush to remove any excess crumbs. Dab a tablespoon of buttercream on each of the 4 squares of cardboard, and place a block of cake on each square. Crumb-coat the cakes (see page 14) and refrigerate for 1 hour.

9. Fill 3 pastry bags with tinted buttercream, one each in pink, yellow, and blue.

10. Remove 1 cake from the refrigerator. Using the #789 icing tip and the blue icing, hold the bag so that the

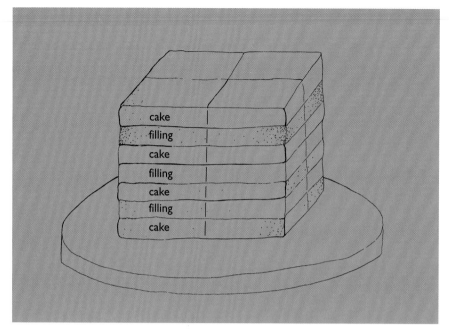

Stacking the Baby Block Cake layers.

serrated edge of the tip faces out. Pipe each side of the cake with 2 wide horizontal stripes across, each stripe just touching the next, to cover the sides of the cake. Repeat, using 3 stripes on top of the cake, so the entire cake is now covered in blue icing. Put a bead on each edge of the cake. Repeat with each block cake, using pink icing on one, yellow on the other.

11. Using an icing blade, start with the top of the cake. Hold the blade at a 30-degree angle and, using almost no pressure, glide it over the top of the cake to smooth out the lines. Place any icing from the blade into a clean bowl. Wipe the blade with a clean, damp towel. Holding the clean blade at exactly the same angle, glide over the top of the cake in the opposite direction. This should remove any air bubbles. Again, clean the blade as above. Move to the sides of the cake, and this time hold the blade at a 45-degree angle with the bottom edge of the blade flat against the turntable. Glide first in one direction, clean the blade, then glide in the opposite direction.

If there are holes or air bubbles in the icing, smooth them out with an offset spatula or an icing blade. If you make a hole, use some of the excess icing from the bowl to fill it.

12. Using a 10-inch icing spatula, smooth the top of the cake. Holding the blade at a 30-degree angle, start at one corner of the cake and pass gently over the cake to flatten the top edges. Clean the blade and repeat with all 4 sides until the edges of the cake are square and smooth.

13. At this point, the cake should be fairly smooth and square. Now go around the cake and remove any crumbs, smooth any repairs, and make sure the cake is completely square and smoothly iced.

14. Slide a spatula or a knife blade under the cardboard base, pick up the blue cake, and refrigerate for 1 hour. Remove the next block cake from the refrigerator and repeat using pink buttercream. Repeat with the third block cake and the yellow buttercream. Set aside the pastry bags containing leftover icing; you will use them again in Step 17.

15. When all of the blocks are iced, place the pink cake off-center to the left on your cake base. Place the blue cake beside the pink, making sure one edge of the pink cake is 1/8 inch from the blue, angling the blocks away from each other. Place a teaspoon of buttercream icing on the corners closest to each other.

16. Place the yellow cake on top of the two bottom cakes, using the two buttercream drops as glue to hold the top in place. It's okay to have a corner of the yellow block hanging off to one side, but not more than 2 inches.

17. Using a knife or a skewer, lightly trace the "A," "B," and "C" on the 3 block faces. Change the tip on your bag to the #6 round tip fitted to the pink icing. Pipe a 2½-inch "A" on the face of the yellow block. Switch to a #13 star tip. Trace the inner and outer edges of the "A" using a close, dragging pearl.

18. With blue icing and the #6 round tip, pipe a 2½-inch "B" on the face of the pink block. Change to the #13 star tip and trace around the inner and outer edges of your "B" using the dragging pearl technique.

19. Using yellow icing and the #6 round tip, pipe a 2½-inch "C" on the face of the blue block. Change to the #13 star tip and trace the inner and outer edges of the "C" using the dragging pearl technique.

20. If you wish, you can repeat with other letters or numbers on the opposite face of each block, using the same colors and piping techniques as in Steps 17 through 19.

21. When piping is completed, use the pink icing and the #13 star tip to pipe a dragging pearl border on all the edges of your pink block. Repeat this with the blue icing and the blue block, then the yellow icing and the yellow block.

22. Refrigerate the cake until serving time.

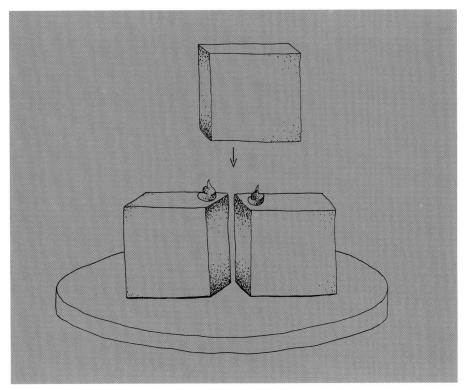

Assembling the blocks.

Balloon Cake

SERVES 12 TO 15

This "bon voyage" cake is so colorful and festive that it could easily be used for a child's birthday.

LEVEL OF DIFFICULTY: 3

TIMING: Buy or order a foam-plastic egg from a crafts store 4 weeks in advance. The confetti and ribbons can also be made up to 4 weeks in advance. The cake can be baked 2 days in advance, and filling and icing 1 to 2 days ahead. The cake may be iced and assembled 1 day ahead of the event.

HINTS: This cake requires a 4-inch square cake. If you have difficulty finding one, you can use an 8-inch square pan and trim the cake down to a 4-inch square. Simply make a 4 × 4-inch cardboard template, lay it on top of your cake, and trim. If you have any leftover cake slices in the freezer, this is your opportunity to use them. Since the 4-inch cake is separate from the 8-inch cake, it doesn't really matter that you might have two different flavors of cake.

You will be using half of a foam-plastic egg as the bottom half of the balloon; the 8-inch cake will sit on top, trimmed to become the upper half of the balloon. There will be plenty of trimmings to help get the top of the balloon as perfectly round as possible.

This is a very bright cake that requires a full range of gel colors, and you will want to use all of them to make the confetti and spirals.

SPECIAL EQUIPMENT

One 8 × 3-inch square cake pan
Two 8 × 3-inch round cake pans
Turntable
Five 8-inch cardboard cake rounds
One 4 × 4-inch piece cardboard
14-inch serrated knife
Pastry brush
Standing electric mixer and paddle or whisk
    attachment
One 4½-quart mixing bowl
Small mixing bowls
Rolling pin

Plastic cutting board
Ruler
Flexible utility knife
Clear plastic wrap
Pastry crimper
2 or 3 half sheet pans
10-inch icing spatula
Icing blade
Flexible icing strip
Two pastry bags
Two sets couplings
    #13 star tip
    #4 round tip

20 bamboo skewers
25 toothpicks
10-inch round cake board or platter

STRUCTURAL SUPPORT
10-inch square cake board or platter
Five $^1/_4$-inch dowels, 8 inches long
10 × 6-inch foam-plastic egg (available at craft stores)

INGREDIENTS
1 recipe Classic Yellow Cake (page 17)
1 cup Vanilla Wash (page 38)
4 cups Chocolate Buttercream Filling (page 32)
1 recipe Basic Buttercream Icing (page 28)

Gel food colors to make the following:
   3 cups orange
   3 cups brown
   2 cups yellow
Vegetable shortening
$3^1/_2$ to 4 cups sugar dough, colored to make the following:
   2 cups purple
   $^1/_4$ cup pink
   $^1/_4$ cup blue
   $^1/_4$ cup yellow
   $^1/_4$ cup red
   $^1/_4$ cup green

ASSEMBLY:

Cut the 8-inch square cake vertically into quarters. Score and slice the cake at 1-inch intervals. You will need only 4 slices in all (you will have extra cake left over). Score and slice the 8-inch round cakes at 1-inch intervals. You will need 5 slices in all.

Cut the foam plastic egg in half, severing the small top from the larger bottom. Using the smaller end of the egg, measure the flat surface of the egg. It should measure approximately 6 inches in diameter. Set aside the larger half of the egg—you will use this later as a model to trim the top of your balloon.

CONFETTI AND SPIRALS

1. Lay all 20 bamboo skewers on a sheet pan and dust with cornstarch.
2. Roll out $^1/_4$ cup purple sugar dough. Cut six 6 × $^1/_4$-inch strips. Pick up the first strip and spiral it around a skewer, then spiral a second strip around the skewer above the first strip. Continue winding the purple strips around the skewer, and let them dry.
3. Roll out the remaining $^3/_4$ cup purple dough, cut into $^1/_4$-inch squares, and place on a cookie sheet to dry.
4. Repeat Steps 1 through 3 with the pink, red, yellow, green, and blue sugar dough. Set aside until you are ready to decorate the cake. You will have 36 spirals in all, using eighteen skewers.

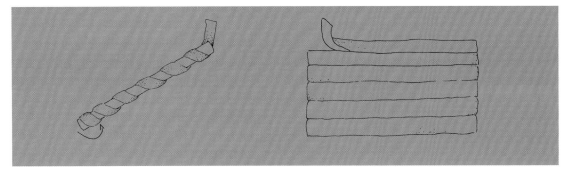

Making the sugar-dough spirals.

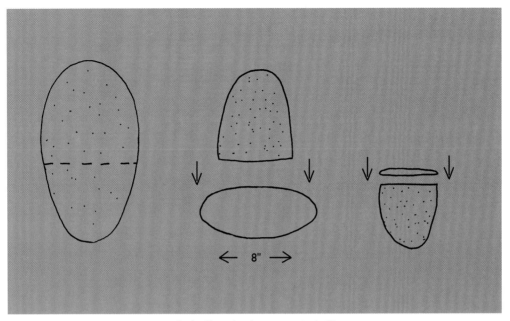

Left: Cut the foam egg in half.
Center: Place the smaller egg half on an 8-inch round cake cardboard.
Right: Center the cardboard on top of the 8-inch cake.

BALLOON AND BASKET

1. Remove the buttercream filling and icing from the refrigerator and allow to come to room temperature. Now proceed with the balloon and basket.

2. Trim and slice the 4-inch cakes. Wash, fill, and refrigerate 4 layers and set them on the 4-inch square cardboard. Slice the 8-inch round cakes and wash, fill, and refrigerate 5 layers placed on cardboard.

3. Place the stacked 4-inch cake on a turntable and crumb-coat. Position four ¼-inch dowels in the corners of the cake, each about ½-inch in from the point of the edge. Press each dowel vertically into the cake to touch the base. Refrigerate the cake for 1 hour.

4. Place the smaller egg half, flat side down, on top of one 8-inch round cake cardboard. Trace around the egg bottom onto the cardboard with a pencil, then cut the cardboard to match the circle. This cardboard will be set between the 8-inch cake (which you will

trim to fit) and the surface of the egg (see drawing at top of page).

5. Poke a hole in the center of the trimmed cardboard round with one of the dowels. Break or cut one of the dowels in half and stick it perpendicularly into the center of the flat surface of the egg half so that 2 inches stick out.

6. Remove the 4-inch cake from the refrigerator and position the round part of the egg so that it rests evenly on the 4 dowels. Very gently press down on the egg so that each dowel sticks slightly into the foam plastic, being very careful not to move the dowels, to avoid damaging the cake below.

7. Center the cardboard cake round (with center hole) atop the 8-inch round cake. Using the larger end of your egg as a visual guide, trim the top of the cake with a serrated knife to fit the top cake round, shav-

ing out and away. Remember that you are trimming the *top* of your balloon, even though it is upside down. Invert the cake so that the round is on the bottom, and begin to trim the cake so that the top is round but still wider than the bottom by almost half. Once you are satisfied with the shape of the cake, seat the cake on top of the foam egg half so that the dowel sticking up from the center of the foam-plastic egg goes into the bottom of the cake through the hole in the cake round (see drawing on the top of page 83). Trim the cake further if necessary to fine-tune the shape, then crumb-coat (see page 14). Use the crumb coating to fill in any holes or to add balance to the upper half of your balloon. Chill the cake for 1 hour.

8. Put the buttercream icing in the bowl of a standing mixer and add the red and yellow colors. Turn the mixer on low and blend for 2 minutes, adding more red or yellow to get the color you desire. Scrape down the sides of the bowl and blend for another minute, or until the color of your icing is uniform and no longer streaky. Fill a pastry bag with the orange icing and attach the icing tip and coupling.

9. Remove the cake from the refrigerator and place the structure on the turntable. Apply the orange icing to the balloon, using the pastry bag, and then begin to smooth the icing, using both an icing spatula and the flexible icing strip. Ice the balloon as smoothly as possible.

10. Fill a pastry bag with the chocolate icing and the #4 round tip. Basketweave the sides of the 4-inch cake, then go back and double- or triple-border the base and the top edges of the cake, using the dragging pearl.

11. Roll out 1 cup purple sugar dough. Cut out four 11 × 2-inch strips (see the drawing at the bottom of page 83). Place a toothpick in the top center of the balloon. Place one end of the first purple strip at the toothpick. Press the strip gently against the balloon. Place the second strip about an inch away from the first strip, repeating with the remaining 2 strips.

12. Fill a pastry bag with the yellow icing and the #4 tip. Pipe a dragging pearl along either side of the purple strips. Pipe dots onto the dowels at random intervals.

13. Place 18 to 24 of the toothpicks at slight angles into the top of the basket of the cake, sticking just the bottom $1/2$-inch into the cake. (Keep the toothpicks about $1/4$ to $1/2$ inch apart.) Remove the sugar-dough spirals from their bamboo skewers gently so that they don't break. Place the first of the spirals over one of the innermost toothpicks in the center of the basket. Continue arranging spirals over the toothpicks, varying the colors.

14. Dot the cake base with icing and sprinkle the sugar-dough confetti around the board. Your cake is ready to serve.

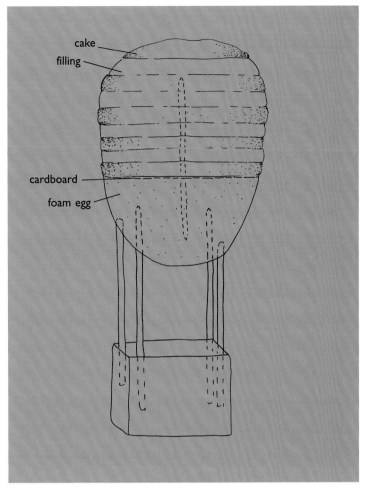

cake

filling

cardboard

foam egg

The assembled balloon cake.

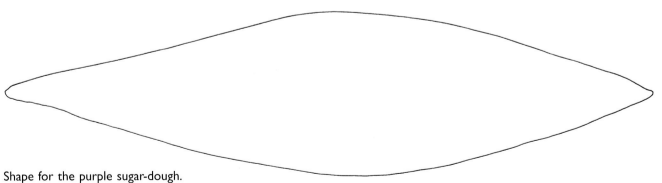

Shape for the purple sugar-dough.
Use a copier to enlarge this by 157 percent.

Box Wedding Cake

SERVES 80 TO 100

This is a beautiful cake, and unusual because most wedding cakes are round. It could be used for almost any other occasion, and could be finished with marzipan fruit instead of flowers. If you wish you can also make a smaller version by using smaller baking pans.

LEVEL OF DIFFICULTY: 3

TIMING: The fruit and flowers should be started 10 to 12 weeks in advance. The cakes can be baked up to 2 days in advance, as can the buttercream filling and icing. Assembling, filling, icing, and bordering can be done one day ahead if the cake is stored in an enclosed box. The fruit and flowers must be added on the day the cake is served.

HINTS: I call this cake "difficult" because of its many labor-intensive fruits and flowers, which should be done well ahead (see Timing). You must use straws for structure—the stacked decorated cakes will be very heavy. Use the sturdiest, most solid cakes. Chocolate Fudge and Classic Yellow are the best choices. There will be a lot of cake left over, and if you freeze the leftover slices, you will definitely have enough to create another cake. Once you have filled and iced the cakes, make sure that they spend at least 12 hours in the refrigerator. (Because the second box cake is placed at an angle above the square cake beneath it, the corners may hang off slightly. Refrigerating the individual cakes will help to firm their shape and keep the boxes from sagging when stacked.)

When decorating with fruit and flowers, you will be going up one side of the cake and down the other. The task will be easier if you divide the fruits and flowers into three groups and then divide each group in half—one for each side of each cake. Start from the bottom and decorate up, placing fruit and flowers sparsely at first and filling in later. You may even want to do both sides of the cake at the same time, using identical arrangements of fruit and flowers. This will keep the cake from looking like two different cakes. Decorate the top of the cake last.

If you intend to refrigerate this cake after adding fruit and flowers, be sure to put it in an enclosed box. (If the cake is refrigerated uncovered for more than 2 hours, you risk ruining the decorations, because moisture will make them wilt and bleed.) The fruit and flowers should go on the cake the day of the event, unless you have a box and a refrigerator large enough to hold the boxed cake.

This is a wedding cake, so you will want to leave flavor choices to the bride and groom. (We have done the cake in chocolate with a hazelnut wash, fresh raspberries pressed into vanilla buttercream filling, and vanilla buttercream icing colored with chocolate.)

SPECIAL EQUIPMENT

Two 8 × 8 × 3-inch square pans
Two 10 × 10 × 3-inch square pans
Two 12 × 12 × 3-inch square pans
One 8-inch round cake pan
One 10-inch round cake pan
Four 8-inch square cardboard cake squares
Four 10-inch square cardboard cake squares
Four 12-inch square cardboard cake squares
Turntable
14-inch serrated knife
Standing mixer with whisk or paddle attachment
Two 4½-quart mixing bowls
Small garden pruning shears
Two 8-inch spatulas
Pastry brush
Icing blade
Four pastry bags
Four sets couplings
   #48 basket tip
   #67 leaf tip
   #13 star tip
   Lily of the valley tip

STRUCTURAL SUPPORT

18 ¼-inch dowels, 6 inches long
16-inch square cake board

INGREDIENTS

3 recipes Chocolate Fudge Cake (page 21)
1 recipe Hazelnut Wash (page 38)
2 recipes Basic Buttercream Filling (page 31)
6 half-pints fresh raspberries
Gel food colors
Food color dust or petal dust
Two recipes Basic Buttercream Icing (page 28):
   2 tablespoons melted chocolate added to 10
      cups buttercream
   Leaf-green food color added to 5 cups butter-
      cream
   4 cups plain buttercream
   2 pounds sugar dough
   5 pounds marzipan

FLOWERS

Small calla lilies:
5 red
4 yellow
4 pale green
5 purple
5 orange
Roses:
15 peach medium roses
25 small rosebuds

MARZIPAN FRUIT

7 bunches of grapes
6 pears
2 plums
8 lady apples

1. Line two 12-inch square pans, two 10-inch square pans, and two 8-inch square pans with baking parchment. Fill the pans three-quarters full with the chocolate cake batter and bake and cool according to the directions. After unpanning, score the cakes horizontally at 1-inch intervals; each of the cakes will yield 4 slices.

2. Remove the buttercream filling from the refrigerator. Trim off the bulging top of each cake so that the top and bottom surfaces are equally flat. Slice the cakes

along the scores, to yield 12 slices, 4 in each size. Place each cake on a cake square. Brush each slice with hazelnut wash. Wrap and freeze any extra cake.

3. Place the first 12-inch slice on the turntable. Spread on 1 to 2 cups buttercream filling and press one-quarter of the fresh raspberries into the filling. (Press the berries into the filling very firmly, so that the next layer will lie flat against the one below it.) Repeat with the next 2 layers, and place the fourth 12-inch slice on top. Return the buttercream to the refrigerator to keep it cool, and freeze any spare layers.

4. Check the cake to be sure the top is level and flat, applying pressure to any places where it is uneven. Remove any oozing filling with a spatula.

5. Repeat the wash and filling for the 10-inch and 8-inch cakes.

6. Remove the buttercream icing from the refrigerator and allow to come to room temperature.

7. Place 10 cups buttercream icing in a bowl of a standing mixer and add the 2 tablespoons melted chocolate. Blend on low for 2 minutes, scrape down the sides of the bowl, and blend for another minute, or until the color of your icing is uniform and no longer streaky. The icing should be the color of coffee with cream.

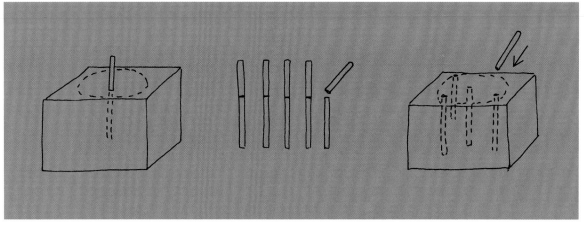

Positioning the dowels and cutting off the tops.

8. Ice the 12-inch cake smoothly with buttercream icing. Use your icing blade to get as smooth a look as possible.

9. Center a 10-inch round cake pan on top of the cake and press gently into the icing to leave an outline. Insert a dowel in the center of the circular outline, and press it vertically down into cake to the board underneath. Mark the dowel where it meets the top of the cake, and withdraw the dowel slowly. Cut the dowel at the mark, and using this dowel as a guide, cut 8 other dowels to the same length. Cut the dowels using the garden shears. Place the first dowel back in the center of the 12-inch cake, then place the next 8, equidistant about ¹/₂ inch inside the circular outline.

10. Ice the 10-inch cake smoothly. Repeat, marking the 10-inch cake with the 8-inch round, marking and cutting 9 dowels. Insert the dowels in the 10-inch cake in the same manner as in step 9.

11. Ice the 8-inch cake.

12. When all the cakes are iced, and with the dowels in place, stack the cakes: Place the 12-inch cake squarely on the cake board. Place the 10-inch cake diamond-style on top of the 12-inch cake, and the 8-inch cake diamond-style on top of the 10-inch cake.

13. Using a pastry bag filled with white icing, and a #48 basketweave tip, border around the base of the 12-inch cake using the flat side of the tip. You want to create a flat band around the perimeter of the base. Repeat this border around the base of the 10-inch cake and then the 8-inch cake.

14. Using a pastry bag with white icing and the #13 star tip, border around the bottom of the band on the 12-inch cake, using the dragging pearl stroke all the way around the cake. Border on top of the band, again using the dragging pearl stroke around the perimeter of the cake. Repeat this border above and below the border band on the 10-inch cake, and then the 8-inch cake.

15. Using a pastry bag with the leaf-green icing and a #70 leaf tip, place leaves in a random fashion on the top and two sides of the 8-inch cake. Orient yourself and the cake so that when you finish the cascade of leaves down one side, you will finish placing leaves on the center and the opposite side of the 12-inch cake. Working from the top, cover almost half of the 8-inch cake with leaves, and then move down, adding leaves to one side of the cake all the way to the base. Repeat on the opposite side. (When you look at the photograph of this cake, you will see that the cascade of fruit and flowers does not cover the entire cake, but only two sides.) Be generous and free with the placement and direction of leaves; remember that the

fruit and flowers will nearly cover them—the leaves are simply a backdrop and will peek out from underneath. The cake can be refrigerated at this point until you are ready to add fruit and flowers.

16. For the top of the cake, use: 1 red, 1 purple, and 1 orange calla lily; 3 medium roses; 5 small rosebuds; 1 bunch of grapes; 2 pears; 2 lady apples. Divide the remaining fruit and flowers into two groups, with the same number of each color and kind in each group, one group for each side of the cake. Reserve the remainder.

17. Start by placing a bunch of grapes on each side of the 12-inch cake near the bottom center. Working upward with one group of fruit and flowers, place one of each fruit and flower up the side, up the corner of the 10-inch cake, and up to the top edge of the 8-inch cake. Keep the fruit and flowers 2 inches apart. Now begin adding flowers (reserving the rosebuds) and fruit. Working in a methodical fashion, with one of each flower and one of each fruit, begin to fill in the line. Fill in any gaps with the remaining rosebuds. Repeat on the opposite side of the cake. (You may even want to work on the two sides of the cake alternately, placing the same fruit or flower in the same position on opposite sides.)

18. Once the two sides of the cake are decorated, arrange the last fruits and flowers on top. Then go back over the cake with the leaf tip and leaf-green icing, squeezing leaves and pulling them out into any spaces or small gaps.

19. Fill a pastry bag with the white buttercream and attach the lily of the valley tip. Pipe lilies of the valley on top of any exposed leaves, or in spots where there are not enough flowers or fruit.

A similar arrangement of fruit and flowers on a round cake.

Cornelli Heart Cake

SERVES 12 TO 15

During one interview I had with a bridal couple, they spoke of their fantasy of a cake that expressed their great love for one another. They wanted a stack of heart-shaped cakes. I pointed out that when hearts are stacked, one loses the shape and ends up with a somewhat rounded cake with points on one side and a cleft on the other. The heart shape would be apparent only if the cake was viewed from above. The couple agreed and settled for a cake that was a single heart with rounded edges, covered in delicate lace cornelli piping and ornamented with a sash garland of flowers. I arranged for a prop to be placed under the cleft end of the cake so that it was tilted up to make the heart shape readily visible. This type of cake would also be appropriate for many occasions such as birthdays, sweet sixteen parties, anniversaries, bridal showers, or engagements.

LEVEL OF DIFFICULTY: 2

TIMING: This cake can be baked and crumb-coated up to 2 days ahead. The cake should be iced, decorated, and refrigerated for at least 4 hours or 1 day ahead.

HINTS: If you don't have heart-shaped pans, you can easily use a regular 10-inch round cake pan. You can buy heart-shaped cake cardboards; use a 10-inch to carve the cake and a 14-inch covered with colored foil to use as the base. You can also make a template using a 10-inch cardboard cake round that has been cut into a heart shape. When the round cake has been washed and filled, place the heart-shaped cardboard on top of the cake and carefully carve the cake into a heart shape. Invert the cake onto the cardboard heart, which becomes the base. Whether or not you use a heart-shaped pan, you will still have to trim the top and sides of the cake to get rounded edges. Use a regular steak knife; just hold it against the cake and carefully shave the cake to get nice, rounded edges. (Be careful not to trim away too much; it's easy to overfuss and wind up with a lopsided heart.) If you don't have #789 icing tip, crumb-coat the cake first. Use the flexible icing blade to get smooth, rounded edges, and after refrigeration use your fingertips to smooth the icing. Run your fingers gently over the rounded edges of the icing; the heat from your hands will melt and help to smooth it. Just be careful to use gentle pressure; the aim is to smooth, not to dent or gouge the icing.

Before you start piping the cornelli design onto the cake, spend a good 20 minutes practicing on a piece of wax paper, unless you are experienced with it. When you finish practicing, scrape the icing up with an icing spatula and put it right back into the pastry bag. This cake takes time to decorate. If you need to take a break, just put the cake in the refrigerator until you are ready to

begin again. Be sure that the icing in your bag is at room temperature when you resume.

If the cornelli seems too daunting a technique, do the whole cake in dots, or make a simple border around the base and then decorate the top of the cake with a band of flowers. We used lace points made from royal icing as a decoration, but this is optional; the cake is beautiful without them.

SPECIAL EQUIPMENT

Two 9-inch heart-shaped cake pans
Turntable
One 9-inch heart-shaped cardboard cake round
Five 10-inch cardboard cake rounds
14-inch serrated knife
Pastry brush
Standing mixer with paddle or whisk attachment
4½-quart mixing bowl for standing mixer
Mixing bowls
Steak knife
Long icing spatula
Icing blade
Palette knife
Clear plastic flexible icing blade, 9-inch strip
Two pastry bags
One or two sets couplings
    #789 icing tip
    #13 star tip
    #3 round tip

STRUCTURAL SUPPORT

12-inch heart-shaped cake board or plate

INGREDIENTS

1 recipe Chocolate Fudge Cake (page 21)
1 cup Vanilla-flavored Wash (page 38)
1 recipe Chocolate Mousse Filling (page 35)
1 recipe Basic Buttercream Icing (page 28)
2 pounds sugar dough
Gel food colors to make the following:
    4 cups pink icing
    ½ cup pale-green sugar dough
Optional: 2 cups Royal Icing (page 36)

FLOWERS

4 medium pink roses
3 small white roses
6 small cream roses
15 miniature pink rosebuds
15 violets

1. Bake, cool, and unpan the cakes. Trim off the bulging top of each cake so that the top and bottom surfaces are equally flat. Score and slice the cakes horizontally at ½-inch intervals and slip a cardboard cake round under each slice. You will be using 5 slices in all. Wrap and freeze any extra slices. Remove the mousse filling and the icing from the refrigerator and bring to room temperature.

2. Wash each of the 5 slices with vanilla wash.

3. Place the first slice on the turntable and spread on about 1 cup of the chocolate mousse filling. Repeat with the next 3 slices, and place the fifth slice on top of the cake.

4. Check the cake to be sure the top is level and flat, applying pressure to any places where it is uneven. Remove any oozing filling with a spatula, crumb-coat the cake (see page 14), and chill for at least 3 hours.

5. Place 4 cups of the buttercream icing in the bowl of

a standing mixer. Add a toothpick dab of red gel food color. Turn the mixer on low, blend for 2 minutes, check the color, and add more red if you need to. Scrape down the sides of the bowl and blend for another minute, or until the icing color is a uniform pale pink throughout, and no longer streaky.

6. Remove the cake from the refrigerator. Using a regular steak knife, round the top edges of the cake. If you have not used a heart-shaped pan, place the heart-shaped cardboard on top of the cake and trim the cake as needed. Crumb-coat the entire cake and refrigerate for 1 hour.

7. Ice the cake with the pink buttercream icing, taking your time to ensure that the finish is smooth and seamless. Ice the top of the cake using the flexible icing blade to make the edges smooth and round. Refrigerate the cake for at least 1 hour, or until you are ready to decorate.

8. Remove the cake from the refrigerator. Smooth any rough edges with your fingers, using gentle pressure; do not gouge or dent the icing.

9. Fill a pastry bag with the plain buttercream icing and attach the #3 round tip. Practice piping the cornelli pattern on a piece of wax paper before you begin piping the pattern onto the cake.

10. Pipe the cornelli pattern over the entire surface of the cake, stopping and refrigerating the cake whenever you need to. When you continue piping the pattern, make sure the icing in your bag is at room temperature.

11. Roll out the green sugar dough to a length of about 10 inches. Cut a ribbon 1½ inches wide by 10 inches long. Drape the ribbon across the cake diagonally, lifting up to create a ripple or drape effect.

12. Begin to arrange the flowers on your cake, following the direction of the ribbon and placing some flowers directly on the ribbon and others on either side. Box and enclose the cake if you intend to refrigerate it after the flowers have been arranged.

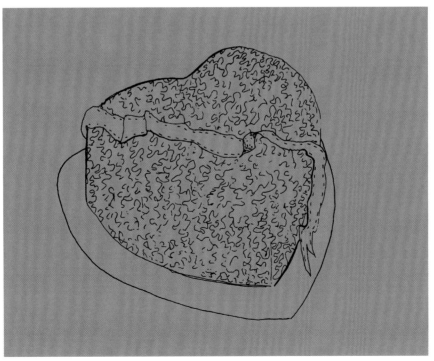

Positioning the sugar-dough ribbon.

Lace-points pattern.

13. If you choose to add lace points, fill a pastry bag with Royal Icing and attach a #2 round tip. Enlarge the template 50 percent. Lay a piece of wax paper over the template (see illustration above) and pipe up to 30 lace points, leaving space between them. Leave at room temperature for up to 3 days; do not refrigerate. Remove the points from the wax paper using a small palette knife. When you are ready to display the cake, carefully stick the lace points into the sides of the cake all the way around.

Calla Lily Cake

SERVES 10 TO 15

I love calla lilies, simple, graceful flowers easy to make in sugar dough. Their art deco appearance and the size of the blossom make them ideal for decorating a cake for a mature bride. Simple, stark, beautiful, the calla lilies will be the perfect flowers to set the scene for the ceremony and celebration. The effect is elegant and sophisticated.

This is a stunning cake; its beauty lies in its simplicity: You can use any cake recipe, any filling, and any additional flowers you like to give the cake your own look. The cake would be suitable for any number of occasions, from a wedding to a garden-club luncheon to an anniversary party.

LEVEL OF DIFFICULTY: 1

TIMING: This cake can be baked 2 days ahead and crumb-coated then. Ice and refrigerate the cake for at least 4 hours, or up to 1 day before you apply flowers. Flowers can be placed on the cake 1 day ahead or the day of the event.

HINTS: You will need lots of calla lilies for this cake; I suggest starting the flowers several weeks in advance. The small lilies are about 2 inches wide and 2 inches tall, while the larger ones are about 4 inches wide and tall. Before you cover the surface of this cake with flowers, cover most of the surface underneath with green leaves, and drape a few over the edges of the cake. (The leaves

add authenticity to the flowers, as well as a beautiful dash of color.) After you begin to place flowers on the cake, use the green icing and leaf tip to fill in around and up the sides of the flowers. You may need to use a pair of clamp-type longnose pliers to push the flower wires into the cake. If you press on the top of each flower, you risk breaking it, and your hands may be too big to reach underneath the flower to stick it into the cake by its wire.

SPECIAL EQUIPMENT

Two 10 × 3-inch round cake pans
Turntable
Five 10-inch cardboard cake rounds
14-inch serrated knife
Pastry brush
Standing mixer with paddle or whisk attachment
4½-quart mixing bowl
Set of mixing bowls
Rolling pin
Plastic cutting board
Ruler
Flexible utility knife with clean blade
Clear plastic wrap
Twenty-five 5-inch lengths of florist wire
One roll florist tape
Long icing spatula
Icing blade
Two pastry bags
Two sets couplings
   #70 leaf tip
   #48 basketweave tip
   #6 round tip
Longnose pliers

STRUCTURAL SUPPORT

12-inch round cake platter or base

INGREDIENTS

2 recipes Chocolate Fudge Cake (page 21)
1 recipe Raspberry-flavored Wash (page 38)
1 recipe Raspberry Buttercream Filling (page 33)
1½ pints fresh raspberries
6 ounces melted unsweetened chocolate
1 recipe Basic Buttercream Icing (page 28):
   2 cups basic buttercream
   5 cups dark chocolate buttercream
   3 pounds sugar dough
Gel food color to make 2 cups leaf-green icing

CALLA LILIES:

3 small red
12 small yellow
14 small white
8 small purple
2 large purple
3 small red
6 large red
14 small white
6 large white
3 large pale green

1. Bake, cool, and unpan the cakes. Trim off the bulging top of each cake so that the top and bottom surface are equally flat. Remove the buttercream filling and icing from the refrigerator and allow to come to room temperature.

2. Place 5 cups buttercream icing in the bowl of a standing mixer, add the melted chocolate, and blend until the color of the icing is uniform and no longer streaky.

3. Place the first cake on the turntable and cut horizon-

tally in ½-inch slices, sliding each onto a cake round. Repeat with the second cake. You will be using 5 slices in all. Wrap and freeze any extra slices.

4. Wash each slice with the raspberry wash.
5. Place the first slice, on its cake cardboard, on the turntable. Apply 1 to 2 cups raspberry filling on the first slice, and press in ¼ of the fresh raspberries. Press the berries firmly so that the next slice will

lie flat against the one below it. Repeat with the next 3 slices and place the fifth slice on top of the cake.

6. Check the cake to be sure the top is level and flat, applying pressure to any places where it is uneven. Remove any oozing filling with a spatula. Crumb-coat the entire cake in basic buttercream icing and refrigerate for 1 hour (see page 14).

Masses of assorted flowers cascade down a tiered cake.

7. Fill a pastry bag with 4 cups of the chocolate buttercream icing and fit on the #48 basketweave tip. Basketweave around the sides of the entire cake.

8. Change to the #6 round tip. Use the remaining chocolate icing to border the base of the cake with the dragging pearl.

9. Fill a clean pastry bag with 2 cups leaf-green icing and the #70 leaf tip. Pipe leaves over most of the top surface of the cake, leaving a little of the basic buttercream exposed.

10. Beginning in the center, place the calla lilies on the cake. Start with the larger flowers in the center and work toward the outer perimeter of the cake surface, placing the smaller flowers toward the outer edges. Fill in any spaces with the smaller flowers. When pressing the flowers into the cake, let the center flowers stand a little higher than the surrounding flowers, so that you get the effect of flowers cascading down from the center.

11. Enclose your cake in a sealed box if you intend to refrigerate it after you have applied the flowers.

Fairy Tree Cake

SERVES 10 TO 15

Here's an opportunity to get really creative with sugar dough. There are all kinds of things you could make to decorate this tree stump: snails, ladybugs, a squirrel or two, birds—the possibilities are endless. This cake is pure fantasy for a little girl's birthday. It was designed for a party where the children were all to dress as fairies, and the favors were wands and crowns. The room was decorated to look like an enchanted forest. It was truly a charming party.

LEVEL OF DIFFICULTY: 1

TIMING: The cake can be baked 2 days ahead, and decorated 1 day ahead.

HINTS: When you trim this cake, keep in mind that you are trying to create a tree stump. It's very hard to make a mistake, as you will cover the cake with layers of icing "strips" that look like bark. When you blend color into the icings, don't blend the colors completely; what you want instead are some natural-looking striations in the browns of the tree stump. Add some yellow gel food color to the chocolate icing to get color variations.

The fairy is really just a simple figure made from sugar dough. I have given you a rough description of how to make her; you can position her sitting up if you like, or sleeping, as we have here. We used sheet gelatin to make her wings, but tissue paper or rice paper cutouts would work just as well.

SPECIAL EQUIPMENT

Small leaf cutter

Rose petal cutter

Calyx cutter

Swivel blade utility knife

Leaf veiner

Fourteen 4-inch lengths florist wire

Florist tape

Standing electric mixer

One 4½-quart mixing bowl

Set of mixing bowls

Rubber spatula

Two 8 × 3-inch round cake pans

One 8-inch round cake cardboard

Turntable

14-inch serrated knife

Small serrated steak knife

Five 6-inch round cake cardboards

Three pastry bags

Three sets couplings

  #3 round tip

  #13 star tip

  Lily of the valley tip

  #48 basketweave tip

  #233 grass tip

STRUCTURAL SUPPORT

14-inch round cake board or platter

INGREDIENTS

1 recipe Classic Yellow Cake (page 17)

1 recipe Raspberry Wash (page 38)

1 recipe Chocolate Buttercream Filling (page 32)

1 recipe Basic Buttercream Icing (page 28)

4 to 6 ounces unsweetened chocolate, melted, to make the following:

  3 cups mocha with addition of yellow gel food color

  3 cups dark chocolate

Gel food colors to make the following:

  2 cups grass-green icing

  1 cup purple icing

2 cups sugar dough colored to make the following:

  ⅓ cup peach or flesh color

  ½ cup leaf-green sugar dough

6 violets

1 gelatin sheet

Nontoxic Magic Markers

FAIRY

The fairy is only 4 inches tall. Fashion her torso, head, arms, and legs from peach or flesh-colored sugar dough, dress her, and let dry. Use nontoxic Magic Markers to add features to the fairy's face.

Pipe on her hair with brown icing and a #3 round tip. Make the top of her dress from green sugar dough leaves, and the skirt from 6 pink sugar dough rose petals; use a rose petal cutter to make these if you have one. Pipe little purple stars around her waist with some purple icing and a #13 star tip. The shoes are tiny leaves pressed onto her feet, with some purple star flowers piped on the top. The hat can be made using a calyx cutter and some green sugar dough. The wings are cutouts made from sheet gelatin, the details added with Magic Marker.

1. Trim the two cakes, score them at ½-inch intervals, and slice horizontally. Slip a cake round under each slice. Reserve 5 slices. Wrap and freeze the remainder.

2. Place the first layer on the cardboard cake round, then wash and fill. Slide the next layer on top of the filling, wash, and fill. Repeat with the remaining three slices. Place the stacked cake on the cake board or platter.

3. Center the 6-inch cake cardboard on top of the cake, place a serrated knife against the edge of the cardboard, and cut down and away to trim off a piece from one side of the cake. Drape this piece against the side of the cake so that half lies against the cake and the widest part rests on the cake board, secured

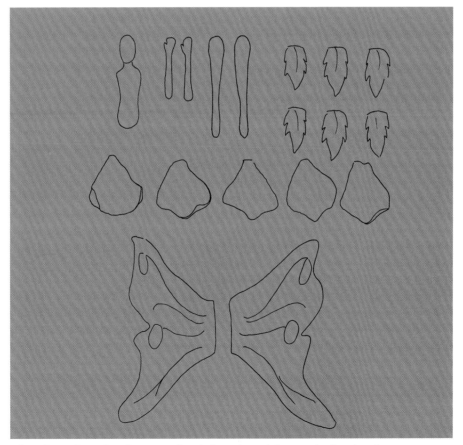

Sample outlines for the sugar-dough fairy, from left to right: head and torso, arms, legs, leaves for dress top, rose petals for skirt, wings.

with a dab of buttercream icing. (See right-hand drawing at the bottom of page 102.)

4. Repeat Step 3 twice more on two other sides of the cake.

5. Crumb-coat the cake and refrigerate for 1 hour (see page 14).

6. Blend the mocha buttercream briefly and add some yellow food color, leaving streaks. Fill a pastry bag with the icing and attach the #48 basketweave tip. Use the flat side of the tip. Starting at the edge of the top of the cake, begin to lay long strips of icing down the sides, overlapping and draping onto the cake board. Continue working around the cake, letting the strips overlap until the sides of the cake are completely covered.

7. Fill a second pastry bag with the dark chocolate icing and attach the #4 round tip. Randomly pipe long stripes into the overlapping mocha strips to simulate striations in the bark of the tree trunk.

8. Replace the basketweave tip on the pastry bag with the mocha icing with the lily of the valley tip. Using the rounded part of the tip, work from the center on top of the cake to pipe a large, open circle on the surface of the cake.

9. Using the pastry bag with the chocolate icing and the #4 round tip, pipe a concentric circle inside the mocha circle. Use the palette knife to flatten the circles, working carefully so that you don't spread the icing as much you flatten it.

10. Fill a pastry bag with the green icing and attach the grass tip. Place a 2-inch spot of grass on top of the cake in the upper right-hand corner. Pipe several clumps of grass around the base of the tree stump.

11. Place the leaves on top of the cake to the lower left, opposite the grass. Arrange the violets in between and around the leaves. Set the fairy on top of the cake, allowing her head to rest on the grass.

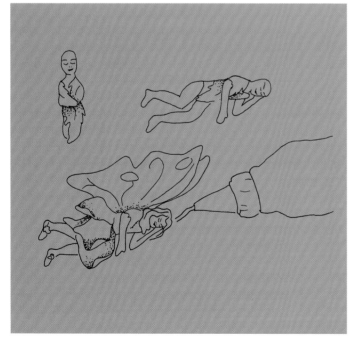

Finishing the sleeping fairy.

Shaping the tree stump.

Another lovely cake for a children's party would be a carousel.

Gift Box Cake

SERVES 10 TO 15

I have created many variations of this cake for birthdays, weddings, anniversaries, and even for corporate functions. It works well for almost any occasion to which you would bring a gift.

LEVEL OF DIFFICULTY: 2

TIMING: The cake may be baked, filled, and iced 2 days ahead, and decorated 1 day ahead. Be sure to box the cake or keep it covered so that the sugar dough stars and ribbons don't break down under refrigeration.

HINTS: This cake requires very little carving, so a carrot cake, or any cake with fruit or nuts in the batter, will work here. The trick to making the cake look like boxes is to create as smooth a surface as possible, as smooth and flat as wrapping paper. Spend some time icing and smoothing, icing and smoothing. Once this is done, chill the cake before adding the icing lid. After the iced cake is chilled, you will be able to place a strip of parchment around the bottom of the cake without ruining the icing job—just remember to use a light touch. No need to press the paper into the icing; gently arrange the paper around the cake, then add the lid. If you wish, make the lid in a different color icing than the cake.

SPECIAL EQUIPMENT
Two 8 × 8 × 3-inch square cake pans
Two 6 × 6 × 3-inch square cake pans
Five 8-inch square cake cardboards
Five 6-inch square cake cardboards
Turntable
Ruler
Pencil
14-inch serrated knife
Standing mixer and paddle or whisk attachment
Two 4½-quart bowls
One 24-inch by 3-inch piece of parchment, or
    two 16-inch by 3-inch pieces

Icing blade
Icing spatula
Three #14 pastry bags
Three sets couplings
    #4 round tip
    #48 basketweave tip
    #789 icing tip
Clean kitchen towel

STRUCTURAL SUPPORT
12- to 14-inch square cake board or platter
5 plastic drinking straws

INGREDIENTS

2 recipes Carrot Cake (page 22)

1 recipe Vanilla Wash (page 38)

1 recipe Cream Cheese Filling (page 32)

2 recipes Basic Buttercream Icing (page 28)

3 to 4 tablespoons melted chocolate to make 8 cups pale-brown buttercream icing

3 pounds sugar dough

Gel food colors to make the following:

2 cups lavender icing

3 cups pale-green icing

6 cups red icing

1 cup yellow sugar dough

2 cups pink sugar dough

2 cups brown sugar dough

1. Remove buttercream filling and icing from refrigerator. Bake, cool, unpan, and trim cakes. Score and slice horizontally at ½-inch intervals.

2. Slide the first of your cardboard squares under the first slice of each cake, set aside. Repeat with the remaining slices. You will need five in all for each cake. Paint each slice with the wash, and place one 8-inch cake slice on its cardboard on your turntable.

3. Fill the first 8-inch slice, smooth, then slide the second slice off its cardboard base onto the first filled layer. Fill and repeat with remaining slices. Chill the 8-inch cake for at least three hours.

4. Repeat Steps 2 and 3 with the 6-inch cake.

5. Remove the 8-inch cake from the refrigerator. Trim the sides of the cake if necessary, using your serrated knife to shave the sides to square them. Brush off the crumbs with a pastry brush.

6. Crumb-coat the 8-inch cake with white buttercream icing and refrigerate for one hour (see page 14).

7. Repeat Steps 5 and 6 for the 6-inch cake.

8. Mix 4 cups of the pale-brown buttercream with 2 cups of the red icing. This will be the icing for the 8-inch cake, and the shade should be a deeper color than that of the 6-inch cake.

9. Ice the cakes using your pastry bag and the #789 icing tip. For the 8-inch cake you will use the icing in step 8, and to ice the 6-inch cake you will use pale-brown icing. When the cakes are iced, smooth out the icing with your icing spatula or your blade. Chill the cakes for at least 3 hours or overnight.

10. Starting with the 8-inch cake, take a ruler and measure the height of your cake. Whatever the height of your cake is, cut the strip of baking parchment 1 inch narrower than the cake's height.

11. For Steps 11 and 12, see the illustration on page 106. Carefully place the strips of parchment around the base of the chilled 8-inch cake, so it just barely touches the icing. Do not apply unnecessary pressure, as you don't want to push the paper into the icing—the object is to let the paper just touch it. About 1 inch of the top of the cake should show above the paper.

12. Using a pastry bag filled with the red/pale-brown icing, and the flat side of a #789 icing tip, pipe icing on top of the cake. **To create an icing lid:** Ice the exposed top 1 inch on all four sides of the cake. Let this strip of icing overlap the top ¼ inch of the parchment.

13. Using an icing blade or an icing spatula, smooth the icing on top of the cake, removing as little icing as possible. Be sure the blade or icing spatula is clean and free of icing each time you touch the cake. Once the top of the cake is smooth, move to the sides of the lid, smoothing the edges, removing as little icing as possible. Do not be concerned about the bottom edge of the lid being uneven. When you remove the parchment, it will correct itself.

14. When you are done icing the lid, carefully grasp one loose edge of the parchment, and turning the turntable slowly, pull the paper gently away from the cake. Refrigerate the cake for at least one hour before proceeding.

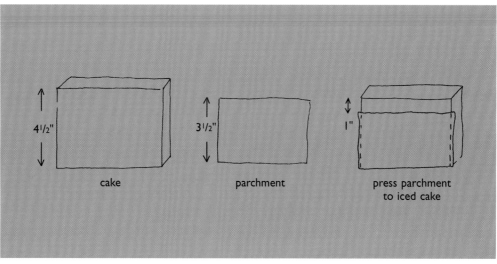

Positioning the parchment on the iced cake.

15. Using the pale-brown icing, repeat Steps 9 through 14 for the 6-inch cake.

16. Remove the 8-inch cake from the refrigerator.

17. Roll out 1 cup yellow sugar dough, made with egg-yellow and lemon-yellow food color, and cut out twelve 1-inch stars. Place the stars randomly around the four sides and on top of the 8-inch cake. Since it is supposed to look like wrapping paper, press a couple of the stars onto the corners of the box, letting the stars wrap around the edges of the cake.

18. Make two small bows with the yellow sugar dough and set aside to dry. Cut four lengths of yellow ribbon, about 5 to 7 inches long and 1 inch wide. Cut upside-down V tabs out of one end of each ribbon, and cover tightly with plastic wrap; set aside. The bows can be left out to dry, but the ribbons must be kept covered. The ribbons should remain pliable, so that when they are applied to the cake they will be flexible enough to drape.

19. Roll out the pink sugar dough to a length of 8 inches by 10 inches. Cut five ½ by 7-inch lengths of ribbon. Make 5 individual Loop Bows (see Loop Bows, page 57) and air-dry. Repeat with the brown sugar

dough. When your loops are dry, gather them in a bouquet, wrap the wires with florist tape, and set aside. (Make the bows at least one day in advance.)

20. Fill a pastry bag with 2 cups red icing and attach the #4 round tip. Starting from the bottom of your cake, pipe dots onto the cake, moving upward so that the dots resemble soda bubbles. Cluster most of the red dots toward the bottom of the cake, with a few rising upward.

21. Fill a pastry bag with 2 cups green icing and attach the #4 round tip. Pipe green dots, starting from the top down, clustering most of the dots at the top of the cake, with a few falling down between the red dots.

22. Using the same green icing, pipe a dragging pearl border along the bottom edge of the cake lid. Pipe the same dragging pearl along the top edge of the lid. Refrigerate the cake for 1 hour.

23. Remove the 6-inch cake from the refrigerator. Using the pastry bag with red icing, attach the #48 basket-weave tip. Using the flat side of the tip, start in the top center of the cake and pipe a straight line across the cake and down the side of the cake. Go back to

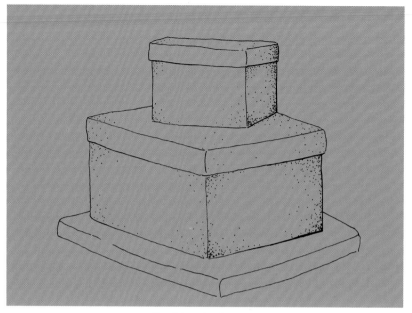

Stacking the boxes.

the top center of the cake and continue piping the line down the other side of the cake. Begin another line about 1½ inches away from the first line. Going in the same direction, pipe across the top and down both sides of the cake.

24. Now pipe one red icing line going in the opposite direction, about 1 to 2 inches away from the center.

25. Pipe a green line between the two red lines, across the top and down two sides of the cake. Pipe a horizontal straight line all the way around the bottom or base of the cake, about 2 inches above your turntable.

26. Using the same green icing, move to the single red ribbon that runs across the top of the cake, and pipe a dragging pearl up against the edge of one side of the ribbon. Rotate the turntable a one-quarter turn and, starting on top of the cake, pipe a dragging pearl ribbon down one side of the cake, and then the other. Repeat this dragging pearl line, placing the second line about 1 inch from the first.

27. Rotate the turntable a one-quarter rotation and, starting about 2 inches from one of the red lines, pipe a straight line ribbon down one side of the cake, then

the other. Rotate the turntable a one-quarter turn, and pipe a straight line ribbon down one side of the cake, then the other.

28. Fill a pastry bag with lavender icing, and attach the #48 basketweave tip. Working on the side of the cake, with the ridged edge of the tip, start about 1 inch below the bottom of the lid and pipe a straight ribbon line all the way around the cake. Move to the top of the cake, and pipe a straight line down one side of the cake, and then the other.

29. Remove the basket tip, and replace it with the #4 round tip. Give the turntable a one-quarter turn and, starting on the top of the cake, pipe a line down one side of the cake, and then the other.

30. Place a 6-inch square cake pan on the diagonal on top of the 8-inch cake. Press the pan very lightly so that the top of the cake is imprinted. Place a plastic drinking straw in the center of the cake, push it vertically into the cake to the bottom, and mark where it is level with the top of the icing. Gently remove the straw and cut at the mark. Using this straw as a guide, cut 4 straws the same length. Reinsert a straw

into the center of the cake, and insert the other 4 straws in the corners of your marked square.

31. Place the 6-inch cake diagonally on top of the 8-inch cake so that each corner rests on top of a straw. Using the bag with the lavender icing and the #4 tip, triple-border using the dragging pearl around the base of the 6-inch cake where it meets the 8-inch cake.

32. Using a pastry bag filled with brown icing and the #4 tip, triple-border using the dragging pearl around the base of the 8-inch cake.

33. Place your yellow bows on opposite corners of your 8-inch cake and drape the ribbon over the corners and edges of the cake. Box and refrigerate your cake.

A gift box cake can be customized to suit a variety of occasions.

Hatbox Cake

"Tell me about the guest of honor," I said. The reply came: "She is very neat. Everything she owns has its own place, and oh, she loves hats and hatboxes . . ." and so the hatbox cake. Perfect for a ladies' lunch or dinner, elegant and beautiful.

This cake calls for two recipes of almond cake, more than you will need. Fill the cake pans first, then use the remainder to make cupcakes. You will need only 1 cupcake to make the hat-pin cushion; the rest you can ice and send to school with the kids.

LEVEL OF DIFFICULTY: 2

TIMING: Order rice paper and dragées from a decorating supplier 2 weeks ahead. This cake can be baked 2 days ahead and crumb-coated then. Ice and refrigerate it for at least 4 hours, or up to 1 day before you pipe on the decorations. The cake and pincushion may be decorated a day ahead of the event.

HINTS: The piping may make this cake seem difficult, but you can pipe on any design you want. The design we have used on the cake in the photograph is rather elaborate. I suggest tracing your design onto a piece of tracing paper and then tracing over the design several times with your pastry bag until you get the hang of it. You can trace the pattern into the icing with a toothpick before doing the design in icing. Don't limit yourself to the template we have provided; feel free to create your own. You might try matching the cake to the decor of the room, or you could do something as simple as a series of concentric circles, or even a dotted swiss pattern instead.

To really dress it up, we put the cake on a silver platter and made two little pincushions out of cupcakes. One of the cupcakes sits in a silver wine coaster, but you could use a small flat dish or an old silver-rimmed ashtray.

We used rice paper to simulate tissue paper; it can be molded into shapes by spraying it with water first. Put a little water in a spray bottle, spray the rice paper, and crumple it gently to look like tissue. Place it in a bowl to help hold the shape until you are ready to use it. We have dusted the rice paper with silver food coloring powder, but you could dust it with pink or lavender, or leave it plain white.

SPECIAL EQUIPMENT

Two 9 × 3-inch round cake pans
One cupcake pan
Five 9-inch round cardboard cake rounds
Standing electric mixer with whip or paddle
    attachment
One 4½-quart mixing bowl
Mixing bowls
Turntable
Icing spatula
Ruler
Tracing paper
Pencil
Two-inch star cookie cutter
Two pastry bags
Two sets couplings:
    #1 round tip
    #2 round tip
Toothpicks

Two to four bamboo skewers
Florist tape
One 7-inch dowel, ½ inch thick
One 3-inch round silver or pewter wine coaster
    with rim
Three pieces 3-inch florist wire
Small scissors
One 12-inch round silver platter or cake base

INGREDIENTS

2 recipes Almond Cake (page 23)
1 recipe Orange-flavored Wash (page 38)
1 recipe Chocolate Buttercream Filling (page 32)
1 recipe Basic Buttercream Icing (page 28)
Gel food colors to make the following colors:
    Copper
    Red
    Leaf green, lime green
    Mauve   (continued)

SPECIAL EQUIPMENT *(continued)*
1 cup sugar dough to make the following:
   ¼ cup red sugar dough
   ¼ cup mauve sugar dough
   ¼ cup leaf-green sugar dough
   ¼ cup lime-green sugar dough

Jelly beans
Gumdrops
9 silver dragées—#3 medium
2 sheets rice paper
Silver food color dust or petal dust for rice paper
   tissue (or any pastel color)

1. Pour enough batter into a cupcake pan to make 3 cupcakes; pour the remaining batter into the cake pans and bake. (Three cupcakes will give you 2 more than you need.)
2. Bake, cool, and trim the cakes. Score them horizontally at ¾-inch intervals and slice. You will use 4 slices for the base cake and 1 layer for the lid—5 slices in all. Dab a bit of buttercream in the center of an 8-inch round cake cardboard. Place the single slice on the cake round.
3. Crumb-coat the single slice and refrigerate; this will become the hatbox lid (see page 14 for crumb coating).
4. Wash the remaining four cake slices, fill, and stack. Crumb-coat and refrigerate.
5. Blend 4 cups of buttercream icing with a dab of copper food color to get a pale pink. Add more color if you like; just be sure to blend well so the color is uniform and there are no streaks. Ice the 9-inch layer cake with pink buttercream and refrigerate.
6. Remove the lid from the refrigerator, ice in white buttercream, and refrigerate.
7. Trace the lace pattern onto a piece of tracing paper. Fill two pastry bags, putting 3 cups white buttercream icing in each. Attach the #1 tip to one bag and the #2 tip to the other.
8. Using a bag with white icing and the #2 tip, pipe a plain pearl border all around the base perimeter and the top edge of the cake.

A sample lace pattern for the hatbox.

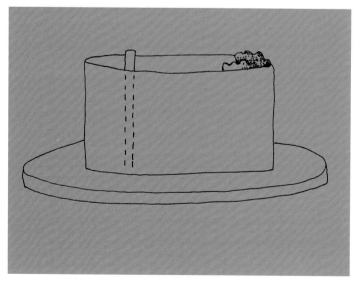

Before positioning the "lid."

9. Practice piping the white icing over the template on tracing paper. Use the #2 tip for the larger designs and the #1 tip for the smaller ones. Go over each of the larger curls twice; pipe on top of the first line with a dragging pearl. When you are comfortable making the patterns, pipe this pattern over all sides of the 9-inch layer cake. Refrigerate the cake for at least 1 hour.

10. Remove the iced lid from the refrigerator and set it on the turntable. Using a bag with white icing and the #2 tip, pipe a pearl border around the bottom perimeter. Pipe a dragging pearl border above the first border. The goal is to cover the cardboard base that the lid rests on so the base is no longer visible.

11. Using the #1 tip and the white icing, pipe groups of 3 dots in a triangle fashion all over the sides and top of the lid. (You may need to pipe a third border to make sure the cardboard is covered.) Refrigerate for 30 minutes.

12. Remove the iced cake from the refrigerator. Squirt a

A similar technique was used for this treasure chest.

mound of about ¼ cup of any color icing off to one side of the top of the cake (don't worry about how it looks—it is being used as glue). Push the 7-inch dowel vertically into the cake opposite the mound of icing, about 2 inches from the edge of the cake. About 1 to 2 inches will stick out of the cake.

13. Remove the lid from the refrigerator and carefully place one edge on the mound of icing, being sure the edge of the lid and the edge of the cake underneath are flush. Let the other side of the lid rest on the dowel.

14. If you like, border around the area where the two cakes meet to fill in any spaces or gaps. We used pink icing and the #2 round tip to border the lid.

15. Dust the crumpled rice paper with the color of your choice. Cut or tear the paper into large pieces and begin to tuck it into the open gap between the two cakes to simulate tissue paper spilling out of the hatbox.

PINCUSHION:

Gel food colors

1½ cups sugar dough to make the following:

    ½ cup red

    ½ cup mauve

    ¼ cup leaf green

    ¼ cup lime green

Jelly beans

Gumdrops

Standard dragées

---

1. Unmold the cupcakes and let cool. Try fitting the bottom of one of the cupcakes into the wine coaster. If it is too large or fits snugly, trim off a little from the bottom. (You will need enough room to fit the cupcake trimmed with sugar dough into the base, so trim accordingly.) Carve the top of a cupcake into a round ball.

2. Roll out an 8 × 8-inch piece of red sugar dough. Cut a 6-inch circle and wrap the dough around the cupcake ball, gathering the edges inward toward the center of the cupcake. Make a small indentation with your thumb in the top center where the dough meets.

3. Roll out the green sugar dough, and make a cutout using a small star cookie cutter. Place the star over the center of the cupcake where the edges of red dough meet and press the center of the star gently into the indentation.

4. Cut three 3-inch lengths of florist wire, and wrap with florist tape. Stick 2 or 3 different-shaped jelly candies or gumdrops on top of each of the wires. Dab a drop of icing on top of the top candy, place a silver dragée directly on top, and then stick the wires into the center of the green star on top of the pincushion.

Lily of the Valley Cake

SERVES 50 TO 60

The delicate, fragrant, exquisite lily of the valley is spring's gift to every bridal bouquet. This tiny lily is a time-honored wedding symbol, but real lily of the valley has no business on a wedding cake. (It is a member of the belladonna family, or deadly nightshade, and it is poisonous.) With a little practice using a pastry bag with a lily tip, you can cover sections of your cake with piped lilies of the valley made of white icing. Complete the look by piping on green leaves, and you will have a beautiful wedding cake.

LEVEL OF DIFFICULTY: 3

TIMING: Order the platform with the columns from a baking supplier several weeks in advance. Bows can be done 1 week ahead, cakes baked up to 3 days ahead, and filling and icing made up to 3 days ahead. The cake can be filled and iced 2 days ahead. Assembly, bordering, and decorating can be done 1 to 2 days ahead if you have a refrigerator large enough to accommodate the cake.

HINTS: **Do not use real lily of the valley flowers on the cake. They are beautiful but also poisonous!** This is an easier wedding cake in that there are no handmade flowers, only piped flowers, and some ribbon, which is easy to make. For this cake you will need to purchase a commercial 6-inch round plastic platform with four 9-inch disposable pillars with rings. You will place the 9-inch columns and 6-inch platform on top of the 8-inch cake. After you arrive at the event, you will place the 6-inch cake on its platform. Do not try to travel with the 6-inch cake in place; it will fall off!

You will need only 3 pastry bags and 3 tips to deco-rate the entire cake, and the cakes themselves are simply round layers. The first 2 cakes rest on top of one another, with plastic drinking straws as support. Pipe leaves up the platform legs if you wish. Be sure to use a colorless vanilla in the buttercream icing; it should be pure white. When coloring the buttercream for icing, use only the tiniest amount of green gel food color. Start with a drop on a toothpick, adding a little more until you get just the palest hint of color. The cake is the backdrop, and the color should be very subtle so that it doesn't compete with the flowers. When piping leaves, cover as much as possible of the top surface of the cake. Let the leaves drape down and over the sides of the cake, with the leaf tips curving in opposite directions, and ending at different points on the cake. Cover about $2/3$ of the leaves with lilies of the valley, piping flowers on top of flowers on top of the leaves to give a look of depth and dimension. Remember that the real flowers grow on a stem, and are full at the bottom but taper to buds at the top.

VARIATIONS: This cake could be made in any cake/ filling/icing combination. Sometimes we have added a

very pale green tint to the buttercream icing, but a pale, pale peach or rose, or even a pale lavender, would work beautifully. I feel that since lily of the valley is a delicate flower, the colors should be very delicate. If you wish, tint the sugar dough ribbons to match the color of the icing.

SPECIAL EQUIPMENT
Two 10 × 3-inch round cake pans
Two 8 × 3-inch round pans
Two 6 × 3-inch round pans
Four 10-inch cardboard cake rounds
Four 8-inch cardboard cake rounds
Four 6-inch cardboard cake rounds
Turntable
14-inch serrated knife
Pastry brush
Standing mixer with whisk or paddle attachment
Two large mixing bowls
Three pastry bags
Three sets couplings:
    #13 leaf tip
    #13 star tip
    Lily of the valley tip
Plastic cutting board
Rolling pin
Ruler
Flexible utility knife

Five 4-inch pieces florist wire
Florist tape
5 white 6- to 8-inch sugar dough bows with wire backs
6 feet 1/2-inch white satin ribbon (optional)

STRUCTURAL SUPPORT
10 drinking straws
Plastic 6-inch round platform with four 9-inch disposable pillars with rings
14-inch round Masonite cake board
6-inch round Masonite cake board

INGREDIENTS
3 recipes Classic Yellow Cake (page 17)
1 cup Orange Wash (page 38)
2 recipes Chocolate Buttercream Filling (page 32)
Two recipes Basic Buttercream Icing (page 28)
Gel food colors to make the following:
    10 cups pale-green icing
    6 cups leaf-green icing
Vegetable shortening

1. Let the cakes cool and remove them from the pans. Slice off the bulging tops so the tops and bottoms are equally flat.
2. Remove the buttercream filling and icing from the refrigerator and allow to come to room temperature.
3. Place 10 cups buttercream icing in the bowl of a standing mixer and add 1/4 to 1/2 teaspoon green gel food color to make a very pale green; add a tiny bit more if necessary to get the color you desire. Turn the mixer on low and blend for 2 minutes, scrape down the sides of the bowl, and blend for another minute, or until the icing color is uniform and no longer streaky.
4. Score each cake horizontally at 1-inch intervals and slice each layer. Slip a cake cardboard under each slice. The 3 finished cakes will each have 4 cake

slices. Wash the 12 layers with the orange wash. Wrap and freeze any leftover slices.

5. Place the first 10-inch layer on its cardboard on the turntable. Spread 1 to 2 cups of chocolate buttercream filling on the first layer. Slide the second layer off its cardboard and onto the filling, spread with buttercream filling. Repeat with the next 10-inch layer. Place the fourth 10-inch layer on top of the cake—do not fill.

6. Check the cake to be sure the top is level and flat, applying pressure to any places where it is uneven. Remove any oozing filling with a spatula. Crumb-coat the entire 10-inch cake with pale-green buttercream and refrigerate for 1 hour (see page 14).

7. Repeat the filling and crumb-coating for the 8-inch cake, then the 6-inch cake, refrigerating each after crumb-coating.

8. Remove the 10-inch cake from the refrigerator and ice smoothly with the pale-green buttercream. Refrigerate. Repeat with the 8-inch cake, then the 6-inch cake.

9. Remove the 10-inch cake from the refrigerator, place it on the platter or cake board, then set it on the turntable. Center the 8-inch cake pan on top and press gently into the icing to leave an outline. Press a straw in the center of the circular outline and mark where it is level with the top of the cake. Remove the straw and cut it at the mark. Using your cut straw as a guide, cut 4 other straws the same length. Set the first straw back in the center and insert the other 4 straws equidistant apart inside the circular outline. Push the straws gently into the cake—they touch the cake base below. The tops of the straws should be level with the top of the cake. Center the 8-inch cake (on its cardboard round) on top of the 10-inch cake.

10. Assemble the plastic platform and the four pillars according to the manufacturer's instructions. Place a ring on each pillar. Holding the rings so they don't slide down, center the pillars and the platform over the 8-inch cake. Apply a gentle, downward pressure to the top of the 6-inch platform, making the tubular pillars press into the 8-inch cake all the way to its cardboard base. Allow the rings to slide down the pillars and rest atop the 8-inch cake. The platform will be about 5 inches above the 8-inch cake.

11. Set the stacked cake on the turntable. Fill a pastry bag fitted with the #13 star tip with 3 cups of the pale-green icing. Triple-border around the base edge of the cake where it meets the plate, first with the dragging pearl, then with the loopy m, then with the dragging pearl stroke again.

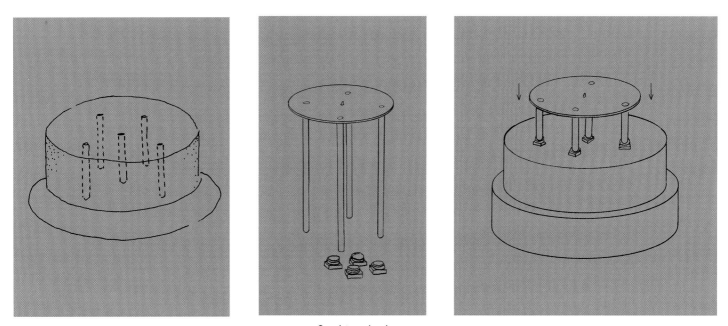

Stacking the layers.
Left: The 10-inch layer with the straws inserted (Step 9).
Middle: The plastic platform, the four pillars, and the rings (Step 10).
Right: The platform in place, with the rings slid down the pillars and resting on the 8-inch layer.

12. Fill a clean pastry bag fitted with a #13 leaf tip with leaf-green icing. Pipe the leaves down the columns, draping over the sides. Work your way down the sides and over the edges and sides of the 10-inch cake. There are no rules. You want to be able to see the pale-green icing but at the same time provide a good base for plenty of lily of the valley flowers.

13. Fill another pastry bag with the white buttercream and attach the lily of the valley tip. Pipe the flowers on top of the leaves, keeping them close together and connected. To give the flowers more depth, pipe flowers on top of flowers.

14. Roll out 2 cups of white sugar dough into a 12 × 16-inch rectangle. Cut 12 lengths of white ribbon, each 10 inches long by 1 inch wide. Cut out an inverted V from one end of each ribbon. Set 2 ribbons at each pillar with the straight edge of each ribbon against the pillar where it meets the 8-inch cake. Drape the ribbons gracefully down the sides of the cake, pressing gently in the spots where the ribbon touches the cake. Place a dried bow at each spot where ribbons meet the pillars, and push the wire into the cake. (There will be 1 bow left.) If you wish, stop at this point and refrigerate the cake in a sealed box overnight.

TOP TIER—6-INCH CAKE

SPECIAL EQUIPMENT

Pastry bag with pale-green icing and #13 star tip
Pastry bag with leaf-green icing and #13 leaf tip
Pastry bag with white icing and lily of the valley tip
3 cups white sugar dough for bows and ribbons

Vegetable shortening
Rolling pin
Swivel-blade utility knife
Plastic cutting board
Ruler

1. When the cake is in place at its final destination, place the 6-inch cake on top of the platform. Pipe on the border, leaves, and lilies of the valley.

2. Roll out the remaining sugar dough and cut four 8 × 1-inch ribbons, cutting out an inverted V on the bottom of each. Place the 4 ribbons on top of the 6-inch cake, the straight edges meeting each other in the center. Stick the last bow in the center of the cake.

3. **Optional:** Pipe lilies of the valley over the knot of the bow on top of the cake. **Optional:** Cut two lengths of satin ribbon, one ribbon 63 inches long, the other 20 inches long. Place the 63-inch ribbon around the edge of the 14-inch cake board and glue where the two ends overlap. Repeat with the 20-inch ribbon on the 6-inch cake board.

4. To serve, remove the 6-inch cake and box it for the bride. Remove the bows and ribbons from the rest of the cake and remove the pillared platform. Cut the 8-inch cake, removing the platform underneath; then cut the 10-inch cake.

Marzipan Fruit Cake

SERVES 18 TO 25

We all have fond memories of playing with clay as children. Here is an opportunity to be a child again. Mold marzipan into flowers, apples, pears, bananas, or grapes, or try pumpkins or squash for a Thanksgiving or harvest cake. I once did an October wedding at a rural country inn, and covered the cake with marzipan pumpkins, gourds, and corn husks and stalks.

Working with marzipan is very tactile. You get both hands in it, using a little shortening to keep it from sticking to your fingers. The resulting fruits and vegetables can be painted with food colors to make them look real, then placed on a cake by themselves or to supplement flowers.

This cake is easy, and fun to make. If you have kids around, they can help shape the marzipan fruit—just be sure their hands are scrupulously clean, and that the children don't eat more than they make! Use real produce as models for shapes and colors.

LEVEL OF DIFFICULTY: 1

TIMING: Order marzipan from your supplier several weeks in advance. You will need approximately 7 pounds to complete the fruit needed for this cake. The fruit should be started one week in advance and stored in airtight containers. The cakes can be baked 2 days ahead, and so may the buttercream filling and icing. Assembly, filling, icing, and bordering can be done 1 day ahead. The fruit should go on the cake the day of the event, unless you have a box and a refrigerator large enough to hold the boxed cake; in that case you can add it the day before the event.

HINTS: People may wish to eat the marzipan, but if it is exposed to air for too long it will become crusty and inedible. If you must leave it exposed, a couple of days won't hurt it. Just be sure you insert the toothpicks (which will anchor the fruit to the cake) before you let the fruits dry out completely.

The same rule for refrigeration applies to flowers as well as marzipan. If you must refrigerate after you have decorated, then the cake must be enclosed in a box. If you leave the fruit exposed to moist refrigerator air, there is a risk of having droplets of water gather on the fruit, which will ruin the color and look. Experiment with colors. I wish I could give specific descriptions, but use your eye to get the right amount of green in the marzipan for pears, orange for oranges, and so on. The same applies to the right amount of food color dust to accent the fruit; only *you* can decide how little or how much. Again, I strongly suggest buying fresh examples of some of the fruits you will be using to help get a true sense of shapes and colors. Remember, you are working in miniature; try to keep all the fruits approximately the same size by starting with golf-ball-sized pieces of marzipan.

SPECIAL EQUIPMENT

Two 8 × 3-inch round cake pans

Two 6 × 3-inch round cake pans

Five 8-inch cardboard cake rounds

Five 6-inch cardboard cake rounds

Turntable

14-inch serrated knife

Pastry brush

Standing mixer with whisk or paddle attachment

Two 4 1/2-quart mixing bowls

One pastry bag

One set couplings

#4 round tip

#233 grass tip

Ivy leaf cutter

Oak leaf cutter

Rose leaf cutter

Leaf veiner

12-inch round platter or cake board

Six small paintbrushes

Florist tape

70 toothpicks

Thirty 6-inch skewers

Scissors

STRUCTURAL SUPPORT

14-inch round cake platter or board

5 plastic drinking straws

INGREDIENTS

2 recipes Classic Yellow Cake (page 17)

1 cup Orange Wash (page 38)

1 recipe Raspberry Buttercream Filling (page 33)

1 recipe Basic Buttercream Icing (page 28)

Gel food colors—red, orange, green, yellow

Food color dust or petal dust—assorted colors

2 cups moss-green sugar dough

7 pounds marzipan to make the following:

25 lady apples

18 pears

18 oranges

18 plums or figs

18 green apples

FRUIT:

Start with a golf-ball-sized piece of marzipan. Using toothpick drops of food color, dab in the color and knead well with hands. Adjust the color as needed, and don't be afraid to mix colors to create whatever shade you prefer. Use a #233 grass tip to dimple the orange skin, and the wooden tip of a skewer to indent the stem areas of the fruits.

Toothpicks and skewers will go through the center of the fruits to anchor them to the cake. Cover all the toothpicks with florist tape and wrap just 3 inches of 25 skewers. (When you skewer the fruit, leave a fraction of the end of each wrapped toothpick just sticking out of the top of the fruit so that it looks like a stem.) Stick the toothpicks through the fruit while the fruit is still soft. If some of the fruit is longer than the toothpicks, use wrapped skewers instead and cut off the extra length with scissors.

Once the fruits are finished, store them at room temperature in airtight containers for up to 3 weeks. When you are ready to apply the fruits to the cake, dust them with appropriate powdered food colors using clean small brushes.

A marzipan rabbit at the harvest.

1. Bake and cool, unpan the cakes. Trim off the bulging top of each cake so that the top and bottom surfaces are equally flat. Score and cut the slices horizontally at 1/2-inch intervals and slip each slice onto a cardboard cake round. You will use 10 slices in all, 5 slices from the 8-inch cakes and 5 slices from the 6-inch cakes. Wrap and freeze any extra slices.

2. Wash each slice with orange wash.

3. Place the first 8-inch slice on the cake board or platter and place on a turntable. Spread on the raspberry buttercream filling and repeat with the next three 8-inch slices, placing the fifth 8-inch slice on top of the cake.

4. Check the cake to be sure the top is level and flat, applying pressure to any places where it is uneven. Remove any oozing filling with a spatula. Crumb-coat the entire cake with buttercream icing and refrigerate for 1 hour (see page 14).

5. Repeat filling and crumb-coating for the 6-inch cake. Refrigerate after crumb-coating.

A cornucopia of marzipan fruits and vegetables.

6. Place all of the remaining buttercream icing in the bowl of a standing mixer. Add 2 drops of green gel food color to make a very pale green, adding a tiny bit more if necessary to get the color you desire. Blend for 2 minutes on low, scrape down the sides of the bowl, and blend for another minute, or until the icing color is uniform and no longer streaky.

7. Take a 6-inch round cake pan and gently center it atop the 8-inch cake. Remove the pan and your cake will be imprinted with a 6-inch circle. Take a drinking straw and insert it into the center of this 6-inch circle. Mark the straw where it is level with the top of the cake, remove, and cut at the mark. Using your cut straw as a guide, cut 4 straws of the same length. Reinsert the straw into the center, and insert the remaining 4 straws ½ inch inside the 6-inch circle, at equal intervals.

8. Ice both cakes to a smooth finish. Center the 6-inch cake on top of the 8-inch cake. Do not remove the 6-inch cake round.

9. Roll out the moss-green sugar dough to a thickness of less than ⅛ inch. Using the leaf cutters, cut out 15 ivy, 15 oak, and 15 rose leaves. Using the shiny side of the leaf veiner, lift each leaf and press it into the veiner. Peel off and gently press the leaves on the top, sides, and edges of the cake. Remember that most of the leaves will be covered by fruit, so don't fuss too much.

10. Working with the photograph of the cake, set aside the fruit in groups as you will want it on the cake. Set aside the fruits you will use for the top. Starting at the base of the cake, begin sticking the skewer or toothpick end of each fruit into the cake, grouping 3 or 4 fruits together to rest on the cake plate. Add fruits above.

Peach Rose Wedding Cake

SERVES 25

This is a gorgeous small wedding cake for an intimate family wedding. The flowers make this cake spectacular, so focus on them. I cannot stress enough the importance of starting flowers well in advance. At our shop, whenever we do a cake with this many flowers, we start making them at least 3 weeks in advance (but then, we also have at least 4 experienced flower-makers working on nothing but flowers). Start early; 3 months ahead if you can. You can do the flowers while sitting in front of the television at night. If you do 6 or 8 of the same flower 4 nights in a row, your flower-making skills will improve. It really pays to have plenty of flowers on hand. Flowers can turn a plain cake into a spectacular one in a matter of minutes.

I store flowers in large rectangular plastic boxes with lids. You can layer the flowers in these boxes, separating the layers with tissue paper or foam egg crates cut to the size of the boxes. Once the boxes are full, cover with plastic lids and stack the boxes. The completed flowers can be stored this way for up to 1 year.

LEVEL OF DIFFICULTY: 3

TIMING: The flowers for this cake should be started at least 6 to 12 weeks in advance. The cakes may be baked 3 days ahead and the buttercream filling and icing made 2 days in advance. Assembly, filling, icing, and bordering may be done 1 day ahead. The flowers should go on the cake the day of the event unless you have a box and a refrigerator large enough to hold the boxed cake, in which case flowers can be added to your cake the day before your event. Be sure you close or cover the box so that moisture from the refrigerator doesn't ruin your flowers.

HINTS: When you are ready to decorate, remember that a row of roses cascades down from the top and swirls around the cake. This should be done on 2 sides of the cake so that the roses appear to twist around the cake.

SPECIAL EQUIPMENT
Two 10 × 3-inch round cake pans
Two 8 × 3-inch round pans
Two 6 × 3-inch round pans
Four 10-inch cardboard cake rounds
Four 8-inch cardboard cake rounds
Four 6-inch cardboard cake rounds
Turntable
14-inch serrated knife
10-inch icing spatula
Pastry brush
Standing mixer with whisk or paddle attachment
Two 4½-quart mixing bowls
One pastry bag
One set couplings
    #13 star tip
Small sable paintbrush

STRUCTURAL SUPPORT
10 plastic drinking straws
14-inch round cake platter or board

INGREDIENTS
3 recipes Carrot Cake (page 22)
1 cup Orange Wash (page 38)
1 recipe Cream Cheese Filling (page 32)
2 recipes Basic Buttercream Icing (page 28)
6 pounds sugar dough
Copper gel food coloring
2 tablespoons copper food color dust
½ to 1 cup cornstarch

FLOWERS
22 large pale-peach roses
38 medium pale-peach roses
44 small pale-peach roses
72 pale-peach rosebuds

1. Prepare two 10-inch round pans, two 8-inch round pans, and two 6-inch round pans with parchment. Fill the pans to the ¾ mark with the carrot cake batter and bake according to directions. When the cakes are done, remove from the pans after they have cooled. Slice off the bulging tops so that the tops and bottoms are equally flat. Score each cake horizontally at 1-inch intervals.

2. Remove the buttercream filling and icing from the refrigerator and allow to come to room temperature.

3. Place 16 cups buttercream icing in the bowl of a standing mixer and add ¼ to ½ teaspoon copper gel food color to make a very pale rose, adding a tiny bit more if necessary to get the color you desire. Turn the mixer on low and blend for 2 minutes, scrape down the sides of the bowl, and blend for another

minute, or until the icing color is uniform and no longer streaky.

4. Set the first 10-inch cake on the turntable and slice horizontally at the score marks. Slide 2 layers from each 10-inch cake onto a cake round. Repeat with the 8-inch and 6-inch cakes, using only 2 slices out of each of the 6 cakes. You will use 12 layers in all, 4 from each of the three sizes. Wrap and freeze extra slices.

5. Wash each of the 12 layers with orange wash.

6. Place the first 10-inch layer on the turntable and spread with 1 to 2 cups of cream cheese filling. Repeat with the next two 10-inch layers, stack, and set the fourth 10-inch layer on top.

7. Check the cake to be sure the top is level and flat, applying pressure to any places where it is uneven. Remove any oozing filling with a spatula.

8. Insert a drinking straw into the center and press it down to the base of the cake. Mark the straw where it is even with the top of the cake. Remove the straw, and cut it at the mark. Cut 4 other straws the same length. Set the first straw back in the center of the

Positioning the flowers.

cake and insert the other 4 straws in a circle around the straw, equidistant apart, about 2 inches out from the center straw.

9. Crumb-coat the entire cake with the pale-peach buttercream, and refrigerate for 1 hour (see page 14).

10. Repeat the filling and crumb-coating for the 8-inch cake, then the 6-inch cake, refrigerating each after crumb coating.

11. Repeat Step 8 with the remaining 5 straws for the 8-inch cake.

12. Remove the 10-inch cake from the refrigerator, and ice smoothly with the pale-peach buttercream. Refrigerate when done. Repeat with the 8-inch cake, then the 6-inch cake.

13. Remove the 10-inch cake from the refrigerator, set on the platter or cake base, and place on the turntable. Fill a pastry bag with the #13 star tip with 3 cups of the pale-peach icing. Triple-border around the edge of the cake where it meets the plate, first with the dragging pearl, then the loopy m, then the dragging pearl stroke again.

14. Center the 8-inch cake on top of the 10-inch cake.

Using the pastry bag with the pale-peach icing and the #13 star tip, triple-border around the edge of the cake where it meets the cake underneath.

15. Center the 6-inch cake on top of the 8-inch cake. Using the pastry bag with the pale-peach icing and the #13 star tip, triple-border around the edge of the cake where it meets the cake underneath.

16. Optional: Mix the copper food color powder with enough cornstarch so that the powder is a shade darker than the roses. Dust the roses lightly by dipping the sable brush into the powder and brushing gently on the outer petals.

17. Starting on the top of the 6-inch cake, stick 4 large roses in the center about 1 inch apart. Begin to fill in the cake with 6 medium roses, and 8 small roses. Once you have placed these roses, fill in with the rosebuds, using up to 18 rosebuds for the top of the cake. You want to create the look of a nosegay of roses.

18. Starting at the base of the 10-inch cake, place 3 large roses together into the cake. Turn the cake base or turntable 2 inches to the right and place 3 large roses

into the base of the 8-inch cake. Turn the cake base or turntable 2 inches to the right and place 3 large roses into the base of the 6-inch cake.

19. Place 12 medium roses in the sides of the cake, working from the top down. Note that the idea is to curve the roses down one side of the cake, and that you want to establish this curving line with the placement of the roses so they spiral down the cake. Place small roses in the cake, beginning to fill in the spaces and give the line definition.

20. Fill in any large gaps or holes with the remaining 4 medium roses and 6 small roses. Stick 18 to 20 rose-buds in between the flowers to finish and fill out the swirl of roses.

21. Repeat Steps 17 through 19, using the same pattern, on the opposite side of the cake.

22. To serve, remove the top (6-inch) cake and box to give to the bride. Remove the remaining flowers and cut the 8-inch cake, and then the 10-inch cake. Serve each cake slice with a rose.

The same techniques and different choices of colors and flowers create an entirely different cake.

Potted Iris Cake

SERVES 12 TO 15

This is a beautiful cake that you can fill with any flower you wish; we used iris in this particular cake, but I have also done it with roses. You could also create a topiary with the pot as the base, and a beautiful ball of tiny roses on top—use your imagination.

Irises and orchids are so much alike to me that I consider the iris the American orchid. Rising to the challenge of a florist friend who said he could always tell a fake flower from the real, I made 3 sugar dough irises and placed them in a bouquet of real irises, telling him to find the fakes. I'm proud to say that his batting average was only 50 percent, and I glowed at his concession and praise. After that, I made a cake that was a replica of a clay flower pot in which I "planted" 3 irises, and used it as a dinner centerpiece. The guests were floored when I began cutting the flower pot to serve as the dessert. Your guests will love it too. Place the flowers in a dry vase so you can continue to enjoy them—and eat the pot!

LEVEL OF DIFFICULTY: 2

TIMING: The cake can be baked 2 days ahead and crumb-coated then. Chill the crumb-coated cake for at least 4 hours before you apply the final icing. Ice and refrigerate the cake for at least 1 day before you apply flowers, which may be placed on the cake 1 day ahead or the day of the event.

HINTS: The easiest way to shape the cake is to center the 6-inch cardboard cake round on top of and in the center of the other filled, crumb-coated sizes. Hold the serrated knife with the blade pointing down and, starting at the very top, carve into the cake and away from the 6-inch circle; the goal is to carve an upside-down clay pot. (Use an inverted pot as a model. Be careful carving; later the pot must be turned right side up, and it will need to be balanced to stand upright. Try to shave off as little cake as possible while creating the look of your flower pot.

This is technically a lid cake, so use the same parchment and icing techniques described for the Gift Box Cake (page 104).

The pot is iced using buttercream containing a fair amount of chocolate and red coloring, both agents that break down buttercream faster than other ingredients do. Play with the red in the chocolate until you get a deep terra-cotta hue. The texture and temperature of the icing is critical here. The pot is shaped in such a way that the top will be heavier with icing than the bottom, so be sure the icing is at just the right temperature. If it is too warm or too loose, the icing may fall off the cake. To be safe, I recommend refrigerating the cake for several hours after each application of icing.

If you decide to use irises for this cake, be sure to cut a 12-inch length of florist wire so you will have plenty of stem to stick into the cake while allowing the irises to stand tall above the pot. Of course you will wrap the stems in green florist tape first. To make irises, see page 48.

If you intend to refrigerate the cake after you add flowers, be sure it is enclosed in a box so that the flowers remain stable.

SPECIAL EQUIPMENT

Two 8 × 8 × 3-inch round cake pans

Five 8-inch cardboard cake rounds

One 6-inch cardboard cake round

Turntable

Ruler

Pencil

14-inch serrated knife

Pastry brush

Standing mixer and paddle or whisk attachment

One 4½-quart mixing bowl

Handheld electric mixer

Mixing bowls

Rolling pin

Plastic cutting board

Flexible utility knife with clean blade

Clear plastic wrap

Icing spatula

4-inch offset spatula

Icing blade

12-inch by 3½-inch piece of parchment, cut into thirds

Palette knife

4 toothpicks

Two pastry bags

Two sets couplings

  #789 icing tip

  #4 round tip

  #67 leaf tip

  #233 grass tip

Five 12-inch lengths of florist wire

One roll florist tape

1 recipe Spice Cake (page 20)

1 recipe Orange Wash (page 38)

1 recipe Orange Buttercream Filling (page 33)

1 recipe Basic Buttercream Icing (page 28)

8 ounces melted unsweetened chocolate mixed with 8 cups Basic Buttercream Icing plus ½ to 1 teaspoon red food color

Gel food colors to make 4 cups grass-green icing

3 cups sugar dough

FLOWERS

5 to 7 irises

8 iris leaves

---

1. Bake the cakes and let them cool. Trim off the bulging top of each cake so that the top and bottom surface are equally flat. Score the cakes at 1-inch intervals and slice horizontally. Slip each slice onto a cake cardboard. Reserve 5 slices in all, and wrap and freeze any remaining slices. Remove the buttercream filling and icing from the refrigerator and allow to come to room temperature.

2. Wash each of the 5 slices with orange wash.

3. Place the first slice on an 8-inch cake cardboard on the turntable and spread on 1 to 2 cups of orange butter-cream filling. Repeat with the next 3 slices, placing the fifth slice on top.

4. Check the cake to be sure the top is level and flat, applying pressure to any places where it is uneven. Remove any oozing filling with a spatula. Refrigerate the cake for 1 hour.

5. To shape the cake, place it on the turntable and center the 6-inch cardboard cake round on top. Hold the serrated knife with the blade pointing down and, beginning at the very top of the cake, carve away from the 6-inch circle; the object is to carve an

If potted plants don't appeal, try a flower arrangement.

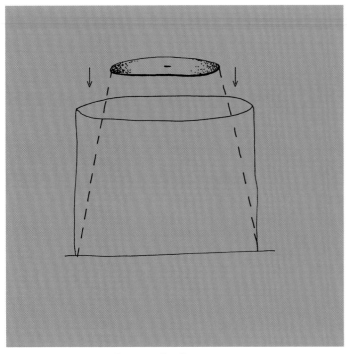

Shaping the flower pot.

Creating the lip of the pot.

upside-down clay pot tapering from 6 inches at the top to 7 inches at the bottom. When you have finished carving, turn the pot right side up so that the 6-inch diameter part of the cake becomes your base. Remove the 8-inch cake cardboard.

6. Crumb-coat the entire cake in basic buttercream icing and refrigerate for 4 hours (see page 14).

7. Place 8 cups basic buttercream icing in the bowl of a standing mixer and add the melted chocolate and ¼ teaspoon red food color. Blend on low speed for 2 minutes. Scrape down the sides of the bowl and check the color. You want a deep terra-cotta hue. If necessary, add a bit more red. Blend for another minute, or until the icing color is uniform and no longer streaky.

8. Stir the grass-green gel food color into 4 cups of basic buttercream. Mix on medium speed for 1 minute. Stop and scrape down the sides of the bowl, adding more green food color if needed. Transfer the green icing to a pastry bag equipped with a #233 grass tip.

9. Ice the cake with the terra-cotta chocolate buttercream icing, taking your time to be sure that the finish is smooth and seamless, and that the edges are sharp. Refrigerate the cake for at least 2 hours before proceeding.

10. Place the strips of parchment around the base of the chilled cake. About 1 inch of the top of the cake should stick out above the paper. Do not apply unnecessary pressure; you don't want to push the paper into the icing—the paper should just touch the icing. Using a bag and the flat side of a #789 icing tip, pipe icing around the top exposed perimeter of the cake; let some icing cover the top ¼ inch of the parchment.

11. Smooth the icing carefully, removing as little as possible. Don't be concerned with how the top edge of the cake looks; it will be covered later. When you

Making the grass.

have smoothed the lip of the pot, gently remove the parchment pieces, pulling them away from the cake. Correct any tears or pulls in the icing using a small palette knife.

12. Fill a pastry bag with the remaining terra-cotta chocolate icing and attach the #4 round tip. Place 4 toothpicks, upright and evenly spaced, around the top perimeter of the cake, inserting each toothpick not more than 1/8 inch from the edge. Pipe 1 swag beginning at 1 toothpick, and ending at the next. Continue piping swags from that toothpick to the next, and the next. Pipe over each swag 3 times. Pipe a dot in the center where each swag meets the toothpick.

13. Change to the #67 leaf tip. Pipe a series of 3 leaves just under the dot, then pipe 3 more leaves over them. Repeat the leaf pattern at each point where the swags meet. Replace the leaf tip with the #4 round tip and pipe 3 dots in a triangular fashion in the center of each leaf series. Remove and discard the toothpicks.

14. Using the pastry bag with the green icing and the grass tip, cover the top of the cake with grass. Point your tip straight down onto the cake, squeeze, and pull up. Cover the entire top of the cake with grass, piping grass on top of grass, until the top surface is covered. Refrigerate the cake for at least 4 hours, or overnight.

15. When you are ready, arrange 2 or 3 irises in the center of the cake, and 4 leaves around the flowers.

Ribbon Cake

SERVES 15 TO 20

This is a stunning cake whose beauty lies in its simplicity. You can use any cake recipe and any filling. I first did a version of this cake for a bride who said "No flowers but I love ribbons and bows." We draped soft-colored, fanciful ribbons with detailed edging all over the cake; it was simply beautiful. The loop bows are easier to make than flowers, and can be done well ahead of time. You can vary the color of the icing and the ribbons to suit your personal taste or that of the bride, or to match the colors in the cake pedestal. This cake is like a good suit; it can stand on its own at a formal celebration yet is equally suitable for a small birthday dinner with close friends. It may be used for a man or a woman, depending on the colors.

LEVEL OF DIFFICULTY: 1

TIMING: Loop bows can be done up to 1 month ahead, but no later than 2 days before. The cake can be baked 2 days ahead and crumb-coated then. The cake should be iced and refrigerated for at least 4 hours or up to 1 day before you apply ribbons. Long, draped ribbons should be applied several hours before serving, and the loop bows should be inserted after the long ribbons.

HINTS: The goal in icing the cake is to make it as smooth and seamless as possible, and to make sure the top is perfectly flat. Ideally, this cake should be served on a pedestal cake stand, and ribbons and bows applied on site. Some of the ribbons drape and hang. Once dry, they will become very brittle, and any unnecessary movement could break them. Particularly if you serve this cake on a pedestal stand, make sure the cake is in place before applying the ribbons. It is best that the icing be at room temperature when you apply the blue ribbon, but this may be difficult. The cake shouldn't be at room temperature *and* sit out for another 6 hours without refrigeration. I suggest that you have a little extra buttercream on hand to act as glue if necessary. To serve the cake, remove the loop nosegay and the long ribbons before cutting.

SPECIAL EQUIPMENT

Two 10 × 3-inch round cake pans
Turntable
Five 10-inch cardboard cake rounds
14-inch serrated knife
Pastry brush
Standing electric mixer with paddle or whisk
   attachment

One 4 1/2-quart mixing bowl
Mixing bowls
Rolling pin
Plastic cutting board
Ruler
Flexible utility knife with clean blade
Clear plastic wrap
Pastry crimper

Twenty-five 5-inch lengths of florist wire

One roll florist tape

Four half-sheet pans

Long icing spatula

Icing blade

Two pastry bags

Two sets couplings

   #13 star tip

   #3 round tip

STRUCTURAL SUPPORT

12-inch round pedestal cake stand

INGREDIENTS

1 recipe Hazelnut Cake (page 24)

1 cup Vanilla Wash (page 38)

1 recipe Chocolate Mousse Filling (page 35)

1 1/2 pints fresh raspberries

1 recipe Basic Buttercream Icing (page 28) and

   gel food colors to make the following:

   5 cups blue icing

   2 cups yellow icing

5 cups sugar dough:

   3 cups yellow

   2 cups blue

Vegetable shortening

1. Bake and cool the cakes. Trim off the bulging top of each cake so that the top and bottom surfaces are equally flat. Place the first cake on the turntable, score the cake at one-inch intervals, and slice horizontally, slipping each slice onto a cake cardboard. Repeat with the second cake, reserving five slices in all. Wrap and freeze any remaining slices.

2. Remove the buttercream icing from the refrigerator and bring to room temperature.

3. Wash each of the 5 slices with the vanilla wash.

4. Place the first slice on a turntable. Spread on 1 to 2 cups of mousse filling and press ¼ of the fresh raspberries into the filling firmly, so that the next layer will lie flat against the one below it. Repeat with the next 3 slices, placing the fifth slice on top of the cake.

5. Check the cake to be sure the top is level and flat, applying pressure to any places where it is uneven. Remove any oozing filling with a spatula. Crumb-coat the entire cake and refrigerate for 1 hour (see page 14).

6. Place 5 cups of the buttercream icing in the bowl of a standing mixer. Add 2 or 3 tiny droplets of blue or lavender food color. Turn the mixer on low and blend for 2 minutes; scrape down the sides of the bowl, check the color, and add more if necessary. Blend until the color of the icing is uniform and no longer streaky.

7. Ice the cake with the blue buttercream icing, taking time to be sure that the finish is smooth and seamless and the edges are sharp.

8. Mix the yellow food color into the remaining 2 cups of buttercream icing. Place in a pastry bag, attaching the #3 round tip. Pipe small dots all over the cake. There is no real pattern; just attempt to space the dots evenly over the entire cake.

9. Refrigerate the cake until you are ready to transport and/or decorate, at least 4 to 6 hours.

10. Carefully place the cake on a pedestal stand. Fill a pastry bag with 2 cups of the blue icing. Attach the #13 star tip and border around the bottom edge of the cake using the dragging pearl stroke. Pipe a second border around the outside of the dragging pearl, this time using the loopy m. You can if you wish make a third border, another dragging pearl directly on top of the first dragging pearl.

RIBBONS AND LOOP BOWS

11. Use a large surface area (at least 36 square inches). Prepare the clean work surface with vegetable shortening. Rub the rolling pin with a thin coating of shortening, and roll out 1 cup of the yellow sugar dough to about 10 inches long and 6 to 8 inches wide. Working with the long edge of the sugar

Dotting the frosted cake.

dough, use a ruler as a guide to mark and cut out a 10-inch × ½-inch length of ribbon. Do not lift the ribbon yet. Move the ruler over and repeat, marking and cutting at least twelve ½-inch wide ribbons. Use a knife to slice a straight line across the top and the bottom of the ribbons so that they are all the same length and have straight ends.

12. Lay a 10-inch length of clear plastic wrap on top of the sugar-dough ribbons; it is not necessary to cover the dough completely. Using the pastry crimper, gently trace a light seam along the edges of each ribbon, being careful to use a gentle touch to avoid cutting through the ribbons.

13. Lift the plastic wrap to lift up one of the ribbons. Cover the rest of the sugar-dough ribbons with the plastic wrap. Hold a length of wire in the middle, straight out in front of you. With the other hand, pick up one end of the ribbon and stick the bottom 2 inches of the wire against the end of the ribbon. Loop the rest of the ribbon up so that the ends meet, and squeeze the ends so that they attach securely to the end of the wire. Lay the ribbon on its side in a half-sheet pan so that one edge of the ribbon is resting on the pan and the other edge is exposed to the air. Gently shape the loop so that it is rounded, and let dry. Continue making loops with the yellow sugar dough; you will need to make 25 loops. Try to keep all the ribbons the same shape to make bunching them together easier. Set aside the remaining yellow sugar dough, covered with plastic wrap.

14. Once the loops are completely dry, bunch them as you would a nosegay. Start with 1 loop and add loops, 1 at a time, until you have a "bouquet" of 20 loops. Now take florist tape and, starting at the top of the wire where the loops meet, begin to wrap the wires with the tape, wrapping the tape around and

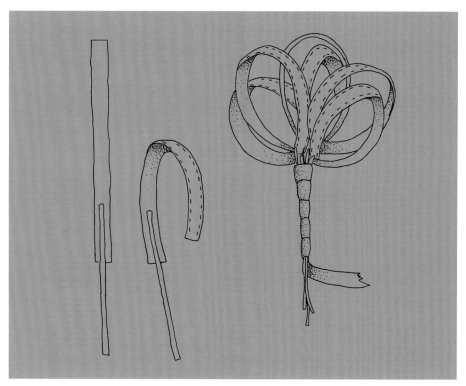

Making the ribbon nosegay.

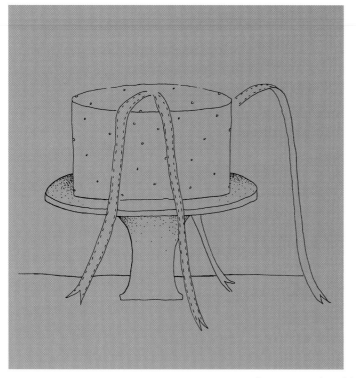

Positioning the ribbons and the nosegay.

around the wire until you reach the middle. At the midway point, take a good look at the loop bouquet. If there are any that need to be pulled up or pushed down, now is the time to make any adjustments. Be gentle and careful; the ribbons are very brittle and will break easily. Pull or push the loops into place by pulling or pushing the wire. If you do break one, pull the broken loop out of the bunch from the top and just add a loop from the extras. Wrap the tape around to secure it to the group. Once all adjustments are made, continue wrapping the wire until you reach the end. Stick the nosegay into a foam-plastic block.

15. Roll out 1 cup of blue sugar dough to about 10 inches long by 6 to 8 inches wide. Working with the long edge of the sugar dough, use a ruler as a guide to mark and cut out a 10 × 1-inch length of ribbon. Do not lift the ribbon yet. Move the ruler over and repeat, marking and cutting at least six 10 × 1-inch

ribbons. Using a knife, slice a straight line across the top and the bottom of the ribbons so that they are all the same length and have straight ends.

16. Lay a 10-inch length of clear plastic wrap on top of the sugar-dough ribbons. Using the pastry crimper, gently trace a light seam along both edges of each ribbon, being careful to use a gentle touch so that you don't cut through the ribbon. To prevent drying, leave the ribbons covered until you are ready to use them.

17. Remove a ribbon, cut an upside-down V out of what will be the bottom of the first ribbon, then lift the ribbon. Place the straight edge of the ribbon on top and in the center of the cake, letting the cutout V end of the ribbon drape down over the side. You can ripple the ribbon so it appears to fall down and curl against the cake. Use your fingers to lift the ribbon away from the cake in places. In spots where the rib-

bon touches the cake, press gently against the ribbon so that it adheres to the cake, using a dab of buttercream if necessary. Repeat, using 3 to 5 more ribbons, arranging them around the cake and letting the top straight edges touch and overlap one another.

18. Repeat Steps 15, 16, and 17 using the remaining yellow sugar dough; make the yellow ribbons slightly thinner in width than the blue ribbons.

19. Arrange the yellow ribbons between the blue ribbons.

20. Holding the wire where it meets the loops, place the loop ribbon nosegay in the center of the cake where the edges of the blue ribbons meet or overlap. Push the wrapped wires down into the cake.

21. To serve, remove the loop nosegay and the long ribbons before cutting.

Shaggy Dog Cake

SERVES 10 TO 12

One day a mother came in with her young daughter, who had an important birthday approaching. I quickly became frustrated at the little girl's rejection of every suggestion I made, when suddenly her mother interjected, "She loves Max." The little girl's face lit up when she explained that Max was an adorable white puppy with long, curly hair that covered his eyes and nose. Enthusiasm greeted my proposal that the birthday cake be a replica of Max. As they were departing, I held the mother back for a second to suggest that after presentation of the cake, it should be cut in the kitchen, because her child might be distressed by seeing a knife cutting into her Max. The cake was a huge hit, and the little girl sent me a photograph of herself holding the real Max next to the cake Max! This is a great birthday cake for a young child. You will have fun with it because it is hard to do anything wrong.

LEVEL OF DIFFICULTY: 1

TIMING: This cake can be baked and decorated on the same day you serve it.

HINTS: It is very difficult to make mistakes with this cake. You will use the grass tip to ice, so even if your carving is not terrific, you will be able to conceal it with icing. When carving, think of a figure 8—the head or the top part of the 8 should be smaller than the body or the bottom part. The dog is lying down, and ears and paws are made with icing. Take a small lump of the leftover cake and roll it around in your palms to make a ball for the nose. Do the same thing for the eyes, or pipe on with a different color icing. Since the icing is what makes it a dog, the cake could easily become a cat—give it two

slits for eyes, pointy icing ears, pipe a long tail and add some florist wire for whiskers. Voila! The little rag rug that is pictured underneath the dog is optional; we made it out of sugar dough. Since you don't have to fill in the center of the rug, make just enough so that it peeks out from underneath the dog or cat; probably 6 or 7 strips of sugar dough will do.

SPECIAL EQUIPMENT

Two 8-inch round and two 6-inch round cake
 pans
Standing electric mixer with paddle or whisk
 attachment
One 4½-quart bowl
Turntable
Pencil
Ruler
One 17 × 27-inch cake cardboard, cut into a fig-
 ure 8 with the top part a 6-inch oval and the
 bottom a 9-inch oval (see page 146)
14-inch serrated knife
6- or 8-inch sharp knife
Long spatula
Pastry brush
One pastry bag (two if you intend to pipe eyes
 and nose)

One set couplings
 #233 grass tip

STRUCTURAL SUPPORT

One 12 × 18-inch rectangular platter

INGREDIENTS

2 recipes Chocolate Fudge Cake (page 21)
1 cup Vanilla-flavored Wash (page 38)
1 recipe Mocha Buttercream Filling (page 33)
1 recipe Basic Buttercream Icing (page 28)
4 cups sugar dough and gel food colors to tint
 the following:
  1 cup purple
  1 cup red
  1 cup blue
  1 cup dark pink or mauve
Vegetable shortening

1. Bake the cakes, let cool, remove from the pans, and trim.
2. Place a cake on the turntable. Score the cake at 1-inch intervals and slice horizontally, slipping each slice onto a cake cardboard. Repeat with the remaining cakes, reserving 4 slices from the 10-inch and 4 slices from the 8-inch. Wrap and freeze any remaining slices.
3. Wash the 8 slices with the vanilla wash. Place a 10-inch layer on its cardboard on the turntable. Spread about ½ to ¾ cup of mocha buttercream filling on the cake. Slip a second 10-inch layer on top of the filling and place filling on this layer. Repeat with the third slice, placing the fourth slice on top—do not add filling to the top slice.
4. Repeat Step 3 with the 8-inch cake. Chill the filled cakes for ½ hour.

RAG RUG

1. Roll out ½ cup sugar dough (color is your choice) between your hands to form a long cigar-shaped piece. Lay it on a clean surface and roll the piece into a thin rope at least 26 inches long. Try to keep the width of the rope uniform. Make a large oval with the rope, connecting the ends, on the cake platter.

2. With another color of dough, make another rope about 25 inches long. Place this rope just inside the first sugar dough oval and connect the ends, pinching off any excess. Continue the same process with ½ cup of another color of sugar dough, placing each consecutively smaller piece just inside the others on the cake platter, until your rug is complete.

DOG

1. Remove the cakes from the refrigerator. Place the 10-inch cake and the 8-inch cake side by side so that they are touching.
2. Lay the cardboard figure 8 on top of the cake and trace and score around it. Carve through the cake and remove the excess pieces; reserve. Remove the cardboard and set aside. Continue carving, shaving away to give the form rounded edges. The goal is to create a round, oval head a few inches smaller than the round, oval body. Brush away any excess crumbs and cake with a dry pastry brush.
3. Slide a long spatula under the carved cake, lift the cake, and place it on top of the cardboard template, which now becomes the base. Arrange the shaped cake on the rag rug so that the edges of the rug peek out from under the dog on either side.

4. Crumb-coat the dog with about 1 cup of basic (white) buttercream icing, reserving the leftovers (see page 14).
5. Fill a pastry bag with the remaining basic buttercream icing and attach a #233 grass tip. Starting at one end of the cake, point the tip to the top of the cake and squeeze the icing out in a long downward motion—the idea is to make it look like a shaggy dog, so you want the icing fur to come out in long downward strokes that end at the rug. Draw the stroke out very slightly so that it splays out onto the rug. Cover the dog entirely in icing fur.
6. To make ears, pipe 2 side-by-side strokes on top of the icing where the ears should go. Pipe a second time directly on top of each of the two side-by-side strokes; then, to give the ears final definition, pipe again directly on top of the second ear layer.
7. Pipe 2 side-by-side 2-inch strokes from the body onto the rug, for the paws. Pipe on a slight angle away from the body. Repeat on each side of the cake where the paws should be. Pipe a tail on the back of the dog, curling around the body.
8. Use some reserved cake and roll it into firm balls to make the nose and the eyes. Refrigerate the cake until ready to serve.

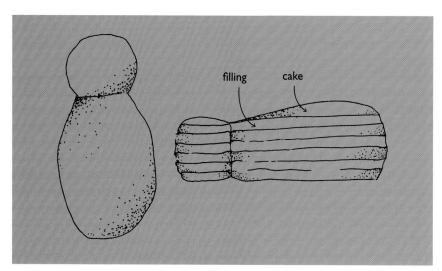

filling   cake

Shaping the dog.

Handbag Cake

I love to serve this cake alongside the Shopping Bag Cake (page 150), but it can stand on its own. If you do serve it with the shopping bag, make sure you have a cake board big enough to accommodate both. I would place a pair of car keys and some gloves alongside the cake, or maybe a wallet or a silk scarf. You can personalize this cake in a number of ways, and don't be afraid to use whatever colors you like.

LEVEL OF DIFFICULTY: 2

TIMING: This cake can be baked, filled, and trimmed 2 days ahead, and iced and decorated 1 to 2 days ahead.

HINTS: If you plan to serve the Handbag Cake and Shopping Bag Cake together, you will need a cake board that measures 17 inches square. The silver dragées needed to complete the look of your handbag will need to be ordered ahead of time from a cake-decorating supplier; they are difficult to find in the supermarket.

SPECIAL EQUIPMENT

Two 8 × 3-inch square cake pans
Five 8-inch square cardboard cake square
Turntable
Ruler
Pencil
14-inch serrated knife
4 bamboo skewers
Standing electric mixer with whisk or paddle
   attachment
4½-quart mixing bowl
Mixing bowls
Icing spatula
Flexible icing strip
4-inch offset spatula or palette knife
8 × 8 sheet parchment or wax paper
Plastic icing strip

Two pastry bags
Two sets couplings
   #734 icing tip
   #3 round tip
   #20 star tip
Tweezers
Twenty-five #2 or #3 silver dragées
Vegetable shortening
Rolling pin
Flexible blade utility knife

INGREDIENTS

1 recipe Chocolate Fudge Cake (page 21)
1 recipe Vanilla Wash (page 38)
1 recipe Basic Buttercream Filling (page 31)
1 recipe Basic Buttercream Icing (page 28)
Gel food colors to make 5 cups pale-blue icing

1. Place a cake on the turntable. Score the cake at ¹/₂-inch intervals and slice horizontally, slipping each slice onto a cake cardboard. Repeat with the remaining cake, reserving five slices in all. Wrap and freeze any remaining slices.
2. Wash, fill, and stack four slices, placing the fifth layer on top. Refrigerate the cake for two hours.
3. Remove the cake from the refrigerator. Use a skewer to trace two lines on the cake top—at the bottom end of the bag the lines will be 6 inches apart, and at the top of the bag the lines will be 4 inches apart. Cut along the lines to remove the two tapered wedges from each side of the cake. Your cake will now be 4 inches across the top of the purse, and 6 inches across on the bottom of the purse.
4. Trim the cake with a steak knife to round all the edges and corners slightly. Crumb-coat the cake and refrigerate (see page 14).

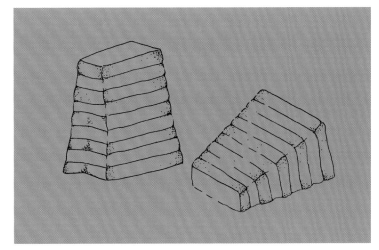

Positioning the filled but not frosted cakes.
Left: The Shopping Bag Cake.
Right: The Handbag Cake.

5. Ice the cake in pale-blue icing, using the icing blade, the palette knife, and the flexible icing strip on the rounded corners.

6. To make the flap of the handbag: Use a skewer to trace a 3-inch half moon at the 4-inch end of the cake. Fill a pastry bag with blue icing, and using a #13 tip, pipe a dragging pearl border over your tracing to outline the flap. Fill another pastry bag with white icing and use the #3 round tip. Border a dragging pearl right up against the blue dragging pearl of the flap.

7. Use the pastry bag with white icing and the #3 round tip. Starting on the flap of the handbag, pipe 5 diagonal lines in one direction, then go back and, starting at the top of the first diagonal line, pipe 5 more lines in the opposite direction so that you have 5 large, connected X's on the flap. Move to the sides of the cake and pipe 5 to 7 smaller, connected X's on the edge to resemble seams. Repeat this on the opposite side and the bottom of the bag.

8. Place one silver dragée at each top point where all the X's connect.

9. Using the pastry bag with the white icing, begin to pipe a looping m border just below the bottom of your X's on one side of the cake. Work all the way around the seams of the cake, ending on the opposite side.

10. Pipe a looping m border along the bottom edge of the handbag flap, then the top.

11. Using the pastry bag with blue icing and the #13 star tip, pipe a dragging pearl border just touching the top of the looping m border on the flap of the handbag, then pipe a dragging pearl just under the white looping m border.

12. Pipe a dragging pearl border just on top of the white looping m that goes around the sides of the cake.

13. Working on the sides of the handbag, pipe a blue dot at the top point where each X meets, all the way around the cake.

14. Pipe a dragging pearl border around the base of the cake where it meets the cake board. Double or triple border if you wish.

15. Attach the #20 star tip to the pastry bag with the white icing. Pipe a series of connected stars to form the handle of the bag, piping onto the base.

16. Place dragées where one end of the handle attaches to the bag, to simulate metal studs. Repeat at the other point where the handbag handle meets the bag.

Shopping Bag Cake

LEVEL OF DIFFICULTY: 2

TIMING: This cake can be baked, filled, and trimmed up to 3 days ahead, and iced and decorated up to 2 days ahead.

HINTS: If you plan to serve the Handbag Cake and Shopping Bag Cake together, you will need a cake board that measures 17 inches square.

SPECIAL EQUIPMENT
Two 6 × 6 × 3-inch square cake pans
Four 6 × 3-inch cardboard cake rectangle
Turntable
Ruler
Pencil
14-inch serrated knife
Steak knife
Standing electric mixer with whisk or paddle
    attachment
Two 4¹/₂-quart mixing bowls
Mixing bowls
Icing spatula
4-inch offset spatula or palette knife
Two pastry bags
Two sets couplings
    #48 basketweave tip
    #4 round tip
    #13 star tip
Vegetable shortening
Rolling pin
Flexible blade utility knife

Ten 8-inch pieces florist wire
Florist tape
2-inch heart-shaped cookie cutter
Wax paper

STRUCTURAL SUPPORT
3 bamboo skewers

INGREDIENTS
1 recipe Chocolate Fudge Cake (page 21)
1 recipe Vanilla Wash (page 38)
1 recipe Basic Buttercream Filling (page 31)
1 recipe Basic Buttercream Icing (page 28)
Gel food colors to make the following:
    5 cups dusty rose icing (2 drops red gel color,
        2 drops purple, 2 drops blue)
    3 cups red icing
    1 cup red sugar dough
2 sheets rice paper
Vegetable shortening
Cornstarch

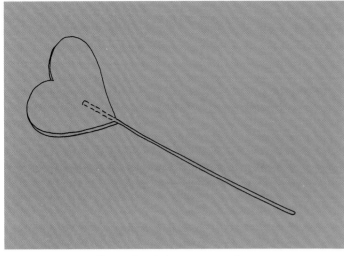

Sugar-dough heart on a wire.

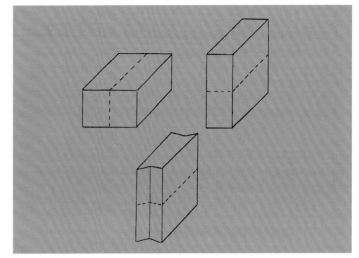

Forming the Shopping Bag Cake (Steps 6 and 7).

1. Wrap 2 pieces of wire with florist tape and bend each piece into a U shape; these will be the handles of the bag. Use just one handle if you wish.

2. Cut each piece of rice paper in half, spray with water, and crumple the pieces gently. The object is to create tissue paper that will stick out of the top of the bag. Place the pieces of tissue paper in separate bowls to maintain their shape.

3. Roll out the red sugar dough. Using the heart cookie cutter, cut out 6 to 10 hearts. Spread them out on pieces of wax paper dusted with cornstarch, then lay a piece of wire on each heart. Cut a tiny piece of sugar dough and, using a drop of water as glue, lay the bits of dough on the wires to secure them to the hearts. Press gently; do not crush the hearts. The object is to attach the wires to the hearts so that you can later stick them into the cake. When the hearts have dried, wrap the exposed wire with florist tape.

4. Trim, score, and slice the cakes horizontally at $1/2$-inch intervals, reserving 4 slices; wrap and freeze the remainder.

5. Wash and fill 3 slices and place the fourth on top. Refrigerate the cake for 2 hours.

6. Using the ruler, find and mark the middle of the cake. Cut the cake in half to make two oblong 6 × 3-inch cakes. Put a layer of icing on top of one cake, then take the other and stick one cake directly on top of the other to give a 6 × 3-inch oblong twice as tall. Place a bamboo skewer into the top of the cake near each end, then one in the middle. Press the skewers all the way into the cake, and snip off the ends so that they are level with the cake.

7. Trim the edges of the cake so that it is absolutely straight. Cut a $1/2$-inch wedge down the center of one 3-inch side of the cake to resemble the crease in the side of a bag. Repeat on the other side.

8. Crumb-coat the entire cake and refrigerate for 1 hour (see page 14).

9. Ice the cake smoothly with the dusty-rose icing, using the pastry bag and the icing tip. Run the tip of a palette knife down the center of each side of the bag where you have made the creases in the bag.

10. Fill a pastry bag with basic buttercream and attach the #48 basketweave tip. Using the ridged side of the tip, pipe stripes onto the bag, keeping them even and equidistant apart with about 1 inch between. After you

have piped all the stripes, pipe a line around the base (perimeter) of the bag where it meets the cake board.

11. Using the same pastry bag with basic buttercream, remove the #48 tip and attach the #13 star tip. Pipe a dragging pearl border on each side of each stripe. Border the stripe that goes around the base perimeter of the bag and border the top edge of the bag, where the vertical stripes end.

12. Fill a pastry bag with the red icing and attach the #4 round tip. Pipe hearts all over the bag. Leave a space across the front and/or back of the bag so that you can pipe on the name of the guest of honor.

13. Place the rice paper tissue on top of the bag, cutting the paper if necessary to make it fit. Place 1 or 2 of the wrapped wires into the top of the cake to simulate handles.

14. Insert the wires in and around the tissue and into the cake so that the hearts peek out above the tissue.

Stack of Books Cake

SERVES 18 TO 20

This cake can be either a stack of horizontal books or a group of vertical books. A stack of books is a perfect graduation cake, and I once made a stack of medical texts as a wedding cake for two doctors. The titles that you pipe onto the volumes will personalize the occasion. Titles like Principles of Ophthalmic Surgery *next to a volume of* Romeo *and* Juliet *can cover a lot of ground.*

LEVEL OF DIFFICULTY: 1

TIMING: Cake can be baked 2 days ahead and iced and decorated 1 day ahead.

HINTS: This cake requires some trimming, and you will have some good pieces of cake left that you may want to ice and serve if you have more than 20 guests. The border work is what really makes this cake special, so plan to double or triple the border.

SPECIAL EQUIPMENT
Two 8 × 8 × 3-inch cake pans
Five 8 × 8-inch square cake cardboards
One 6 × 8-inch cake cardboard
Two 5 × 3-inch cake cardboards
Turntable

Ruler
14-inch serrated knife
Mixing bowls
Standing electric mixer with whisk or paddle attachment
4¹/₂-quart mixing bowl

Icing spatula

Icing blade

Icing comb

Small offset spatula or palette knife

Plastic icing strip

Parchment paper

Three pastry bags

Three sets couplings:

  #79 lily of the valley tip

  #13 star tip

  #3 round tip

Small paintbrush

STRUCTURAL SUPPORT

10 × 10-inch cake board

INGREDIENTS

1 recipe Carrot Cake (page 22)

1 recipe Hazelnut Wash (page 38)

1 recipe Cream Cheese Filling (page 32)

2 recipes Basic Buttercream Icing (page 28)

Gel food colors to make the following:

  4 cups burgundy or dark-red icing

  4 cups dark-green icing

  4 cups brown icing

1/2 cup white sugar dough

Vegetable shortening

Gold petal dust

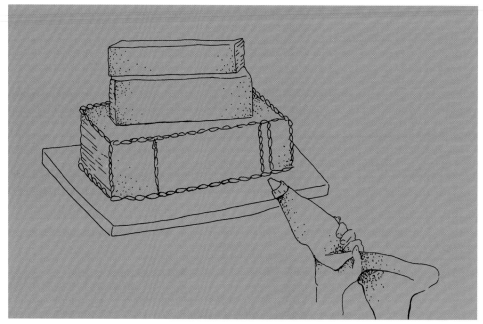

Piping the book binding.

1. Score and slice the two 8 × 8 cakes horizontally at ¹/₂-inch intervals, reserving 5 layers; wrap and freeze the remaining slices.

2. Wash, fill, and stack 3 slices (do not put filling on the third slice); then use a ruler to measure and slice off 2 inches on one side of the cake. Using a long spatula, carefully place this 6 × 8-inch cake on the 6 × 8-inch cardboard. Refrigerate.

3. Wash the remaining 2 slices, fill between them, then cut the cake in half. Use a ruler or the 5 × 3-inch cake cardboard to trim each cake to 5 × 3 inches. Place each slice on a 5 × 3-inch cake cardboard.

4. Measure the height of each cake, then the length of 3 sides of each cake. Cut 3 strips of parchment to match the height and length of 3 sides, and set aside.

5. Crumb-coat the 3 cakes and refrigerate for 1 hour (see page 14).

6. Take the 6 × 8-inch cake out of the refrigerator, and ice *three sides* with basic buttercream. Slide the icing comb along the icing to simulate pages. Refrigerate this cake for ¹/₂ hour.

7. Remove the first 5 × 3-inch cake from the refrigerator and ice and comb 3 sides of the cake, as in Step 6. Refrigerate, and repeat with the remaining 5 × 3-inch cake.

8. Take the 6 × 8-inch cake out of the refrigerator and place the corresponding piece of parchment around the 3 sides (pages) of the cake you have just iced and combed. There is no need to press the parchment into the icing; just stand it against the 3 sides, pressing around the top edge only if necessary.

9. Ice the top and the 1 back side of the cake with the burgundy icing, icing smoothly with a long icing spatula. Remove the strip of parchment carefully and clean up the edges with a small palette knife or a small offset spatula.

10. Fill a pastry bag with the remaining burgundy icing and attach the #79 lily of the valley tip. Pipe a long, straight border along the edges and the spine of the book. Remove the lily of the valley tip, replace it with the #13 star tip, and border on each side of the lily of the valley line using the dragging pearl stroke.

11. Remove the #13 star tip, attach the #3 round tip, and pipe a title on the spine of the book. Refrigerate.

12. Remove one of the 5 × 3-inch cakes from the refrigerator, place a parchment strip around the combed icing, and ice the top and fourth side in the green icing, icing smoothly with a long icing spatula. Remove the strip of parchment carefully and clean up the edges with a small palette knife or a small offset spatula.

13. Fill a pastry bag with the remaining green icing and attach the #79 lily of the valley tip. Pipe a long, straight border along the edges and the spine of the book. Remove the lily of the valley tip, replace it with the #13 star tip, and border on each side of the lily of the valley line using the dragging pearl stroke.

14. Remove the #13 star tip, attach the #3 round tip, and pipe a title on the spine of the book.

15. Stack this cake on top of the 6 × 8-inch cake, slanting the book slightly askew. Correct or add any border to the base of this cake where it meets the cake underneath. Refrigerate.

16. Repeat Steps 12, 13, 14, and 15 with the remaining cake and the brown icing. Refrigerate.

17. To make the sugar dough page marker and tassel: roll a golf-ball-sized piece of dough between your hands to form a 6-inch pencil shape. Repeat with a second

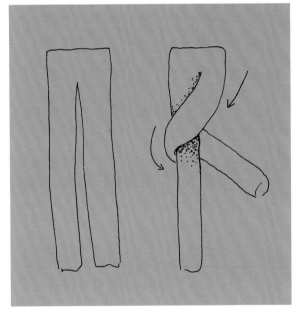

Making the page marker.

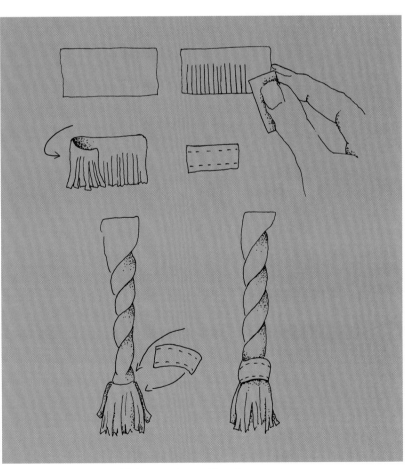

Making and attaching the tassel.

piece of dough. Hold the ends together and twist the 2 pieces of dough around in one direction to form a rope. Slice off each end with a utility knife to get a clean edge.

18. Attach 1 end of the rope to the red book, placing the rope in the pages close to the spine of the book.

19. Roll out a grape-sized piece of sugar dough into a 1-inch square. Using the utility knife, make 10 slices in the dough, cutting from one edge to almost the top edge of the square but not slicing all the way through. This will be the tassel. Roll the tassel around your pinkie, then place on the end of the rope. Cut a small piece of sugar dough to place like a cuff over the spot where the tassel and the rope meet. Dust the rope and tassel with a paintbrush dipped in gold petal dust.

Straw Hat Cake

SERVES 15 TO 20

The original inspiration for this cake came from a bride who owned a hat shop. She collected hats, and had a country home called "Le Chapeau." The bride was open to a different look in a wedding cake, and that is how this cake came into being. I can only imagine the surprised looks on the guests' faces as they realized the hat was actually the wedding cake; evidently it caused quite a sensation. Try this cake for a bridal shower, a birthday, an anniversary, or a retirement. You might pipe a design or a logo on the brim. This cake could be your crowning glory.

LEVEL OF DIFFICULTY: 2
More patience than skill is required here.

TIMING: This cake can be done 1 or 2 days ahead of time.

HINTS: This cake is simple to assemble, and you will be a pro when it comes to basketweaving skills after piping it. The most important thing to remember with basket weaving is to keep the vertical lines equidistant. You can even mark the cake with toothpicks or dot it with icing before beginning, to plot the measurements.

The next most important thing to remember is that there should be the same number of horizontal lines in every row. This will get difficult when you have narrow spaces, but keep a rhythm or a count going in your head. This is important when you have come all the way around the cake and are ready to join the weave. If you've kept

the same number of horizontal lines, the finish will look smooth and seamless. If the lines are irregular or uneven, mistakes may be covered with the sugar ribbon and bow. Also, note that the horizontal lines at the top of the brim and crown will be narrower than those at the bottom. Start the vertical line on the crown of the hat in the same spot where you began and ended the lines on the brim. Practice basket weave on a plate or a tabletop before starting to get used to the rhythm and feel of the technique.

You may be interrupted while weaving; it can take some time. If you need to stop, put the cake in the refrigerator until you are ready to begin again. Just be sure that the icing in the bag is at room temperature when you resume.

When it is time to place the ribbon and the bow on the iced cake, it is easier to attach the sugar dough to the basket weave if the icing is at room temperature. However, if the cake is cool, use a dab of buttercream icing on the back of the ribbon or bow to help it stick.

SPECIAL EQUIPMENT

10 × 3-inch round pan

Two 6 × 3-inch round pans

Four 10-inch round cake cardboards

Four 6-inch round cake cardboards

Ruler

10- to 14-inch serrated bread knife

Standing electric mixer with whisk or paddle
   attachment

4½-quart mixing bowl

Turntable

Three pastry bags

Three sets couplings:

   #6 round tip

   #67 leaf tip

   #80 lily of the valley tip

Rolling pin

Plastic cutting board

Rolling pastry cutter

24-inch length of clear plastic wrap

Small scissors

Bamboo skewers

STRUCTURAL SUPPORT

10-inch cake round

14-inch cake base

INGREDIENTS

1 recipe Classic Yellow Cake (page 17)

1 recipe Orange-flavored Wash (page 38)

1 recipe Orange Buttercream Filling (page 33)

4 ounces melted bittersweet chocolate

1 recipe Basic Buttercream Icing (page 28)

Gel food colors to make the following:

   1 cup green buttercream icing

   6 cups straw-colored buttercream icing

   1 cup pink sugar dough

   2 pansies

   Vegetable shortening

1. Fill the 6-inch cake pans to three-quarters full; the remaining batter goes into the 10-inch pan.

2. Bake the cakes, let cool, and remove from the pans. Place a cake on the turntable. Score the cake at ½-inch intervals and slice horizontally, slipping each slice onto a cake cardboard. Repeat with the remaining cakes, reserving 4 slices from the 10-inch and 4 slices from the 6-inch. Wrap and freeze any remaining slices.

3. Paint each 6-inch slice with orange wash. Place 1 slice on a cake cardboard on the turntable. Spread ½ cup of orange buttercream filling to the edges, add the second slice, fill, stack, and repeat with the third slice. Set the fourth slice on top.

4. Trim about ¼ inch of the outer edges of the top layer, to give the top a slightly rounded edge. Remove from the turntable and refrigerate.

5. Place the 10-inch cake on the turntable; trim off the outer and top and bottom crusts.

6. Again, using a ruler as a guide, score the side of the cake at 2 inches. Slice the cake at the 2-inch mark. You will need only this 2-inch slice as the base of your cake. Wrap and freeze the other slice.

7. Place on a 10-inch cardboard cake round. Center the cake on the 14-inch base, and place on the turntable.

8. Center a 6-inch cake round on top of the 10-inch cake. Using a serrated knife, hold it so that the blade slants upward, and trim away the entire outer perimeter of the cake so that the 6-inch center area of the cake is slightly higher than the outer edges. The cake should slope gently downward from the center to the board. Crumb-coat the cakes and refrigerate for 1 hour.

9. Place a dollop of buttercream in the center of the

brim of the hat and center the 6-inch cake (the crown of the hat) directly on top of and in the center of the brim.

10. Blend about 1/2 cup basic buttercream into the melted bittersweet chocolate, add this to the remaining 5 cups basic buttercream, and blend gently. Add 1 teaspoon of yellow food color, blend, and continue adding small amounts of color until the buttercream is the color of straw.

11. Place 3 cups of the buttercream in a pastry bag, attach the #6 tip, and shake down the bag to remove any air. Make the first radial line. These are the lines that extend from the base of the crown all the way out to the edge of the brim and 1 inch beyond onto the cake board. Now make a series of short perpendicular lines across the radial, spacing between the lines as far apart as the width of the tip. Basketweave the brim. It is critical that you try to keep the radial and perpendicular lines equidistant. You should have the same number of perpendicular lines in each row of basketweave.

12. Place a bamboo skewer in the center of the hat crown. Starting at the point of the first radial line on the brim, place the first vertical line on the hat crown, starting at the skewer. Basketweave around the entire crown of the hat. Remove the skewer.

13. With the pastry bag, pipe a dragging pearl around the outer edge of the brim of the hat. The tip will be touching the outer edge of the basketweave, and the cake board. The idea is to give the edge of the brim a clean, uniform, finished look.

14. In the center top of the hat crown, pipe the same dragging pearl in a 2-inch circle. Fill in the center of the 2-inch circle with the dragging pearl until it is completely filled in. Again, this will give the top of the crown a more polished look. Refrigerate the cake for at least 1/2 hour.

RIBBON

15. Cover the plastic cutting board with a thin coat of vegetable shortening. Roll out the pink sugar dough 22 inches long and about 5 inches wide. Using a ruler, measure 2 strips, each 20 inches in length by 1 1/2 to 2 inches wide. Cut the strips with a pastry cutter, using a ruler as a guide. Lift the scrap edges of sugar dough away from the strips; do not lift your strips yet.

The carved and assembled hat.

16. Cover the strips with a length of plastic wrap. Lay the ruler on top of the first sugar-dough strip with not more than $\frac{1}{8}$ inch of sugar-dough edge showing on the left side of the ruler. Using a pastry roller and guided by the edge of the ruler, press very gently into the sugar dough, just enough to make an indentation that looks like a line of stitching. (Do not cut through the dough.) Move the ruler so that the line runs the entire length of the strip and repeat the process on the right side of the ribbon, again not more than $\frac{1}{8}$ inch away from the outer edge of the strip. Repeat with the second strip.

17. Remove the hat from the refrigerator and place it on the turntable. Gently pick up the first strip and, holding it with both hands, gently press the beginning of the strip to the base of the crown, so that the bottom edge of the strip just rests on the brim. Turn the cake and gently press the length of ribbon around the crown until it meets the beginning. Put a small dab of buttercream on the beginning length of ribbon; attach the end of the ribbon to this buttercream (it will act as glue). Drape the remaining length of ribbon (you should have approximately 3 to 4 inches left) on the brim of the hat. At this point you may want to cut the very end of the ribbon into two points.

18. Cut a 3-inch length of ribbon from the second strip—the one that is still on the cutting board. Using scissors, cut 2 points on one end. Gently join the other inside the point on the cake where the first ribbon meets itself. Drape this second piece of ribbon on the cake.

BOW

19. Cut two 4-inch lengths from the remaining ribbon on the cutting board. Loop the first length of ribbon so that the ends touch. Where the ends touch, cut away a V, then press the two ends together. Repeat with the second length of ribbon. Lay the loops on their sides.

20. Dot one side of the V on the first loop with buttercream, and attach the buttercream side to the spot on the cake where the ribbon meets itself. Use your fingers on the inside of the loop to puff out the bow; you want it to be rounded, not flat against the cake. Repeat using the other piece of the bow, placing it opposite the first half.

21. To make the knot, cut a 2-inch length of ribbon, fold it over your finger so that the ends touch, and gently squeeze the ends together; remove from your finger and cut the ends into a V. Place a tiny dab of buttercream on the outside of the V and, with your finger in the hole of the loop, press the buttercream side gently into the center of the bow.

22. Stick 1 pansy into the point just above the ribbon knot and the other just below it. Press them into the knot.

23. Fill a pastry bag with 1 cup of green icing. Attach the #67 leaf tip and, starting above the right half of the bow, pipe a leaf in the space between the two pansies. Just below the bottom of the right half of the bow, pipe 2 more leaves. Repeat this process on the left side of the bow, placing leaves wherever they look as if they might fit.

24. Fill a pastry bag with 1 cup basic buttercream and the #80 lily of the valley tip. Pipe lily of the valley flowers on top of the leaves, starting at the tops and working downward. Pipe a few or many; there are no rules here. If you wish, go back and pipe on extra leaves so that leaves appear to be coming out from under the blossoms.

Sunflower Cake

SERVES 12

This cake reminds me of Mediterranean summers. There is something so warm and inviting in the yellow color and the openness of this flower. The client for whom I originally created this cake dismissed garden flowers such as roses and lilies. She showed me her china pattern, all covered in glorious sunflowers. This cake was for a summer luncheon, and all the decorations were sunflowers, with the table linens in greens, blues, and yellows.

LEVEL OF DIFFICULTY: 1

TIMING: The cake can be baked 2 days ahead and decorated the day before or on the day of the event.

HINTS: You will be adding chocolate to buttercream twice, the first time adding 1 ounce to make the cake icing and the second time to make the center of the sunflower. If you don't think the icing for the center flower is dark enough, add another ¹/₂ ounce chocolate, then another, until the color is right.

SPECIAL EQUIPMENT
Two 6 × 3-inch round cake pans
Turntable
Four 6-inch cardboard cake rounds
14-inch serrated knife
Pastry brush
Standing mixer with paddle or whisk attachment
One 4¹/₂-quart mixing bowl
Long icing spatula
Icing blade
Three pastry bags
Three sets couplings:
   #70 leaf tip
   #66 leaf tip
   #233 grass tip
   #4 round tip

STRUCTURAL SUPPORT
10-inch round cake platter or base

INGREDIENTS
1 recipe Almond Cake (page 23)
1 recipe Hazelnut-flavored Wash (page 38)
1 recipe Raspberry Buttercream Filling (page 33)
1¹/₂ pints fresh strawberries, sliced
1 recipe Basic Buttercream Icing (page 28)
1 ounce melted unsweetened chocolate added to
   3 cups Basic Buttercream Icing (to ice cake)
3 ounces melted unsweetened chocolate added
   to 2 cups Basic Buttercream Icing
Gel food colors to make the following:
   4 cups leaf green
   3 cups sunflower yellow

1. Bake and cool the cake in two 6-inch round pans. Trim off the bulging top of each cake so that the top and bottom surfaces are equally flat. Remove the buttercream filling and icing from the refrigerator and bring to room temperature.
2. Place 3 cups of buttercream icing in the bowl of a standing mixer, add 1 ounce of melted chocolate, and blend until the color of the icing is uniform and no longer streaky.
3. Place the first cake on the turntable, score, and cut horizontally into 1-inch slices. Repeat with the second cake. You will be using 4 slices in all. Wrap and freeze any extra slices. Set the 4 slices aside separately.

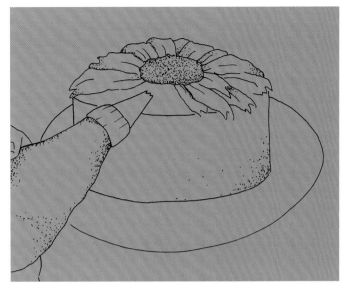

Making the sunflower petals.

4. Wash each of the 4 slices with hazelnut wash.

5. Place the first cake slice on the turntable. Spread 1 to 2 cups of raspberry buttercream filling on the first slice and press ¹/₃ of the sliced strawberries into the filling, really pressing the berries in firmly so that the next slice will be flat against the one below it. Repeat with the next 2 slices; place the fourth slice on top.

6. Check the cake to be sure the top is level and flat. Apply pressure to any places where it is uneven. Remove any oozing filling with a spatula; refrigerate for 1 hour.

7. Crumb-coat the entire cake smoothly in light-brown buttercream icing (see page 14) and refrigerate for 1 hour.

8. Fill a pastry bag with dark-brown icing and attach the #133 grass tip. Starting in the center of the cake, begin to pipe grass in a circle about 3 inches in diameter.

9. Fill a pastry bag with the yellow icing and attach the #70 leaf tip. Begin piping the petals of the sunflower onto the cake, working from the center rim of grass outward to the edge of the top, using one long stroke for each. Place the petals side by side, just touching. Once the top of the cake is covered, pipe petals that are shorter by half on top of the first petal layer, piping over the lines where the first ring of petals underneath meets the next.

10. Fill a pastry bag with the green icing and attach a #4 round tip. Pipe dots around the entire outside of the brown center, letting each dot touch the next.

11. Using the same bag and tip, pipe a green vine all around the base of the cake, letting it swirl and loop. Remove the #4 tip and replace it with the #66 leaf tip. Pipe small leaves randomly, attaching them to the vine. Pipe a border of small leaves around the base of the cake, letting all the leaves touch one another.

12. Refrigerate the cake until ready to serve.

Teacup Cake

When I learned that the theme of a pending bridal shower was chinaware, I asked what pattern the bride had selected, and designed the cake as an oversize replica of the cup and saucer for that pattern. She was thrilled and delighted, and exclaimed that the cake had been the hit of the party!

For this little teacup, I used a dinner plate that I like very much, and then made the pattern on the teacup match that of the saucer. I suggest you do the same: find a plate with an interesting pattern and create your own template to match the plate so that your cup and saucer match. I have listed the colors that I used, but you will want to change them to suit your own pattern. We put flowers in the top of the teacup, but you could place a couple of flowers on the edge of the saucer instead, then color the icing to give the illusion of coffee or tea in the cup.

This cake could also be scaled down to cupcake size so that it could be an individual dessert; try that for your next dinner party. My sister-in-law collects teacups in many patterns; imagine dessert cakes in the style of collectors' teacups.

LEVEL OF DIFFICULTY: 2

TIMING: This cake can be baked, trimmed, and filled 2 days in advance, and iced and decorated then. Note that the handle for the teacup should have at least 3 days' drying time before it is attached.

HINTS: To shape the cake, center a 6-inch cardboard round on top of the filled cake. The idea is to shave the cake to round the sides of the teacup, and to make the base of the cup smaller than its lip. When trimming the cake, try not to hack off big pieces; slice away thin slivers, working around the cake to maintain a certain balance to the rounded sides. This is necessary, or the cup will be too lopsided to stand on its own once you invert it.

The hardest part of this cake is the little lip around the edge of the teacup. You will definitely need the offset spatula both to trim and ice this little lip. When icing it, you will need the 4-inch offset spatula to get inside for a smooth, clean, well-defined edge.

The design for the teacup is on page 168. It can be enlarged 10 percent or used as it is. When you are ready to pipe the design shown or your own on the cup and saucer, make a template from tracing paper and practice piping over the tracing. Make all your mistakes on paper first, when you are comfortable; then scrape the icing back into the bag and move to the cake. Use one continuous motion when piping the pattern onto the cake, to avoid broken lines.

SPECIAL EQUIPMENT

Two 8-inch round cake pans

One 6-inch round cake cardboard

One 10- or 12-inch plate

Standing electric mixer with whip or paddle
    attachment

4¹/₂-quart mixing bowl

Turntable

4-inch offset spatula or palette knife

Serrated knife

Plastic icing strip

Four pastry bags

Four sets couplings:
    #13 star tip
    #3 round tip
    #4 round tip
    #67 leaf tip

Rolling pin

14-inch length of heavy-gauge wire

Florist tape

Small sable paintbrush

INGREDIENTS

1 recipe Chocolate Fudge Cake (page 21)

2 cups Vanilla Wash (page 38)

1 recipe Chocolate Mousse Filling (page 35)

1 recipe Basic Buttercream Icing (page 28)

Gel food colors to make the following:
    2 cups dusty rose icing
    2 cups red-brown icing
    2 cups pale-brown icing
    2 cups pale-pink icing
    2 cups leaf-green icing

4 cups sugar dough

Gold petal dust

Pink food color dust or petal dust

3 bunches mauve hydrangeas

6 medium white roses tipped in pink

You can use these techniques to create a teapot.

TEACUP HANDLE

1. Roll the sugar dough between your hands to a long, thick strip. Lay the strip on a flat surface and gently roll over the strip until it measures 8 × 1 inch, and about ½ inch thick.

2. Wrap the entire 14 inches of florist wire in florist tape.

3. Lay the wire in the center of the sugar dough strip, leaving an overhang of about 3 inches at either end of dough. Press the sides of the dough up and around the wire to enclose it completely, except for the ends. Roll the strip to get an 8 × 1 × ½-inch strip with the wire inside and 3 inches of wire showing on either end.

4. Curl the dough into a teacup handle shape and set aside to dry for 3 days. When dry, paint handle of cup gold and set aside.

5. Bake and cool the 2 cakes. Remove the buttercream icing from the refrigerator and bring to room temperature. Score and slice the cake layers horizontally at ½-inch intervals, reserving 5 slices. Wrap and freeze any leftover slices.

6. Paint the slices with vanilla wash and fill with chocolate mousse.

7. Center the 6-inch round cardboard on top of the filled cake. You will use this to carve the teacup. Carve out and away from the cardboard circle to make the base of the cup. Slice out and away, carefully round-

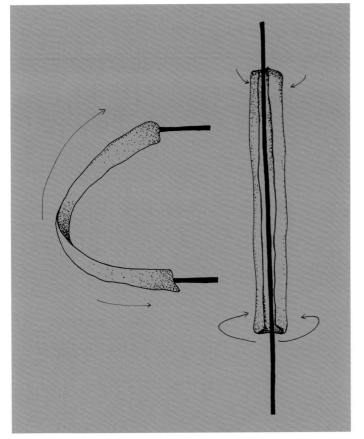

Shaping the teacup handle.

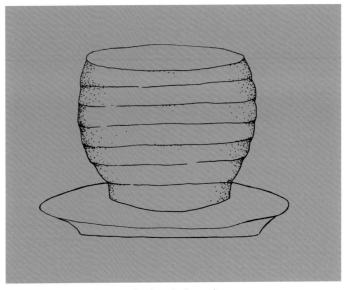

The stacked and shaped teacup.

ing the sides of the cup. Once you are satisfied with the shape of the cup, invert the cake and place it on the plate (saucer) and on the turntable.

8. Insert the tip of a steak knife pointing down into the cake about ½ inch in from the edge. Cut down into the cake about ½ inch and, working carefully, move the turntable around slowly while allowing the tip of the knife to cut a large 7-inch circle on top of the cake. Trim the cake out of the center using an offset palette knife or tiny offset spatula, again rotating the turntable with one hand and carving with the other. Don't be concerned about removing all of the cake from the center at once; start with the outer edge and work inward, removing small pieces of cake as you go. When most of the area is clear, flat-ten it by slicing across the surface with the offset spatula.

9. Crumb-coat the cake and chill for 1 hour (see page 14).

10. Ice the cake in basic buttercream with an icing spatula, or a pastry bag and a #789 icing tip. Use the flexible icing strip to get a smooth, clean finish on the rounded sides of the teacup, and the offset 4-inch spatula or palette knife to ice inside the lip of the cup.

11. Place the teacup on the plate you intend to serve it on. Fill a pastry bag with basic buttercream and attach the #13 star tip. Pipe a triple border of dragging pearl around the base of the teacup.

12. Using a toothpick or a bamboo skewer, trace the pattern into the sides of the teacup. You can enlarge the pattern by 10 percent if you like.

The teacup china pattern.

Attaching the handle to the finished teacup.

13. Fill a pastry bag with dusty rose icing, and attach the #4 round tip. Begin to pipe the pattern on the sides of the teacup.

14. Fill a pastry bag with pink icing, attach the #3 round tip, and continue piping the pattern.

15. Fill a pastry bag with the pale-brown icing, and using a #4 round tip, finish piping the pattern and the dots.

16. Fill a pastry bag with the green icing and attach the #67 leaf tip. Pipe leaves randomly over the top of the cake, letting some drape over the edge of the lip of the cup.

17. Place the flowers in the top of the cup, starting in the center and working outward.

18. Use a paintbrush to dust the dry handle with gold petal dust. Attach the handle to the teacup.

19. Box and refrigerate the cake.

Thatched Roof Cottage Cake

Lincoln's birthday, a fairy tale party, a sleep-away camp send-off, a house-warming: all of these occasions would make this cake the perfect symbolic treat. What's more, it's easy to make. The icing needn't be smooth because you want a rough, rustic structure that can easily be personalized. If you are ambitious, make a small sugar-dough or marzipan figurine of an elf or a wood nymph.

One of my triumphs was a Fiddler on the Roof cake that I made for a woman who owned one of Chagall's paintings. She was kind enough to telephone and tell me she wasn't sure whether she liked her cake or her painting better!

LEVEL OF DIFFICULTY: 2

TIMING: The cake may be baked 1 day, then carved and decorated as soon as it cools. It requires several hours to decorate, but can easily be done in 1 afternoon.

HINTS: Once the cake is iced, take a toothpick and carefully trace out where the door and windows will be so you can simply pipe over the tracing later. By tracing the door and windows ahead of time, you will be able to see whether they are the right scale, and can adjust accordingly. We used a silver dragée for the door handle, but you could pipe it on in blue or light brown icing. You can be very free with your piping on this cake. Using the star tip and the dragging pearl technique, get as creative as you like to add more depth and details. Don't be afraid to double or triple border around the windows and door.

SPECIAL EQUIPMENT

Two 8 × 8-inch square cake pans
Five 8 × 8-inch square cake cardboards
Two 8 × 5-inch cake cardboards
Turntable
Ruler
Pencil
Tracing paper

14-inch serrated knife
Standing electric mixer with whisk or paddle
   attachment
4$\frac{1}{2}$-quart mixing bowl
Icing spatula
Icing blade
Kitchen towel
Four small mixing bowls

Five pastry bags (or two bags and 5 inserts)
Two to four sets couplings
    #47 basketweave tip
    #13 star tip
    #2 round tip
    #12 round tip
    #233 grass tip
    #67 leaf tip (optional)

STRUCTURAL SUPPORT
Four 8-inch skewers
One 14-inch square platter

INGREDIENTS
1 recipe Lady Baltimore White Cake (page 19)
1 cup Vanilla Wash (page 38)
1 recipe Mocha Buttercream Filling (page 33)
One recipe Basic Buttercream Icing (page 28)
1 ounce melted unsweetened chocolate to make
    3$\frac{1}{2}$ cups pale-brown icing
3 ounces melted unsweetened chocolate to make
    2 cups dark brown
Gel food colors to make the following:
    3 cups sunflower yellow
    1 cup pale blue
    2 cups grass green
6 pale-blue or lavender hydrangeas
One #14 silver dragée

1. Bake the cakes, let them cool, and remove them from the pans. Score and slice the two cakes horizontally at ½-inch intervals, reserving 5 slices. Wrap and freeze any leftover slices. Wash and fill the slices, crumb-coat (see page 14), and refrigerate for 2 hours.

2. Place one of the 8 × 5-inch cake cardboards on top of the cake so that three sides of the cardboard are flush with three sides of the cake. Carefully cut along the edge of the cardboard at its 5-inch edge, slicing vertically all the way down and through the cake to get a cake measuring 8 × 5 inches. Carefully set aside the extra 8 × 3-inch piece of cake. Slide the cardboard rectangle underneath the 5 × 8-inch cake and place it on the cake plate or board.

3. Spread some icing along the top center of the 5 × 8-inch cake. Carefully center the 3 × 8-inch cake lengthwise on top. There will be a 1-inch gap along both sides of the 3 × 8-inch cake. Insert a skewer vertically into the center of the top and push down until the skewer touches the base of the 5 × 8-inch cake. Insert four more skewers into the top of the cake in the same manner, placing the skewers at equal intervals. Cut the tops of the skewers so they are all level with the top of the cake.

4. With the serrated knife, cut a level slope from the center line of the 3-inch cake down to where its edge meets the 5 × 8-inch cake, and continue to cut into the 5 × 8-inch cake to make the sloping line of the cottage roof. Do the same thing on the other side, so the cottage has a peaked roof.

5. Ice the 4 sides of the cake in pale-brown buttercream icing. Crumb-coat the roof (see page 14). Reserve the remaining icing for cobblestones in Step 11. Chill the cake for 1 hour.

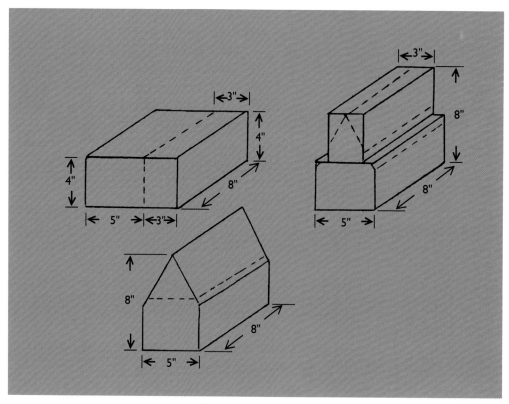

Shaping the cottage.

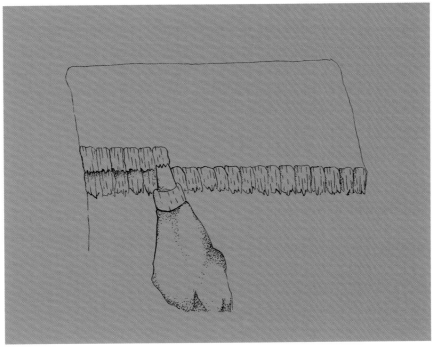

Making the thatched roof.

ROOF, WINDOWS, DOORS

6. When piping the roof with the basketweave tip, use the serrated edge to make the shingles. Be sure to try to keep the shingles the same length so that the roof looks neat, not ragged and uneven. (You will use the #47 basketweave tip twice, once with the yellow icing for the roof, and later with the brown icing to do the door and windows.)

7. Using the serrated side of a #47 basketweave tip, and the yellow icing, start at the bottom of one side of the roof where it meets the house. Work lengthwise across the long side of the cake. Using a downward pulling short stroke, pipe a series of ¹/₂-inch shingles, touching and side by side, all the way to the opposite long side of the cake—you should have 20 to 25 shingles that hang down over the edge of the roof line.

8. Start the next row ¹/₂ inch above where you began your first shingle, and pipe a series of shingles directly above the first row, letting the bottom of the

second row overhang slightly down and on top of the first row.

9. Do the third row above the second row, overlapping the row below in the same manner. Repeat this process until you reach the peak of the roof; you will have 5 to 7 rows of shingles on one side of the roof.

10. Repeat the process on the opposite side of the roof.

11. If you don't like the way the peak of the roof looks where the 2 sides meet at the top, pipe 2 straight lines along the center of the peak using the ridged part of the tip, side by side. If you wish, pipe a third line on top to finish the peak.

12. Using the brown icing and the flat side of the #47 basketweave tip, pipe the outline of the door first, and then fill in the center using vertical strokes. If you need to smooth the lines out to make the door smooth, use a small offset spatula or palette knife. If you wish, place the dragée on the door where a handle would go.

13. On the triangular end of the peak of the roof, using

the same tip and brown icing, pipe about 5 to 7 horizontal lines across the face of the peak. Repeat on the opposite peak.

14. With the blue icing and the flat side of the #47 basketweave tip, pipe several 2- by 2-inch windows, using 3 vertical strokes, side by side. Pipe a blue window into the peak of the roof, on top of the brown icing.

15. Using brown icing, change to the #13 star tip. Pipe around the edges of the windows and the edge of the peak of the roof using the dragging pearl technique. Give extra detail under the windows by piping 3 lines to create the effect of window boxes; pipe 3 more lines directly over the first 3 lines to give depth. Pipe around the front door, adding extra detail above the door by piping a half round over the top of the door. Double or triple the piping over the half round. Pipe all the straight edges of the house and around the bottom edge where the house meets the board.

16. With the #2 round tip and brown icing, pipe 2 vertical and then 2 horizontal lines to create windowpanes in the windows.

17. Dot the ground with the remaining pale-brown icing and the #12 round tip to create a cobblestone walk leading to the front door.

18. With the green icing and the #233 grass tip, pipe bushes on the two front corners of the house using a short squeeze-and-pull motion. Pipe over the top and center of the bushes 2 or 3 times to give them definition and depth. Pipe grass around the perimeter of the house. Stick 1 or 2 bunches of hydrangeas into the bushes and into the cake.

19. If you like, use a #67 leaf tip and green icing to pipe small leaves draping over the window boxes. With a #2 round tip and the blue icing, pipe a series of small dots on the leaves to resemble flowers. Refrigerate the cake.

20. Optional: You can fashion a chimney from cake scraps, and ice accordingly.

Round Cakes

Clown Cake

SERVES 15 TO 18

It's hard not to laugh and have fun in the presence of a clown. This clown cake is perfect for a child's birthday. If it is a big party, the clown head can be placed on a larger sheet cake as a base.

LEVEL OF DIFFICULTY: 3

TIMING: The cake can be baked 2 days ahead; it should be filled, carved, iced, and decorated 1 day ahead.

HINTS: When rolling out the sugar dough for the clown's ruffle, break the rule of trying to get the dough as thin as possible. Instead, keep it about ⅛ inch thick. The thicker dough will be less likely to tear when ruffled.

When you decorate with hair and a face, note that the clown's face should be slightly upturned. The cake will probably be placed on a table where people look down at it, and they will have a better view that way. Center the nose on the face first, placing it slightly higher than you think it should go. It will serve as a reference point for all the other features. Use a toothpick or skewer to lightly trace the mouth and eyes into the icing before you pipe. I strongly suggest that you first pipe the face onto a plate or a piece of paper. It is always helpful to practice, and this way you won't make your first mistake on the cake.

To make the black icing, take whatever icing you have left over—the color doesn't matter—and add a few drops of black food color. Make sure the cake is cold when you begin piping the lines. This way if you make a major mistake, you can simply lift the warmer icing off the cold cake with a palette knife without destroying the icing job.

SPECIAL EQUIPMENT

Two 8 × 3-inch round cake pans
Turntable
10 × 10-inch square cardboard
Standing electric mixer with whip or paddle
    attachment
4½-quart mixing bowl
Mixing bowls
Pencil
Scissors
Serrated knife
Plastic icing strip
Small offset spatula or palette knife
Rolling pin
Cornstarch
Clear plastic wrap
Swivel blade utility knife
Tissue paper
Three pastry bags
Three sets couplings
    #13 star tip
    #4 round tip
    #3 round tip

Toothpick or bamboo skewer
1-inch star cookie cutter
½-inch star cutter

STRUCTURAL SUPPORT
14-inch platter

INGREDIENTS
1 recipe Chocolate Fudge Cake (page 21)
1 recipe Vanilla Wash (page 38)
1 recipe Basic Buttercream Filling (page 31)
1 recipe Basic Buttercream Icing (page 28)
Gel food colors to make the following:
    4 cups red icing (mix red and lemon yellow)
    3 cups black icing
    1 cup blue icing
    1 cup lime-green icing
5 cups sugar dough:
    3 cups lime green
    1 cup yellow
    1 cup red

Shaping the cake using the template.

1. Bake the cakes, let cool, and remove them from the pans. Place a cake on the turntable. Score the cake at $1/2$-inch intervals and slice horizontally, slipping each slice onto a cake cardboard. Repeat with the remaining cake, reserving 6 slices in all. Wrap and freeze any remaining slices.

2. Center the 8-inch round cake pan on the 10 × 10-inch cardboard. Trace an 8-inch circle onto the cardboard, using the cake pan as a guide. Cut out the circle and then fold the cut cardboard in half so that all 4 square edges are even. Cut at the 2 folds to give 2 half-moon cutouts. These will be the templates to carve a round cake.

3. To begin carving the cake, first see Carving Round Cakes on page 179. Place one of the half-moon templates next to the stacked cake to get a visual idea of where and how to begin to carve. Start from the top of the cake, shaving thin slivers of cake out and away. Keep in mind that the midpoint (the middle of the cake) will remain 8 inches across, and try to carve from the top out and down toward the middle, then

from the bottom up toward the middle. From time to time replace the template on the top and sides of the cake and trim accordingly.

4. Crumb-coat the carved cake and refrigerate for 1 hour (see page 14).

5. Ice the cake as smoothly as possible with the basic buttercream icing, using the plastic icing strip and a palette knife or a small offset spatula.

6. Roll out $1/2$ of the green sugar dough and cut 3 lengths of dough, each measuring 18 × 2 inches. Cover two of the strips with plastic wrap. Lay the other dough strip flat around the bottom of the ball, tucking one edge of the strip in and under the ball. Use your fingers, work with the front edge of the dough to make a ruffle; this is the beginning of the clown's ruffled collar. Ruffle the next length of dough and tuck it inside and under the ball immediately next to the first strip. Repeat with the third length.

7. Roll out the remaining green sugar dough and repeat Step 6, layering and ruffling the lengths of dough on top of the first ruffle. Use crumpled tissue paper to

The clown face. Using a copier, enlarge this drawing by 191 percent.

stuff into the ruffles to help hold the shape; you can remove the tissue when the ruffle is dry.

8. Roll out the yellow sugar dough. Cut a length of dough 15 × 3 inches, and another length 4 × 2 inches. You will use the longer length to fashion the bow tie, the smaller length to make the knot of the bow. Press the bow into the ruffle, add the knot, and use tissue to puff the loops of the bow if you wish. (Remember that the bow must be in the front, or below the face of the clown.) (For more on bows, see page 56.)

9. Fill a pastry bag with the red icing and attach the #13 star tip. Pipe a dragging pearl border on both edges of the bow and on both sides of the bow's knot. Pipe polka dots onto the bow tie, 8 to 10 dots on each loop of the tie and 4 to 6 on the knot.

10. Fill a pastry bag with the black icing, and attach the #4 round tip. Pipe a series of dots in a triangular pattern between the red polka dots.

11. Using the bag with the red icing and the star tip (you could also use a grass tip), begin to pipe the clown's hair. The clown is bald on top; pipe hair on the sides and back only. Hold the tip against the cake and squeeze the bag and pull it back, using this motion to cover the area with hair. Be very free with the piping; it is impossible to make a mistake.

12. Roll a piece of red sugar dough a little smaller than a golf ball into a nose. Using a little dab of buttercream as glue, center the nose on the face of the clown, placing it about 2 inches higher than the center.

13. Trace the mouth, the eyes, upside-down teardrops, and the eyebrows into the icing, using a toothpick or a skewer.

14. Using the pastry bag with the red icing and the #4 round tip, pipe the mouth over the tracing.

15. Fill a bag with the lime-green icing and attach the #3 round tip. Pipe the round circles that will be the eyes, then pipe over the circle again using the drag-

ging pearl. Use the bag containing black icing to pipe the eyeballs in the center of the green circles.

16. Fill a pastry bag with the blue icing and rinse and attach the #4 round tip. Pipe the half-moon circles under the eyes. Move 1 inch above the green circles and pipe an upside-down teardrop above each eye.

17. Using the bag with the black icing, rinse and attach the #4 round tip. Pipe an arched eyebrow over the tracing, beginning on one side of the eyebrow 1/2 inch away (to the left if you start with the left eye, or to the right if you start with the right eye) from the blue half-moon circle, and ending at the nose. Repeat to make the second eyebrow.

18. Moving back to the mouth, attach the #4 tip to the bag with the red icing. Fill in the mouth. You can also use a small palette knife to spread or to flatten the icing.

19. Use the bag with the black icing and the #3 tip to add the inner detail to the mouth.

20. Roll out the remaining yellow sugar dough, and using the 1-inch star cutter, cut out 2 stars and place them on the cheeks. Using the small star cutters, cut out 6 more tiny stars and place 1 above and 2 under each of the larger stars.

21. Gather up any remaining pieces of sugar dough and shape into balls. Roll a golf-ball-sized piece of any color dough between your palms to a 4-inch cigar-shaped piece. Repeat with 2 more pieces of dough in different colors.

22. Hold the 3 pieces of dough together in one hand, grasping them from the top. Twist the dough pieces around, then roll the dough lightly with your hands so that the pieces are now 1 piece (roll gently so that the individual colors remain; don't blend the colors), and cut off 1/4 of the dough. Roll the larger piece of dough into a ball, then use your fingers to fashion the top hat with straight sides, a flat bottom, and a flat top. Roll the smaller piece of dough into a ball, then roll it out into a circle about 3 inches in diameter. Cut a circle with a water glass to make the flat brim to go underneath the top hat.

23. Place the hat on top of the clown head.

24. Optional: pipe a dragging pearl border around the hat where the brim meets the top. Use any leftover icing to pipe a dragging pearl border on the edge of the ruffled collar.

CARVING ROUND CAKES

Making a template to help carve a round cake will take most of the guesswork out of the job. However, making a perfectly round cake is hard work. Most is done free-hand; the template gives visual guidance, then it is removed and the cake is carved accordingly. You will very quickly begin to see the spots where the cake is lopsided, so you shave a little off here and there until you have made the cake as perfectly round as possible. Allow plenty of time, and work carefully and slowly. Use the template often as a guide on the sides and the top. The cake will not slide off the board it sits on once you begin shaping, so be sure to set it on the serving platter before you begin.

Basketball Cake

SERVES 15 TO 18

For the birthday of a youngster (or a youngster at heart) who is crazy about a sport, there's no problem designing a cake. The kid who lives, loves, watches, plays, and dreams of basketball will love this cake. The same goes for baseball, football, soccer, or golf. Get the colors right and decorate with the symbols of his or her favorite team, and you will wow the birthday boy or girl. Add to the sports theme by placing certain props around or near the cake—a baseball glove if it is a baseball cake, a baseball jersey, sports cards or the newspaper headlining the team's latest victory. You can really have a lot of fun if you let yourself explore and expand on a theme.

Use these same directions for any round sports cake.

LEVEL OF DIFFICULTY: 3

TIMING: The cake can be baked 2 days ahead, iced and decorated 1 day ahead.

HINTS: Give yourself plenty of time, and work carefully and slowly. Use the template often as a guide on the sides and the top. If you really get into trouble, remember that you can do some damage control with icing, building up or filling in where you may have taken off a little too much cake. Your cake will not move off the board it sits on once you begin carving, so be sure to position it before starting.

Keep a basketball (or soccer or other appropriate ball) handy because you will need it for visual guidance when it is time to pipe the appropriate lines.

To make the black icing, take whatever icing you have left (the color doesn't matter) and add a few drops of black food color. Piping black icing against any lighter background will make even the most experienced decorator feel like a beginner; you see every little mistake. I suggest going over the first piped line using a dragging pearl stroke; this way the first black line will serve as a guide, and you can cover any mistakes with the dragging pearl border. Also, make sure the cake is cold when you begin piping the lines. This way if you make a major mistake, you can simply lift the warmer icing off the cold cake with a palette knife without destroying the icing job.

For the banner, customize the color to your team color(s). We used green for this cake, but you will use whatever color is appropriate.

SPECIAL EQUIPMENT
Two 8 × 3-inch round cake pans
Six 8-inch round cake cardboards
Turntable

10 × 10-inch square cake cardboard
12-inch round cake base or platter
Pencil
Scissors

Serrated knife

Standing electric mixer with whip or paddle
  attachment

4½-quart mixing bowl

Plastic icing strip

Small offset spatula or palette knife

4 pastry bags

4 sets couplings
  #4 round tip
  #13 star tip
  #47 basketweave tip

STRUCTURAL SUPPORT

14-inch platter or cake board

1 recipe Chocolate Fudge Cake (page 21)

1 recipe Vanilla Wash (page 38)

1 recipe Basic Buttercream Filling (page 31)

1 recipe Basic Buttercream Icing (page 28)

Gel food colors to make the following:
  5 cups orange icing
  3 cups yellow icing
  4 cups black icing

2 cups green sugar dough (or color of your
  choice)

1. Bake the cakes, let them cool, and remove them from the pans. Place a cake on the turntable. Score the cake at 1/2-inch intervals and slice horizontally, slipping each slice onto a cake cardboard. Repeat with the remaining cake, reserving 6 slices in all. Wrap and freeze any remaining slices.

2. Wash the cake slices. Place the first slice on its cardboard onto the cake platter and then the turntable. Spread 1/2 to 3/4 cup of the buttercream filling on the first cake layer. Slide a cake layer off its cardboard and onto the filling below. Repeat the stacking and filling with the remaining slices, placing the last slice on top—do not put filling on the top layer. Refrigerate the filled cake for 1 to 3 hours.

3. Center the 8-inch round cake pan on the 10 × 10-inch cardboard. Trace an 8-inch circle on the cardboard, using the cake pan as a guide. Cut out the circle, and then fold the cut cardboard in half so that all 4 square edges are even. Cut at the 2 folds to give 2 half-moon cutouts. These will be the templates to carve a round cake.

4. To begin carving the cake, place one of the half-moon templates next to the stacked cake to get a visual idea of where and how to start. Begin to carve from the top of the cake, shaving thin slivers of cake out and away. Keep in mind that the midpoint (the middle) of the cake will remain 8 inches across, and try to carve from the top out and down toward the

A golf ball crowns the perfect cake for Dad.

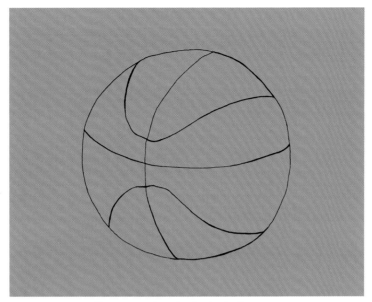
Placement for the basketball seams.

middle, then from the bottom up toward the middle. From time to time replace the template on the top and sides of the cake and trim accordingly.

5. Crumb-coat the carved cake and refrigerate for 1 hour.

6. Ice the cake as smoothly as possible with the orange buttercream icing. Using a toothpick or a bamboo skewer, begin tracing the lines into the basketball. Once all the lines are traced, refrigerate the cake for 1 hour.

7. Fill a pastry bag with the black icing and attach the #4 round tip. Pipe a single line onto the tracings. Flatten the single line by lightly going over the top with a small offset spatula or a palette knife. Pipe over the single line using the dragging pearl stroke.

8. Roll out the green sugar dough to measure 14 × 5 inches. Use a utility knife to cut the 2 long edges of the dough into a narrow triangle, so that one end of the banner ends in a point. Cut 2 small tabs, each 2 × ½ inches.

9. Lift the banner and arrange it so that part rests on the cake and part on the cake board or platter. Use a dab of icing to glue the banner to the cake. Drape the banner around the basketball, adding icing as glue wherever you need it. Place the two tabs on opposite sides of the wide end of the banner.

10. Fill a pastry bag with the yellow icing and attach the #48 basketweave tip. Using the flat side of the basketweave, pipe a flat line border all around the edge of the banner.

11. Remove the #48 tip and replace it with the #13 star tip. Border a dragging pearl around the inner and outer edge of the flat line border.

12. Reattach the #48 tip and pipe the team name on the banner, using the flat side of the #48 tip. Remove the #48 tip and replace it with the #13 star tip.

13. Border a dragging pearl around the inner and outer edge of the team name.

14. Using the pastry bag with the black icing, rinse and attach the #13 star tip. Border a dragging pearl around the inner and outer (yellow) dragging pearl borders of the team name.

15. Refrigerate the cake until ready to serve.

Globe Cake

SERVES 15 TO 18

We had an international client who wanted an immense globe. The size was dictated by the opening of our doorway and elevator. After the globe was completed, we planned to do the final artwork in the lobby of the building where the party was to be held. The day of the party it poured rain, which always complicates travel in New York. As luck would have it, four big, strong chefs had come to visit our shop, and they offered to help with the delivery. So with the aid of the chefs, three of my shop assistants, three large umbrellas, and $1/2$ inch of clearance on each side of this enormous cake, we finally got the globe into our truck. We drove 2 miles an hour—creeping to avoid New York City potholes—while my husband Ben and my chef Michael held onto the stem of the globe, and Richard, our driver, called "Slowing down, stopping for red light, passing pothole, coming to a curve." We arrived at the site, finally, and with the help of the entire catering staff, were able to situate the cake and finish the final artwork.

Since we can make round cakes, we are now empowered to create the world, including the continents and oceans (in icing), and even the Arctic and Antarctic ice caps. This is a great cake for travelers, as well as for corporations with numerous international offices. Plot the vacation route on the globe cake, and it is a great send-off for a lucky traveler. This cake is for the artist in you. We did the cake freehand; I suggest that you open the atlas to a world map view, and take it from there.

LEVEL OF DIFFICULTY: 3

TIMING: The cake can be baked 2 days ahead, filled and carved 1 day ahead, and iced and decorated 1 day ahead.

HINTS: This cake is decorated using icing and a palette knife. Look at the colors on a world map—greens, yellows, and browns for mountain ranges and land, blues for bodies of water, white for snow. Experiment to get the colors you want to use.

When we did this cake, we started by marking the Arctic circle, and then marking the continents and oceans in relation to that. Use toothpicks or skewers to mark, trace directly onto the iced cake, and then add the appropriate colors in icing with a palette knife. To do this, pick up the icing on the bottom of the knife and dab it onto the cake using a light tapping motion. This motion will give your land areas three-dimensional depth and height.

SPECIAL EQUIPMENT

Two 8 × 3-inch round cake pans

Turntable

10 × 10-inch square cardboard

Pencil

Scissors

Serrated knife

Standing electric mixer with whip or paddle
   attachment

4^1/$_2$-quart mixing bowl

Plastic icing strip

Small offset spatula or palette knife

5 pastry bags

5 sets couplings
   #3 round tip
   #13 star tip

Map of the world

Rolling pin

Swivel blade utility knife

Clear plastic wrap

Optional: 10 to 20 small toothpick flags (available
   at party stores)

STRUCTURAL SUPPORT

14-inch platter or cake board

1 recipe Chocolate Fudge Cake (page 21)

1 recipe Vanilla Wash (page 38)

1 recipe Basic Buttercream Filling (page 31)

Two recipes Basic Buttercream Icing (page 28)

Gel food colors to make the following:
   3 cups pale-blue icing
   3 cup darker-blue icing
   3 cups moss-green icing
   2 cups light-brown icing
   2 cups yellow icing

1 cup sugar dough:
   ^{1}/$_2$ cup red
   ^{1}/$_2$ cup white

Vegetable shortening

1. Bake the cakes, cool, and unpan. Place a cake on the turntable. Score the cake at ^{1}/$_2$-inch intervals, and slice horizontally, slipping each slice onto a cake cardboard. Repeat with the remaining cake, reserving six slices in all. Wrap and freeze any remaining slices.

2. Wash the cake slices. Place the first slice on its cardboard onto the cake platter and then the turntable. Spread ^{1}/$_2$ to ^{3}/$_4$ cup of the buttercream filling on the first cake layer. Slide a cake layer off its cardboard and onto the filling below. Repeat the stacking and filling with the remaining slices, placing the last slice on top. Do not put filling on the top layer. Refrigerate the filled cake for 1 to 3 hours.

3. Center the 8-inch round cake pan on the 10 × 10-inch cardboard. Trace an 8-inch circle on the cardboard, using the cake pan as a guide. Cut out the circle, and then fold the cut cardboard in half so that all 4 square edges are even. Cut at the 2 folds to give 2 half-moon cutouts. These will be the templates to carve a round cake.

4. To begin carving the cake, place one of the half-moon templates against the stacked cake to get a

visual idea of where and how to start. Begin to carve from the top of the cake, shaving thin slivers of cake out and away. Keep in mind that the midpoint (the middle) of the cake will remain 8 inches across, and try to carve from the top out and down toward the middle, then from the bottom up toward the middle. From time to time replace the template on the top and sides of the cake and trim accordingly.

5. Crumb-coat the carved cake and refrigerate for 1 hour.

6. Ice the cake as smoothly as possible with the pale-blue buttercream icing. Refrigerate for 1 hour.

7. Using the map of the world as a guide, begin to trace on the cake with a toothpick or a skewer.

8. After completing the tracing, begin to paint with the icings and the palette knife.

9. Banner: Roll out the red sugar dough to a length of 12 by 4 inches and cut an upside-down V (or a deep notch) out of each end. Roll out the white sugar dough to a length of 10 × 3 inches and cut an upside-down V out of each end. Lay the red banner on the cake board and center the white banner directly on top so there is ¹/₂ inch of red banner peeking out around the white.

10. Using the pastry bag with the blue icing and the #4 tip, pipe Bon Voyage (or another message) on the banner. Pipe a dragging pearl border around both edges of the banner.

11. Optional: Placement of small flags. Fill a pastry bag with the remaining green icing, attach the #4 round tip, and border the dragging pearl around the continents.

An elegant shoe for the old woman and her children.

Index

Metric Equivalencies

LIQUID AND DRY MEASURE EQUIVALENCIES

Customary	Metric
¹/₄ teaspoon	1.25 milliliters
¹/₂ teaspoon	2.5 milliliters
1 teaspoon	5 milliliters
1 tablespoon	15 milliliters
1 fluid ounce	30 milliliters
¹/₄ cup	60 milliliters
¹/₃ cup	80 milliliters
¹/₂ cup	120 milliliters
1 cup	240 milliliters
1 pint (2 cups)	480 milliliters
1 quart (4 cups)	960 milliliters (.96 liter)
1 gallon (4 quarts)	3.84 liters
1 ounce (by weight)	28 grams
¹/₄ pound (4 ounces)	114 grams
1 pound (16 ounces)	454 grams
2.2 pounds	1 kilogram (1000 grams)

OVEN-TEMPERATURE EQUIVALENCIES

Description	°Fahrenheit	°Celsius
Cool	200	90
Very slow	250	120
Slow	300–325	150–160
Moderately slow	325–350	160–180
Moderate	350–375	180–190
Moderately hot	375–400	190–200
Hot	400–450	200–230
Very hot	450–500	230–260

"*The Forgotten Home Child* is a poignant, edgy, and skillfully written portrayal of a Home Child's experience that typified so many. The absence of any sugar coating makes this story come to life and brings a level of reality that is often lacking—an emotional journey well worth reading."

Lori Oschefski, CEO of the British Home Children Advocacy and Research Association

Praise for

The Forgotten Home Child

"Drawing on a dark, yet little-known chapter in Canada's history, Graham paints a searing portrait of a childhood shattered by isolation and brutality. I was profoundly moved by this tale of courage, fortitude, and the heart's ability to open again in the wake of great injustice. A powerful and engrossing read, brimming on every page with both heartbreak and hope."

Roxanne Veletzos, bestselling author of
The Girl They Left Behind

"If there's one thing that defines *The Forgotten Home Child*, it's the essence of the past. In these pages, one family discovers the truth about their personal history and realizes that while our pasts are imperfect and multifaceted, and can bind us or set us free, in the end, they inform our identity. Genevieve Graham captures the reader's attention from the beginning in this exquisite journey to the heart of what makes us human."

Armando Lucas Correa, bestselling author of
The German Girl and *The Daughter's Tale*

"Another gem from one of my favourite historical fiction authors. Graham reveals our past—both the shame and the hope of it—in the truest possible light. In doing so, she offers promise that the future can be changed by the telling of such important stories. This novel is heartbreaking yet romantic, distressing yet charming—and perfect for fans of Joanna Goodman and Jennifer Robson!"

Marissa Stapley, bestselling author of
The Last Resort

Praise for
Genevieve Graham

"Time and time again, Genevieve Graham shows us just how fascinating our shared past as Canadians is."

Jennifer Robson, bestselling author of *The Gown*

"From icy gales on the Chilkoot Trail to the mud and festering greed in booming Dawson City, *At the Mountain's Edge* gives new life to one of the most fascinating chapters in Canada's history. Fast-paced and full of adventure, this novel is an exciting take on the raw emotions that make us human and the spirit required to endure."

Ellen Keith, bestselling author of *The Dutch Wife*

"A story of resilience and fortitude in the face of nature's harshest conditions, and of love breaking through the barriers of battered hearts. I practically read it in one sitting, savoring every page."

Kim van Alkemade, international bestselling author of
Bachelor Girl* and *Orphan #8*, on *At the Mountain's Edge

"Graham continues her worthy crusade of recounting pivotal Canadian history in this poignant story [about] the travesties of war both on the battlefield and the home front."

RT Book Reviews*, on *Come from Away

"The talented Genevieve Graham once again calls upon a fascinating true story in Canadian history to remind us that beneath the differences of our birth, and despite the obstacles we face, we're all human underneath. Vividly drawn and heartwarming, *Come from Away* is a beautiful look at the choices we make in the face of both love and war."

Kristin Harmel, international bestselling author of
The Room on Rue Amélie* and *The Winemaker's Wife

"At once dizzyingly romantic and tremendously adventurous, this novel also serves as a poignant reminder of the senseless toll the violence of war can take—and the incredible lengths of heroism humans will go to in order to survive and rescue the ones they love."

Toronto Star, on *Promises to Keep*

"[Graham] has delivered a book that reads like a love letter to a time and place that figures largely in our national identity: Halifax in 1917."

The Globe and Mail, on *Tides of Honour*

"Fans of Gabaldon and other historical fiction/romance writers will lap this up for the classy, fast-moving, easy-to-read, and absorbing book that it is— with some Canadian history to boot."

Winnipeg Free Press, on *Tides of Honour*

The Forgotten
Home Child

GENEVIEVE GRAHAM

Published by Simon & Schuster
New York London Toronto Sydney New Delhi

SIMON &
SCHUSTER
CANADA

Simon & Schuster Canada
A Division of Simon & Schuster, Inc.
166 King Street East, Suite 300
Toronto, Ontario M5A 1J3

This Simon & Schuster Canada edition March 2020

SIMON & SCHUSTER CANADA and colophon are
trademarks of Simon & Schuster, Inc.

For information about special discounts for bulk purchases,
please contact Simon & Schuster Special Sales at 1-800-268-3216
or CustomerService@simonandschuster.ca.

Interior design by Lewelin Polanco

Manufactured in the United States of America

1 3 5 7 9 10 8 6 4 2

Library and Archives Canada Cataloguing in Publication
Title: The forgotten home child / by Genevieve Graham.
Names: Graham, Genevieve, author.
Identifiers: Canadiana 20190130105 | ISBN 9781982128951 (softcover)
Classification: LCC PS8613.R3434 F67 2020 | DDC C813/.6—dc23

ISBN 978-1-9821-2895-1
ISBN 978-1-9821-2896-8 (ebook)

To the memory of Canada's British Home Children, and to the over four million descendants of those children, now living across Canada. Many of these can trace back their family's lineage thanks to the tireless efforts of passionate volunteers. Because of their selfless work, the British Home Children will never be forgotten.

To my daughters, Emily and Piper, who will always know who they are.

And to Dwayne, my one true home.

Being unwanted, unloved, uncared for, forgotten by everybody, I think that is a much greater hunger, a much greater poverty than the person who has nothing to eat.

—MOTHER TERESA

From All Such, Good Lord Deliver Canada

Dr. Barnardo prays with much fervor that God will put it into the hearts of people to give him money with which to gather up the "waifs and strays" of the slums of London, wash off the slime and filth from their bodies, put clean clothes upon them and dump them down in Canada. These "waifs and strays" are tainted and corrupt with moral slime and filth inherited from parents and surroundings of the most foul and disgusting character, and which all the washing and clean clothes that Dr. Barnardo may bestow cannot possibly remove. There is no power whatever that can cleanse the lepers so as to fit them to become desirable citizens of Canada. Dr. Barnardo is probably doing a good thing for London in decreasing, as far as he is able, the vicious and criminal classes there; but he is certainly doing a great wrong in dumping his human warts and excrescences upon Canada.

—**The Honourable Frederick Nicholls,**
Canadian Manufacturer and Industrial World Magazine,
April 17, 1891

PART
— one —

WINNY

— Present Day —

My life is spilling onto the street, and I am as helpless as a child to stop it. Through the living room window I watch my treasured Ulster coat tumble into a mound on the pavement, followed by a flutter of faded grey cotton when my frock lands on top. The old woollen stockings, mended so many times, slip out and cushion the books as they fall, then come my boots.

My granddaughter, Chrissie, is staring down at the little pile with a sort of guilty curiosity, but she sobers when she glances toward the house and sees my stricken expression. She stoops and gathers my things, placing them gently back inside the little wooden trunk I have kept with me for over eighty years. As she snaps the rusted hinge closed, I curse the rotted metal for releasing a secret I have kept to myself for so long.

Moments later, Chrissie comes into the house and quietly sets the trunk on the floor next to the rest of my things.

"I'm sorry, Gran, the hinge broke." She puts a warm hand on my shoulder, and I pray she will be able to contain the questions flickering in her eyes. "But that's the last of it," she says, and I exhale. "I have to go pick up Jamie from school—it's my turn in the carpool. Will you be okay for a bit?"

She'll only be out for a few minutes, and yet I am glad she asked. I've never been comfortable being alone. The silence is too loud, full of so many voices I've loved and lost.

I pat the arms of my chair. "I'll be fine. I promise to sit right here and not die while you're gone."

Chrissie frowns slightly but grabs her keys and heads to the doorway, where she pauses and glances back at me.

"I'll be fine," I say again, ashamed of my snide remark. I had only been trying to lighten the mood, but it came out wrong. I'm thrown off by the scene in the street. My gaze drops to the trunk, and I wonder if I have enough balance to carry it all the way to my room and put it away before she sees it again. Out of sight, out of mind.

I had hoped the trunk would outlive me. That once I was gone, someone could dust it off, open the latches, and discover the treasures old Gran had hidden away. Without me to tell the story, no one would be able to figure it out. It would remain forgotten. Like the rest of us.

I watch Chrissie drive away and my chest tightens with gratitude. My dear granddaughter has become quite protective of me ever since she lost her mother, my daughter, Susan, two years ago. Susan and I had shared an apartment, which had suited us both beautifully. Until she'd gotten sick, the high point of our week had been playing bridge at the Seniors' Centre or shuffling through the mall to see the lights and the people. I should have valued those moments more, but I had always assumed I would be the one going first. It didn't turn out the way I'd hoped, but I am grateful to have had a long and enduring bond with my daughter. Not all of us can be so lucky. It has been difficult living without her, but it is getting easier. These days I see Susan less and less as a woman in pain. My memories of her now are of when she was so small she needed to hold my hand everywhere we went. So small I couldn't resist hugging her on impulse, marvelling that she was mine. And his, of course.

Just after Susan's seventy-first birthday, cancer stole her from me, and it was obvious to everyone that I could no longer look after myself. Every morning and every night my creaking joints and wasting muscles remind me that the sand in my glass is running low, so when I moved from the apartment to the Shady Pines Retirement Home, I resigned myself to sitting and waiting for that last grain of sand to fall. Shady Pines was not the worst part of my life, but it was not how I'd imagined it ending. Chrissie and her son, Jamie, saw through my facade and asked me if I wanted to come live with them. I jumped at the chance. The two of them are a small but good family, and I love them with all my heart. They have no idea how important it is for me to be with family. It's all I've ever wanted, really.

The front door swings open, bringing a curtain of fresh summer sunshine into the kitchen along with my tall, dark, and handsome great-grandson. When Chrissie's husband left her for another woman ten years ago, Jamie became the man of the house by elimination. Jamie is sixteen, smart, and the spitting image of his great-grandfather.

"Hey, Gran," he says, shrugging out of his backpack. "Enjoying the new digs?"

"I am." I smile. "Thank you."

Chrissie bustles in behind him and makes her way to the kitchen. She had set a chicken to roast to celebrate my first night in their house. I've lost track of how many first nights I've had in my life. How many times I've had to start again.

Over dinner, Chrissie pries out details about Jamie's day from him, and I listen as he talks about his math teacher, his soccer game, and the fact that one of his friends is getting a car. Jamie is a teenager with teenager things on his mind, but he is a good boy, and he loves his mother. It's easy conversation, and it takes me back so many years. I almost feel like I'm home again.

"I have homework," Jamie says when he's done clearing the plates. He edges toward the door, his eyes on his phone. "I'll see you tomorrow, Gran."

"Actually," Chrissie says quickly, "I wanted to talk about something with you and Gran."

He winces, then glances apologetically at me. "Yeah, sure."

"Let's go to the living room. It's more comfortable there. I'll bring cookies."

They help me shuffle to my armchair, and Chrissie sets me up with a cup of tea. She is a nurse, following in my footsteps and those of her mother, and she always seems to know what I would like before I ask for it. There's something reassuring in that.

She sits beside Jamie, across from me. "I just thought maybe we could do this sometimes after supper. Get to know each other a bit."

Jamie's expression is pained, and I can't really blame him. I'm sure he'd rather be doing just about anything other than talking to his ninety-seven-year-old great-grandmother.

"Don't look that way," she scolds, and I see regret in her eyes. "It's just that now that your grandma is gone, we can't ask her things about when she was growing up, you know? We can't hear any more stories from her. Don't you ever wonder where our family comes from, Jamie?"

Unease stirs in my chest. I do not want to have this conversation, but I can hear the sadness in Chrissie's voice. She yearns to know more about her family. About her mom.

He gives a weak shrug. "I guess. But isn't that what the internet is for?"

"Oh, my life wasn't interesting," I assure them. "I can tell you stories about your grandmother, but to be honest, we lived a pretty average life together."

Chrissie gestures with her chin toward the trunk, which hasn't been moved since she first brought it inside, and I am instantly reminded of all that it holds.

"I was wondering if you could tell us about the little suitcase," she says. "I don't mean to be snoopy, but it looks like it holds more than an average life."

I'm sitting perfectly still, and yet I feel myself toppling backwards, as if a lifetime of secrets is unravelling before me. My gnarled fingers curl around the arms of the chair, holding me in place.

"Gran?" Jamie is by my side now, and oh, it is as if eighty years have flown away.

My hands unclamp. "You look so much like your great-grandfather." The thought sticks in my throat. "So, so much like him."

He grins, and again, it's as if I'm looking at my husband, the way he was at Jamie's age—though he had been underfed and toughened by street life. But when he smiled, he lit up my world.

"Do I?" He settles back on the couch. "What was he like?"

"I loved Pop," Chrissie tells him. "He was quiet, and he . . ."

She pauses, so I help her out. "He had a bit of a temper."

"Maybe, but I didn't see that very often. I was going to say that he was a good man. He always had time for me. And he loved Mom so much. That was obvious."

"Yes, he did."

"He wasn't from Ireland, was he?" she wonders. "I mean, he didn't have the same accent as you."

"I thought I'd mostly lost mine," I say. "I haven't been there in a very long time."

Jamie shakes his head. "Nope. You're still real Irish. I wish I had an accent."

I wink and reach for my thickest brogue. "Come on you, boyo. Oi'm not the one who'd be havin' an accent."

Jamie grins and takes a bite of a cookie as his mother leans toward me. "Mom said your family left for London when you were little, is that right? And you had four brothers? Why did your parents decide to leave Ireland?"

How long had it been since I'd thought of my little brothers? I imagine they're all gone now. "London was where everyone was going. Jobs, money, a better life. . . . Almost all the English, Irish, and Scots living in the countryside moved to the city back then."

"Was it better?"

"No. Just more crowded."

"What about Pop?" Chrissie asks. "Where was he from?"

"Oh, he was from London."

"Did he have any brothers or sisters?"

"He had a sister," I reply, then I stop, unable to say any more.

Only one person in the whole world knows my story, and he has been gone for fifteen long years. Not even my beautiful daughter, Susan, knew the humiliating truth about her parents.

Chrissie and Jamie are watching me, waiting, and my heart races as if I am standing on the edge of a cliff. I am ashamed to tell my story, but now I have no choice. My family deserves a history. As much as I don't want to talk about my past, I do not want them to wonder, as I always have, about their roots. I am haunted by the truth that I have kept from everyone I know, everyone I love.

Everyone but him, of course.

Nowadays, doctors have words to describe the way our minds can construct a wall to keep it strong—blocking painful memories in order to help us survive. But youth no longer maintains my walls, and I feel them giving way, brick by brick, spilling long overdue sunlight onto my truths. I have seen enough days to know we have no say over any of them. Life picks us up and drops us where it will. My friends and I were thrown into a whirlpool, and we did what we could, but we were only children after all. We had no idea how to swim.

I take a deep, shuddering breath and stare at the trunk. "I never expected anyone to ever open that trunk."

"I really am sorry, Gran. I don't want to upset you, and you don't have to tell us anything if it's too hard to talk about. We all grieve in our own ways."

"I know, sweetheart." I hesitate, daring myself. "Jamie, can you put that trunk up on the table here?"

It looks small in his hands, and the once-dark wood has faded to a dull, lifeless brown. It's the size of a small suitcase, like those bags they call carry-ons these days. I still remember when it was my carry-*all*. All my worldly possessions in one little box.

When he sets the trunk before me, I stare at it, wondering where to begin. I tentatively rest my hands on its surface, feeling the familiar grooves and coarse lines. Like my hands, the wood shows the ravages of time—though not nearly so vividly—and my fingers go to the long, deep scrape on top, then the notch on the back corner. The trunk and I both bear scars.

I turn it around so they can see the letters of my name carved into the back. "I made this trunk when I was a little girl."

Jamie looks impressed, and he runs his young fingers over the old seams.

"What's in there, Gran?" Chrissie asks.

If only she knew what she was asking. The answers will change the way she and Jamie see their own lives.

With a sigh, I unfasten the latches and the old trunk creaks open. I haven't looked inside for a very long time, but other than the fact that its contents had been hastily repacked that afternoon, nothing has changed. I pull out an old hairbrush and comb, then I fold back a piece of material and dig out my copy of *The Pilgrim's Progress*. Such a terrible book to give to children. I set it aside, then sort through the bits and pieces of cloth until I find my soft, black leather Bible.

This is where I must start, I realize. The cover falls open, and I slide the book toward Chrissie so she can see the sticker where my name is printed on the inside of the cover.

"'A memento of the old Country from the British and Foreign Bible Society,'" she reads, then she looks to the page on the right. Her finger taps a black-and-white photograph of a stately, spectacled gentleman with waxed ends on his moustache. "Who's this?"

"Dr. Thomas Barnardo," I say softly. His name hasn't passed my lips in probably seventy-five years, and yet I still speak it with a twisted blend of admiration and loathing. "I'm afraid I haven't told you the whole truth about our family and how we ended up here."

two

WINNY

❧

— 1936 —

The shadow of the huge steamship flooded the pier and loomed over Winny, and she shivered despite the warm morning. She'd been on a boat once before, but back then she'd been with her family, leaving Ireland for England. When they'd arrived, those two countries hadn't felt so different from each other. Where she would be going this time was another matter entirely, and so many questions filled her head.

She studied the movement on the pier, and her eyes rested on the assembly line of men stowing baggage on board the ship. As they passed trunk after trunk to each other, Winny wondered which one was hers. The wooden cases all looked the same, and from where she was standing, it was impossible to see the different names carved onto the back of each one. For a moment, a panicked thought raced through her that maybe hers had been left behind, forgotten back at the Home. But no, she remembered seeing the men at the London station load it onto the train to Liverpool, along with the others. That little trunk held everything she'd ever owned. She didn't know what she would do without it.

At the end of the pier, smaller fishing vessels were unloading their catch. Despite the foul smell that hung in the air, Winny's stomach growled. They hadn't had a bite to eat since the night before. Miss Pence, their chaperone from the Home, had said the combination of breakfast and ocean might make them sick, but the train ride had taken a full day, and she was so, so hungry. Her legs felt weak from it. Some of the younger girls had sunk to the ground and were sitting cross-legged on the dock, and Miss Pence's fair brow creased as she worried over their frocks getting dirty.

"I'd give anything for a biscuit," Winny said.

Mary, her best friend in the whole world, stood beside her, scrutinizing the dock. As long as Winny had known her, Mary had studied her surroundings as if scouting for an escape route. It was a habit from the time they'd spent living on the streets with Mary's older brother, Jack, their friend Edward, and his younger brother, Cecil.

"You're always hungry," Mary replied, still peering around.

Mary wasn't wrong. After growing up never knowing where her next meal was coming from, hunger had become habit for Winny.

"I wonder what people eat in Canada."

Mary's hand closed around hers. "I reckon we'll find out soon enough."

Winny was doing her best to think of today as the beginning of an adventure. That's what Mrs. Pritchard, the matron at the Barkingside Girls' Village, had assured them this would be. How many children could say they'd travelled across the ocean and started new lives in Canada? Winny and the others had been told over and over what lucky girls they were to have been chosen to go. But try as she might to imagine the bright, exciting future ahead, Winny couldn't help feeling as if she was stepping into a thick fog where she couldn't see a foot in front of her nose.

She wished she was still at Barkingside. She and Mary had lived there for two years and she had loved almost every minute of it. For Winny, the Home had been the answer to her prayers—sheer heaven after the wretched year she and Mary had spent in the orphanage. Instead of fighting for space with hundreds of other girls in the cold, close quarters of the orphanage, the girls at Barkingside were divided between seventy cottages—sixteen girls and a housemother in each one. There was even a house just for babies. Winny and Mary were given neat dresses and pinafores to wear and cheery white bows for their hair, and they ate three meals a day off clean dishes.

When they'd first arrived, it was all Winny could do not to gobble her food down in case it might vanish before her eyes. Over time, she began to trust that at Barkingside, there would always be enough for everyone. That unfamiliar sense of security had lifted a heavy weight from her shoulders, freeing her to laugh again. Together, she and Mary learned to read, sew, cook, and clean, all in preparation for someday becoming a lady's maid, a house servant, or a cook. She particularly liked caring for the younger girls at Barkingside, and one of the teachers suggested she consider studying to become a nurse one day. She even gave Winny a book to read about Florence Nightingale.

At the Home they worked hard and were disciplined when they broke any rules, but Winny no longer worried about an unexpected blow from a cane hitting her backside as it had at the orphanage. Punishments at Barkingside weren't doled out simply for the matron's enjoyment. The Barkingside Girls' Village had been created by Dr. Thomas Barnardo, a generous, good-hearted man who had opened many other homes to help take thousands of poor children like Winny and Mary off the dangerous streets and help them become productive citizens. Every night, after they'd included the good doctor in their prayers, the girls snuggled into clean, warm beds and whispered in the darkness until sleep overtook them.

"What do you suppose he's doing now?"

Winny never had to ask who Mary meant. It was Jack. Always Jack. "Same as us. Lying in bed, wondering what you're doing."

"Think he's all right?"

"I think so. He's smart. And he has Edward and Cecil. They'll stick together."

"You're right. I'm glad they have each other." Mary gave Winny a soft smile, barely visible in the dark room. "I'm glad I have you."

Hearing Mary voice her own thoughts filled Winny with warmth. "I don't know what I'd do without you," she admitted. "I can't imagine my life if I hadn't met you that day."

"You might still be free," Mary said wryly.

"I'd rather be with you in here than out there alone. Besides, I like it in here."

"Yeah, it's all right. It's just . . ."

"I know. I miss him too. But I'm sure we'll see him again someday."

"Someday."

On a good night, their muted conversations were more hopeful.

"What'll we do when Jack finds us?" Winny asked. "Where should we go?"

Mary was a practical, straightforward girl, and Winny loved that about her. Even more, she loved when Mary could relax enough to imagine possibilities. The dreams seemed far-fetched, but on those wonderful nights with Mary, Winny let herself believe almost anything was possible.

"We'll get our own place to start," Mary began. "You and I shall open a small shop, and Jack will open his own, right next door, with the brothers."

"That sounds lovely. What will we sell?"

"We know a lot now," Mary said quietly. "We can make and sell dresses."

"Oh, yes. For all the ladies. And hats and shoes. All of it."

"We'll have to earn some money first, maybe work in a shop before we can have our own."

"Of course."

"The sooner we can get out of here, the sooner we can live our lives the way we want to."

But once Winny was happy, comfortable, and well-fed, she stopped thinking about running away. Mary, on the other hand, never had. Her plan had always been to get away from Barkingside, find Jack, and carry on with life as it had been. Winny understood her feelings, since she missed Jack as well, but she couldn't imagine leaving all the wonders of Barkingside behind to return to a dirty, meagre life on the street.

And then one day, almost two years from the day they'd first arrived, she and Mary were working in the laundry when they were called to the matron's office.

Winny picked nervously at her fingernails as they headed across the courtyard. It was a habit she'd always had. "What did we do?"

"We'll soon see," Mary replied, steady as ever.

In the office, they stood in front of a wide desk, waiting for a woman with a handful of paper to take her seat. "My name is Mrs. Pritchard," the woman said, indicating that they should sit as well. "I'm the new matron of Barkingside." She lifted a paper off her desk and studied another underneath. "Winnifred Margaret Ellis is your name, am I correct?" she asked, looking at Winny.

Her voice wasn't unkind, just matter-of-fact. Winny nodded, transfixed by the woman's face. Her hair was swept back into a dark bun just as Winny's mother had worn hers. Her nose was a little smaller, and her eyes had little lines in the corners that Winny guessed had come from smiling. She couldn't recall if her mother had any of those. The lines *beneath* her eyes had always been much darker than this woman's, but she couldn't remember any at the sides. It had been a long time since she'd last seen her mother.

"You'll say, 'Yes, ma'am.'"

"Yes, ma'am."

"We haven't been able to locate your mother. The last place she was living was on William Brown Street."

"Yes, ma'am. Near Steple Fountain."

"Do you have any idea where she might have gone?"

Winny pictured the cramped, ugly rooms she'd shared with her family in London, the constant screaming and crying, the way her mother seemed to age by the day. If she wasn't there, what had happened to her? What had happened to Winny's brothers?

"I don't know, ma'am," Winny said. "I ain't seen her in three years."

"And your father? Where is he?"

"Da died when I was eight, when we first came from Ireland."

"What about your brothers or sisters?"

"I've four younger brothers, ma'am, but I ain't seen them since I left home."

Mrs. Pritchard turned her attention to Mary, confirmed her name, then asked about her family.

"Da's dead, Grammy's dead, and we left our mother to her gin," Mary said. "It's only me and Jack now."

"Jack is your brother?"

"Yes, ma'am." Mary leaned forward. "Last I saw him was before the orphanage, and I need to find him. He's a year older than me, hair straight and black as mine, aye? And he'd be looking for me as well. Can you help me find him?"

Mrs. Pritchard didn't appear to be listening. She made a couple of notes then sat back in her chair. "I hear you're both doing well with your studies, that you'll make fine maids one day." She tapped the table with the tips of her long fingers. "Have you heard about other children going away from here on a ship and living somewhere else?"

"No, ma'am," Winny said slowly. She knew some girls had left Barkingside, but that was only when their parents came to claim them, or when they were too old to live there any longer.

"It's only for very special, fortunate children willing to work hard and make something of themselves. And because you two are such good girls, it's your turn. How would you like to go to Canada?"

Winny had never heard of Canada and didn't know what to say. Beside her, Mary stilled.

Mrs. Pritchard smiled when they didn't answer. "Canada is a wonderful place with fresh air and horses and mountains and a great deal for girls and boys to do."

Butterflies swooped in Winny's stomach as she recalled a photograph she'd seen in her schoolbook of unfamiliar, wide open spaces. The image had been in black and white, of course, but in Winny's eyes, it came alive with blue sky and green grass and spectacular, towering mountains. Never in her wildest dreams had she imagined she might see that in person.

"Like what?" she asked.

"The children we send over from here will live with families, go to school, learn new things, and work."

"Is it far?" Mary's voice was quiet.

"Why, yes. It's on the other side of the ocean, Mary."

"Then we can't go," Mary said firmly. "I can't leave England. What if my mother comes looking for me? And what about my brother? I can't leave Jack."

The picture in Winny's mind vanished. "And I can't go without Mary," she said. She'd sworn never to be alone again. She'd left that awful life behind.

Mrs. Pritchard's mouth set in a straight line. "Mary, has your mother come to see you even once while you were here or at the orphanage?"

Mary shook her head.

"I didn't think so. I believe it's fair to say she won't come looking anytime soon. As for your brother, I'm afraid I don't have any idea where he is. Regardless, you can't let that stop you from making a better life for yourself."

"Can't we stay here?" Winny asked. "We will work hard so you won't need to send us away."

"Girls, you are looking at this the wrong way. It is an *opportunity*, and you are very lucky to be included. People in Canada are looking for children like you to work in their homes and farms, to tend their children, and to live with their families in a beautiful new land." She got to her feet. "You must trust that we know what's best for you. Anyhow, everything is all arranged. You will be leaving here in two weeks."

Winny opened her mouth to speak, but Mrs. Pritchard had no time for conversation. "Out you go. Back to work."

Mary had gone very pale, her eyes round as dinner plates, so Winny took her hand. They walked numbly down the corridor, and Winny dug through the fog for something to say.

"It'll be all right," she tried.

"We can't leave Jack," Mary whispered.

But as Mrs. Pritchard had said, the arrangements had been completed, and the subject was closed. Winny and Mary had to prepare for the voyage. The first time they were brought into a woodworking shop along with the other chosen girls, it felt strange. They'd never learned that sort of trade before. The hammer and nails were unfamiliar at first, and the agony of missing a stroke and hitting her thumb was excruciating, but it was all part of their next lesson—building their very own travel trunk for the journey to Canada.

Now Winny stood on the pier, watching those trunks be swallowed up by the ship.

"Stay in line, girls," Miss Pence called, corralling the children into place. "We cannot get on the boat until everyone has been counted."

Winny looked down at her coat where her nametag fluttered from a buttonhole. Each girl had one with her destination on it. Winny's said *Winnifred Ellis, Toronto.* Mary's said *Mary Miller, Toronto.* She had never heard of Toronto before, but it was a comfort to know that she and Mary would end up in the same place. Her gaze passed over the crowd and paused on the little ones, some of whom were only five and six years old. Winny couldn't help but wonder what good those young children would be in Canada. Were they being sent over as housemaids? Who would expect a baby to clean a house?

For the voyage, all the girls were dressed in matching black coats and skirts, straw hats perched on their heads. Unfortunately, the fine job the ladies at Barkingside had done of combing out the girls' freshly washed hair had been wasted by the wind. At least they had taken everyone's photographs in advance of going to the pier. Winny heard them say the pictures were "for their files," but she wasn't sure what that meant. She would have liked to keep hers.

A gust of wind pushed at them and Winny slapped her hand onto her hat, holding it in place. One of the littlest girls lost hers and stepped out of line to retrieve it. Without thinking, Winny reached for her, wanting to keep her safe.

"Stand still." Mary grabbed Winny's arm. "Miss Pence will see to it."

But Miss Pence was distracted by something on the other side of the dock. "Wait here, girls."

Winny popped up on her tiptoes. At fifteen, she was still shorter than many of the younger girls, probably because she hadn't had much to eat as a child. It didn't help that her mother had also been small. Between the other girls' heads and shoulders, Winny spotted another group of children approaching the ship, and she took in the matching navy coats, caps, and short pants with interest. It was a group of boys.

"Mary, look!" She pointed, practically jumping in place. "Could it be . . . ?"

Beside her, she heard Mary catch her breath. "Do you see him? I can't see him."

"Excuse me," Winny muttered, pulling Mary through the group.

"Get off me!" a girl cried when Winny accidentally trod on her foot.

"We just need to see is all."

"I'll thank you not to do it on my foot."

"Keep going, Winny," Mary urged, squeezing her hand.

Once they stood on the outside edge of their group, the two girls scanned the crowd of boys.

"Anything?" Winny asked.

"Not yet. Keep looking."

It had been so long since they'd seen Jack and the others. He'd be sixteen now. How had the last three years been for him? Had they been anything like hers? Would she recognize him? Would he recognize her?

"Edward!" Mary suddenly cried. "Edward! Over here!"

Winny squealed, spotting their old friend's sandy-coloured hair and the laughing blue of his eyes. "Edward! It's us!"

The girls waved with both arms so he couldn't miss them.

"Mary? Hey, Winny!" Edward called, then he turned back to the other boys and dragged his brother Cecil forward so that the sun shone like copper off his thick red hair. Then, just like that, there was Jack.

three
JACK

Jack didn't care what Mr. Keller said. He broke from the group and sprinted toward Mary, gathering her into his arms before either of them could speak. She held him tight, her frame racking with sobs, and it was all he could do not to cry with her. From the day his sister was born until the day they'd been separated at the orphanage, the two of them hadn't left each other's side, and for the past three years, Jack had felt as if a piece of him was missing. Holding her now, he felt truly alive for the first time in ages.

She stepped back, her red-rimmed eyes taking him in as he did the same with her. She was taller than he remembered—as was he, of course—and she looked so grown up in her uniform. So many questions rose inside him that he couldn't speak at first.

"I thought . . . ," she said, wiping her face with the back of her hand. "I was afraid you . . . I thought I'd have to go without you, and—"

"Me too. No one would tell me where you were. I didn't know if you were still at the orphanage, or if Barnardo's people had come for you, too. I'd never thought to see you here today!"

From his first moments in the orphanage, he'd questioned anyone and everyone in authority, demanding to know where his sister had been taken. Answers had come in the form of beatings, sometimes followed by days locked in the black, earthy pit of the cellar, but he never stopped asking. How many nights had he lain awake, wondering how and where she was? Praying she was eating well, that she was safe and warm? Mary had always prided herself on being tough, but Jack knew how fragile she could be.

By the time he, Edward, and Cecil had been transferred from the orphanage to Barnardo's Stepney Causeway Home for Boys, he had almost accepted that he'd never see his sister again. But here she was. He took a step back and saw Winny hopping on her toes at Mary's side, her cloud of curls bouncing under her hat.

"Hi, Jack," she said. Her wide brown gaze was just as intense as it had been the first day he met her.

"Hey, Irish," he said, pulling her in for a hug. "God, it's good to see you."

"We missed you so much," she said into his ear.

Edward and Cecil took turns embracing the girls. "You two sure are a sight for sore eyes!" Cecil said, grinning.

"Thought I'd seen the last of you," Edward said quietly to Mary, and Jack heard relief in his friend's voice.

Mr. Keller strode over, separating the boys from the girls with a wide sweep of his arms. "Back in line, children," he said.

But Jack didn't move. "Can't I have a moment with my sister?"

"It's all right, Mr. Miller. You'll have time to talk when we're on board. We're travelling together."

Happiness surged through Jack at the news, so he nodded and returned to his group. All that mattered was that Mary was here, safe and sound. From this point on, he could take care of her and Winny again, just like he used to.

Winny's chipper voice rang out from across the dock. "See you on board, Jack!"

Her teacher scolded her for shouting, but as soon as the woman moved away, Winny looked back at him, still beaming. Her smile was as contagious as ever.

———

The first time he'd met Winny, there had been no smile on her face. Mary had found her down the street from the market, dirty, shivering with cold, and stooped with hunger, and she had brought the little waif to their hideout in the tunnel. The girls were the same age, but Winny looked much younger. A tiny little thing. They gave her some of their food, then Mary took her under her wing and explained how their gang worked. He was glad to see Winny didn't argue when Mary told her she'd have to contribute to the pot if she wanted to stay with them, whether that was by earning money fair and square or by stealing, as most of them did.

"I took a plum yesterday," she'd said in her singsong Irish accent. "On my own."

"That's a good start. Just grabbed it, did you?" Mary said. "Jack can teach you some tricks too."

He liked how Winny watched them all—Mary, him, Edward, and Cecil—and how she seemed to ingest everything that happened around her. Her eyes were big and as brown as nuts, and Jack was well aware that those were valuable to a little group like theirs. He knew from experience that folks would do just about anything for a kid who looked like her.

By the time Winny joined them, he and Mary had been scraping by on the streets for about two years. Their father had been a tight-lipped, hard-fisted man who couldn't stand children, and their mother cowered before him. Jack was eleven and Mary was ten when he'd abandoned them. They'd hoped their lives would get better after he was gone, but their mother blamed the children for driving him away and making her life miserable, and she turned to gin.

One day, three solemn-faced women from the Children's Aid Society showed up at their door. They had taken one look at Jack's mother, unconscious on her bed, then said that for the children's own safety, they had to go with them. Jack and Mary had always been able to communicate without words, and when he glanced at his sister he could see the idea didn't sit right with her. It certainly didn't with him. Feigning agreement, Mary assured the women they'd collect their things and be right back. Instead, they escaped through a rear window and never looked back.

Jack sometimes toyed with the idea of going back to the old place just to make sure their mother was all right, and once in a while, he and Mary dreamed about a happy ending for their family, but they knew it would never come true. The truth was, their mother had probably barely noticed they were gone.

Life on the street was difficult, but they were used to fending for themselves. Finding shelter was the hardest part. One cold winter morning they came across a woman's frozen body, curled against a wall like a snail, and Jack had peeled her shawl off to wrap around his sister's shoulders. Living rough was the price they paid for not going to an orphanage or workhouse, where they'd have to pick oakum, smash rocks, or do some other kind of miserable labour for a roof over their heads and food to eat. But there, they would be separated from one another. That was the one thing they couldn't face.

Other children, including Cecil and Edward, had met up with them along the way, but only the brothers stayed. No one knew where the others went. They might have returned home, they might have gone into a workhouse, they might have died. With so little certainty about what might happen on any given day, no one ever thought to say goodbye.

And then Winny came along.

A few days after she joined their group, they had gone to the market, and he'd asked if she was ready to try something new. She'd nodded eagerly, and he was glad to see there was already a bit more colour in her cheeks.

"Today, you're the bait," Jack said.

She blinked once. "What's a bait?"

"Don't be daft."

"I'm not daft. I just dunno what a bait is."

"Sure you do. Like a worm when a fella goes fishing," he'd said, though he'd never fished in his life. "It's easy. You're real small for twelve, so they'll think you're just a tyke. You don't gotta say nothing, just look up at them with them eyes of yours. So you distract 'em, see? Try it. Show me them eyes."

She looked up at him, eyes wide.

"That's it. As big and sad as you can."

"But—"

"Is ya hungry, Irish?"

"I am," she said.

"Then let's go." He spun her around so they both could watch the crowd milling about the stalls. "There. See the lady with the big hat and the black feather?" He pushed her gently forward. "That's the one for you. Go over and look sad. So she sees you."

"Then what?"

"You'll see. Sad as you can."

He left her there, but as he wound his way between the merchants, he kept a protective eye on her. He didn't want her getting hurt in the bubbling stew of people. She stopped behind the woman with the black feather hat and sought Jack out, but before she saw him he'd ducked behind a stack of crates. She had to do this herself. She needed to know how to get her own food if she was to survive. After this first time, it would get easier.

"Go on," he urged. "Do it."

As if she heard him, Winny stepped into the woman's line of sight and heaved a deep breath before gazing soulfully up. She bit her lower lip and looked through her eyelashes at the woman, making her saddest face. It was the juiciest piece of bait Jack had ever seen.

"Oh my! What a pretty little thing you are. Where's your mother, dear?"

Winny just looked at her, not saying a word, then the woman leaned down and asked the magic words.

"Are you hungry?"

Winny nodded, and the woman gave the grim-faced seller a coin before handing Winny an apple. Jack was especially glad he wasn't with her in that moment, because the man knew him and their gang well. He'd chased them away from his stall many times. Then again, he most likely wouldn't say anything as long as this woman handed him her coins. A sale was a sale, after all.

The woman smiled with appreciation as Winny bit into the apple. Quiet as a cat, Jack wound his way back toward her and waited for his cue.

"What a dear little thing you are," the woman said, producing a small sack from within her coat. "Here now." She peered into it and Jack braced to run. "I've enough here to—"

He snatched her purse before Winny or the woman saw him coming, then he vanished back into the crowd. He could hear the woman screaming, "Thief! Thief!" but they'd never catch him. As he ran, he glanced behind, but Winny wasn't there. She must have stayed put. He circled back at a safe distance and spotted her standing in the same place, looking around for him.

"Winny!" he called, just loud enough for her to hear.

Looking slightly annoyed, she headed toward him. "You never told me if I should run or—"

But the seller was right behind her, hollering for the police.

"Run now, Irish! *Run!*" he said, shoving her ahead of him. "I ain't getting caught 'cause of you!"

Winny got going as fast as her legs would carry her, her arms pumping like mad. When she started to lag, Jack scooped her up and carried her lickety-split out of the market. He ran until he reached an alley, then he let her go, his chest heaving against his threadbare shirt.

"You gotta run faster next time, Irish."

"My name is not Irish," she said, gasping for breath. "It's Winny."

"I know that. But you're from Ireland, ain't ya? That's your home."

"I live in England now, so England's my home."

"Nah. That's not the way it is." He took a few big gulps of air. They both needed to get their breath back before they could run again. "This is my home because I was born here, but it's more than that. Mum said—" He hesitated. He never liked to think about Mum. "When I was little she told me home is where your heart is."

Winny cocked her head to the side. "In Ireland I lived in a dirty wee house in the middle o' nowhere. In England I lived in a dirty wee house in the middle of a city, until I met you lot. Now I live on the streets. I dunno where my heart is."

"Maybe you just have to wait and see."

She looked thoughtful for a moment. "I feel like I'm home when I'm with you and Mary."

He laughed. A person couldn't be a home, he wanted to say.

"Coast is clear," he said, ducking his head out of the alley, and they started off again. Jack reached the tunnel first, and when Winny arrived, puffing behind him, he was already telling them about her success.

"There she is!" Edward said, grinning. "Well done, mate."

"Whatcha get?" Cecil asked.

Jack handed over the purse. "You mean what did Irish get," he said, giving Winny a wink.

Cecil squinted into the bag, one finger stirring the coins within. "Looks like ten pence, maybe."

"Your first steal," Mary said. "Now you're one of us."

Winny smiled, but her brow creased.

"What's wrong?" Mary asked.

"I feel bad for doing it. That lady was kind to me, then we stole from her." She looked at Jack. "It feels like a lie."

They all knew stealing was wrong, and Jack was plenty guilty of that, but he was also responsible for making sure he and the others ate. In his mind, those two things balanced each other out. He'd never actually thought of stealing as *lying* until now. Somehow that was a harder thing to swallow. It made what they did feel more personal.

"Would you do it again?" he asked.

The crease in her forehead disappeared. "Oh, well. If it means we don't starve, then I'll do it again."

And that was all Jack needed to know.

————

From his place on the pier, Jack watched the group of girls begin to cross the gangplank and board the ship. At the last second, Mary glanced over her shoulder at him, and their eyes locked.

I'm here, he thought hard, needing her to know. *And I ain't leaving you again.*

When she nodded with understanding, he grinned. It was astounding how much life could change in a moment. Minutes before, he'd been dragging his heels, torn apart that he'd be travelling to Canada and leaving Mary behind. Then she'd appeared as if by magic, and now he was impatient to board the ship. When it was his turn, Jack stepped forward then grasped the rope banister when the gangplank swayed. The seawater looked very black beneath his feet, and Jack had no idea how to swim.

Once everyone was on board and gathered on the main deck, Mr. Keller and the girls' teacher, Miss Pence, explained where on the ship they were permitted to wander. To Jack's relief, it was announced that as long as they all behaved with decorum, the boys and girls were allowed to socialize during the voyage. Jack could hardly wait to hear about the girls' lives and tell them about his.

Edward clapped him on the back, looking happier than Jack had seen him in a while. "We're all together again, just like the old days."

Cecil snorted. "For how long? Once we're over there, we'll probably never see each other again."

The reality of what Cecil was saying smothered Jack's joy, and he looked away. He knew his friend was probably right, but he didn't want to think about that just yet.

"Ain't you a bringer of glad tidings," Edward muttered to his brother.

"What? You're daft if you think this is gonna go well for us. They said we're being sent to different places. They're sending us over to work."

"And live," Edward reminded him. "Which means maybe we *will* see each other."

"Doubt it," Cecil muttered, and Jack heard the fear behind Cecil's words. The brothers had never lived apart from each other.

"Shhh," Jack said, noticing the girls coming toward them. "No more moping."

"There you are," Mary said, hugging Jack again.

"I still can't believe you're here," he replied, stepping back to take a better look. "Or how grown up you both are." He turned to Winny. "You've gotten bigger. You must be eating all right."

"I'm fifteen," she said, as if he didn't remember. "Practically a lady."

"I can see that." And it was true. She'd always been small, and she still was, but she stood taller now, and her wild mane of hair had been slightly tamed under her straw hat. Those big brown eyes were as deep as ever, though.

"And look at you." She gestured to his cheeks. "Shaving like a man."

"I'm sixteen," he copied her. "Practically a gentleman."

Winny laughed just like he remembered, but when he glanced at Mary, her tense expression was unfamiliar. Every gaze, every lifted eyebrow or shoulder had always carried an implication that he understood, but he couldn't quite read her now. Maybe the past three years had taken away more than time spent together.

"What's wrong?" he asked.

"This shouldn't be happening," she said, wringing her hands. "Cecil's right. We shouldn't leave England. We know nothing about Canada or what they'll have us do there. Jack, tell me you have a plan to get us out of this."

"A plan? I suppose if you'd asked me an hour ago, I'd have agreed with you, but that was before you lot showed up. Canada don't seem so frightening now we're together again. Sure, they're sending us to work, but—" He elbowed Cecil. "There'll be no more marching in lines, no more 'yes sir, no sir.' Right?"

Cecil wrinkled his heavily freckled nose at the memory.

Just the thought of living without those restraints made Jack feel as if he could fly. No more living in a cage. Whether at the orphanage or at Stepney Causeway, he'd always felt trapped. It was true that once they'd been taken to the Home, they'd had better food to eat and books to read, but they'd still been inmates in a prison of sorts.

"They say we'll be cowboys in Canada," Edward put in, trying to lighten the mood. "We'll live good."

Mary shook her head. "I don't believe it."

"Don't believe what?"

"Any of it. That Canada will be a good thing," she said. "Who knows where we'll end up?"

Jack caught Edward's eye, recalling an incident where they'd both ended up at the wrong end of a teacher's belt. "It's gotta be better than here."

"It wasn't so bad in the Home," she insisted.

"That's true. I liked Barkingside," Winny said. "We always had food and warm beds, and they taught us loads. I can sew and cook now, and I never knew none of that before. We used to sing, too. I liked a lot of things there."

Jack didn't remember Stepney Causeway with that much fondness. He remembered the discipline, the drills, the work, and the everyday drudgery. He remembered staring past the black iron gates, wishing he could run through them.

"Never mind that. The point is we're free now," he said. "Mr. Keller said folks want us so bad out there that they *pay* the Home to bring us. And nobody wants us here in England. *Nobody*." He looked at Winny. "What do you say, Irish? Anybody gonna miss you when you're gone?"

Her face fell. "Nobody."

He suddenly wanted her smile back. "Don't worry. I bet you'll get the very best family over there. They'll love you and take care of you, and one day you'll marry a prince."

"The ship's moving," Edward said quietly.

Seeing the gangplank had been raised, they ran to the side of the deck and watched as the thick ropes connecting the boat to the pier were tossed loose. The black line of water between ship and land widened, and Jack's heart thudded with the sense of being trapped yet again. The coast of England faded into the distance, becoming smaller and smaller until it was blocked out altogether by the ship's oily belch of smoke.

"Aren't you scared?" Mary asked him softly.

"We've faced worse," he reminded her. "Everyone says this is a good thing for us. We've no choice but to believe them." He turned and leaned his back against the rail. "Would you rather be hiding in doorways? Or back in the tunnel, eating whatever you can steal?"

"I didn't mind that," she said. "As long as we were together."

"Jack will make sure we are," Winny said. "He'll take care of us again."

He swallowed hard and drew the girls in close as the familiar, welcome weight of responsibility returned to his shoulders. For so long, he'd had no idea where the two of them were and if they were all right, and not knowing had made him feel unsteady. Now that he had them again, it was a relief to carry that burden. But the truth was, he couldn't look into Winny's trusting eyes and assure her that everything would be fine. They were going into the unknown, and he couldn't make her that kind of promise. He would do everything he could to protect them, but he couldn't lie. Not to Mary, and not to Winny.

four
WINNY

❧

What do you say, Irish? Anybody gonna miss you when you're gone?
Jack's question had burrowed into Winny's mind. Even now, tucked into a bunk in the belly of the ship with a scratchy grey blanket tickling her chin, she couldn't shake it. She stared at the metal slats over her head and listened to the quiet breathing around her, feeling all alone in a roomful of girls.

When the ship rocked slightly, moving with the sea, Winny rolled her head toward Mary. Just like at the orphanage, then at Barkingside, Mary had secured the bed right beside hers. It comforted Mary to know Winny was safe. It comforted Winny to watch Mary sleep. Winny still recalled those nights at the orphanage when she'd heard Mary crying to herself, missing Jack so much it hurt. Winny had gone to her every time, crawling into her friend's bed and curling up around her. Here on the ship, Mary's sleeping expression was calmer than Winny had seen it in three years. She had her brother again, even if it was only for now.

Winny wondered about her own brothers. Did they miss her? They'd been so young when she'd left. Only Harry would have been old enough to even remember her. Her mother would, of course. Unless— could a mother ever completely forget her child? Winny pictured her as she'd last seen her, hunched over a bucket, scrubbing a filthy brush over a filthier frock, and wondered if she ever thought of her only daughter. Did she question where Winny was? Would she care that her little girl was sailing across the ocean right now, miles and miles away from home?

Barkingside had done more for Winny than her mother ever had. Maybe someday, once she'd made something of herself—a lady's maid or a governess, perhaps—Winny would go back to England and find her family again. What would her mother think of her then? Wouldn't it be grand to one day return to the Home and show all the little girls there that it was possible to do well? All they had to do was put their life in the right person's hands.

Jack called her Irish, but the truth was Winny didn't remember much about Ireland. As an eight-year-old child, she'd huddled with her family in the belly of a reeking boat, and her father had told them stories he'd heard about England, trying to brighten the shivery darkness with hope. Winny had clung to every word just as she had clung to his hand when the family finally disembarked. To her disappointment, England was no warmer, the sky no bluer than in Ireland, but the sudden, overwhelming noise and bustle of the city had been terrifying.

Harry was six back then, Freddy was four, Jimmy was two. Sam was born a few weeks after they landed. They all squeezed into two rooms of an old stone building that housed two other families, and they all fought the rats for space. The air was choked with soot from grimy chimneys, and Jimmy had coughed constantly. At least they were protected from the rain, until the puddles seeped under the door, anyway.

Despite London's filth and the lack of food, her father always claimed this was where their lives would start fresh. He'd toss Winny in the air until she cried with laughter, and say they'd soon have so much money they'd be spreading butter on bacon. Less than a year passed before he died in the factory, caught up in the machinery. *Stupid man*, Mum had said. *Stupid, stupid man.*

The next two years had been hard and hungry. Winny had done what she could to help, but they barely scraped by. When she was ten, her mum brought home a strange man named Stuart, who gave them each a stick of candy.

"He's going to stay with us," Mum had said.

"Doesn't he have his own family?" Winny asked.

Her mother told her no and to stop asking rude questions. Stuart was there to help them. He would be their new father. Winny eyed him skeptically, but she couldn't deny that he brought home enough money to pay the rent. The boys were so young they didn't seem to mind this new member of their family, but for Winny, no one but Da could ever be Da.

Stuart had a big, booming voice because he was partly deaf from the machines in the factory. He'd bellow for her mother to bring him his meal; he'd bellow at Winny to keep the boys quiet. His face grew alarmingly red if Winny didn't do as he said right away, and she was sure his shouts could be heard down the street. It didn't take long for Winny to know she was right, and her mother was wrong. This man was not her new father; he was a brutish lout who got worse with every order he gave.

"Bring me gin," he roared at Winny one night.

She glared back. "You can get it yourself. I'm making supper."

"Bring it now."

"I won't."

She'd never seen him move so fast. He shot to his feet, his chair falling back with a clatter, took one long stride, and slapped her. The unexpected sting of his hand blazed like fire through her face. Behind her, her brothers gasped. Her mother looked taken aback, but she didn't come to her daughter's aid.

"Don't hit me, Stuart," Winny said through tight lips, her eyes streaming from the impact. "You can't hit me. You're not my father."

So he hit her again, told her not to talk back or he'd give her a whupping she would never forget.

Winny pressed her hand to her cheek, still hot from the slaps and wet from her tears. "Mum?" she whispered, afraid to look away from him.

"Stuart," her mother said carefully. "Leave the girl. Here, I've your gin for you."

He wheeled on Winny's mother this time, and she cried out when he struck her. The cup flew from her hand and smashed on the floor, splashing gin on Winny's bare toes.

"Get me my gin!" he roared, turning back to Winny. She quickly found a cup and filled it without another word.

After that, Stuart's strikes became a regular occurrence. When he hit baby Sam a couple of weeks later, Winny rushed over and snatched the baby out of his reach, which only made him angrier. He chased her down and, just like he'd said, he gave her a whupping she would never forget.

The next morning after Stuart left for work, Winny went to her mother. Dried blood rimmed her lips, and her right eye had swollen completely shut. "Please, Mum. Make him leave," she said, picking at her fingernails. "We don't need him."

Her mother raised tired eyes from the washing and took in the terrible sight of her daughter's bruised face, then she looked back down and continued to scrub. "But we do, Winny. Is ye paying the rent? Does ye want to eat? Stuart pays for us, so he ain't leaving."

"Then I am," Winny said softly.

Her mother nodded, and to Winny's dismay it looked like she'd been thinking about that very thing for a while. "You're a smart girl. You'll do fine."

For a week or so, Winny lived by herself on the street, huddling in doorways, shivering in the rain. Hunger twisted through her, and she wobbled unsteadily when she stood. Desperate for company, she reached out to strangers, smiling, wishing them well, but they took her for a beggar and pushed her away. Worse than the pain in her stomach was the cold she felt on the inside, the deep hurt that came with being unwanted. She'd never felt so alone.

Then along came a tall, willowy girl with a mop of long black hair.

"Think of us as your family," Mary told her that first night. They'd found an open space where they could lie on their backs and look up at the heavens, bundled close together for warmth, and Winny had never felt so calm. "It may be rough out here, but as long as you're with us, you have a home." Mary turned her head so she could smile at Winny. "I'm glad to finally have a sister."

Winny held on to Mary and the boys like a lifeline and swore never to let go.

One day, Cecil asked her to go to the market with him, and Winny knew he needed her to be the bait. He let her pick out a mark by herself, and she chose a young lady wearing a pale-coloured coat, her hood rimmed in shiny white fur. To Winny, she looked like a snowflake in a coal mine.

Cecil scouted for threats, then nodded. "Right. Let's go. Be quick, though. Looks like she's almost done her shopping."

Moving to her usual spot, Winny gazed up with her saddest expression, but the woman didn't notice her. She was laughing at something the handsome young baker was saying, her lovely eyes sparkling. Winny sniffed to get her attention, and the woman glanced down. Disgust bloomed on her face, and she waved a pale grey glove at Winny.

"Get away from me, you vile little beggar. Probably covered in fleas."

"I don't got fleas," Winny said, scratching her head and hoping that was true. "I'm only hungry is all."

"What are you staring at? Don't come near me. I'll call the police." The woman turned to the baker. "The brat stinks. How do you—"

In dashed Cecil. He snatched the purse from that pale grey glove, and Winny chased after him, blood pounding. Her heart nearly jumped from her chest when she heard the tweet of a policeman's whistle right behind her, but she kept on running, darting through the crowd even after she lost sight of Cecil.

Then suddenly, the ground was gone from beneath her feet.

"Hold up, girly," a man said, tossing her over his black wool shoulder. "You're coming with me."

"Let me go!" Winny kicked, but the bobby held her tight. Across from her, Cecil stood panting and sweating, red circles burning on his cheeks. A second policeman's hand was clamped on his shoulder.

"We wasn't doin' no harm," Cecil tried. "Let us go."

"Give it here, lad. Give it without a fuss and I might go easy."

Cecil reluctantly handed over the purse, and the policeman passed it to the simpering woman who had appeared beside them.

"What'll you do with them?" she asked, eyeing Winny and Cecil as if they were rats.

"Workhouse, I s'pose."

Winny gasped and caught Cecil's eye.

The woman frowned. "Not prison?"

"Not much difference, ma'am."

The policeman grabbed Cecil by the back of the neck and shoved him ahead. The one holding Winny started marching as well, but she couldn't see where they were going.

"Please, sir!" she cried, pounding her fists against his back. "Put me down! I'll be good!"

"Quiet, girl."

"But please!"

He stopped suddenly, then Winny heard a familiar voice and her heart grew wings.

"Excuse me, sirs. These children are with me." Jack's voice was low and deep, though it cracked on the last word. "I'll just take them—"

"With you, eh? How old are you, boy?"

"Sixteen, sir," he bluffed. Winny knew very well he was only thirteen. "Their parents asked me to watch them, but you know how children are. I looked away for a second and they were gone."

Mary was with him, and she walked around the bobby so she could gaze up at Winny. "He'll put you down soon, love. I'm sure he will."

Instead, the two policemen produced their nightsticks. "You might be a good storyteller, boy, but you'll all be coming with us now. We've been watching you lot for a while."

"Get your hand off me," Winny heard Edward say. Of course he was there too. He wouldn't leave Cecil.

She twisted around so she could see, and that's when she spotted two more uniforms. One held Jack's arm, another had grabbed Edward. No one needed to hold Mary. She wasn't going to run off on her own.

"'You know how children are,'" Cecil muttered to Jack, clearly offended. "Nice."

"Don't you worry, sweetheart," the bobby said, patting Winny's bottom. "Nobody's going anywhere."

But that had been a lie, hadn't it? The policemen had dumped them at the orphanage, then the Barnardo's people had come for them, and now they lay in cold bunks on a ship, on their way to a strange land across the ocean. No, the policeman had been wrong about no one going anywhere.

Not all the girls at Barkingside had been chosen to go to Canada. Winny couldn't imagine what she would have done if Mary hadn't been picked as well. Sometimes when Mary had worried about leaving Jack behind, Winny thought about their friend Charlotte, who had arrived at Barkingside a few months after they had. A pale blond thing, meek and silent as a shadow, Charlotte stayed huddled on a cot in the far corner of the room. Every time any door swung open, she swivelled toward it, crystal-blue eyes wide with expectation, and every time she slumped with disappointment.

"Do you see that girl there?" Winny had asked Mary. "The bonny little one in the corner? She looks sad. She needs a friend. I'm going to say hullo."

As Winny approached her cot, the girl eyed her warily.

"I'm Winny," she said. "What's your name?"

"Charlotte Mary McKinley." Her voice was almost a whisper.

"Can I sit a spell with you?"

After a moment, the girl shifted, making room for Winny to sit on her bed. "I'm only here for a little while."

"Oh? Why's that?"

Charlotte explained that her mother had left her at the Home, but only temporarily, while she got back on her feet. She'd be back soon, Charlotte insisted, then they'd go home together. Winny hadn't seen any sign of Charlotte's mother, but she didn't feel it was her place to question the girl's plan, so she just sat with her and talked. Before long, Charlotte had become Winny's welcome companion. She was a sweet, delicate girl, and Winny was happy to take care of her. But Charlotte had not been chosen to go to Canada, so a little piece of Winny's heart remained in Barkingside with her.

"You still awake?" Mary whispered groggily. "Go to sleep."

"Just thinking," Winny whispered back.

"About what?"

"Charlotte. Do you think her mum has come for her yet?"

"Doubt it."

Most of the time Winny tried to avoid the subject of mothers around Mary. It wasn't that hard to do, because Winny didn't like to think about the last time she'd seen her own mother. She didn't like remembering that sudden, cold wind at her back as the door slammed behind her. She knew that sometimes Mary still thought of her own with a sort of re-signed longing. But Charlotte clung to a *need* for her mother, convinced she would return for her one day. As much as Winny wanted Charlotte to be happy, she was quietly envious. What would that be like, knowing her mother still wanted her? To know someone wanted her?

Winny closed her eyes at last and let her thoughts drift.

No, Jack. No one will miss me when I'm gone.

five

JACK

❧

On the morning they were supposed to arrive in Halifax, Jack stepped onto the deck and spotted Winny and Mary leaning against the rail, scouting for land. With the thick fog blanketing the sea, he doubted either of them would see anything for a while.

Edward and Cecil lounged behind them, backs against the wall, long legs stretched in front.

"I can't wait to get off this boat," Edward muttered.

"If I never see another plate of fried tripe and onions it'll be too soon," Cecil agreed.

They'd had practically the same food every day for two weeks. To Jack it all smelled like seasickness. He was looking forward to being on land again, but now that their arrival was imminent, he felt apprehensive. Though he'd tried to ignore them, Mary's and Cecil's words had gotten under his skin. He didn't want to think about the fact that this reunion with the girls might be temporary.

"Doing all right?" he asked, bumping Mary's shoulder with his.

She gave him that searching look he knew so well from their childhood, and his stomach knotted. She knew he didn't have the answers, but she looked to him just the same. She was waiting for something, trusting that he would never let her down.

"It'll work out all right," he told her, because he had to say something.

"Don't worry too much, Mary," Edward said. "I think Canada will be good for us. Think about it. They taught us so much at the Home that we'll know how to do just about anything out there, and we can get paid work once we're eighteen. Wouldn't have happened that way if we were still in London. No one was ever gonna offer us jobs back there."

"But what if this is it?" Mary replied, then she turned to Jack. "What if we get separated and I never see you again? No one ever promised they'd keep brothers and sisters together. This is the first time I've seen you in three years. Why would they think twice about separating us now?"

Edward nudged the brim of his cap upward and glanced sideways at his brother, but Cecil was scowling at his hands. The only one in their little group without a family member was Winny, and she kept her eyes resolutely on the horizon.

Jack reached out and touched the name tag dangling from his sister's coat. "We'll just have to make sure that doesn't happen."

"I guess we'll find out soon," Winny said, pointing into the distance.

A dark shape appeared out of the fog like a spectre, growing in size and coming into focus. As they sailed closer, the terminal emerged from the gloom, a long barrier of two-storey buildings alongside a number of docks, jutting out into the sea like long, flat tongues. Smaller fishing boats were hitched here and there, and two larger ships steamed past theirs at a safe distance, going the opposite direction. Theirs was the only big ship docking, and the captain steered the massive bow alongside the dock with surprising grace.

The pier itself was crowded with travellers, creating a moving obstacle course for the working men and wagons loaded down with crates.

Despite the crowds, Jack was disappointed. Somehow he'd imagined Canada would be more exciting, that they'd be met by cowboys or mounted police or something equally impressive. From what he could see, there was nothing remarkable about this pier. It was even smaller than the one they'd left two weeks before, and the stink of dead fish was just as bad.

Below Jack, the sailors set expertly to their work, some of them carrying luggage while others secured the ship to the dock then extended the gangway to the passengers' deck. Mr. Keller eventually appeared and directed the children toward it, shepherding the girls up first. Then, with his heart beating in his throat, Jack grabbed the banister and followed, heading to the terminal. Once inside, they were guided up a wide set of stairs to an assembly hall on the second floor, where they joined a long queue. Despite the weeks of travel and everyone's exhaustion, the space buzzed with questions and speculations, and heads turned this way and that. From his vantage point, Jack could just see above the other children's heads, and he spotted a number of desks and offices at the far end of the room. He turned to Mary to describe the scene just as Miss Pence held up her hands for quiet.

"Children, it is very important that we stay together here and not get separated. Mr. Keller and I will be watching, but there are more than a hundred of you and only two of us, so we shall need your help."

"What's this line for, Miss Pence?" a small voice in the crowd asked.

"When you reach the front of the line," she explained, "you will each see the Canadian doctor, then you will meet with the immigration officer. After that, we will board a train and be on our way. Remember, you *must* stay together. This is a new country to you. It would be easy to get lost, and there are hazards here you know nothing about. Do you understand? All right. Stay together, and keep each other safe."

The urge to flee the stuffy, unfamiliar space was gnawing at Jack. It felt too much like a trap. He scanned the crammed room, searching for a way to disappear into the crowds and dash through the doors into the open air. Cecil caught his eye and tilted his head towards the clearly marked exit, but Jack shook his head. He knew escape was impossible.

A ripple of movement started up behind the boys as a couple of men pushed by in a hurry, all elbows, and Jack shuffled out of the way. Up ahead, the girls weren't so lucky. Set on their path, the men shoved Mary against Winny and the girls toppled sideways like dominoes. Jack reached out just in time to catch Winny, and Edward grabbed Mary's arm, steadying her.

"You and Mary stay close," Jack said into Winny's ear, his heart beating wildly. If she had fallen in the crowd, he feared she would have been trampled. Winny gripped his arm, and Mary closed in on her other side, flanked by Edward and Cecil. It gave Jack a sense of security, seeing the five of them shoulder to shoulder again, despite the uncertainties before them.

The line inched forward then stopped again. Winny popped up, dancing on her toes.

"What's happening? Where's Miss Pence?"

"She's here somewhere. She won't leave without you."

A woman standing just in front of them scowled over her shoulder at Winny. "Would you look at that," she said to the woman beside her. "It's *those* children. I've read about them in the newspaper. Had I known any of *them* would be here, I'd have made alternate travel plans."

Jack stiffened.

"Careful not to touch them," the other woman replied, placing a gloved hand on her friend's elbow and turning her attention ahead. "You know what they say about these little gutter rats. They're all diseased and contagious."

"It's a travesty," the first went on. "Shame on England for dumping their garbage on us, and shame on our government for actually paying for it. Can you imagine? I read somewhere that there's thousands of these creatures infesting the country now, and they're degenerates, every one of them. Criminals. You just know the girls will all end up as prostitutes, if they're not already."

The air was suddenly thick, and a sick sense of dread tightened Jack's throat. Crowds of strangers pressed in around him, staring at the children with a sort of horrified fascination, and he realized that once again, he was cornered.

They hadn't been wanted in England, and they weren't wanted here.

"Was she talking about me?" Winny asked softly.

"Don't listen to them," Mary said. "They don't matter."

Jack refused to let his fear show. The others needed him to be strong. He straightened and rolled back his shoulders, just as he had done that day in the market when the police had caught them. A desperate sense of courage wrapped itself around him like a suit of armour, and he forced it into his heart, hardening him against whatever was to come. Winny glanced at him for reassurance, and he gave her a nod.

"Mary's right."

When they finally reached the front of the line, a clerk took their information then directed them one at a time toward a doctor's examination room, curtained off behind the clerk's desk. Jack went first, head held high.

"Your name?" the doctor said. He was sitting at a small wooden desk, checking his paperwork. He wasn't old. Perhaps thirty. His short brown hair was slicked back and he wore a buttoned white coat.

"Jack Miller."

The doctor wrote something down on a card which lay on the desk in front of him, then he got to his feet. "You're how old?"

"Sixteen."

"Open wide, please." He stuck a flat piece of wood on Jack's tongue and peered inside. "Tonsils gone?"

"They took everyone's out at the Home before we left." That was something he preferred not to think about.

He tried not to flinch when the doctor peeled back his eyelid and aimed a tiny light at his eye before poking another thing into his ear. Apparently satisfied, he asked Jack to step on a platform so he could check his weight and height.

"You seem pretty healthy," the doctor said, stamping the card and handing it to Jack. "Surprisingly strong compared to some of these other boys, actually. You should do just fine here."

Jack looked down at the card. He couldn't make out the doctor's writing, but the stamp was clear as day. FIT FOR ENTRY, it said.

"Go through there," the doctor said, indicating a curtain at the back of the examination room, "and give that card to the man at the second desk."

Jack did as he was told, and the clerk marked something in his ledger before giving Jack a tired smile. His eyes looked very small behind his smudged spectacles.

"Welcome to Canada," he said.

Canada. The word sent an unexpected thrill through Jack. "Is it true you can pick gold off the streets here?"

"Gold?" The clerk scratched his chin. "I can't say as that's so. But it's a nice place all the same."

Jack hoped he was right. He had crossed the sea, and there was no going back now—even if he wasn't wanted here. Canada was massive—he'd seen the map—and he couldn't help but believe that a land that large had to have opportunities in it, possibilities he never could have imagined back in England. He would simply have to find them. Or create them.

"You passed?" he asked when Winny emerged.

"The doctor said I was underweight." She wrinkled her nose. "I told him he should have seen me before."

Mary joined her at Jack's side and took in the crowd, her expression unreadable. She reminded him of a sphinx he'd seen in a book about Egypt. Hard and distant.

Once everyone had been cleared, Miss Pence guided them downstairs where Mr. Keller was waiting by a mountain of wooden trunks. Jack spotted his right away. On purpose, he'd hammered in a darker board back in the carpentry room, wanting to make it look different from the others. When it was time, the children were called up one by one to collect their own trunks. Only the four- and five-year-olds got away with leaving theirs in a wagon, which Mr. Keller paid a man to bring outside the terminal.

The fog had cleared while they'd been inside, and sunlight blinded them as they stepped through the door and onto a platform toward a waiting train. Before boarding, Miss Pence had them all stop, then she took out a piece of paper and announced that she would read a list of the children who would be staying in the area.

Jack froze. He'd seen some of the name tags, the ones that indicated those children would remain in the Halifax area, and though his said *Jack Miller, Toronto*, the realization that they were about to lose some of the party here still shocked him.

"I told you," Mary whispered, clenching his hand. "They're splitting the group up. It starts here."

The children on the list were gathered to the side and put under the care of a woman they hadn't seen before. They clung to each other, many of them crying, bewildered by the sight of their friends and siblings boarding the train to Toronto without them. All Jack could think was how glad he was that it wasn't him standing there.

They climbed onto the train and Jack led the way down the aisle, claiming one of the booths halfway down the car. He and Edward swung the trunks onto the rack overhead, then they all sat. Winny and Mary claimed the seats across from Jack, and Edward and Cecil lounged in the booth ahead of them. When the train jarred forward, Jack closed his eyes, expecting the noise and the gentle rocking would lull him to sleep. His body was more than willing. It felt as if it was filled with stones, dragging him underwater. The trouble was, his mind kept bobbing to the surface, bubbling with questions.

What if Mary was right? What if they were separated? Of course he'd hate it, but maybe it would be all right. They'd survived being apart before, he reasoned. He cracked his eyes open, studying the girls as they slept, piled onto each other like kittens. He hated seeing the lines of exhaustion on his sister's face, the way her brow seemed permanently creased with worry. She had always been so alive on the streets of London, unafraid and ready to take on the world. Back then, they'd been more than brother and sister; they'd been partners. She had always been the serious one, but she had been fun as well. Now she was guarded, suspicious of just about everyone. He missed her laugh—never mind that, he missed her smile. The years apart had taken their toll on her, and he couldn't help but wonder if she could handle another separation.

What felt like hours later, Mr. Keller walked down the aisle, handing out sandwiches. "Next stop: Toronto," he said. "We've a few hours to go, but this ought to hold you over."

Mary and Winny were still sleeping soundlessly, so Jack collected their food as well.

"Don't eat them all," Mr. Keller warned.

"I wouldn't."

Jack leaned across and tucked the sandwiches under Mary's coat, spread like a blanket over them both. He didn't hate Mr. Keller, but the constant drone of his reminders and lessons, punctuated by glares, was like a rock in Jack's shoe. He could go along without noticing for a while, then one would poke him the wrong way and he couldn't get it out of his head.

Once Mr. Keller had moved on down the aisle, Cecil peered behind him at Jack. He and Edward had been talking quietly between themselves the whole trip, but Edward was asleep now, his head pressed against the window.

"If they don't want it, I do."

Jack gave him a wry smile. "You try to wrestle this out of their hands when they wake up. I'd bet on the girls."

The sandwich was dry and tasteless, but it eased the cramping in his gut, and that's all he really needed. Jack had known hunger his whole life. Until he'd ended up at the orphanage, he couldn't recall a time when he and Mary weren't sneaking or stealing food. Now food was provided to them, but despite what the Barnardo people said, Jack had never believed the children were being fed out of the goodness of these people's hearts. Just as fuel turned the wheels of the train, food kept the children working. Sure, the lessons in tinsmithing and blacksmithing, carpentry, printing, brush making, tailoring, and boot making were valuable lessons for their futures, but where did the money from all those boots and brushes and coats go? Right back into Barnardo's bank account. Barnardo's fed the children, but the children fed them as well.

Jack gazed out the window, watching miles and miles of trees pass by, letting it sink in that he was here for at least another year. Whatever happened, he had to make the best of it. Mr. Keller had told the boys they would be in some kind of service until they were eighteen. They'd be paid a little for their labour until then, but they wouldn't receive that money until they turned twenty-one. He'd said Barnardo's was holding it "in trust," whatever that meant. Jack didn't know how much he'd get when the time came, but as long as he could make a start with it, the amount didn't really matter. The important thing was that it would be the first honest money he had ever earned. And then, he'd be free to choose what he wanted to do.

The shrieking brakes jolted Jack awake, and he shot upright, briefly forgetting where he was. He rubbed the sleep from his eyes then peered into the night. Raindrops peppered the windows, glistening like gold as they reflected the city lights.

"We're here," Winny told him. She and Mary were sitting up. Sandwich crumbs littered their laps.

"We are indeed," Mr. Keller said as he came down the aisles. "Welcome to Toronto, children. After the train has stopped, everyone is responsible for carrying his or her own trunk off the train and into Union Station. Stay close to one another. It's a large building, and you won't want to get lost."

From the moment they stepped into Union Station, Jack's attention was everywhere at once. "Large" didn't come close to describing this place. From the clatter and screech of the trains, they entered a wide, open corridor, and their steps echoed as they walked across the shining marble floor. Following Mr. Keller upstairs, they arrived at a great hall dwarfed by an arched stone ceiling four storeys high. A vast window almost completely filled one wall.

"Imagine how bright it gets in here during the day," Winny said beside him. "Look up there."

High up on the walls and wrapping around the hall was a strip of stone etched with the names of various cities, and it struck Jack that he might soon be living in one of them. *North Bay*, he read. *Sarnia, Sherbrooke, Toronto, Ottawa*, then *London*! He pointed the last one out to Mr. Keller.

"How's a train supposed to get from here to London?" he asked.

Mr. Keller glanced up at the stone then shook his head. "There are cities here named after cities in England. That's all. You'll see a lot of that."

Beside him, Cecil hooted loudly in the open space, and the sound bounced through the building. Some of the other boys followed suit, unable to resist the temptation. Mr. Keller picked up his pace but didn't try to quiet them. Maybe, Jack thought, he was just as tired as the rest of them.

Outside, the streets glistened with rain, and the gentle mist reminded him of home. He picked up his pace, anticipation building.

"Where are we going?" someone finally asked.

"To Northwold," Miss Pence said, rain dripping from the edges of her hat. "Dr. Barnardo's head office and receiving home. It's not far."

As they walked, Winny caught up to Jack, lugging her trunk like everyone else. "What do you think of this place?"

"It looks real interesting. I'd like to see it in the daylight. See, look there." He pointed at a shoe store across the street. "I wasn't bad at boot making back at Stepney. Bet I could do pretty good as a cobbler, stitching boots for rich folks' feet."

From the corner of his eye, he spotted one of the littlest girls shivering, her body drooping badly from exhaustion. He stopped and handed Winny his trunk. "Hold this, would you?"

With his hands free, he crouched by the little girl. "Climb up here, pet."

She didn't hesitate, and when she was comfortably perched on Jack's back, he picked up her trunk as well. Just up ahead, Cecil did the same for another little one.

"I'll take my trunk now, Winny."

"It's all right," she said. "I can carry it a while. Let me help you for a change." She studied the wide streets around them with their shops and houses, windows darkened for the night. "Do you think we'll get to stay here?"

"I wish I knew."

Behind him, he heard Edward speaking to Mary in a low voice. "I've been thinking, Mary. I've a thing to say to you, and if this . . . if it's true that we don't have a lot of time left together, I figure I should just go ahead and say it. You might laugh, but that's all right." He sniffed. "The thing is, I fancy you, Mary. Always have."

Winny smothered a gasp, and Jack resisted the urge to turn around and stare at his friend. Mary would already be doing that, he was sure, because she wasn't saying anything.

"Don't look so shocked," Edward said. "I just thought you should know."

"I did know," Mary said softly. "I just never thought you'd tell me."

"It's all right if you don't want to say anything, but I wanted to tell you. I missed you the last time, and I expect that won't change this go around."

"I'll miss you too."

"Good for him," Winny whispered to Jack. "Never thought he'd work up the nerve."

Jack snuck a peek behind and was surprised to see the two were holding hands, and a small smile played on Mary's face. An odd sense of loss rolled in his chest, but he let it go. He was glad for her. And it would change nothing between him and Mary. Nothing ever could.

Eventually Mr. Keller turned onto a driveway and they passed beneath a domed brick entrance big enough for a car to drive under. A large, red stone mansion loomed before them, its round turrets walled with windows.

Jack gave a low whistle as he lowered the little girl from his back. "That's posh, ain't it?"

"It's like a castle," Winny said.

The children followed Mr. Keller and Miss Pence into the front room of the building, where a crackling fire welcomed them. The heat felt like a blanket after the cold rain outside, and the children rushed towards it with their hands held out for warmth. As their shivers died down, Jack looked around in awe, taking in the panelled walls, the lofty ceiling, the elaborate cornices that made doors and windows into pieces of art, and the wide, carpeted staircase that stretched to the second floor.

"Boys and girls," Mr. Keller said, drawing their attention to a large, moustached man standing beside him, wearing a neat suit and leaning on a cane. "This is Mr. Hobday, Dr. Barnardo's manager here in Canada. I know you're all tired, but it is very important that you pay attention to what Mr. Hobday has to say to you."

"Good evening, children," Mr. Hobday boomed. "Welcome to Northwold, Barnardo's exquisite receiving home here in Toronto. On the second floor are your bedrooms, which your teachers will assign to you, and in the morning, you will enjoy your meals in our elegant dining room. You may not leave the second floor unless directed. This ground floor is reserved for the servants' quarters, and my family and

I live on the third floor." His gaze slid over every sopping child as he spoke. "Over the next few days, we will receive word from the families who are waiting for you. You will either leave here with them, or you will be put on a train to meet them. Until then, we expect your best behaviour, of course."

They were divided boys from girls, but this time Jack wasn't concerned. He'd see them in the morning, and knowing that made everything easier. It was a relief to peel off his wet clothes, to rub a blanket over his pruned skin before changing into his pyjamas. Their bunks were soft and inviting, and Jack and the others sank into them with pleasure.

"I may never get up," Edward groaned into the darkness.

"You'd better," Jack teased. "Otherwise I'll have to explain to Mary where you are."

Edward paused. "You don't mind, do you, Jack?"

"Of course not."

"I'm glad," Edward replied, "because I think she's brilliant."

"All right. That's enough," Cecil said from an upper bunk. "This lad's ready to sleep if you'd only shut it."

"Good night," Jack said, and he drifted off to sleep within the first few breaths.

———

The next morning, Mr. Keller came into their room well before the sun rose and switched on the overhead light. "Up we get," he announced, shaking Jack's shoulder. "We must get you to the station."

Jack swept his hand over his face, hoping he had misheard. "Today, sir? I thought we had a few days."

"Some of the children will be leaving sooner than others, and it happens that we have a call for some strong lads this morning, so you'll be going right away."

His mouth went dry. "I need to say goodbye to my sister."

"No time, I'm afraid. We're behind schedule already. Come along," he said, waking the other boys. "Time to go. Get up, get dressed. You can sleep on the train."

Edward frowned at Jack. "We're leaving? But the girls—"

Jack's heart was racing as he pulled on his clothes. "Mr. Keller," he said. "I can't just leave my sister or Winny. We promised we'd see them."

"I'm sorry, Jack. I cannot allow you to wake them. You'll see them again soon."

"Will we really?" Jack asked.

Mr. Keller took a breath as if to speak, then he dropped his chin. "I am not sure. But we shall hope."

Hope wasn't enough. Jack ducked past Mr. Keller and burst into the corridor. "Mary!" he yelled, banging on the first door. "Mary! We're leaving!"

"Jack, stop that!" Mr. Keller called. "You'll wake the whole house."

"Mary! Winny!"

Edward and Cecil joined in, running down the long hall and bellowing the girls' names while they hammered on every door, Mr. Keller on their heels.

A moment later, a flustered Mr. Hobday appeared from the upstairs rooms. "What is the meaning of this?"

One by one, the doors opened and curious faces peered into the hall, blinking sleep out of their eyes. Miss Pence hurried out of her room, tying her belt around her robe as she came, trying to block the girls and ordering them all back to bed. Finally, Jack pounded on the right door, and it swung open.

"Jack!" Mary cried. "What's happening?"

"They're taking me and the lads away right now." He reached for her and hugged her tight, panic surging through him. "I'm so sorry, Mary. You were right. They're separating us."

Miss Pence grabbed Mary's arm and tried to drag both her and Winny back to their room, but Jack hung on, and Winny fought back.

"Please," she begged. "Please let us say goodbye!"

Mr. Keller reached Jack and pried him off Mary, shoving him back toward the stairs where Mr. Hobday and a couple of the servants had a hold on Edward and Cecil. "Back to your rooms, girls. Now!"

"I won't go!" Mary cried, her voice shrill. "I need to say goodbye! Have you no heart at all? He's my brother! I need to say goodbye!"

"I'll find you!" Jack yelled, struggling against Mr. Keller. "I promise I'll find you both."

Smack! Jack bent in half, reeling from a searing blow to his side, and he looked up with disbelief at Mr. Hobday. Edward and Cecil surged forward to help him, but Mr. Hobday's cane came down again. *Smack!* Edward stumbled under another strike, and Cecil went to him.

"That's enough," Mr. Keller ordered flatly, and everyone stopped, including Mr. Hobday. "It's time to go."

Edward's hand reached for Mary, but Mr. Keller pulled him back. The boys moved down the stairs, their eyes on the girls, who clung to the banister, sobbing.

"I'll find you!" Jack promised, but even as he said the words, doubt crept into his mind. How could he ever do that in this vast, strange country? How would he even know where to start? But the girls would be counting on him, and he would never let them down.

I will find them, he told himself as they stepped out into the cold morning, *if it's the last thing I do.*

six

WINNY

❦

Winny didn't have time to fall apart. Mary collapsed in her arms, and Winny swore to herself that she would hold her friend until the end of time if she needed to. Thankfully, Miss Pence took pity and left them alone in the bedroom.

Winny had never seen Mary like this. Being separated from Jack at the orphanage had been terrible for them both, moving away to the Home had been bad as well, but this was a new level of sadness. Once the sobs slowed and the tears dried, it was as if there was very little left of her.

"It'll be us next," Mary said, picking at the blanket on her bed, not meeting Winny's eyes.

Winny wasn't sure how to answer. She was terrified at the thought of losing Mary, but she couldn't show it. What Mary needed most was support. She took a deep breath and thought of Jack. He was always so strong for them. It was her turn now.

"Maybe we'll end up living close to each other," Winny said, then she realized she was picking anxiously at her fingernails. If Mary looked up she would see Winny was scared. So Winny consciously separated her hands from each other and pressed them to her sides. "Then we can visit all the time. And then one day, Jack will find us and we'll be together again."

"I wish I could believe that." Mary's voice was no more than a whisper.

"We *will* see each other again," Winny replied softly, though even she had begun to doubt it.

It was another two days before they learned where they were going. To Winny's relief, Miss Pence called Mary's name and hers at the same time, along with a few others. As she pinned new name tags to their coats, she told the girls they would take a train to Peterborough, a couple of hours away, where the families who had paid for them would come and pick them up. Miss Pence would be staying in Toronto with the rest of the girls.

Once they were out of the city, the sight of the green, flowing countryside calmed Winny somewhat. Though this land was very different, a memory surfaced from long ago of the little cottage where she'd once lived in Ireland. Life had been hard there, but she remembered happy moments. She remembered feeling loved.

"Have you ever seen so much green?" She nudged Mary. "It goes on forever. Look, Mary! Cows!"

Mary allowed herself a small smile. "I've never seen a cow before."

"It's lovely, isn't it?" Winny asked. "Everything looks so bright and happy."

"Maybe it won't be so bad."

After another hour, they reached the Peterborough station, and when the brakes shrieked, Winny's heart thundered like the wheels on the tracks. "Stay close to me," she said to Mary, as much for her friend's benefit as her own.

No one was there to greet them, but their trunks were unloaded near a bench on the end of the platform, so the group of girls headed toward them. As they did, Winny eyed every stranger she passed with a kind of terrified optimism.

After the platform had cleared of the other passengers, Winny noticed wagons, automobiles, and trucks waiting across from the station, and people began to approach in ones and twos, studying the girls as they walked. Most were dressed in faded shirts and overalls, their straw hats circled by wide brims. Farmers, she thought, taking Mary's hand. What would a farmer need with a housemaid?

The first person to approach the group was an older, bearded man, and he strode directly up to one of the younger girls. Without a word, he reached for her name tag, checked it, then moved on to read the others. Winny made a silent plea that he wasn't there for either of them. He stopped at a brown-haired girl a few spots before them.

"I'm Mr. Chisholm," he told her, his voice unexpectedly gentle. "You're to come with me."

Every girl still standing on the platform watched her pick up her trunk and go, and no one said a word.

"Miller," someone called.

Mary's hand jerked in Winny's, and their eyes went to a round woman in a blue dress, on her way up the stairs to the platform. Her hair was swept into an untidy bun. She wasn't old, Winny didn't think, but she looked tired.

"Miller," the woman repeated, scanning the girls.

"It'll be okay," Winny whispered. "We'll find each other."

"Take care of yourself, Winny," Mary said, then she stepped forward, the hem of her skirt shaking.

"Not much meat on you," the woman said, scowling at Mary's name tag. "I paid a full three dollars. I should get what I paid for." She glanced at Winny. "At least you're bigger than that one."

Winny wrapped her arms around herself, wishing she could disappear.

"I guess you'll have to do. I'm Mistress Renfrew. Get your things and come with me."

Mary's chest rose and fell in a bolstering breath, then she turned and trailed behind her new mistress, her trunk gripped in her hands. Every nerve in Winny's body pulled towards Mary, and she wondered how she could possibly survive without her.

"Wait!" Winny blurted, rushing forward.

Mary dropped her trunk and wrapped her arms around Winny, digging her fingers into her back. "I hope wherever you end up they treat you good."

"Oh, Mary!"

"That's enough," Mistress Renfrew said, pulling the two apart. "I don't have all day. It's bad enough that I had to be the one driving in for you. We've got a long ride ahead."

Through a sheen of tears, Winny watched Mary follow the woman to a dusty green truck, where a brood of children sat in its open bed. Winny counted nine.

"Get in, girl." The woman jerked a thumb then climbed into the front cab. "Best you get to know the kids right off."

At first, the children stared at Mary, then they shifted, making room for her and her trunk. As the truck began to pull away, Mary's shining eyes held on to Winny's.

It's not goodbye, Winny promised silently, tears streaming down her cheeks. She watched Mary until she was just a spot in the distance. *I will find you.*

One by one, the other girls were picked up by their new masters, but Winny remained. She sat on the bench by her trunk, baking in the heat of the sun, feeling as insignificant as the pebble by her shoe. At one point, the station master walked out of the building and looked at her. She opened her mouth to ask for help, but he went back inside without saying anything. She dropped her eyes to her tortured nails and picked at what remained. What if no one came for her?

Two hot hours later, a dented blue truck with a cracked windshield pulled up to the station, and a haggard-looking woman called out from the cab.

"You the Home Girl?"

Winny nodded.

"I'm Mistress Adams. Get over here."

Winny jumped to her feet and clutched her trunk. Her heart raced as she ran towards the truck, and she was so nervous she nearly lost her balance on the platform steps. When she got closer, she could see Mistress Adams a little better, sitting behind the steering wheel. She was thin, and the brown hair pulled back into a bun was wispy around her angular face. Beside her, Winny saw a girl she thought might be eighteen or so, with the same drawn face as Mistress Adams.

She stopped at the window of the cab and offered a tentative smile. "My name's Winny."

"What are you standing there for?" Mistress Adams demanded. "Put your trunk in the back and get in with it."

Winny's smile wavered, but she did as she was told.

"She's so *small*," she heard the other girl say.

"You're right, Helen. I am disappointed," her mother agreed. "I think we might have gotten a bigger one if we'd ordered earlier. The other farms took the good ones."

"Only good thing I see is from the size of her, she won't eat much. What's she gonna be able to do with those scrawny arms of hers?"

"That is no concern of yours, is it? You won't even be around. She will do whatever she's told. Do not speak to her unless you have to, and she will not speak to you. If she does, don't listen. She'll just tell lies." She glanced back at Winny as she climbed into the back of the truck. "And do not touch her, because she probably has a disease. Or fleas. They say all these Home Children do."

Winny felt the words like a punch to her gut. She'd taken special care that morning to wash her face and brush her hair, and she'd cleaned her clothes the best she could. She wanted to speak up, to explain that she'd been checked over by the doctor, and he'd said she wasn't sick, only small. Most of all she wanted to tell them that it was safe to talk to her because she wouldn't lie. She never lied. But her mistress's cruel words brought back the voices of the other women at the Halifax pier, and all the ugly things they had said about Home Children. Was this what everyone thought of her and Mary and Jack and the brothers? Why had the Home gone to all the trouble of sending them here if they were so clearly unwanted?

Helen scowled back at Winny, then Mistress Adams started the engine. As they drove away from the station, Winny gripped the sides of the bed, trying to stay upright even as her head spun with a sense of helplessness. Had Mary arrived safely at her farm? Was it nice? Was her mistress kind? What about Jack, Edward, and Cecil? What had happened to them after they'd left Northwold on that dark, rainy morning? All Winny could do was hope they were all right. Because hope was all she had left.

They bumped along the dirt road, dust billowing behind their wheels, and Winny stared out at the endless farm country that had so delighted her before, the rolling hills and the stands of trees quivering in the breeze. Where was Mary in all of it? And where would Winny end up? For the rest of the long, lurching ride, the Adams women never looked back. It was as if they had forgotten about her.

With every lonely mile, Winny felt herself shrinking away, becoming smaller and smaller. Eventually, she wasn't sure she was really there at all.

PART
— two —

seven
WINNY

❦

— Present Day —

The summer grass crackles underfoot as I shuffle through the yard, leaning on my cane. My doctor suggested I start taking daily walks to keep myself strong, and when the sun finally started to shine, I agreed. Despite my slow pace and the toll the exercise takes on my wasted muscles, I'm ever so glad she suggested it. Today I make it as far as Chrissie's fine little vegetable garden. She's there, tending to the pea pods and green beans that hang from their climbing stems, plump with promise. My fingers twitch, remembering the feel of the task, the countless hours spent shelling pods at the farm where I learned to go through them like the wind. I cannot imagine crouching in the dirt at my age. I might never get up again.

"It's hot today," Chrissie says, squinting up at me. "You sure you're okay to be walking in this heat?"

She's wearing her mother's favourite old straw hat, which takes me back. Until recently, she's avoided dealing with Susan's boxes, letting them gather dust in her basement rather than deal with her grief. I'm glad to see she's finally going through them, though I can't deny a pang of sorrow at the memory of a different face beneath that brim, a different smile.

I recover quickly enough that she doesn't notice. "I feel fine, sweetheart. Your garden is looking lovely."

She rises and sweeps the back of her hand across her brow. "Jamie loves green beans. It's a good thing they're easy to grow. I'd be in trouble if he liked artichokes or something."

"He's fortunate to have them straight from the garden. People don't grow their own as often these days."

"The world is a busier place. No time or space for gardens. But I like gardening."

"Me too," I say softly. "It always took me away from less pleasant things."

Chrissie picks up her pot, brimming with beans for tonight's dinner, and takes my arm as we turn toward the house. "I've been thinking about the stuff you told us last night," she says carefully. "It must be difficult to talk about."

Difficult. Yes, that's fair to say. Last night I'd watched Chrissie and Jamie's eyes widen in disbelief as I told them about my childhood in England. Every time they asked a question, my memories were more than willing to chase down the particulars, and I'd felt as though I was reliving those moments: walking barefoot on the slick wet cobblestones in London, running into the rain to rinse dirt from my face, seeing the disdain in people's eyes as they passed by me. Meeting Mary that first time, the way she'd been the one to take my hand, to rescue me. How I wish I could have done the same for her.

"I suppose I had hoped it would all just go away," I admit.

"I feel bad that it took me this long to find out. I had no idea what you'd been through. Did Mom know?"

"She knew what you knew. That I'd come here from England as a child. Not much more than that." I give her a small smile. "I can be evasive when I want to be."

"So I've learned. You and Pop. He never said anything either."

"No. He had his own reasons." I look away, not quite ready to explain that part yet.

"It must have been hard to keep such a big secret."

"Not really. I've discovered that if you don't want to talk about something, you just don't."

Chrissie opens the door on the back porch, and I feel her eyes on my back as I hobble past. "So you're all right talking about it now?"

"It's not that simple." I stop and turn to face her. "My life is made up of secrets, and for a long time, I thought it was easier to keep them to myself than to share them. But I'm tired of carrying them around. I think when you accidentally dropped the trunk yesterday, it was a message to me that it's time to let those secrets go."

Chrissie doesn't reply, but she nods her head thoughtfully, and we go inside. The front door bangs shut, and I realize Jamie must be home from his soccer game.

"Hi, Mom. Hi, Gran," he says as he enters the kitchen and makes a beeline for the refrigerator.

"Don't eat anything," Chrissie says. "Supper will be ready in no time if you help with the beans. Come and sit at the table, Gran. I'll bring you lemonade while you wait."

"Should we clear this off the table to make room for supper?" I ask pointedly, looking at Chrissie. My trunk is taking up a good portion of the tabletop, and I'm certain it didn't make its way from the living room into the kitchen on its own.

"I thought it might provide food for thought."

"I think it looks cool there," Jamie says. "Very retro."

Chrissie's expression softens. "Unless you'd rather not talk about this tonight."

"I don't mind," I say, which is the truth. The revelations from the day before did weigh on me, though. They'd brought back dreams I have not had in many, many years, and I stayed in bed longer than usual this morning. But there is no reason to delay the story. The latches of my battered old trunk look like staring eyes, a silent witness to those days, holding me accountable. "It can stay."

I sip my lemonade as Jamie helps Chrissie with the beans, and I smell the meaty aroma of pork when she opens the oven. When all is prepared, they come and sit with me at the table.

"This looks delicious," I say.

"Thanks, Gran," Chrissie replies, placing a small pork chop on my plate. She turns to Jamie. "How was school?"

He gives a vague shrug. When his phone lights up, he reaches for it, but Chrissie pries it from his hand.

"Not at the table. Pass the beans to Gran, please."

He mutters something under his breath and passes me the steaming bowl. Only then does Chrissie hand the phone back and Jamie tucks it into his back pocket.

The beans are fresh and delicious and I eat them as quickly as I can, which isn't that fast anymore. Chrissie and Jamie's plates are empty long before mine, but they wait for me to finish. As Jamie clears the dishes, Chrissie slides the trunk toward me, a question in her eyes. I hesitate just for a moment, then I unlatch it and pull out an old cotton frock, its white fabric long ago dulled to grey and speckled with stains. It's been so many years since I last wore it, it feels foreign. Like it belonged to someone else entirely.

Jamie, already done with the cleanup, is taking out his phone and heading towards the stairs, but he stops and lingers in the doorway. "You know, I still don't understand why those policemen put you in an orphanage," he says. "You weren't an orphan."

"A lot of us weren't," I reply. "Not in the technical sense of the word. We might as well have been, though. You must understand that poverty in those days was rampant. When the Industrial Revolution started, families everywhere came from the farms to the city, hoping for work, but there wasn't enough room for them all, and there certainly weren't enough jobs. Most of the children I knew in the orphanage and at Barnardo's had at least one parent still alive."

"Really?" Jamie says, inching back toward the table. "That seems wrong."

"Sometimes when parents were struggling to support their children, they brought them to the Home for a time. Many planned to take them back with them again when they were able, but sometimes the children had already been sent away by the time they returned."

"What was it like going to an orphanage? I mean, I've seen movies, like"—Jamie pulls up a chair beside his mother—"*Annie*? Was that it? Oh yeah. And *Oliver Twist*. Was it like in those movies? I don't mean with all the singing and dancing, of course. But the rest?"

"Not quite." In a flash, I am back in a cold grey room with Mary on the day we'd arrived at the orphanage. I wince, remembering the sharp pain of the woman's comb scraping and snagging in my tangled hair, and I press my hand against my soft grey curls.

"The first thing they did was shave our heads." Even now, I can still recall the coarse, unfamiliar terrain of my young scalp, like sandpaper against my fingertips. In that moment, I'd thought cutting my hair was the worst thing they could do to me. How naïve I had been. "Then they gave us matching dresses, tights, and shoes, then they sent us to the matron's office and asked what our names were. When I told her, she informed me that Winny was no longer my name. She said no one would call me Winny for as long as I lived in the orphanage. She told me my name was now Four-Seventeen, and Mary was Two-Thirty-Seven." I take a shaky breath. "She was right, too. Everyone there called us by those numbers, never our names. Everyone but Mary and me. I think I might have forgotten my name along the way if it weren't for her. She always called me Winny. And I always called her Mary."

"Oh, Gran." Chrissie's gentle hand covers mine. "What a terrible thing to do to a child."

I meet Jamie's stunned gaze. "Not quite like the movies," I say.

Chrissie reaches for my old Bible and opens the cover. "Tell me about Dr. Barnardo. It seems unbelievable that he could just send children across the ocean like that. Did anything ever happen to him?"

"Oh no," I say quickly. "He died before I was born, but from everything I understand, Thomas Barnardo was a well-intentioned man with a good heart. He dedicated his life to helping destitute children get an education and improve themselves." I take a moment to fold the frock. "There is a story we were told about Dr. Barnardo from the mid-1800s, just after he opened his first shelter for boys. One night the place was so full they had to turn some boys away. A couple of days later, one of them was found dead in the street from hunger and exposure. After that, Dr. Barnardo hung a sign over the door that said, 'No Destitute Child Ever Refused Admission.' I remember seeing that sign myself." My fingertip absently follows a worn line of stitches on the old cotton. "I believe Dr. Barnardo was a good man. When I was at his Home for Girls, I got my name back, and I left that miserable Four-Seventeen behind. His plan to send children to Canada was supposed to be a good one. This country was young and it needed people, and England was overwhelmed by poor children with no foreseeable future. A win-win situation, you'd call it these days." I falter, my gaze going to the trunk. Its presence makes me uneasy. As if I might need to carry it somewhere else, change my life again. "It's just that things didn't always go according to his plan."

Jamie points at two faded cards in the trunk. "What are those?"

"Oh, dear." I take the cards out, turn them over in my hands. "They're from Barnardo's. Before we left for Canada, every child was given two of these cards. One was to confirm that we'd arrived safely at our new home, and the second was for us to send an update later on, to show how we were progressing in our new life." I tuck them back in the trunk. "It was a nice thought."

"Yours were never sent?" Chrissie asks.

"No. Even if she'd known I had them, I'm sure my mistress would never have offered to mail them for me."

"Why not?" Jamie asks. "If this was such a good plan for all you kids, then why wouldn't she mail them?"

I swallow, tasting the bitterness of the question. They have no idea. "Yes, it was a good plan, in essence. The trouble was that they greatly underestimated what would be needed once we arrived here. There simply weren't enough people to monitor all of us. Canada is much larger than England, and without proper checks in place . . ." I drop my gaze. "A lot of people took terrible advantage of the children in their care."

Chrissie and Jamie exchange a glance, but they don't speak, and I'm grateful for that. I need a moment to let grief release its grip on my throat. When I am able, I lift my eyes and offer a small smile.

"So you were all alone out there." There's a familiar loss in Chrissie's face. She knows what it is to be alone, since her mother had died the same year her husband had left her. How far she's come since then. "Did you . . . ever look for your friends?"

"I tried to, but once we reached the farm, I couldn't get off it. It's not like today." I look at Jamie. "There were no cellphones, of course. I couldn't text an Uber, could I? I was in the middle of nowhere, and I had no way of finding out where any of them were." I close my eyes briefly. "But at night, when I was all alone, I saw them." I remember those nights so well. "Every night, I said their names, one by one, and I pictured their faces. I couldn't ever let myself forget them."

eight
WINNY

— 1936 —

"Follow me, Home Girl." Mistress Adams slammed the truck door behind her. "Leave your trunk here by the barn."

Winny climbed stiffly out of the back of the truck, taking in the world around her. A large, rundown barn towered above her at the side of the drive, and the earthy aroma of hay hung in the still air like laundry. Farther ahead, she spotted two more sheds. A flock of brown chickens surrounded the smaller one, and a massive garden flanked the other. In the distance stood the farmhouse, a two-storey, ramshackle place with grimy windows and a crooked chimney, and Helen swiftly disappeared within. Besides the buildings, just about everything else Winny saw was grass. And it went on forever.

"You planning on standing around all day?" Mistress Adams called as she strode toward the chickens. "Because I did not pay for that."

Winny ran to catch up, ducking and squealing with terror when the chickens panicked and took flight, their wings drumming the air around her head. Ignoring her distress, Mistress Adams shoved a basket at Winny then opened the door to the coop. Winny followed her inside, catching her breath as a putrid smell hit her square in the face. She swallowed hard against bile and braced herself against a shelf, but when she drew her hand away, it was smeared with warm, wet chicken poop. Taking shallow breaths through her mouth, Winny tried to wipe the mess off her hand with a piece of straw.

"Eggs must be collected twice a day," Mistress Adams was saying. "In the winter, you'll need to do it more often because you cannot allow the eggs to freeze and go to waste. Return the basket to the house when you're done or else the raccoons will get them."

Raccoons? What's a raccoon? But she was too afraid to ask.

"Go on, then." Mistress Adams glared pointedly at the empty basket then left Winny alone in the henhouse.

Winny looked around the bleak hut, wondering what to do. Chickens wandered in and out of the filthy building through a hole in the wall while others sat in boxes, puffed like mushrooms on the straw. One nesting box was vacant, and inside it lay four eggs. Winny carefully placed each egg in her basket and stepped outside.

"Four?" Mistress Adams balked. "What is the matter with you? Did you even look?"

Back inside, Mistress Adams reached under a sitting hen and pulled out more eggs, paying no mind to the chicken's indignant outburst, then she gestured toward the next one. Winny stared at the pointy beaks and sharp claws, daring herself to copy her mistress. As much as she feared the birds, she had a feeling Mistress Adams could be crueler. Bracing herself for an angry peck, Winny thrust her hand under a chicken and felt around within the bird's soft, warm down. At first, she felt nothing but straw and feathers, then her fingers bumped against something hard. She closed them around two perfect ovals then pulled them out, quietly thrilled by the sight of the eggs in her palm. While Mistress Adams observed, Winny continued, visiting each of the ten nesting boxes and filling her basket to the top.

"Come along," Mistress Adams said, already on her way toward the house, "and don't trip over yourself. We can't have you breaking any of those."

Winny swore to herself she would never do that. She couldn't imagine what her mistress might do.

At the door to the house, Mistress Adams stopped short, and Winny instinctively placed her hand over the basket to keep the eggs in place.

"Put the basket on this table, then leave. Understand? No looking around, no asking questions. You are never to come inside this house."

Winny blinked, baffled. "Where will I eat, Mistress? Where will I sleep?"

"By the time we're done with our meal, you should be done with the cows. Leave the milk here, then you can get your plate and bring it to the sheep barn. You will eat and sleep there."

Winny swayed, her knees suddenly weak. "The cows, Mistress?"

Mistress Adams's lips hardened to a thin line. "Have they sent me an *idiot*? Do you know how to do *anything*?"

"I do," Winny whispered, her chin quivering. "I'm happy to cook for you, or sew, or any number of things. It's just—"

"All of that is useless to me. I need someone who can do farm chores."

"I'm sorry, Mistress. It's just that I've never seen a cow in my life."

"Helen!" Mistress Adams shouted. "Helen! Come here now!"

Winny heard a thump from inside the farmhouse, then Helen appeared in the doorway. "Yes, Mum?"

"Show the Home Girl how to milk a cow, would you?"

Helen's jaw dropped. "But I was reading."

"Just do it." Mistress Adams turned to face Winny. "This will not happen again. You are here so Helen can plan her wedding. She is not to be disturbed. Do you understand that?"

"Yes, Mistress," Winny said.

"Come on, Home Girl," Helen said, storming past.

"My name's Winny."

"I don't care."

When they entered the cow barn, Winny noticed a tall, thin boy just leaving one of the stalls. At the sight of her, he practically bolted outside.

"Who was that?" Winny asked.

"The Home Boy. He sleeps in here."

Winny's jaw dropped. A Home Boy?

"Stop standing there looking like a fool, and watch. I'm only going to show you once."

Winny turned her attention to the massive beasts before her and tried to slow the hammering of her pulse as Helen dragged out a stool. She watched as Helen's long fingers wound around a teat then pulled and squeezed, spraying the bucket with a neat line of steaming milk. After a few minutes, she let go then stepped back and shoved Winny onto the stool. With shaking hands, Winny took ahold, but no matter how she tugged, she couldn't coax out any milk. When she finally managed to pinch out a little, the cow kicked the bucket over.

Helen huffed with exasperation. "Well, I've shown you how, haven't I?" She headed toward the door. "Don't come out until they're all done."

In silence, Winny watched her leave, then she gazed up at the thick, crusted spiderwebs lining the rafters, seeking out the sky through holes in the roof. "What am I doing here?" she whispered.

The cow slammed a back hoof on the floor and turned her sad eyes on Winny.

"All right. I'll try again."

After a while, the rhythm of milking finally came to her, and she felt a rush of elation as a steady stream of milk shot into the bucket. When the supply petered out, she moved to the next cow, a little less wary of its teeth and hooves. By the time she finished milking all the cows, her fingers were curled into claws. Her body was stiff and ached with hunger. She stood with a groan and stretched to ease the tension in her back, then she lifted the bucket by its thick rope handle and lugged the milk to the house, watching carefully to make sure not even one drop lapped over the side.

Mistress Adams was waiting by the door. "Finally done?"

Winny nodded, setting the pail on the table outside the house as she'd been told. The smell of cooked food wafted from inside, and her mouth watered.

"Mistress, might I have some supper?"

Mistress Adams turned back into the house and called out her daughter's name.

"Yes, Mum?" Helen called from somewhere inside.

"Where's the leftover food?"

"Gave it to the dogs. Didn't want it drawing flies."

"That was for the girl, Helen."

"Oh, right. Sorry, Mum!"

Mistress Adams sighed. "You'll have to be quicker tomorrow so the dogs don't get your breakfast too."

Winny blinked back tears, stunned. She needed to eat. Her mind flew back to the marketplace years ago, to the ladies with their shopping, to Jack and Cecil and their quick, dirty fingers closing around purses— *Folks'll do just about anything for a kid with eyes like that*—and she offered her saddest, most pitiful expression to Mistress Adams.

"Mistress, please. There must be something left."

"Don't beg. I won't have it."

"But—"

Mistress Adams's hand shot out, and pain bloomed in Winny's right cheek. She took two steps back, hand on her face.

"That's enough. Now pay attention, Home Girl. You're here because of my charity, and you'll eat if you get your work done in time. That is the way it will be, so get used to it. In the morning, you'll start with the cows again, and you'd better get faster at it or the milk will spoil before I can use it." She handed Winny a thin blanket. "Come with me. I'll show you where you will sleep."

Afraid to say a word, Winny followed her mistress mutely back to the barn and past the cows' door, then all the way around to the opposite side, where her trunk still waited. She squinted through the door and into the darkness, smelling dust and wool.

"The sheep won't be in here during the summer, so you'll have more room than you need. The Home Boy sleeps with the cows on the other side of this wall. Don't you mess with that boy. He has his own work to do and some whore girl has no business around him."

Winny didn't have the strength to tell her that she had never even kissed a boy.

"Yes, Mistress," she said quietly.

"Get some sleep. You have a busy day tomorrow."

Hugging the mildewed blanket to her chest, Winny reached for the familiar handle of her trunk. Night had fallen, its chill seeping into her bones, but the moon was bright enough that she could still see endless fields of grass and the long dirt road cutting through it all. A fleeting thought played in her mind, and she imagined following that road and disappearing into the darkness. If she left now, no one would see her go, and she might get a good distance before the sun came up. She could scavenge for food along the way, sleep in *other* people's barns, and then maybe she could find Mary. Maybe even Jack.

Tears blurred her vision as courage left in a rush. She didn't know which direction they had come from when they'd left the station, and she hadn't seen many houses on the long drive here. Even if she had, what could she do? No one would help her. She knew that now. No one wanted her. No one ever had. Not her mother. Not the orphanage. And not the Adamses. Here, she was the Home Girl. And she would be nothing more than that for five more years, when she finally turned twenty-one.

Winny turned from the landscape, the handle of her trunk clutched in her hand. The barn was pitch black inside, so she skimmed her hand along the rough wall to feel her way to the far corner, where she slid down and sat on the straw. She fumbled with the clasps of her trunk; it didn't matter that it was too dark to see what lay within. She knew everything inside by heart. Her fingers brushed over one of her three cotton night-gowns, and she felt a pang of nostalgia for those comfortable nights at Barkingside with Mary in the next bed. She set the nightgown to the side. No one but her would sleep here, and she would only have to change back into her clothes in the morning. The nightgown might as well stay in the trunk.

Her fingers continued their exploration, finding her drawers, petti-coats, stockings, pinafores, and the two straw hats underneath: one for Sundays, one for travel. In the corner of the trunk was her hairbrush and comb, a copy of *The Pilgrim's Progress*, and her Bible, along with two cards from Barnardo's. What would she write on those cards? She couldn't imagine ever telling anyone that she felt at home here. It was probably better not to send them at all.

Beneath everything else was her warm, brown Ulster coat, which she had last worn on the ship. She'd felt so ladylike, walking around the deck in its pretty cape and sleeves, the belt snug around her waist. She dis-carded the smelly blanket Mistress Adams had given her and pulled her coat over herself instead, stopping short when she heard paper crinkling in the outside pocket. Had she tucked something in there and forgotten about it? Curious, she dug inside and pulled out a piece of folded paper, but she couldn't read what it said in the dark.

Suddenly it seemed the most important thing in the world that she see what was written on that paper, no matter what it was. If it was simply the remnants of a ticket, that would be enough, because it would be proof that somewhere beyond these walls there was another world. No longer bothered by the darkness, she hurried to the door and angled the paper toward the moonlight.

But it wasn't a ticket at all. It was a letter, and her throat tightened when she recognized the neat script. Mary.

My dearest Winny,

My mother used to say: "We do not know where we might end up, but we know where we have been." What I know is that whenever I've been with you, I've had a sister, and she is the truest, most wonderful sister I ever could have wished for.

You always looked at me like I was the strong one, but I have seen what you can do. You are courageous and honest. Whatever happens to us, I know you will be okay.

Your sister always,
Mary

Winny pressed the letter to her chest as if it might heal the open wound inside her, but nothing could ever do that. She squeezed her teary eyes shut, needing desperately to see Mary's dear face again, then those of Jack, Edward, and Cecil. She knew how easily they could be lost—the faces of her mother and father were long gone—and she needed to keep her friends safe in her heart.

"Mary, Jack, Cecil, Edward," she whispered slowly, imprinting each face in her memory as she said their names. She turned back to her makeshift bed and lay on the Ulster coat, trying in vain to forget where she was. "Mary, Jack, Cecil, Edward," she repeated over and over, bringing her dear friends close enough that they could carry her to sleep.

nine

JACK

❦

Jack tilted the bucket of water over his upturned face, his mouth open wide. Never in his life had he tasted anything so exquisite as the musky well water that trickled down his neck and under his shirt like tiny fingers. When it was empty, he set the bucket down by the base of the well and considered the plot of land the boys were clearing of maple trees. The stumps were putting up a fight. Edward had taken a break and was sitting in the dry grass, his head in his hands. Cecil was leaning on a shovel in front of a stubborn tree trunk, his face dripping with exertion. Quinn, a quiet boy who had come to the farm with them, stood a few feet away from Cecil, swinging an axe in a wide arc over his head, chopping a felled tree to pieces. His dark brown curls were pasted to his scalp, and sweat cut lines through the grime on his face. Quinn would chop that tree until he fell down himself, Jack thought.

Sunshine poured over the fields like honey, but there was no sweetness to it. During their first week on the farm, it had left the boys dizzy and sunburned and sick. Now, in their third week, their skin had toughened into a rugged shade of brown, but the sun continued to beam down on them as if it had a point to make. The wall of dark clouds brooding over the horizon were a welcome sight.

London had been shades of grey, her smells oily and urban, and the noise had been constant, whether from the screech and crack of engines or the yells and cries of the people living there. Here, the fields were a thirsty green, the trees still but many. The warm air was ripe with the fragrant perfume of crops and a hint of the coming storm. Jack found the constant quiet strange. He longed for the soothing familiarity of London's chaos.

Where was Mary in all this? he wondered for the thousandth time. Was she anywhere nearby? He'd asked Mr. Keller where she was going when they left Toronto. He hadn't known, but he'd promised to get word to Jack with any news. That was all Jack had to go on.

Edward got to his feet and waded through the grass toward Jack. "Never thought I'd wish I was back on that boat," he said, lowering the bucket with a clunk down the well. "Don't think I've ever been so tired in my life."

"Maybe we'll get used to it. We're getting stronger, anyhow."

"What good's muscle when you can't stand up any longer?"

"Shall we ask Warren?" Jack quipped.

Edward took off his cap and dumped the bucket of water over his head. "I'll ask Warren."

"Yeah, sure," Cecil said, coming over. "Ask him real nice like. You'll just get hit again."

It had become obvious within the first few minutes of meeting Master Warren that the man's main objective was to make sure the boys never forgot he was in charge. His beard couldn't hide his permanent scowl, and the stick he used to punish them at will was always in plain sight. In the first couple of days, Jack had accidentally spilled a bucket of fresh milk, and Warren had descended on him with that stick. He'd borne those bruises for a week.

Since then, they'd all experienced Warren's wrath. When his decrepit wheelbarrow cracked and fell apart, he punished Edward. Cecil had made the mistake of disagreeing with Warren about the most efficient way to clear the field, and he'd learned the hard way that Warren was not to be challenged. Quinn had done nothing wrong, but he moved too slowly for Warren's liking, and his back had bled for it. They all lived in fear of Warren's temper, and Jack suspected they weren't the only ones. The boys only saw Mistress Warren at mealtimes, and that was enough to show them what kind of husband he was. The woman would have shied from her own shadow. None of them had seen any sign of children, which partially explained why the Home Boys were there.

"It ain't right how he treats us," Edward said. "We signed a contract, didn't we? Didn't he promise to take care of us?"

"You tell me. You're the one who spent all day reading that paper."

"It did say we could petition Barnardo's if we weren't treated well. They could send us somewhere else." Edward combed his fingers through his wet blond hair. "Course we'd have to figure out how to petition first. We can't even get our hands on paper since he ripped up those cards from Barnardo's."

"Think Warren can even read?" Cecil muttered.

A deep rumbling shuddered across the fields, and the boys' attention went to the distant clouds. Jack's skin cried out for the storm to come closer, to cool him, to clean him.

"We gotta figure something out," Edward replied. "Do you want to stay here until you're eighteen?"

"Don't matter what the contract says, I reckon we don't have much choice if we want to stay together," Jack cut in. "I don't think too many other folks are gonna want to take all three of us."

The brothers fell silent. Out in the field, Quinn still swung his axe. Quinn was a big lad, and he could work like an ox without stopping, but something always seemed to be missing from his eyes. Edward figured Quinn had been born that way, that it could be his mother was a drinker or something had happened to him as a baby. He barely spoke a word—except in his sleep, and even then they couldn't understand a thing he said.

Jack waved him over. "Come on, Quinn. Take a break."

Cecil cooled himself down with the water then refilled the bucket. He handed it to Quinn, who poured it over his head then shook the water out of his hair like a dog.

"You don't look so good, Quinn," Jack said. "Where's your hat?"

Quinn scratched his head. "Don't know."

"Take mine for now." He passed his faded cap over. "It'll keep the sun off your head."

Quinn nodded a thank you.

"What home did you come from, Quinn?" Cecil asked.

"Weren't no home. Workhouse, it was."

The boys exchanged a glance. "Even Stepney's better than that," Cecil said.

"I reckon we had it pretty good at Stepney," Jack agreed. "I never used to think so, but . . . three square meals, a comfortable bed, clean clothes, lessons. The chores were hard, but not like this."

Edward grunted. "Never thought I'd miss those days."

"I miss football," Cecil said. "Ever play football, Quinn?"

He shook his head.

"Remember how they thought we was gonna run away that first time?" Edward mused. "How they stood around like bobbies, folding their arms all wary-like while they watched us play? Where did they think we'd go?"

"I would have run," Cecil admitted.

Jack wasn't surprised. Cecil's first instinct was always to defy, to go head to head with any challenger, while Edward tended to wait things out and strategize the smartest move. Jack figured he fit in somewhere between the two of them.

"Maybe we should have," he said.

The only thing about Warren's farm that Jack was glad about was that he had the lads with him. On the day their train pulled into the station, they'd laughed at the irony: of all the places to end up in Ontario, they'd landed in a town called London. After they'd disembarked and claimed their trunks, a small, studious-looking man with a leather bag and a thin moustache had come out to meet them. He'd briefly introduced himself as Mr. Brown, Barnardo's representative in the area, and he'd explained that the farmers would be there soon to choose the boys they wanted.

"So you'll want to stand tall and show them you're strong," he'd advised.

When the farmers arrived, Jack stood with Edward and Cecil, his heart thumping as he waited for their futures to unfold. That's when it hit him that this might be the last time he'd ever see the brothers. The thought made him feel very small, as if bits of him were being chipped off every time someone was taken away. What would be left of him when he'd lost them all?

On that day, they'd stood together like a battalion. The way they held themselves, he supposed, was why they were chosen. That, and the fact that of all the boys on the platform, they were the biggest and strongest. None of them had known if the stocky, bearded farmer striding toward them would be a good master, but they'd all tried to impress the man by puffing out their chests even as he sneered at them over the broken angle of his nose. He jabbed a thick finger into Cecil's side as if he were a piece of meat, and Cecil grunted, startled, almost setting the boys off in nervous laughter. It was only natural that they all wanted to win this competition, but none of them had any idea what the prize would be. If he'd known then what he knew now, Jack would have curled up on the platform and whimpered like a child. Anything to stay away from Warren.

Warren had pointed at the three of them plus Quinn, standing on Jack's other side. "I'll take these four. I can send them back if they're not good enough, right?"

"Oh, yes, sir. We want you to be completely satisfied," Mr. Brown replied, holding out a handful of paperwork. "Here are the indenture papers for each boy, which we'll need you to sign."

One by one, Mr. Brown called the boys over to read and sign their papers alongside their new master, who already looked impatient to leave. They'd all been shown the contract—four typed pages—ahead of time, so they knew that Mr. Warren would be their legal guardian until they turned eighteen, and then they would be out on their own. Over the next two years, Mr. Warren would pay "$100 In Trust" to Barnardo's for each boy, which they would receive when they were twenty-one. Working a farm wouldn't have been Jack's first choice of employment, but he reminded himself it was only for a time. And he'd admit it was a better, more respectable line of work than stealing from market stalls and running off with purses.

When Mr. Brown signalled to them, Edward went first, and as was his way, he took a considerable amount of time checking the pages to make sure nothing had been changed. Satisfied, he nodded at the others, then Cecil, Quinn, and Jack all signed as well.

Once they'd collected their trunks, they climbed into the back of Warren's truck. Throughout the train journey from Halifax, Jack had seen farmland pass in a smooth, lulling landscape. Now they were in the very heart of it, riding the dips and jolting over bumps as the truck crested hills. After a while, Warren rolled off the main road onto a rough, two-track trail bordered by a leaning fence that corralled a herd of cows. The big black brutes stood like statues, staring at the truck with what Jack guessed was malevolence, based on their size alone. He had seen lots of horses in the streets back home, but those were small compared to these cows. He figured just one of their massive hooves could stomp him to death.

At the end of the road was an old grey house, its roof withered by weather. Off to the side stood a barn, and a couple of small sheds huddled under the shadows of maple trees. Warren stopped in front of the barn and got out of the truck. As he walked toward the house, he yelled over his shoulder, "Bring 'em in, get 'em milked."

"Bring who in?" Cecil asked the other three.

Jack raised an eyebrow at the cows. "I reckon we're about to become cowboys, mates."

Ever since that moment when they'd first arrived on the farm, they hadn't stopped working. They were up at four thirty every morning and closed their eyes somewhere after ten each night. They slept in what Warren called a bunkhouse, an old shed with four walls and a questionable roof. Each boy had a narrow wooden pallet with a moth-eaten blanket tossed on top. There were no windows, there was no light, and the mosquitoes were a plague that worsened after dark. The familiar, comforting sounds of Jack's friends sleeping were forgotten when the whine of a bloodsucker sang in his ear. The creatures drove him mad, and he hunted blindly for them, occasionally crushing one between his palms. Until the morning light revealed proof, he wouldn't know whether he'd gotten it before it got him.

When the day's first round of milking had been completed, Jack and the others lined up at the door to the house, and Warren's timid wife dropped a lukewarm lump of oatmeal into each boy's bowl, her eyes never leaving the pot. The glutinous cereal sat like a ball in their bellies, and it had to tide them over until suppertime, when they lined up again for a dry biscuit along with some kind of meat in broth.

Almost everything the boys did at Warren's farm was new to them. Barnardo's had trained them to make boots and brushes, taught them metalwork and other trades, but no one had thought to tell them what would be demanded of them on a Canadian farm. Their hands and feet blistered as they slaughtered chickens, milked cows, built fences, pitched hay, chopped firewood, and dug out rocks, turnips, and tree trunks. The work took over Jack's mind. Sometimes he forgot there was anything beyond the farm.

Now his gaze travelled to his shovel, the handle sticking up from the dry dirt like a flagpole. Thunder came again, closer this time, and he rolled his head around his neck, preparing to get back to work. Maybe they could finish clearing this one trunk before the rain came.

In the end, they cut down four more trees but could only pry out one trunk before the clouds finally burst and they finished for the day. They held their faces to the fat, warm raindrops, soothing their parched skin, but when lightning sliced through the air, they bolted to the farmhouse for their supper.

The door opened, and Jack caught a brief, pained expression on Mistress Warren's face before her husband barged past her.

Warren took up the entire doorframe. "Those stumps ain't dug out yet."

"They'll come out tomorrow, once the ground's wet." The words were out before Jack could stop them.

Warren strode through the door, forcing him backwards. "Did I tell you to take them out *tomorrow*? You saying I did, you lying limey bastard?"

"I didn't. I just said the trees are stuck till tomorrow. The rain'll help them loosen up."

Warren's fist caught Jack in the jaw, and stars exploded in his vision. He stumbled back and landed on the fresh mud.

"Master Warren!" Cecil shouted. "Leave him be."

"Don't tell me what to do, boy. Don't forget who's in charge," Warren said, low and deliberate. He turned back to Jack, who tried to scuttle away, but he couldn't get out of reach fast enough. He heard the *whoop!* of Warren's stick as it cut through the air, and he braced just as it sliced down on his stomach.

"Get off him!" Cecil yelled.

The stick sang and snapped again. When Jack opened his eyes, he saw a bright red line cutting Cecil's cheek.

"It ain't right," Edward said through his teeth. "It ain't right how you're treating us. We don't none of us deserve this. You'll never get away with it."

"Is that right? Who's gonna stop me?" As if to make his point, Warren wheeled on Jack again. "I'll do as I please. I paid for you. You're mine."

Jack curled into a ball so the blows bit into his back rather than his front, wishing he was anywhere but right there, squirming in the muck. Anywhere—on the boat, in the Home, in the orphanage, on the streets of London, running free and happy with Mary, the two of them dressed in rags with barely anything in their bellies. *Mary!* he grasped for her name between flashes of pain. Was she all right? Was she safe? Was she alone? With every one of Warren's blows he clung tighter to the hope that she and Winny had been taken together into a fine, caring home to be ladies' maids. It was too much to imagine them alone and afraid in the pouring rain somewhere, lying in the mud at the whim of a cold, cruel master.

Be strong, he thought, as much for his sister as for himself. *When this nightmare is finally over, I swear I will move heaven and earth to find you.*

ten

WINNY

❦

Winny sloshed through the mud and slid the bushel of cucumbers onto the bed of the truck before turning back to the garden to gather more. Rain had poured down all night, turning the garden to muck, but she had to keep working. Mistress Adams had told her two days before that she needed the whole garden harvested by this morning. This field was the last one to be cleared. When Winny heard the farmhouse door creak open, she picked up her step.

"You'll never get this done in time," Mistress Adams snapped. "You're too slow."

She was going as fast as she could, Winny wanted to say, but she'd learned long ago that it wasn't worth a bruised cheek to argue.

"Home Boy!" Mistress Adams shouted, stomping through the puddles toward the cow barn. "Get over here!"

Minutes later, the Home Boy appeared and got to work beside Winny without a word. Appeased, Mistress Adams retreated into the house.

Since she'd arrived on the farm three months ago, Winny had done no more than peep a quick hello at the Home Boy in passing, and only when she felt absolutely certain no one else was around. She had discovered that his name was David, because she'd heard Master Adams call him that once. Winny had never spoken to Master Adams. She'd only ever seen him across the field, sometimes with David, sometimes on his own. From a distance, she got the impression that Master Adams was gentler than his wife. He walked with an easy lilt, slow and steady, and she'd never once heard him yell.

Winny twisted a cucumber off its vine and glanced sideways as she tossed it in the basket. "Thanks for your help."

He looked up, startled.

"You're David, right?"

He nodded.

"It's awful nice to work with someone. To . . . to talk with someone."

David focused on the plants in front of him. "You work harder than a girl ought. I'm sorry about that, Winny."

It had been so long since anyone had called her by her name or said a kind word to her. "I'm all right," she said, but her voice wavered. She reached for safer ground. "How long have you been here?"

"Oh, five years or so."

"Five years! I can't imagine that. You must be so lonely."

"You get used to it. And Master Adams is good company sometimes. He's the one who told me you was coming."

That answered her question about how he'd learned her name.

"Did you talk with Helen at all?" David asked. "I mean, before she left."

Helen's marriage three weeks ago had been a small affair but demanding for Winny. Nothing had ever been good enough for Helen, and if dirt could be made to shine, she would have made Winny clean it. Winny wouldn't miss her at all.

"Oh no. I wasn't allowed near her."

"Right. Diseases and all that."

Winny gasped. "I ain't got a disease!"

"None of us does. But they say we do. That's why they won't touch us. That's why we can't sleep in the house."

"I can't imagine sleeping in the same house with such horrible people."

"That's the spirit," David said with a smile.

They settled back into the silence of their work, picking vegetables and dropping them into the bushel. Despite the calluses that had toughened Winny's hands, her fingers were swollen and tender from cucumber prickles, and when she lifted the full bushel, it felt as if she were squeezing bits of glass. But just like the unrelenting hunger pangs, and just like the ache she constantly felt for her friends, she had learned to put the pain in a box, shut the lid, and tuck it in the back of her mind. Winny's life was crowded by stacks of boxes filled with different kinds of hurt, all of which she feared might one day tumble down and crush her.

But she couldn't ignore everything. These days it was her feet, or rather her boots, that weighed on her mind. Her body had shrunk due to hunger and hard work, but her feet kept growing, stretching the limits of her old boots. Every step was excruciating. Taking her boots off at the end of each day was sheer bliss. A week ago, she had worked up the nerve to ask Mistress Adams about getting new boots before the weather turned cold, but that had thrown the woman into a rage.

"You want *boots*?" Mistress Adams had shrieked, her face bright red. "We're in the middle of a depression and some people can't even afford to eat! Selfish, ignorant girl! You're lucky I give you a roof to sleep under."

In the beginning, Winny had thought the worst part about being at the farm was the heap of straw she had for a bed, but she found she was so tired at the end of every day she could have slept on dirt. One time she'd fallen asleep in a haystack in the middle of the day. Mistress Adams had found her there, and Winny was soundly whipped. She'd learned her lesson, swearing she would never again let herself close her eyes and rest. Not until her workday was over.

Then she'd thought the wrenching emptiness in her stomach would be the hardest thing to handle. She'd learned to time her days just right so she could get her meals before the dogs did, but sometimes the pitiful allotment of leftover scraps was hardly worth the effort. No one cared that she was weak and dizzy. At night, she snuck out to the vegetable garden and dug up what she could find, always making sure to fill in the holes and cover her tracks after, in case anyone noticed carrots or potatoes were missing.

But working with David now, she realized that the bleakest thing about her life was the loneliness. Day after day, night after night, she had no one with whom to share stories, no one to share kindness.

"Why are we loading all this?" Winny asked as David slid a bushel into the truck, tight against the peas.

"It's a big family party. They do this once a year. They can vegetables and trade things." He pointed toward the front. "She had me load up all the yarn you made, did you see?"

Winny nodded, privately admiring the covered baskets. She knew every inch of that yarn, could still feel its twisting fibres winding through her thumb and fingers. When she had first arrived at the farm, the sheep had already been sheared and a mountain of wool waited for Winny. It had taken her a week to soak the pounds and pounds of stinky raw wool in water and lye, then stir it over a fire until the stubborn oils and dirt finally rose to the surface. When the wool was clean, she'd set it all out on racks to dry and prayed it wouldn't rain. That was the afternoon Mistress Adams had caught her sleeping on the hay. Her back still stung the next day when her mistress showed her how to turn the dried wool into yarn.

"Now watch closely," she had said, sitting outside the barn with Winny, "because I'm not spending all day out here teaching you."

In her hands were two large square brushes. Winny watched her press the wool onto one brush then use the other to sweep the strands across over and over again, taking out all the tangles and rolling the wool into a smooth sausage shape.

"This is called 'carding,'" she explained, handing over the brushes. "I taught each of my daughters how to do this, and we used to get it done quickly between the four of us." She corrected Winny's hands with a surprising gentleness. "It was something we looked forward to every year, doing the carding together."

Winny moved the brushes back and forth, back and forth, until a long tube of wool formed. She held it up for inspection, and Mistress Adams nodded.

"That's it. When you've got it all carded, tell me and I'll get you spinning." She turned and began walking back to the house. "Don't fall asleep while you're at it," she called over her shoulder.

Turning wool to yarn took forever, but it was light, repetitive work, and it gave Winny time to think about better days. She called up foggy memories of her family gathered around the table in Ireland, back when Da was still alive and there was warmth and love in their house. It was a shame, she thought, that memories could not bring back sounds, because she would dearly love to hear his laugh again. The clearest moments, and the ones she loved to relive, had happened after she'd met Mary and Jack and Cecil and Edward, when they'd become a family of sorts. Just as she did every night, she focused on bringing each of their faces to mind while she worked, because unlike her, the memories could and often did escape.

"Do we go with the Adamses?" she asked David. She was curious about the party, but at the same time she did like the idea of spending a day without Mistress Adams hovering over her.

"Yeah, we walk out then unload everything, and you'll get stuck chopping and cleaning and the like. The ladies like to say they work, but they'll give you a lot to do."

"What will you be doing?"

"I'll be cutting firewood, most likely. There's always firewood. Or maybe fencing. Master Renfrew is the biggest dairy farmer in the area, so there's always lots of that."

Renfrew? The image of a round woman in a blue dress appeared in

Winny's mind, and for a moment, she couldn't move. There must be plenty of families with that name, but what if . . . oh, what if Mary was there? Her entire body buzzed with nerves.

"Do you know if they have a Home Girl named Mary Miller?"

David cast a look back at the house. "They used to have a Home Girl a year ago, but she's gone now."

Winny fought off disappointment. Then again, a lot of things could change over a year. Maybe David just didn't know about Mary. "Do they have any Home Boys?"

He shrugged. "Some."

"Have you ever heard of one named Jack Miller? Or maybe Cecil or Edward Drury?"

"I don't know those names. Sorry, Winny."

It had been a long shot, she knew. Still, David couldn't know everything. What if her friends were there? Suddenly she couldn't wait to be done with the work and get going.

They finished harvesting the cucumbers just as the sun came out in a burst of brilliance and Mistress Adams bustled out of the house. "The weather is on our side," she said, a rare smile on her face. She inspected the goods in the back of the truck. "Bring the eggs too, girl."

Master Adams loped towards the truck from behind the barn, and he frowned sideways at the full basket of eggs in Winny's hand. "Why do we need all those? Surely Doreen has enough eggs already."

"Lots of families will be there. One of the others will trade for jam, I hope," Mistress Adams said cheerily. "With such a wet spring I didn't can as many strawberry jams as I would have liked."

Her husband paused by the back of the truck, surveying the load. "You'll walk behind," he said to David. "Might be room for you on the way back, though."

He climbed into the truck without a word and started the engine, a signal to his wife that it was time to go. She squeezed in beside him and they chugged down the road, Winny and David trailing behind.

For the first half hour, Winny welcomed the heat as it dried their rain-soaked clothes and warmed their bodies. When it became too much, she tied a rag around her head like a scarf in an attempt to lift her thick waves off her neck, but the material couldn't keep all the stinging sweat from her eyes. Worst of all were her feet. What was left of her boots pinched them terribly, and she had to keep stopping to empty out dirt and pebbles.

"Why don't you just take them off?" David asked. "We've a long walk ahead of us. If Mistress Adams gets angry about it, I'll take the blame."

"You're not to blame."

"No, but I imagine you'd let your feet fall off before you chanced a whipping."

He was right about that. "I just—"

"It's all right, Winny."

She'd slipped them off and he held out his hand for the boots. He tied the laces together and slung them over his shoulder. "Better?"

The rocks on the road were hard under her tender soles, but that discomfort was infinitely more bearable than the restrictive boots. "So much better. Thank you."

Knowing they had miles to go, Winny distracted herself from her feet by asking David where he was from. He told her he'd been born in a workhouse then moved to an orphanage as a baby.

"Never knew my family. It was better that way," he said, and it struck Winny that maybe her life wasn't all that bad, compared to his. At least she had a few fond memories of her family to call on when the loneliness got to be too much. David had none. Then again, did it hurt less if you didn't know what you were missing?

"Tell me about you. How old are you?"

"September's my birthday," she said, swatting at a horsefly. "I'm almost sixteen. You?"

"Seventeen."

The same age as Jack and Edward. Even though she had barely met

David, she felt a pang of loss. "You're almost free of this place. What will you do when you're eighteen? Where will you go?"

David looked out over the sleeping fields. The harvest was done, the dried stalks broken and bent. "I'd like to be a farmer. Master Adams says he'll help me. Who knows? I may not even leave when I'm eighteen. He still needs help here."

She stopped in her tracks. "You want to stay here?"

"I like being outside and working hard. My life here is better than the one I had in England."

Perhaps to a boy with nothing to lose, coming here might feel like a good thing, she thought. Canada was beautiful and the birds sang with such happiness. But it was still a cage to Winny.

"I know that's a surprise to you," David said, filling the silence. "You've had it hard with Mistress Adams, but her husband is a good enough bloke. He's a quiet man. Keeps to himself mostly. What you probably don't know is that the family used to have a young son, but he got killed last year when a wagon rolled on him. He was only eight. Master Adams has never been the same since Frederick died. He spends most of his time in the fields or in town now. Can't blame him. Mistress Adams was always strict, but she's much worse these days."

Winny peered ahead at her mistress, feeling as if the woman was a stranger to her all over again. She had never made mention of a son. "I had no idea."

"No, they don't talk about him. He was a good lad, though. I liked him."

"What about Helen and her sisters? Where are they?"

"All of them married and moved away. I never thought Helen would even have a suitor, she being who she is and all."

Winny suppressed a laugh. "You're mad, talking that way!"

"Made you smile, though, didn't I?"

There was no mistaking the Renfrews' farm. When they crested the last hill, fields of cows spread out as far as the eye could see, and Winny's hands ached at the thought of all that milking. In the midst of the greenery stood a bright red barn surrounded by sheds, two silos, and a large windmill. Set to the side was a brick farmhouse, its cheery, wraparound porch and gabled windows decorated with intricate swirls of white wood trim. Beyond all the buildings rolled another wide, open pasture with a cluster of trees where a group of children played. She could hear their happy shouts and laughter from where she stood.

"You said the Renfrews' farm was big, but this is . . ." She was at a loss for the right words.

"Master Renfrew is very wealthy. Sort of a king out here. Some say he might run for mayor."

Something in David's tone made Winny glance up at him. "You don't like him?"

"No. He comes off as a friendly sort, but he's cruel with his Home Boys. He's locked them up without food for days, tied them outside in the winter. He's just rotten."

"But how can he run for mayor if that's the kind of man he is?"

"It's all about appearances. The people who know about him are either working for him or they're intimidated, so they keep quiet."

Winny could clearly see what David meant about appearances. The house's clean white exterior gleamed, and the windows sparkled in the sunlight. She was sure Mistress Renfrew had all the finest things, and she imagined the wonders she might see if only she could look inside.

While the Adamses got out of the truck, Winny reluctantly tied her boots back on then followed David's lead and began unloading the food and yarn into a small tent that had been set up next to the house. As they passed the front door of the house, a woman emerged with her hands in the air, a wide smile on her face, and Winny almost dropped the bushel she was carrying.

"There you are! There you are!" the woman cried, her arms held out toward Mistress Adams.

It was *her*, the same Mistress Renfrew, the woman who had taken Mary from the station. If she was here, that meant Mary was too.

eleven
JACK

❦

Jack sat on his bunk, absently scratching dried blood off his lip. Almost every day over the past month, Warren had come after him with some complaint or threat. If it wasn't him it was Cecil, and that was usually because Cecil put himself between Warren and Jack when things started getting rough. Warren was like one of those horseflies that chased them all over the fields, only the boys couldn't outrun him.

Jack didn't remember why Warren had hit him this time. Didn't really care anymore. He'd had enough.

"I'm gonna fix this," he said to the brothers one night.

Edward and Cecil were lying quietly on their pallets, wrapped in their blankets. The temperature outside had dropped as the sun went down, and the air in the bunkhouse was raw and cold. If this was autumn weather, Jack couldn't imagine what winter would be like here.

"Mr. Keller promised they'd look after us," he continued. "But they ain't been doing that. I reckon we've been forgotten. So we gotta remind them."

"What's the plan, Jack?" Edward asked, propping himself onto one elbow.

The door creaked open, and Quinn's bulk filled the frame. As the boy squeezed between the cots toward his own, Jack heard a tiny sound.

"What's that you got, Quinn?"

Quinn's face widened with a smile, and he dug a tiny grey cat out of the bib of his overalls. "Got a cat," he said, holding the little creature up. She mewed her hellos at the boys, and Quinn turned her so he was nose to nose with her. "She likes me."

"Looks that way," Cecil agreed. "What are you gonna call her?"

Quinn lay down and the kitten curled contentedly on his chest. "Cat."

Edward chuckled. "Good enough, mate. She looks happy as a queen."

Quinn drew his finger along the soft line of the kitten's back and quietly began to sing. "God save our gracious cat, God save our noble cat—"

"God save our cat," the other boys chorused.

Back in the orphanage, Jack and the brothers had sung that tune every morning before their porridge with milk and molasses. They'd sung to avoid the master's cane.

"Think our king knows we're over here?" Cecil asked. "Think old Eddie would help us out if he knew?"

"Doubt it," Edward said.

"Cat's purring," Quinn murmured. A low, contented rumbling vibrated within the broken wooden walls, and they all paused to listen.

"At least someone's happy," Cecil said.

"Jack," Edward said, shifting his attention back. "What's the plan?"

"It ain't without risks," Jack replied, "but it's all I got."

"Everything we've ever done has been risky. Let's hear it."

"We need to get word to Barnardo's. If I can get into town and find the post office, I can write a note to Mr. Keller. They'll have to come get us if I do that. I'll tell them about Warren, and I'll ask about the girls."

"How are you gonna do that?"

"I'll hitch a ride in the back of Warren's truck next time he goes in."

"I don't like it," Cecil said. "He'll see you. He ain't that stupid."

"Don't know about that," Edward put in. "But I agree it's too dangerous. Even for you, Jack."

Jack had thought that at first too, but there were no other options. "He always drives around with those seed sacks and crates in the back. I can hide in there, wait until he parks, then jump out. He'll never think to look for me there."

"Maybe we should all go," Edward said. "Look out for each other."

"A group of us would get caught. If I'm on my own, I can hide easy. I just have to find the post office, then it'll be fine. I'll hide in the back again and be back before you know it."

"What if he catches you?" Cecil asked.

"What does it matter? He's gonna beat me no matter what I do. I might as well get beat for a good reason." Jack took a deep breath, let it out slow. "The only problem is if Barnardo's takes us out of here, they may split us up. But which is worse: splitting up or living here with Warren for another year? Either way we lose."

For a few moments, Cat's purr was the only sound in the bunkhouse, then Edward asked, "When will you go?"

"The next time Warren goes to town."

———

It was two more weeks before Warren decided to head in, and every day leading up to that dragged on forever. On that morning, he yelled for the boys to come and load some heavy crates onto the truck, and as they worked side by side in silence, Jack knew his friends' hearts were pounding just as his was. When Warren headed inside the house, Cecil leaned towards Jack.

"Get in," he whispered.

Jack hopped onto the bed then snaked between the crates, letting his friends stack the rest around him until he couldn't see anything beyond the pine box in front of his eyes. Trapped inside a cage of his own making, he clenched his jaw, trying to keep calm. Maybe he couldn't do this. Maybe it was a stupid idea. Warren would kill him if he found him. But no, he reasoned. If he couldn't see out, that meant Warren couldn't see in. He'd be all right. He had to be. He swallowed his fear, determined to see this thing through for all their sakes.

"Come back to us safe," Edward murmured from some place Jack couldn't see.

Minutes after the boys left him there, Jack heard Warren return and get into the truck. He breathed a sigh of relief as the engine started. He hadn't seen Jack.

The trip into town took half an hour, but to Jack it felt like much longer. Crammed between the crates, he flinched whenever Warren hit a bump, and his face knocked against the wood so many times he lost count. When the road evened out, Jack let himself breathe a little easier, but he couldn't escape the suffocating sense of dread. He was outside the prison walls, but he sat a mere two feet behind his jailer.

Eventually, the truck slowed and pulled to a stop, and Warren got out. Jack could tell they were in town, because he heard voices and vehicles all around. Then, all of a sudden, he could see sky. Jack held his breath as Warren lifted one of the crates and carried it off. He hadn't looked down, hadn't noticed Jack. *This is where it gets tricky*, he thought. He was still too deeply buried to attempt escape; he'd have to wait until he could move, and pray Warren didn't see him before that happened.

Warren carried a second crate inside the shop then came out again. After two more trips, Jack was only partially covered. He had to move now. As soon as he heard the squeak of the shop's door, he quietly pushed the remaining crates off him, leapt up, and vaulted over the side of the truck, then dashed across the street and out of sight. He knew he stuck out like a sore thumb, marked by the ragged condition of his clothes and face, so he kept to the shadows, backing between buildings when anyone looked in his direction. If anyone knew how to hide, it was Jack.

The town of London, Ontario, was larger than Jack had thought it would be, with more people than he'd expected walking along its sidewalks, more cars on the roads. Stone buildings bordered the wide street, and the sky was lined with electric wires. Down the middle of the lanes stretched two pairs of metal rails for streetcars, which rattled past and clanged their bells when people strolled in front.

Scanning the street from an alley, Jack saw numerous places of business: a bank, a hotel, offices, and storefronts, but where was the post office? After a moment, he spotted it farther up the street. He'd have to cross the road. Tugging his cap low, he kept his head down and stepped into the crowd just as a strong hand clamped onto his shoulder from behind. He whirled around, came face-to-face with a man in a policeman's cap, and froze like a cornered rabbit.

"Who might you be?"

"Jack, sir." He hadn't seen a policeman since the day they'd been taken to the orphanage, and he didn't trust them as far as he could throw them. "I'm off to the post office is all."

"Is that an English accent I hear?" The man's thick grey moustache twitched as he took in Jack's disheveled appearance. "You're one of them Barnardo boys, aren't you?"

He nodded. "Please, sir. I don't mean no harm."

"I bet your master is looking for you. What's his name?"

Jack stalled, hoping to avoid any trouble. "I need to send a letter off to Barnardo's, sir."

"What sort of letter?"

Jack thought about lying, but then he wondered if maybe this accidental meeting was a good thing after all. Maybe the policeman would help him. Wasn't that what they were supposed to do?

"Sir, Barnardo's said they need to hear how we are doing, and my mates and I, we're not doing so well. Our master is a cruel man. I've come to write to Barnardo's because we need them to come and take us away from his farm."

"You haven't given me the man's name."

"Mr. Warren, sir."

One eyebrow lifted beneath the black cap. "Mr. Warren, huh? You know, I might be tempted to lock you up just for lying, never mind trying to damage a good man's name."

Jack's mouth went dry. "Are there two Mr. Warrens living around here? Because the one I know is as mean as they come, sir."

"Don't be smart, boy. No, there's only the one, and I've known him a very long time." He glanced over Jack's shoulder and a smile crinkled his eyes. "As a matter of fact . . ." He held up a hand. "Hey, Warren! I've got something here I believe belongs to you."

Jack's urge to flee was overwhelming, but the policeman gripped his arm. Despite the quaking in his knees, Jack lifted his chin defiantly as Warren approached.

"Why thanks, George. This *is* a surprise." Warren's smile was as hard as flint. "Didn't expect to see you here, boy. But I guess it would be too much to expect a lazy halfwit to follow the rules and stay put." His hand had curled into a fist, and his thumb slid back and forth over his fingers. He nodded to his friend. "I'll take it from here. I appreciate your help."

As soon as the policeman turned and disappeared around the corner, Jack tried to wrestle out of Warren's grasp. He knew what would happen once they were out of sight of the town.

"Help!" he yelled as Warren dragged him toward the truck. "Somebody help me!"

But no one did. One couple dropped off the sidewalk to go around him, hostility drawn in tight lines on their faces. Other people walked by, some staring with interest, others offering friendly greetings to Warren.

"Can someone help me? Please!" Jack cried, but it was as if the entire town was deaf.

"What is it with you, boy?" Warren hissed in his ear. "You like to get hit?"

"I just want to send a letter," Jack tried. "Please, can't I just—"

He shoved Jack against the truck and pulled his arms behind him, then he grabbed a coil of rope and wound it tightly around Jack's wrists. The other end was attached to the bed of the truck.

"I ain't done what I came here to do," Warren said, yanking the knot snug. "So you'll just wait here. Keep your mouth shut if you know what's good for you. We'll leave soon enough." That terrible smile returned. "I hope you're feeling spry, because you ain't riding back."

twelve

WINNY

❧

Winny forced her eyes away from the sight of Mistress Renfrew embracing Mistress Adams and caught up to David inside the tent. She set her bushel on a table then followed him back to the truck and grabbed the next one. The whole time they unloaded the produce, she scanned the crowd, looking for Mary, but she could see no sign of her.

"Who are all these people?" she whispered to David.

"I told you. The Adamses have an annual family party. Mistress Adams has four sisters and seven brothers, and I think two of Master Adams's brothers are here as well," he said. "Everyone brings their children and grandchildren, so there's well over a hundred folks coming today."

Winny's gaze went to Mistress Adams. "So Mistress Renfrew is . . ."

"Mistress Adams's sister," David confirmed, picking up another bushel.

Winny couldn't keep the smile from her face. If the two were sisters, surely that meant they visited each other fairly often. And if Winny could convince her mistress to bring her along . . .

"I think my friend Mary is here."

David stood straighter, surprised, then he peered around. "Your friend? There's a Home Girl here?"

"Yes. Mrs. Renfrew picked her up from the train station when we first arrived. I recognized the name when you mentioned it, but I wasn't sure it was really her until I saw her just now. Do you think I'll be able to find Mary? Will I get a chance to talk with her?"

"Yeah. Should do, anyway. After you're done with your work, they'll want you out of the way." He smiled. "I'm happy for you."

Winny felt giddy with excitement. *I'm here, Mary!* she wanted to yell. *I'm coming!*

After he'd put his bushel down, David lifted his chin toward a heavy-set man with slick dark hair and a laugh that drowned out everyone else's. He had his arm wrapped around one of the women's waists. From the way she was moving, Winny thought she looked uncomfortable, despite the polite smile on her face.

"That's Master Renfrew," David said. "Listen, when all this welcome dies down and people get to work, you'll want to keep your distance from that man. He wouldn't think twice about coming after you. He likes pretty women no matter who they are, and he's not likely to take no for an answer."

The woman slid out of Master Renfrew's reach, but not before he gave her behind a squeeze.

"Thank you," Winny said to David, unsettled. She hadn't seen that kind of behaviour since the streets of London. "I will."

Mistress Adams strode towards them. She was like a locomotive speeding out of a tunnel, the way she could roar into sight. "Why are you just standing here? You've got everything under the tent? Good. All right. You can start cutting up those cucumbers now, girl." She turned, already on the move again, and tossed David's orders over her shoulder as she went. "You're to meet the Home Boys behind the barn with the firewood."

As Winny sliced vegetables, she listened to the sounds of children playing and adults laughing over cider and biscuits. So this is what a happy family sounds like, she thought, and she grinned. *I'm going to see my family today, too.*

After what felt like hours, Mistress Adams told her she could go. "We'll do the rest ourselves."

Winny looked skeptically at the table, still holding her knife. "Really? There's a lot still to be cut."

"Yes, really. My sisters and I get most of our talking in while we're canning. It makes the work go quickly. You may wander around the property, but don't go far. There'll be plenty of dishes to wash when we're done."

Breathing in her first taste of freedom in ages, Winny left the tent and floated toward the happy voices in the field. She slipped off her boots and stretched her feet, savouring the feel of soft grass beneath them as she scouted the pasture. Where was Mary? Since Winny hadn't seen her with the adults, she figured she'd be with the children, so she headed that way.

At the bottom of the hill, a group of older boys was playing some sort of game. They stood in a semicircle while one of the boys threw a ball to another, who tried to hit it with a stick. She was impressed when he did, then even more when another lad farther afield caught the ball. He chased the hitter around until everyone cheered and yelled, including Winny.

A younger group of children stood a ways over, holding hands in two facing rows. "Red Rover, Red Rover, we call Ronny Renfrew over!" one line chorused.

The other line gathered in a group around one boy, talking about something, then they all stood back and watched him run across the field toward the other team.

"Faster! Go faster!"

"Don't let him through!"

"You'll never make it, Ronny!"

But Ronny did make it, bursting through the line with a cry of victory, his arms over his head.

Winny had never seen games like these. In England, people played dice in doorways and alleys, but nothing like this. As she watched them play, she felt an unexpected pang of longing. She'd never done that. She'd never run in the grass with friends, laughing.

"Where are you, Mary?" Winny asked out loud, impatient to find her.

In another corner of the field, a couple of toddlers staggered through the grass, toppling over then struggling to their feet again. Bundled nearby, in baskets repacked as cradles, slept two little infants. An older girl with long black hair stood in the midst of the little ones, her back to Winny. There was something about the set of her shoulders, the slight tilt of her head . . . Winny took a step forward, holding her breath. If it wasn't Mary, she'd be crushed, but—

The girl turned toward her, and the world dropped beneath Winny's feet. "Mary!" she cried, already running.

Mary glanced up, and her mouth formed Winny's name. Then she was racing as well, her face collapsing as she began to cry. The girls came together like two halves of a magnet, and Winny held on for all she was worth. She could feel the bumps of Mary's spine against her palms, hear Mary's sobs in her ear. Winny let her knees go, and they dropped onto the grass, a weeping tumble of long-lost sisters.

When they could breathe again, they laid on their sides and faced each other. Winny was deliriously happy to see Mary again, but what she saw troubled her—the sharp jut of her collarbone, the dark rings beneath her dear friend's eyes, and—

"Your face," she said softly, reaching for Mary's cheek.

Mary covered the bruise with a trembling hand before Winny could touch it. "It's nothing."

"Are these nothing?" Winny's fingers skimmed Mary's neck, dotted by bruises in a pattern that looked a lot like fingertips.

"Bruises don't matter, Winny."

"Who put them there?"

Her smile quivered. "You can't tell anyone."

"Of course I won't, if you say so."

"It's Master Renfrew. He . . . he comes after me something bad."

David's warning and the memory of Master Renfrew's thick arm wrapped tight around the woman's waist flashed in Winny's mind. Apprehension coiled in her belly like a snake. Was this more than beatings? "What's happened?"

Mary sat up and glanced at the toddlers, now rolling contentedly in the grass. "I want to hear about you. Is everything all right where you live?"

"I'm fine. It's you I'm worried about. Mary, you know you can trust me."

"I can't talk about it!" she cried, and she covered her face with her hands. "I can't even let myself think about it. Please don't ask me." She dropped her hands and reached for Winny's. "Every night I dream of you and Jack and Edward and Cecil, and I wonder how you all are, and now that you're here . . . Oh, Winny, I kept thinking that if you was livin' like me—" She pressed her lips together, keeping the words trapped inside.

"Have you contacted Barnardo's?"

She let go of Winny's hands and sagged in defeat. "How am I supposed to do that when I can't leave this farm? All I do is milk cows and tend to other people's children."

"I will. I'll make sure Barnardo's knows about you."

Mary's nostrils flared. "Do you know how powerful the name Herbert Renfrew is around here? He owns everyone. He's gonna be mayor or something. No one is going to do anything against him. Especially not for some Home Girl."

"Let me help you," Winny whispered. "Mary—"

"There's nothing you can do."

The finality in Mary's voice told Winny everything she needed to know, and her entire being ached for her friend. She had to get Mary out of this place, away from Master Renfrew. Mary had always been the strong one, standing up to bullies and protecting Winny, but something had changed in Mary that Winny couldn't put into words. Other than the bruises she still looked like herself, but it was as if Mary was hollow, as if the fight had gone from her.

"Have you seen Jack?" Mary finally asked.

Winny shook her head. "Have you?"

"No." Mary set her jaw. "But he will survive. He always has."

"So will you. Do you remember the letter you put in my pocket?"

She nodded.

"You told me in that letter that I was stronger than I thought. The truth is, so are you. You're just as strong as Jack is, and smarter."

Mary's lips lifted slightly at the corners. "Don't tell him you think I'm smarter than he is."

"Well, you are."

The brief light she'd seen in Mary's eyes faded. "He said he would find us, so he will. He's never lied to me. And when he comes for us, we can all run away together, all right?"

Winny squeezed her hand again. "I wish we could go now."

"Me too," Mary replied. "Now, tell me about you, Winny. Give me something else to think about."

So she did. She told her about the Adams farm, about making yarn, and about David. "He's even more alone than I am," she said. "He has no one."

They reminisced about the streets of London and the comforts of Barkingside, with its classes and choir. Winny did all she could to bring back the happy times, because when she did that, when she spoke of the boys, she saw Mary relax a little, even smile.

The sun was beginning to set, the shadows of maple and birch reaching their long fingers down the hill. The children playing in the background were making their way up, toward the smells of food. Winny shivered as dusk stole the day's warmth. When she heard Mistress Adams call from across the field, she stood slowly then held out a hand to help Mary to her feet.

"Will you come do the washing with me?" Winny asked.

"I'm not allowed up there. I live here." Mary gestured toward a small shed mostly concealed in the trees. "I have to stay here."

"But . . . but I have to go."

"I know." Mary looked at the ground between them. "Will you come see me again? Please?"

"I will." She had no idea how she would manage it, but she had to for both their sakes. "I will come back soon. I promise."

She threw her arms around Mary and held her tight, as if she could keep all the pieces of her dear friend in place. "Be strong," she whispered. "I will be back."

But when she pulled away, the Mary she remembered was already gone.

Winny climbed the hill alone, passing by a pile of red and yellow leaves stirred into a clattering dance by the wind. She turned away, shivering at the sight. The autumn wind was cold and the fallen leaves were dead, and all she could think of was her last glimpse of Mary's eyes.

thirteen
JACK

❧

The sound of Warren's truck rumbled up the drive, and Jack turned from the replacement board he was hammering onto the barn and watched the vehicle approach from across the snow-covered field. He would never forget what it had been like to be tied to the back of that truck as it sped along the bumpy roads, returning to the farm. The burn of the dirt and gravel grinding into his skin every time he fell would never leave him. Every time he'd gone down, Warren had stopped the truck just long enough for him to get to his feet before he'd hit the gas once more.

None of the boys had said a word when he'd returned from town, defeated, but they'd tended his cuts and bruises and brought him supper. The next day, they all got back to work, including Jack. But every nail he hit, every fence post he drove into the ground was Warren. In the months following that day, Jack's physical wounds healed, though they left scars, but something else had changed. The hurt inside him had spread and thickened, like sap in winter, and when his anger flared, it rushed in without warning.

"Who's that?" Cecil asked as two girls, clad in layers of skirts and fur-collared coats, emerged from the truck with Warren. Jack thought they looked about his age, but they obviously weren't Home Girls: they were too well dressed.

"It's girls," Quinn said softly.

Except for during Jack's recent trip to town, it had been months since any of them had seen a woman other than Mistress Warren.

"His daughters?" Jack guessed. None of them had considered the possibility that Warren might have children, but who else could they be?

They watched the girls follow Warren inside the house, then Cecil picked up his hammer. "They sure are pretty."

"Funny how something so nice can come from something so ugly," Edward said, and Quinn barked out a laugh, surprising them all.

They turned back to work, anxious to be done and out of the cold. They were almost finished with the barn wall when they heard the unexpected sound of giggling coming from behind them. The girls were strolling toward the barn, their hands warm inside fur muffs and their cheeks pink from exposure. They stopped at the fence, just a stone's throw away from the boys.

Cecil paused in his work.

"Ain't worth the beating," Jack muttered to him.

"Hello, Home Boys," one of the girls called, her voice like honey. She was the taller one, with long black hair neatly arranged over one shoulder.

"Hello," Cecil replied. "Who are you?"

"We're your mistresses," the other one said, and they both laughed with delight.

"What's that mean?" he asked.

"Our father's your master, boy. That makes us your mistresses."

They might look sweet, but the tone of their voices and the haughty expressions on their faces told Jack everything he needed to know.

"Cecil, get back to work," he said quietly, nudging him with a board. "Help me with this one."

"What's going on out here?" Warren yelled, storming toward them. Jack and the others quickly turned back to the barn. "These boys causing trouble?"

"We're only having fun, Daddy," the tall girl said sweetly. "Saying hello is all."

"You stay away from these conniving bastards, Stella," he told her. "Can't trust them an inch."

"Don't worry, Daddy. We know how to look after ourselves, don't we, Agnes?"

"Of course we do." She rolled her eyes, then sighed. "I wish we were back in Toronto. I'm bored already."

Warren banged his stick on the fence post to get the boys' attention, then he locked eyes with Jack. "If any of you touch my daughters, I'll kill you with my own hands, you understand?"

Jack had no doubt that he meant it.

"Yes, sir," they replied.

"Come on, girls. Your mother's got supper ready."

They left, but once Warren's back was turned, Agnes glanced behind and gave Cecil a coquettish wave. Jack caught Edward's eye.

"They're bad news, Cecil," Edward said. "You gotta stay away."

Cecil shrugged and picked up another board. "Yeah, yeah. I'm not stupid."

———

A few nights later, a vicious snowstorm blew in, and the blizzard consumed the farm all day and night. But that evening, the boys were sheltered and safe inside the newly repaired barn, and that was just fine with Jack. On nights like this, they would all prefer to sleep with the cows rather than shiver in the bunkhouse. They were in the midst of milking, the warm steam of the milk like a balm to Jack's chilled skin, when the barn door creaked open. They spun toward the sound, braced for Warren. At the other end of the barn, always near Quinn, Cat spooked and leapt silently into the rafters.

But it wasn't Warren. It was his daughters. The boys hadn't seen them since that first day, and Jack had hoped they were gone.

"Evening, boys," Stella purred. The girls' smiles shone in the light of their lanterns. "My sister and I thought tonight would be a perfect night to get better acquainted with you."

"Evening, ladies." Cecil's voice was confident, but Jack could hear the strain within. This was dangerous territory, and they all knew it.

"Isn't that nice. A Home Boy with manners," drawled Agnes. "Do you have names?"

"Other than *Home Boys*." Her sister giggled.

"That's Edward, Jack, and Quinn. And I'm Cecil."

As he spoke, the girls' keen eyes examined each boy in turn.

"You talk funny," Agnes noted.

Stella wandered toward Jack, her head tilted coyly. "They're from England, silly. That's the way they talk. They aren't like us. They're poor and stupid and dirty. Nobody wants them, so we bought them."

At least we're not hateful like you, Jack wanted to say. Instead, he asked, "Why are you here?"

"We're home for Christmas." She scanned the barn. "Toronto is *so* much more fun than this place. There's nothing to do here."

"Although, things are more interesting now," Agnes noted, skimming her gloved fingertips across Cecil's chest. Jack could see sweat shine on his forehead despite the cold. "Maybe we can have some fun."

"I don't think your father would like that," Jack said.

"Oh poo. He'll never know."

"You should go," Edward said.

"That's rude," Agnes snapped. "It's our farm, not yours. You're just the help. Bunch of dirty gutter rats who got nothing to say for themselves.

You work for my daddy, which means you're ours." She took a step toward Cecil. "We can do whatever we want to you."

She kissed two of her fingers then touched them to Cecil's cheek. He turned his face away, but she took his hands and placed them on her waist. "Just like that, see? Not so bad."

"Not so bad," Cecil murmured.

"And not so boring."

"Cecil . . . ," Edward said, but his brother didn't move away from Agnes.

Stella smiled at Jack and came closer, but all he could see in her eyes was her father's malice. He held up his hands and took a step back. "Your father would beat me to death."

"Looks like Cecil isn't scared," she said, glancing over her shoulder. "I guess he's just a whole lot braver than you."

Jack snorted with disgust as Cecil leaned in to kiss Agnes. "Or stupider."

Stella lifted her chin and walked deeper into the barn. "I can choose from any of you. How about you?" she asked, strolling towards Quinn.

"Leave him alone," Edward said.

"Why should I?"

"Hey, Stella, leave him alone," Jack repeated, following her. He could see the frightened look on Quinn's face in the glow of the lantern. The boy was a full head taller than she was, and strong enough to physically throw her out of the way, but he had no idea how to escape. "He don't understand what you're up to. Come on. I'm sorry about what I said. You and I can—"

"No," Stella said, a smile in her voice. "I want this big fellow."

She put her palm on Quinn's chest, and he made a small sound of alarm. Jack rushed in and grabbed her arm before she could go any further, and he pulled her away. Quinn retreated behind one of the cows and hid there. At the commotion, Cecil broke apart from Agnes, looking sheepish and concerned.

"Let go of me," Stella cried, shaking out of Jack's grasp. "He's his own man. Just because you're too chicken, that doesn't mean he can't enjoy himself."

"He doesn't want you," Jack said.

"Why, I never!"

"You're putting us all in danger. You have to leave. Now."

"What do you think?" Agnes slid back toward Cecil, but he moved away from her and toward Edward.

"Sorry," he said, "but Jack's right. A bit of fun ain't worth your father's belt buckle."

Agnes seethed. "Oh, Jack's right, is he? You think you can tell us what to do?"

"I guess we just did," Jack replied, nerves racing.

"We'll see about that." Stella gave Jack a withering glare as she pushed past him. "Let's go, Agnes."

A gust of snow blew in as the door opened, and then the girls were gone. Quinn crept out from his hiding place, eyes wide.

Jack let out a long breath. "That was bad."

Edward shoved his brother's chest, knocking him backwards. "What were you thinking, you fool?"

"I'm sorry. I wasn't." Cecil looked away. "You all right, Quinn?"

Quinn nodded, but he was pale.

"Sure he is," Jack said, reaching toward the hayloft. He wrapped his hands around Cat's slender chest and laid her in Quinn's hands. "Just a couple of girls, aye? Nothing to fuss over. Let's finish up here and go. We'll forget it happened."

But inside he knew it wasn't going to be that easy. There was no way the girls were going to let this thing go.

The next morning Warren stormed toward them from the house with Stella and Agnes trailing behind, making a show of tears.

"It's my fault," Cecil said quietly. "I'll take the belt."

"No, mate. We're all in this," Jack told him.

"You *dare* hurt my daughter?" Warren roared in their faces. In his hand, he carried a pitchfork, which he jabbed in the air as he yelled. "You dare to even *touch* her? You're gonna be sorry you even thought about it." He spun toward Stella. "Which one?"

Sniffing dramatically, Stella stepped toward them, her boots crunching on the new snow, and a cold certainty shuddered through Jack. He was the one who had put his foot down and pulled her off Quinn. He was the one her father hated the most. What would Warren do to him this time?

She started on the left, slowly passing Edward and Cecil. When she came to Jack, vengeance sparkled under her lashes, and he braced himself. But she kept walking. With her eyes on Jack, she stopped in front of Quinn.

"This one," she said.

Jack stared at her in disbelief. "Quinn didn't—"

Warren's face was red as beets. "You three get in the bunkhouse."

They hesitated, and Quinn started to follow them, not understanding.

"Not you, moron," Warren said, shoving Quinn. "Don't you move." He turned to the other three, swinging the handle of the pitchfork. "Get in there!"

Jack's stomach curdled with fear for Quinn. Desperate, he tried to reach him, but fast as a snake, Warren jabbed Jack's side with the sharp end of the pitchfork. At first, Jack didn't understand. It felt like he'd been punched, but when he looked down, blood was blooming through the thin material of his shirt. Then everything seemed to happen at once— Edward was yelling and Cecil was trying to get past Warren, but Warren used the fork to shove them all into the bunkhouse then slid a board across the door, locking them in.

For a moment, they heard nothing over their thundering heartbeats, then there was a sharp cry of pain outside, and the boys pounded on the door, but it wouldn't budge. When Quinn's sobs grew louder, they started kicking a loose board on the wall, and Jack felt a jolt of pain in his wounded stomach every time he slammed the heel of his boot against the splintering wood. The board finally gave way, and they pulled it back so they could see outside.

It was too late. Quinn sagged, unconscious, against the pole where he'd been tied, and still Warren's buckle came down. Off to the side, the sisters held on to each other, pale with shock. Did they understand what they'd done? Did they regret any of it? *Only having fun*, they'd said. *We can do whatever we want.*

That was true. They could. But one day Jack would be able to do whatever *he* wanted. And as he watched the farmer pummel Quinn, his strikes cold, cruel, and purposeful, he clutched the wound in his side and vowed that someday he would do the same to Warren.

fourteen
WINNY

⁕

Winny pressed her cheek against the cow's bristled side, warming her face as she milked. Her fingers no longer cramped from the grip, and her rhythm was strong and confident. She'd never have thought cows would be her saviours, but the heat in the barn every morning was heavenly. It was after she finished, when she carried the full buckets of milk to the house and began her list of chores, that winter chased her down and her feet went from sharp, constricted agony to frozen numbness. Only when she finally laid her head down at night, with the sheep cuddled around her, did she feel warm again. But she could never truly rest. Not when she knew Mary was suffering elsewhere.

Every day since the Renfrews' party, Winny had wracked her brain trying to think of ways to see Mary again and to help her get away from that farm, but with all her chores and Mistress Adams watching her like a hawk much of the time, there was no way to escape. She'd never make it to the Renfrews and back without being missed. One time she'd even asked her mistress if she might go to the Renfrews on any errands, but Mistress Adams had waved her away and told her to get back to work. Winny didn't know what else to do.

Her milking done, Winny shuffled through the barn door with the buckets and made her way through the fresh snow and to the house. Mistress Adams was waiting in the doorway as if she'd been expecting her.

"I'll be right back with the eggs, Mistress," Winny said quickly, setting the milk down.

"Good," Mistress Adams said. "And then you will go to school."

Winny almost knocked over the buckets. "This morning?"

Joy buzzed through her veins at the very thought. She'd loved lessons at Barkingside, and at school she could be away from the farm, and . . . maybe Mary would be there too!

"Yes," her mistress said, matter-of-fact. "Sending you to school is a requirement on our contract with Dr. Barnardo, and since there is less for you to do here in winter, this is a convenient time for me."

"Will David be going?"

"No. He's already finished school."

Winny suddenly didn't know what to do with her hands. Part of her wanted to reach out and touch her mistress, let her see how happy this news made her, but she clenched them together instead.

"Thank you, Mistress."

"I expect you to do your very best at school." Mistress Adams's expression softened slightly as she studied Winny. "When you are no longer living here, you will need to depend on your education to do well in life, Winnifred."

Winny couldn't believe her ears. Her mistress had never said her real name. Not in front of her, anyway. "I promise I will work very hard."

"There's one more thing." Mistress Adams stepped back into the house for a moment then reappeared. "You cannot go to school in those terrible old boots. Take these."

She held out a pair of worn but solid leather boots. Stunned by the gesture, Winny wordlessly took them from her, removed her old ones, and slid her stockinged feet into the new boots. Her toes wiggled, confused by all the unexpected space.

"Thank you, Mistress," she whispered.

"I should have given them to you earlier, but money is tight. I can only do what I can."

"I'm just so grateful that you did now, Mistress."

"You'd better get going," she said brusquely, pursing her lips. "Don't make a fool of yourself at school. Listen to the teacher and mind your own business."

A half hour later, Winny started up the road toward the school, her mind racing ahead. Would Mary be there too? If she was, and if they saw each other every day, she knew Mary would get stronger, and they could work together on a real plan to get her away from Master Renfrew. Maybe, given time, Winny could even convince Mistress Adams to take Mary in. It seemed like a faraway dream, but then again, until this morning, she'd never thought she'd be going to school again. Especially in new boots. What if, one day, instead of going to school, she and Mary just ran away?

A cold, raw wind sliced across the fields, and she came to her senses. They could never run away in the winter. They'd freeze to death.

When she reached the school, she scanned the faces of the children outside, but she couldn't see Mary anywhere. A small, young woman with a practical black coat wrapped around her shoulders stepped outside the school's door and rang a shiny brass bell.

"Good morning, boys and girls," she called. "Welcome back from your Christmas holiday. Come and line up now, in rows of two."

Winny fell into line beside another girl and gave her a smile, wondering if she might manage to make a friend here. But the girl's nostrils flared as if Winny had stepped in sheep manure—which she knew she hadn't.

"You're a Home Child, aren't you?" the girl hissed, moving away. She turned to a friend, standing behind them. "I won't go to school with a stupid Home Child. The whole place stinks now that she's here."

"She's not allowed in our school," her friend agreed loudly. "She'll make us sick. We need to tell Miss Burton."

A third girl chimed in, and they formed a small semicircle around Winny. "She's a sick, disgusting orphan," she declared. "Not even her parents wanted her."

"We've got two more over here," a boy shouted up ahead.

"Home Child! Home Child! Home Child!" the children chanted, louder and louder.

Winny covered her ears, crushed by sadness and reminded of her first day at the orphanage many years ago. She'd been excited to meet new children and make friends, but the girls there had pointed and laughed cruelly at her shorn head. Back then, Mary had stepped in and set things straight, and none of the girls had ever come after Winny again. But Mary wasn't here now. How Winny wished she was. She'd always known how to handle bullies. Or at least she used to.

Winny felt a hard shove from behind, and she fell to her knees on the hard, snowy ground, landing beside two boys. Above them the other children crowded, taunting and yelling, throwing hard, icy snowballs, even kicking one fallen boy in his side. When one of the girls rubbed a handful of snow in Winny's face, she instinctively pushed her away, and the girl staggered back, cursing with words Winny had never heard before. Her friends rushed forward, and Winny curled into a ball, covering her face with her hands.

"That's enough!" Miss Burton's voice called out. "Get back in line. You should be ashamed, resorting to violence. For shame. Really, I don't know what to say."

Winny peered up through her fingers and watched Miss Burton usher the other children into the school. The two Home Boys were watching

Winny, and she offered them a cautious smile. It didn't matter that she'd never seen either of them before. In that moment, they were kin.

"You all right?" one of them asked, getting to his feet. He looked about fourteen. His nose was bleeding, and there were red splatters on his shirt.

"Yes, I think so." She pulled a rag from her pocket and offered it to him. "You're bleeding."

"Thanks. I'm Ralph," he said, wiping his face. "And this is Jim."

"I'm Winny."

"What do we do now?" Jim asked, looking at the school. "I can't go back to the farm yet."

"I dunno. I—"

"You three." Miss Burton had reappeared, and she let out an unhappy sigh as she considered them. "That was hardly the welcome I would have liked to extend to you, but I suppose it was to be expected. We're not used to having Home Children in our school, and I've never actually taught a Home Child. Tell me, have you had schooling before?"

"Yes, ma'am," Ralph said. "Dr. Barnardo's made sure we had regular lessons."

"So you can read and write?"

"Yes, ma'am," Winny replied.

"Good," Miss Burton said kindly. "You're here to learn, just like the other children. We will all work together, and over time, I hope they will learn to be more civil. I will expect good behaviour and attitude from you three just as I do from them. Of course, if there are any problems, I am obliged to tell your masters."

They nodded and followed her quietly into the school. Winny kept her eyes averted from the other children, ignoring their stares. She was here, in school, and she was determined that nothing else would take away from this day. Only after she and the two boys had taken their seats at the empty desks at the back of the classroom, far from the warmth of the stove, did she let herself look around. The three girls who had started the fight in line were sitting together on the far side of the room, casting seething looks Winny's way. Beside them sat another girl with beautiful, flaxen hair. She was facing front, so Winny couldn't see her face, but she couldn't help staring at her lovely pink dress, with its clean white lace and soft cotton sleeves. Winny could only ever dream of owning anything so pretty.

As if the girl felt Winny watching her, she turned, and Winny caught her breath.

Charlotte.

Winny almost burst from her chair, she was so happy to see her friend. The last time she'd seen Charlotte was at Barkingside, where she'd been waiting for her mother to return for her. There had never been any talk of her coming to Canada, so what a welcome surprise this was! But Charlotte was shaking her head, slow and deliberate, her baby-blue eyes wide, and that's when Winny understood. The other children didn't realize Charlotte was a Home Child. Winny gave a tiny, imperceptible nod to assure Charlotte she wouldn't let on, and she saw a hint of a smile touch her friend's face.

For most of the day, Winny stared at the back of Charlotte's head, wondering when they might have an opportunity to speak. She had trouble focusing on what Miss Burton was saying because of all the questions in her mind. How on earth had Charlotte come to be here? Had her mother never returned for her? When had she arrived in Canada? Where did she live? The family who had taken her in must be good people, because Charlotte looked healthy and immaculate.

After school, Winny dawdled in the schoolyard, hoping Charlotte would stay behind, but she left with the other girls. Winny's heart sank with disappointment as she watched them go, laughing to each other about something. Maybe they were even laughing about Winny. Maybe after all this time, Charlotte didn't want to be her friend anymore. Why would she, since she could be with all the other girls? Suppressing a shiver,

Winny started out on the road alone. She'd only walked a short way when she heard Charlotte's call.

"Winny!"

"Where are you?" Winny asked, peering around.

Charlotte popped out from behind a cluster of snow-covered bushes, her smile bright as sunshine. "Here!"

Winny raced over to her, and they hugged tight, squealing with happiness.

"I thought you'd changed your mind, that you might not want to—" Winny started.

"I pretended I forgot something at school and told the girls to go on without me," she replied. "I would never forget you, Winny. Oh, you're absolutely frozen." She unwrapped her scarf and wound it around Winny's neck. "Here," she said, holding out her muff for Winny's hands.

"Oh, I couldn't."

"It's all right. We'll take turns."

The rabbit fur was soft and warm on Winny's cold, chapped hands. She almost cried at the exquisite sensation. "I want to know everything," she said as they began to walk again. "When did you come? Are you living with good people?"

"I left a month after you. I live with a very nice family in town."

"Why, that's wonderful! You look so happy!"

Charlotte dropped her gaze, and her fingers picked at her coat. "It's not all been happy news, I'm afraid. Before I left, the Home told me my mother had died."

"Oh, I'm so sorry." She reached for Charlotte's hand and gave it a squeeze. "I know how much you loved her."

"I knew there was a reason she hadn't come. In a way, I reckon hearing she was gone made it a little easier to take. At least I knew she hadn't forgotten about me. And then I was lucky to be taken in by a lovely family."

"Tell me about them. Do they treat you well?"

"Oh yes. Mrs. Carpenter is often ill, and they couldn't have children of their own, so she decided she'd like to take in an older girl. I've become her adopted daughter as well as a helper around the house." Her eyes glistened. "They want me to call them Mum and Dad, so I do, but it still doesn't sit right with me. I mean, I know she's gone, but in my heart I still have a mum. I can't just pretend she never existed."

"Oh, Charlotte. Of course not," Winny replied gently. "But look at you now. You're being cared for by a loving family and doing so well. Your mum would understand. I know she would."

Charlotte nodded, blinking back tears. "You always knew what to say, Winny. I'll never forget how you made me feel less alone when I first arrived at Barkingside."

The girls walked on in companionable silence for a while, then Winny asked if she'd been going to school long.

"Oh, yes, since September. The Carpenters said they will send me to Toronto for nursing school when I'm eighteen if I keep my marks up."

"Nursing school! You're so lucky."

She hadn't meant to sound envious, but Charlotte's gaze was sympathetic. "I know I am, Winny. I feel guilty at how lucky I am, really. I look at you and the other Home Children, and I know I should be with you, but because of the Carpenters, I can hide among the regular people here and pretend."

"Don't feel bad, Charlotte. I'm glad at least one of us is being looked after. It's just the luck of the draw, ain't it?"

"I suppose." She glanced shyly over. "No one but the Carpenters knows I'm from Barnardo's. My new mum says I don't have to tell, and I'd rather not."

"Don't worry. I won't say a word." She passed Charlotte the muff, her hands deliciously warm for the first time in a long while.

"What about you? Tell me what is happening with you."

Winny told Charlotte everything from meeting up with the boys on the ship to the long, quiet ride to the farm. She told her about Mistress

Adams and the sheep in the barn where she slept, and she showed off her new boots. But when Charlotte asked about Mary, Winny melted into tears.

"I knew something was wrong as soon as I saw her. She talked about her master, saying the most awful things. Oh, Charlotte. I have a terrible feeling that he might have—"

"Oh no," Charlotte said, suddenly pale.

"Mary said he wouldn't leave her alone, and then I saw bruises on her neck." She squeezed her eyes shut, wishing away the memory. "I promised I would come back to her as soon as I could, but it's so hard to get away from the farm. Mistress Adams has me so busy, and now with school . . . all I can do is hope I see her again soon. It breaks my heart that I can't do anything for her."

"That's terrible. When you do see her, please tell her I send my love."

"She'll be ever so glad to hear about you. We've been wondering, you know." The road split, and Charlotte turned onto a trail Winny hadn't noticed before. The town must be in that direction, she realized. She wondered if she would ever see it.

Winny tilted her head the other way. "This is my road." She reached out and embraced Charlotte again. "I wish I could stay longer with you, but I've chores to do, and they must all be done in time for me to get some supper. If I'm late, I'll go hungry."

Charlotte's concern was all over her face. "I'll bring you something to eat so you won't have to worry next time." Then she smiled, lighting Winny's heart. "I will see you tomorrow, Winny."

"I love hearing those words," she replied.

———

True to her word, Charlotte began bringing Winny a bit of food every day, whether it was a bun, meat, or a biscuit, and she hid it in their secret spot. Once, she even left Winny a hat and mitts, her own scarf, and a warm, woollen pair of stockings. During school, Charlotte kept up her end of the charade, rarely glancing at Winny, and Winny never made any attempt to speak with her. It was difficult to be so close to her friend and not talk, but they always had their walks home together, which Winny treasured. She was still lonely, but she was no longer alone.

Winny also got along well with Ralph and Jim, who she learned had been at Stepney Causeway at the same time as Jack, Edward, and Cecil, and they told her stories about them she hadn't heard before. Talking about the boys kept them alive in her mind, and imagining them somewhere near helped Winny overlook the snide comments and insults the other classmates constantly tossed her way.

Despite their taunts, Winny began to feel almost happy at school. She loved learning, and when Miss Burton praised her accomplishments in front of the whole class, she couldn't stop smiling. Winny had finally found something she was good at, and when she thought about how far she'd had to go to find it, she was proud of herself. Like that heap of stinky old wool that had awaited her months before at the Adams farm, she had transformed, becoming something strong and useful—even praiseworthy. Thinking of that, a small dream began to take shape in her heart. Maybe someday, she might even go to nursing school herself.

As the weeks went by, she spent an increasing amount of time studying, staying up later at night just to squeeze in more. Mistress Adams didn't complain so long as she got her work done, and when Winny read ahead in her textbooks, Miss Burton brought her more.

She was sitting in the barn one evening, reading a schoolbook by the light of her lantern, when David appeared in the doorway. He rarely came to her side of the barn: they both knew it was safer to keep their distance from each other. Seeing him now gave her a sinking feeling in the pit of her stomach.

"Has something happened?" she asked.

"Mistress Renfrew was here while you were at school," he said. "She came to see her sister, and I heard them talking. I couldn't hear everything, but I'm pretty certain she was talking about your friend."

Winny sat up straight. "About Mary? What did she say?"

"She sounded angry, and she said something about 'the girl' being trouble. From the sound of her voice, I thought maybe you should know."

fifteen
JACK

ꝏ

"We gotta do something," Jack said.

It had been four days since Warren had attacked Quinn, and the boy's poor, torn skin hadn't healed. Quinn lay on his front, barely breathing, and the noxious smell of sickness rose in a cloud around him. He hadn't spoken a word since it had happened. Not even Cat could rouse a smile on his pasty face, though she nestled in as close as she could.

"Warren has to get him to a doctor." Edward was doing what he could, dabbing gently at the mess on Quinn's back with a wet rag, but it wasn't helping. It wasn't enough. "He's got to."

"He won't," Cecil said. "And don't tell me it's in the contract. So's school, and you don't see us going there neither, do ya?"

"We have to take him to one then," Jack said, his heart drumming with new purpose.

Edward glanced up. "To a doctor? How?"

"We gotta run."

The brothers stared at him, digesting what he'd said, then Cecil looked down at Quinn's back. "And go where?"

Jack took a breath, remembering his last big idea and its painful result. "Town. We might not have to go all the way, because I saw houses outside of it, and maybe someone . . ." He didn't want to sound desperate, but the truth was that there was no one they could trust, no one who wanted them here. He cleared the emotion from his throat. "We got no choice. He'll die if we stay here."

Edward dipped the rag into the bucket and squeezed a trickle over Quinn's back. "We all will."

Up until now, they had resigned themselves to serving their remaining time at Warren's farm, but after the attack on Quinn it had become alarmingly clear that Warren could actually kill them. Maybe not outright, but there were a myriad of other ways he could break them.

"How can we carry him?" Cecil asked. "He can't get up. Can't walk."

"We'll take the door off the bunkhouse and use it like a sled," Jack said, a plan growing in his mind. "We can lay all our blankets on top to keep him comfortable. Whoever's not pulling carries the trunks."

"You strong enough?" Edward asked, eyeing Jack's side.

"I'm all right," he said, though the pitchfork wound did hurt when he moved. At least his skin looked nothing like Quinn's.

Cecil's brow lifted. "So you're saying we're leaving for good."

"We have to," Edward said. "There's no coming back from this."

"We'll go tonight," Jack told them. "There'll be a good clear moon." He knew the brothers were afraid. He was too. But he was also riding a wave of conviction that he hadn't felt in some time. "It'll be all right. We survived the streets of London, and we've managed this. We can do it." His gaze went to Quinn. "We have to."

The moon was almost full, and its cold light flooded the fields. The white glare against the snow helped the boys move quickly along the road, but it also meant there was a greater risk they could be seen. The worst part of the trek was the cold. Every tattered blanket they had was layered over Quinn, and Cat did her part by curling up tight between his shoulder and his neck. Quinn and the sled were heavy, but the boys' muscles were solid, their hands calloused from work.

They'd agreed not to talk until they were a long way from the farm, but the farther they got, the more exhilarated Jack felt. He could see it in his friends' expressions as well.

"We did it," Cecil whispered. "We got out."

"He could come after us still," Jack warned quietly. "Or he could find us in town. We have to be watching."

"Thank you," Quinn said, soft as fresh snow. He hadn't said anything for days, and the sound of his voice brought tears to Jack's eyes.

"Never you mind," Edward told him gently.

"That's what friends do for one another," Jack said.

Quinn's eyes cracked open, and Jack saw the corner of his mouth lift in his lazy half smile. "Friends," he murmured, then he sank back to sleep.

After a while, they caught sight of a few scattered houses, and though it was late, they spotted a candle in one window. What were the chances the person behind that glass might be willing to help?

"Take Quinn down to the ditch there," Jack said. "I'll go to the door, see what's what."

Cecil squinted at the house. "I don't like you going alone."

"They won't want a crowd at their doorstep," Edward replied, jaw set. "But neither of you is going. I can run faster than both of you."

Their eyes followed Edward as he crossed the road and approached the house. He hesitated at the door, his hand poised to knock, and moments later it opened. Jack couldn't see who was behind it, and Cecil crouched beside him in the ditch like he was on springs. He'd be on the doorstep quick as lightning, defending his brother if anything went wrong.

"What's he saying?" Cecil whispered.

"I don't know, but he ain't been chased off."

The longer Edward stood there talking, the more Jack dared to hope.

"It's all right, lads!" Edward called across to them. "Bring him over!"

When an elderly couple stepped outside to greet them, Jack nearly wept to see the kindness shining in their eyes. After going so long without seeing a friendly face, he almost hugged them both, the little boy inside him craving their goodness. But he wasn't a little boy anymore, and he never would be again. Out of habit, he forced the need back, behind the wall he'd built in his heart.

"Welcome," the man said. He was stooped and grey, but when he noticed Quinn's covered body, he moved quickly to the side. "Bring him inside."

"Come in, come in, let's get you warm," the woman agreed.

Jack felt a quiet thrill, hearing their British accents. It wasn't the same as the boys' Cockney, but it sounded a lot more like home than anything else had in a long time. They followed the woman upstairs to a room, where they carefully unloaded Quinn onto a bed then folded back their tattered blankets. Her husband leaned in close and studied Quinn's back.

"He's a doctor," Edward whispered to Jack.

Jack blinked. "He's *what*?"

"Yes, dear," the woman said sweetly. "You've come to the right house, haven't you? I am Mrs. Cogan, and this is my husband, Dr. Cogan. You're very welcome here."

"This boy's been beaten badly," the doctor said, his voice grave, then his gaze went to Jack's side. "You're hurt as well."

"I'm all right, sir."

"Let me see, lad. I'll tell you if you're all right."

Jack lifted his shirt, watching the doctor's expression. He felt the man's warm fingers press around the hole in his side, and he held his breath so he wouldn't make a sound.

"What's this from?" Dr. Cogan asked.

"A pitchfork," Edward answered for him, his tone bitter.

"Who did this to you boys?" Mrs. Cogan asked softly. "Where is it you've been living?"

Jack met his friends' eyes. Should they tell? What if she reacted like the policeman had and defended Warren at their expense?

"Your wound is clean. It'll heal over time." Dr. Cogan let Jack's shirt fall back into place and looked him in the eye. "Whoever it was who did this, we will not tell him you are here. You have our word."

Edward nodded at Jack.

"We're Farmer Warren's Home Boys," he said.

Mrs. Cogan lifted a soft hand and placed it on Jack's cheek. "You poor, poor lads. I can't imagine."

He drew away, tears springing to his eyes at the simple gesture.

She smiled sadly. "We don't know Mr. Warren personally, but if he did this, he shouldn't be trusted with a dog, let alone a child. You did the right thing coming here. My husband will do what he can for your friend, and I will do what I can for you. Come with me. Let me get you something to eat and then we shall figure out the next step."

After she'd gone downstairs, the three of them stood in the corridor outside of Quinn's room, and Jack felt his friends' uncertainty as if it were his own. Quinn was as safe as he could be here, and they were out of Warren's reach for now. He wanted to believe he could trust the Cogans, to feel certain that Warren wouldn't come for them, but trust was a difficult thing to come by. But if these people were genuine, what then?

For the first time, Jack dared to think about the future.

sixteen

WINNY

❧

Winny pulled her scarf as high as she could, her teeth chattering against the wind. In the school, the stove would be burning, and Miss Burton would have the students pull their desks closer to it to keep warm. Winny could have been there as well, but today she was not going to school. She was going to see Mary. After what David had told her the night before, Winny couldn't wait another day. Heart pounding, she'd headed out for school as usual that morning, but as soon as she knew Mistress Adams wasn't watching, she turned the opposite direction and ran as fast as she could. Now she only hoped she would remember the way to the Renfrews' and be able to find it through the blizzard. If all went well, she'd be home at the usual time, and Mistress Adams need never know she'd gone.

With the wind and the added burden of a fresh blanket of snow from the night before, Winny's walk to the Renfrews' took almost three hours, and by the time she arrived at the farm, she felt frozen to the bone. But she couldn't stop now. She'd come all that way for a purpose, and she moved swiftly toward the hut in the woods where Mary had said she lived.

"Mary," she said, knocking on the door. "Are you in there?"

When there was no reply, she gripped the door handle and pulled, but it wouldn't budge. A ripple of concern shivered through her, and she circled the building, searching for a window. There was none. She returned to the door and pounded on it this time, glancing nervously over her shoulder at the farmhouse, fearing Mistress or Master Renfrew might hear her.

"Mary, if you're in there, open the door. It's me, Winny."

The wind was the only response.

Where was she? Winny's mind painted the most awful pictures—what if Master Renfrew had beaten her badly enough that she'd had to go to the hospital? Could they have sent her back to Barnardo's? Or to another farm? That would be good for Mary, but how would Winny ever find her?

There was only one way to find out the truth. Holding tight to what courage she had, Winny bowed her head against the cutting wind and made her way back up the hill, to the main house. At her knock, Mistress Renfrew opened the door, a puzzled look on her face. Behind her the house glowed a warm gold, and Winny smelled what she thought was beef soup.

"I'm sorry to bother you, Mistress," Winny said, pulling her scarf down.

"Why, you're my sister's Home Girl! What are you doing here? Is everything all right with Florence?"

Winny blinked, then realized that was her mistress's name. "Yes, she's fine. I'm . . . I'm looking for your Home Girl, Mary."

"Does my sister know where you are?"

"No. It's only, I need to see Mary—"

Mistress Renfrew narrowed her eyes. "She'll be gone for a while now."

"For a while? When is she coming back?"

"In the spring."

Winny felt as if she'd been slapped. "The . . . the spring, Mistress? I don't understand. Why?"

"I should have known," Mistress Renfrew said, folding her arms. "I never should have said yes to this scheme all over again. Boys are one thing. At least they're useful. But letting a cheap piece of garbage like that into my farm—"

"What happened?" Winny cried. "Where is she?"

The woman leaned forward, her round, judging face so close to Winny's she could feel her hot breath. "Listen, girl. Your friend is a whore. Just like all your mothers. Got herself pregnant with one of those Home Boys, and I won't have that."

Pregnant. The news hit Winny like a kick to the stomach, and for a moment, she couldn't breathe.

"That can't be true," she stammered. Mary hadn't mentioned any Home Boys when she'd seen her before, and as far as Winny knew she'd never been interested in anyone but Edward.

"It's not me who's a liar," Mistress Renfrew replied. "Now get out of here before my sister starts wondering where her own little slut has run off to."

And with that, she stepped back into her warm house and slammed the door, leaving Winny open-mouthed in the cold.

All the way back to the Adams farm, Mary's words rang in Winny's ears. *He comes after me something bad.* No Home Boy had done this, Winny was convinced. It was Master Renfrew. She knew it to the bottom of her soul. David had warned her about him, saying how he liked pretty women, saying he wouldn't take no for an answer. Winny already knew he had beaten Mary, and now she was certain he had done more.

At her first sight of the Adams house, Winny broke into a run and didn't stop until she reached the sheep barn, where she collapsed in the straw, sobbing. Where was Mary now? In a strange place, alone and pregnant with her master's child? Winny had never felt so helpless in her life.

"Winny? Is that you?" David asked, coming into the barn. "You're home early."

Winny turned to face him, hot tears rolling down her face.

He was instantly at her side. "What's happened?"

"It's Mary," she said. "She . . . She—"

She couldn't force the words past the swelling in her throat. He knelt and wrapped his arms around her, and though his coat was covered in ice, she buried herself in it. When she could breathe again, she pulled away and wiped her face with shaking hands.

"After you said you'd heard Mistress Renfrew talking about Mary, I went to see her instead of going to school. I had to. But she wouldn't come to the door, so I went to the house, and . . . and she's . . . she's gone! Mistress Renfrew says she's . . ." Her breath caught. "She says she's gone to have a baby."

He closed his eyes. "I'm so sorry, Winny."

"I knew something was wrong when I saw her, but I . . . I never thought she might be pregnant, and now they've sent her away, and she's on her own somewhere, and I can't get to her—"

"Anywhere away from that farm is the best place for her," David assured her. "No one can hurt her now."

"But if only I'd known! Maybe I could have—"

"You couldn't have done anything, Winny. You couldn't have stopped it. Master Renfrew always gets his way."

"Mary told me he wouldn't leave her alone."

"What's going on here?" a terse voice demanded from the doorway.

At the sight of Mistress Adams, Winny and David shifted farther apart from each other. Winny held her breath as she strode toward them.

"You're supposed to be in school, not out here, luring the Home Boy." Her eyes burned. "I let you go to school. I feed you. I gave you boots. And now I find you hiding out here doing absolutely nothing." She took a step closer and glared pointedly at David. "Or perhaps *worse* than nothing."

"It's not what you think, Mistress," David said, his voice solid.

"How *dare* you talk back—"

"It's about your sister."

"What about her?"

"Tell her, Winny."

Winny didn't know where to start. Just looking at Mistress Adams had her trembling, and she worried at a hangnail, drawing blood. "My friend Mary works for your sister. She's her Home Girl."

A wave of disgust crossed Mistress Adams's face. "Yes, I know about her. She's got herself into some trouble, hasn't she? What has this got to do with Doreen?"

From her expression, her mistress obviously considered Mary to be a whore too. Of course she would. She'd have heard the whole story from her sister already. How could Winny convince her?

"Spit it out, girl. I don't have all day."

Mary's face appeared in her mind, and Winny suddenly knew the only way she could help her was to speak the truth. "It wasn't a Home Boy that got her pregnant," she said. "She wasn't whoring around. It was Master Renfrew. He did it."

Winny squeezed her eyes shut, bracing for a blow, but none came. When she looked again, her mistress was staring at her. Her face was very pale.

"I will insist that you not say anything about this incident to anyone else."

What did that mean? Who would she tell? Besides, from what David had said, telling anyone wouldn't make any difference. Master Renfrew would get away with it anyway.

"I wouldn't think of it," Winny replied.

Without another word, Mistress Adams turned and walked back outside, into the blustery dusk. It wasn't until later that evening that Winny realized her mistress hadn't disagreed with what she had said.

The next morning, as Winny was doing her chores, she heard the truck start up, and she peered out of the barn in time to see Mistress

Adams driving away. David stood outside the door, leaning on a shovel and watching the truck.

"Where's she off to?" she asked.

"The Renfrews," he said, offering Winny a hopeful smile. "Maybe she listened to you."

JACK

❧

s there anything else I can get for you boys? More tea?" Mrs. Cogan asked.

While her husband was upstairs concentrating on Quinn, she had set a table in the living room with a delicate tea service, cheese, and biscuits despite the late hour. The room was plain but comforting, its simple rose wallpaper complemented by two green velvet armchairs, a small sofa, and three little tables. The heat from the fireplace felt like an embrace.

"No, thank you, ma'am," Jack said, though he was certain the three of them could eat twice what they'd already had. "But thank you for everything. We've not eaten this well in ages."

"Actually," Cecil said, glancing sideways at Jack, "I'd love another cup of tea, maybe another biscuit?"

"Surely," Mrs. Cogan replied sweetly. "I'll just get us a little more. We haven't a lot these days, but what we have, we're happy to share."

As she disappeared into the kitchen, the boys looked wordlessly at each other. It had been so long since anyone had helped them that this moment almost felt like an illusion.

"Does this belong to anyone, or do we have a stowaway?" Dr. Cogan asked, emerging from the stairway. A small grey bundle peeked out from inside his hands. "She seemed quite comfortable in among the blankets."

Cecil stood and held out his hands. "Oh, she's Quinn's. Her name's Cat."

"A good name, that."

The doctor set Cat in his arms, but she immediately leapt free and began investigating the warm room, her pink nose touching every surface with interest. Cecil offered the doctor his chair and went to stand by the fire, then they all waited in silence until Mrs. Cogan returned with a fresh tray. Once she had sat down herself, everyone's attention went to the doctor.

"I should say up front that I cannot make any promises for your friend's recovery. He has a bad infection and is in grave condition," he said solemnly. "You must understand that. I've given him something for the pain, and I have cleaned the wounds. I'll do all I can, but I must admit I am not feeling optimistic."

Jack had known Quinn was in bad shape, but it still hurt to hear it. He didn't need to look at the brothers to know they were feeling the same way. Silently, he cursed Warren and his daughters, then he cursed himself for not having done something to stop the beating.

"Let's hear about you," Dr. Cogan said, his voice a low, easy rumble. "Where are you lads from? How long have you been here?"

"London," Jack said. "London, *England*, I mean. We came this past June."

"We both grew up outside London," Mrs. Cogan said. "We moved here many years back. It's nice to hear a familiar accent."

"It's nice to have proper tea again," Cecil said, leaning in for another biscuit.

Dr. Cogan smiled kindly, then he tilted his head toward Jack. "From what I have heard, your indenture is until the age of eighteen, correct? And how old are you?"

"Seventeen, sir, and so is Edward." He held out a hand. "Cecil is Edward's brother. He's the runt, you might say."

"I'm sixteen," Cecil explained wryly.

"Quinn's sixteen as well," Edward put in.

"So you've a year or so to work off the payments owed to you."

Mrs. Cogan put her hand on her husband's arm. "You can't think to send them back to that awful man."

"Not at all. But these things must be done properly. I shall contact Barnardo's this week and inform them of what happened. They, I assume, will want to speak with Mr. Warren. And after what I've seen, I imagine the authorities will be called in." He paused. "Do you have an education?"

"Yes, sir," Jack said eagerly. "In England. We can read and write and all, and we've been trained for all kinds of trades. Metalwork, carpentry, the like. Warren was supposed to send us to school out here, but he never did."

"You're smart lads. I can tell," Mrs. Cogan said. "And what do you plan to do when you are done with your indenture?"

"I must find my sister. After that, I've no idea."

Edward gave a small shrug. "I don't suppose it matters much what we do. We just want to make an honest living, and maybe not have to look over our shoulders all the time. A bloke does get tired of that after a while."

"I can imagine he would." Dr. Cogan tapped his chin. "I know of a few men who would be happy to employ a couple of strapping young lads such as yourselves. I do have some influence in this town that I should be glad to finally use, though if you're inclined to work around this place, we'd pay you for that. Whatever you decide, I shall make sure it's done right with Barnardo's, then you'll have nothing to fear."

"In the meantime, you're welcome to live here," Mrs. Cogan said. "We've a couple of spare bedrooms since our children moved out long ago. Your friend Quinn is in one of them now."

"We're happy to sleep in the barn, ma'am," Jack said.

"Nonsense. Whatever for, when there's room inside?"

The boys exchanged a glance. "We assumed, us being who we are, you'd rather us sleep out there is all," Edward said.

Mrs. Cogan frowned, confused. "Who you are?"

"Home Children," Jack quietly reminded her.

There was an awkward pause while Mrs. Cogan waited for further explanation, but they didn't offer one.

"The barn is for animals," she said reasonably, "and it's far too cold for you lads out there. No, no. You'll sleep in comfort while you're here."

Jack dropped his chin to his chest, dangerously close to tears, and Cecil and Edward did the same. After a moment he looked up again, his heart shining in his eyes. "We can't thank you enough for taking us in. You don't know what this means to us." His voice cracked. "You really don't."

"We're only sorry you've been through this," Mrs. Cogan said. "Such a shame. The government had no right to interfere in your lives."

"To be honest, ma'am, I don't think it were done out of malice," Edward said. "The truth is, what they say about us was mostly true back in England. London's so crowded there's no room to breathe, and we was dirty, ragged waifs living off what we could steal. Somebody had to figure out what to do with us. As much as we hated it, the orphanage and Barnardo's fed us and took care of us, but they ran out of room. By sending us over here we reckon they thought they was doing the right thing for everyone. London gets cleaned up, the farmers here get help, and we get to live a better life."

"It's just that they forgot about us once we got here," Jack said. "I think that's the easiest way to explain it. There were too many of us to keep watch over."

Dr. Cogan clicked his tongue. "The papers say there are thousands of children like you being sent out here."

"I don't reckon everyone ended up like we did," Edward said. "We were supposed to have a good life out here."

Cecil snorted. "Maybe some did, but we didn't."

"Have you seen any other Home Children?" Jack asked, always hoping for news.

"No, dear," Mrs. Cogan replied, getting to her feet and reaching for the dishes. "You're the first."

Jack nodded, his heart sinking. He was starting to lose hope that he would ever find the girls.

"You boys must be tired," she said. "Let me show you your room, and we can talk more in the morning."

When they reached the top of the stairs, Jack paused outside Quinn's door. He couldn't stand the thought of their friend waking up to an empty room, thinking he'd been forgotten.

"I'll come in a little while," he told the others. "I think I'll sit with Quinn for a bit."

He opened the door and Cat slid in ahead of him, leaping onto the bed and curling up by Quinn's shoulder. The air in the room was still and heavy with the smell of sickness, and a terrible sadness washed over Jack. Just days ago, they'd been working side by side on the barn, Quinn smiling placidly as he hammered in boards. Now he lay on his stomach, his shredded back exposed, his shallow breaths filling the room. Since coming to the Cogans' home, it seemed the boys finally stood a chance of having a better life, and he couldn't bear to think that Quinn might not be around to share that with them.

He pulled a chair toward the bed. "Hey, Quinn. Cat told me you might want a little company. Exciting day today, huh? You ever been on a sled before?" His smile slipped. "I wish you could wake up and see where we are. These are some real nice folks, and I know you'd like Mrs. Cogan's biscuits. Best things I ever tasted. I was lucky to get any, though. I thought Cecil might eat every one of them before I got a chance."

Jack didn't expect a response, but it felt better to speak out loud. The silence was too much. He stood, then he walked to the window and peered out at the white world beyond. What a big, big world. Where would they go from here?

"Jack."

He turned. Quinn blinked slowly up at him.

"Hey, Quinn," he said gently, resuming his seat. "You're safe here."

"Where are we?"

"Can you believe we found you a doctor? We're in his house, and you, mate, are lying on an actual bed. No more wooden shelf for you. Cat's right here."

Quinn's cheek lifted slightly in a smile.

"She wouldn't leave you."

"Take care of her, Jack. When I'm gone."

He was surprised. He hadn't thought Quinn understood what was happening to him, but maybe he did.

"I will, if she'll let me." Cat had never shown any interest in being with any of the other boys. "She don't like us much."

Quinn's eyes closed, and Jack wondered if he'd gone back to sleep, but a moment later he was staring at Jack again. "I'm scared, Jack."

Jack's throat jammed with emotion. "It's okay," he said, trying to keep his voice level. "You don't need to be scared. I'm right here. And the doctor will help you."

A tear rolled across the bridge of Quinn's nose. "You were my first mates," he said. "My only mates."

"You're a good friend, Quinn. A good man."

"Good man." He sighed. "I hope you find Mary and Winny."

There was no stopping Jack's tears now. Quinn had never met the girls, but now Jack knew he'd listened in the dark to his stories. "I hope so too."

He heard a thump from the room next to Quinn's, and Jack imagined the brothers getting into bed, lying beneath warm quilts. He leaned back in his chair and folded his arms, stretching his legs in front to be more comfortable. Wasn't it ironic how Warren's cruelty had chased them here, to this peaceful place? His farm had been the worst place in the world . . . and yet Jack would go back without so much as a whimper if only Quinn could get better.

He jerked awake a little while later when he almost fell off his chair.

"Don't fall," Quinn said. His voice was thinner than before. "Go to bed, Jack."

Jack shook his head. "I'm not leaving you."

Quinn's deep brown gaze held fast, though his lids looked impossibly heavy. "Thank you, Jack. For being my friend."

He closed his eyes, and Jack held his breath as Quinn's back rose and fell for the final time. His face softened, and the gentle curl of his lip returned now that the pain was gone.

No, Jack thought. He stared at Quinn, wondering how many times a heart could break before it finally stopped beating. *No, Quinn*, he thought. *Thank you.*

As Jack wiped away his tears, his mind returned to Warren, and he felt a shift within his chest. It was a tightening, a hardening of sorts, as if his heart had sealed itself back together. Warren had killed Quinn, the sweetest, most innocent boy Jack had ever known. Someday, Warren would pay for what he had done. Jack would see to that.

———

The Cogans were kind and understanding, and they gave the boys space to grieve in their own way. They promised that as soon as the ground was soft enough they would bury Quinn in the churchyard where they went each Sunday. In the meantime, Dr. Cogan wrote to Barnardo's and told them not only about the boys' abuse and subsequent escape, but also about Quinn's death. In the letter, he stressed that Warren must never be told where the boys were now living. Then they waited for a response. Jack could only imagine how furious Warren must be, and the thought made him smile.

Despite the tragedy, the Cogans were pleased to have the boys in their home, and they made sure they were warm and fed. In return, the boys made themselves useful, working hard around the house and yard, fixing things that had fallen into disrepair, adding to the woodpile, taking care of the animals in the barn. Cecil fell naturally into the farm work, and the other two let him take charge.

Edward had other interests. Over supper one night, he mentioned to Dr. Cogan that he was interested in learning more about medicine. Dr. Cogan patted his mouth with his napkin and smiled.

"Is that right? Come along with me on my rounds tomorrow, if you'd like. See if it is something that appeals. The world can always use a man of science."

Later Edward told the boys what it had been like for him to accompany the doctor as he identified and treated people's complaints. "He just seems to know," he said, obviously impressed. "They would tell him what ailed them, and he'd ask questions, and from their answers he'd know just what to do most of the time. It was like doing puzzles, except he was helping people."

"You gonna do more of it?" his brother asked.

Edward's eyes danced. "I think so. I really enjoyed it."

Pleased to have an eager pupil, Dr. Cogan provided Edward with thick, heavy books which he read well into the night. Jack peered over his shoulder a couple of times, curious about some drawings he'd seen on the pages, but after Edward described what they depicted, he kept his gaze elsewhere. Some things weren't meant to be seen. Not by him, anyway.

Two weeks passed before they heard back from Barnardo's. The letter said they were sending a man out to speak with the boys and Farmer Warren separately, to get both sides of the story. The night before the inspector was due to arrive, the boys stayed up late, arguing about what to say to him. All of them wanted justice, and not only for Quinn. But it was complicated.

Just thinking about what that man had done made Jack want to hit something. "He should hang," he said quietly.

"I agree," Edward said. "But Dr. Cogan says we mustn't call it murder."

"But it was!" Cecil cried.

"It would be Warren's word against ours," Edward said. "And you remember what that policeman said to Jack about Warren. About what a model citizen he was."

Edward was right, and they all knew it. No one would side with Home Boys. As much as Jack wanted revenge for Quinn, that would have to wait. If Warren was declared innocent, there was a good chance the boys would be sent right back to where it had all happened. No, they needed to get out of Warren's clutches, and that meant giving the inspector the bare facts, telling him how they'd been starved and beaten and treated worse than dogs. The specific details about Quinn's death would have to remain vague.

Barnardo's designated inspector for the area was Mr. Brown, the man from the train station so many months before. Today he wore a jacket and tie under his overcoat. Jack liked that. It showed a certain amount of respect for their situation.

Dr. Cogan brought the inspector into the living room and they all took a seat. Mr. Brown pulled out a small notebook and a pencil.

"The boys have been ever so helpful since they've come here," Mrs. Cogan said, setting down a tray of tea. "We're just too old to run this place on our own."

Mr. Brown nodded. "I'm glad they've made themselves of use. We at Barnardo's are very proud of our boys." He turned to Jack and the brothers. "Now I understand you'd like to lodge a complaint against your master, Mr. Warren. Would you tell me the details from your standpoint?"

From your standpoint. Jack didn't like the sound of that. "Farmer Warren," he said, wondering how on earth to be civil about it, "is—"

"He's a monster," Cecil finished for him. "Me and the lads have grown up in a lot of different places, and we're used to gettin' beat on, but before we came here there was usually a reason for it."

Edward nodded beside him.

"You're saying Mr. Warren's attacks were unprovoked?"

"Yeah," Cecil said. "Unprovoked is right. Unprovoked and—"

"Excessive," Edward said.

Mr. Brown looked at Jack. "Would you say the same?"

Jack took a deep breath. "Yeah. If you drop an egg, you're not sup-posed to get your head punched in or cow dung spread in your face. If you answer a question the wrong way, you're not supposed to get whipped so bad you can't sit for two days." He glanced at the others. "If you talk to a girl, you shouldn't get knocked down to the point where you'll never get up again."

Mr. Brown didn't move for a moment, and Jack wished he could read past the man's thick round spectacles. Could he guess from their tone what had happened? Did he understand why they couldn't say anything more about Quinn's death?

"It was terribly sad news to hear about your friend. I am very sorry for your loss," Mr. Brown said eventually. "Is there anything in particular that happened that you would like to report? Anything that explains why, after all these months, you all decided to run away on the night in question?"

The words were on the tip of Jack's tongue, but Edward spoke first.

"No, sir. I think you could safely say that we'd had enough of Master Warren's abuse. Also, we needed to get Quinn to a doctor, and Master Warren wouldn't do anything to help him. The truth is, sir, we're just sorry we didn't run sooner."

Mr. Brown wrote something in his notebook, then he removed his spectacles and pinched the top of his nose. "I'm afraid I cannot do much without specific complaints. I can record that there was abuse or neglect, but without an actual charge there is little more I can do."

Warren would get away with this, Jack thought bitterly. And with-out a charge, did that mean the three of them would be returned to his farm? Jack ground his teeth, swearing that would never happen. If they were sent back, he and the brothers would run again. They'd never stop running.

Dr. Cogan cleared his throat. "Jack, would you please stand up?"

Confused, Jack got to his feet.

"I have a particular charge. Pardon me, Jack." The doctor lifted up the bottom of Jack's shirt, revealing the ugly evidence of Warren's pitchfork, still healing. "I believe stabbing an unarmed boy with a pitchfork warrants serious attention, don't you, Mr. Brown?"

The inspector paled. "Yes," he said. "I see now. You boys will not be returned to Farmer Warren, and I will file a report." He flipped through his book, frowning at the names. "There are other farms still waiting for a Home Boy—"

"We'd like all three of them to stay here," Mrs. Cogan said.

Her husband agreed. They'd already completely outfitted the boys in their sons' old clothes and were paying each boy eight dollars a week for working. Their room and board was free.

Seeing there was little left for him to say, Mr. Brown closed his book and got to his feet. "I'm very sorry you've had to go through this, boys," he said, meeting each of their gazes. "We try our best, but sometimes that's not enough." He looked at the Cogans. "But I'd say you've been very fortunate, finding good people like this."

It wasn't an apology, but Jack could see the sincerity in his expression. "Sir," he said, mustering his courage one last time, "I wonder if you might do me a kindness, seeing as you are the inspector for this area."

"Quite possibly. What is it you'd like, son?"

"I'm looking for my sister and her friend."

———

Jack watched with apprehension as Dr. Cogan slid a knife through the envelope and pulled out a folded piece of paper. Here, at last, was Mr. Brown's report. The boys crowded around the kitchen table as the doctor read the letter out loud. When he neared the end, he leaned back in his chair and regarded the boys.

"Barnardo's has decided to fine Mr. Warren for negligence," he told them. "No charges are being laid."

"That's it?" Cecil asked. "A fine?"

Hardly an eye for an eye, Jack thought, his blood simmering. Warren would pay a hundred dollars to Barnardo's as Quinn slowly turned to fertilizer beneath the dirt.

"What of my sister?" Jack asked. "Have they found her?"

Dr. Cogan flipped the paper over then checked the envelope for another, but Jack knew the answer before he spoke.

"They've said nothing of the girls, I'm afraid. I imagine they'll keep looking and let us know. You'll have to make do with that."

Jack reached for another piece of paper and began to write back to Mr. Brown, detailing both girls' full names and histories as well as anything else he could think of.

"No, sir," he said. "I can't make do. Not anymore. Not when it's about Mary."

eighteen
WINNY

❧

— 1937 —

Winny was up to her elbows in mud. Spring was a pretty time to live on a farm, but it also meant endless, dirty work. As the fields beyond sprouted with corn and wheat, Winny tended the smaller vegetable garden—a chore she'd come to love. Seeding, weeding, and harvesting gave her a feeling of accomplishment like she'd never known before. She was digging rows and dropping in seeds when Mistress Adams's shadow fell over her.

"Your friend is back at my sister's home," she said.

Winny jumped to her feet. "Is she all right?"

"My understanding is that she is well." Mistress Adams scanned the fields. "As luck would have it, I have to go and visit my sister today. You may ride with me after you're done planting here."

Without thinking, Winny grabbed her hand, remembering the mud on her own too late. "Thank you, thank you, Mistress. You are very kind."

To her surprise, Mistress Adams said nothing about the dirt, only wiped her hand on her apron and walked back to the house. Her heart racing with anticipation, Winny finished the garden as fast as she could, and soon she was sitting in the front seat of her mistress's truck, bumping along the pitted road toward the Renfrews' farm. The closer they got, the more her thoughts filled with Mary. Was she really all right? Would the baby be with her?

"I'll be in the house with my sister," Mistress Adams told her when they arrived. "You may go and see your friend, and I will come for you when I am ready to go."

"Yes, Mistress."

As soon as the door closed behind her, Winny sprinted down the slope toward the little shed where Mary lived. It felt like another lifetime when she'd last been here, rushing around the frozen hut, searching in vain, but today would not end that way. She knew for certain that Mary was here. When she reached the bottom of the hill she spotted her, standing just outside the hut.

"Mary!"

Mary spun toward her, and Winny could have cried with joy. Mary's eyes were still shadowed with fatigue, but there was a light within. She stood straight, not cowering as before, and as she got closer, Winny saw no bruises.

"Winny," Mary breathed, wrapping her arms around her as if she were hanging on for dear life.

Winny blinked back tears, slightly unsettled to feel the soft cushion of Mary's still-swollen belly against her own thin frame. "Mary, I—" She didn't know where to begin. "Are you all right?"

Mary stepped back, her eyes lowered with shame. "You know what happened?"

"What he did to you was never your fault. You know that, don't you?"

"They call us sluts, Winny. They call us whores. Maybe that's all we are."

"No, we're not. We never were. Oh, Mary, you know that."

All at once the tight lines in Mary's face melted away, and she gave Winny the most beautiful smile. "It doesn't matter now. None of it does," she said. "Winny, you changed everything for me. I don't know how you made them believe you, but because of whatever you said, Master Renfrew has left me alone since I've been back, and my mistress promises he won't bother me again. I thought I was lost. I thought there was nothing anyone could do, but you saved me. Thank you."

"You know I would do anything for you, Mary. I only wish . . ."

The unspoken words hung in the air between them, then Mary turned away. "Come inside," she said softly.

Winny entered the tiny, dark hut where her friend had lived by herself for so long, and she ached at the emptiness within. The walls were bare, the furnishings primitive, and yet Mary had set her bed as neatly as if she'd still been at Barkingside. That's when Winny noticed Mary's trunk, mostly hidden beneath her cot, and she assumed everything Mary owned was in there.

But Winny saw no baby clothes, no crib. There was no sign of an infant.

"Where's your baby?"

Mary's hands went to her stomach. "Can you believe it, Winny? That I had a baby? It's still a wonder to me." She sank onto her cot, and Winny sat beside her, fascinated by the sudden tenderness in her voice. "When he was inside me, everything felt so different. Even with Master Renfrew about, I felt like I had something to live for as long as I had my baby. I knew he was going to be a boy, Winny. I knew it all along. My little son."

As Mary spoke, her expression changed, the dark places filling with light. "I felt him move, Winny. It was the most magical thing, knowing he was in there, growing, and I was the one person in the world who could keep him safe. I touched his little elbow and foot when it pressed inside me. I sang to him, and I talked to him every night. He was all I had in the whole world." Her gaze dimmed slightly, and her hands moved to her knees. "He gave me hope."

Winny was afraid to break the spell, but the question had to be asked. "Where is he now?"

Mary took a deep, shuddering breath and stared straight ahead, somewhere beyond the rough, grey wall of her hut. "I never really saw him. The nurse called me an unfit mother. The minute he was born, she wrapped him up and took him away, and all I could see was a glimpse of black hair sticking out from inside the blanket. I heard him crying in her arms." The broken sob that escaped her throat was like nothing Winny had ever heard. "Not *my* arms, but *hers*. How could I be an unfit mother, Winny, when I never even got to touch my baby? He was mine, and they took him away from me."

Winny was crying before Mary had finished speaking. She didn't know what to say, didn't know how to comfort her. She wrapped her arms around Mary, and they wept together until they could hardly breathe.

"I sit here day after day," Mary gasped through her sobs, "night after night, needing my baby, but I shall never see him. He was mine—as much as he was that monster's—and I feel broken without him. And now his life is ruined as well as mine."

"Why? Why is his life ruined? Surely they will take care of him, wherever he is."

"Because he's a bastard!" she exclaimed. "Think about it, Winny! No one will want anything to do with a Home Girl's bastard baby. Nobody will ever want my son but me."

Winny had seen far too many orphans in her lifetime. She knew Mary was right.

"What does your mistress say about the baby?" she asked carefully. "Will she not let you keep him here?"

"Of course not. She wouldn't want any sort of reminder of her husband's indiscretions, would she? Oh, I know that I should be thankful that she's been kind to me in other ways since then—she brings me my food now and has given me a lock for my door. But she tells me I must forget my baby and move on with my life. She doesn't understand." Her eyes filled with fresh tears. "How can she say that? How can she think I could ever forget him?"

Winny couldn't imagine a way that she or anyone else could ease Mary's pain, and her helplessness made her feel even worse. Then she thought of the light that had come on in Mary's eyes when she'd first spoken of the baby, of the hope that unborn child had given her. Winny could give her hope. She reached for Mary's hand and held it between hers.

"You and I will find him when we're free. We'll find him, and we'll find Jack and the others as well," she told her. "We'll raise him together, like a family."

"Do you promise?" Mary whispered, her eyes gleaming with urgency.

"I promise."

Something eased in her expression, and Winny caught a glimpse of the old Mary. The stronger, more confident Mary she'd known so well.

Just then the door opened, and Mistress Adams stood in the doorway. She looked from Winny to Mary. "You are Mary, I presume."

"Yes, Mistress."

Mistress Adams took in the room, her jaw tight. "I am sorry for your situation, and I hope it has improved of late." Then she turned to Winny. "It's time to say goodbye. I'll be waiting in the truck."

As her mistress left, Winny pulled Mary into her arms. "I will come back soon. I promise. Oh, Mary. I love you so much."

"I love you too, Winny. You're the best friend anyone could have."

Winny gazed into Mary's eyes, searching for the strength she'd seen before. "Will you be all right?"

Mary didn't look away. "I think so. I'm safe, and I've been shown kindness. Knowing you are near makes it easier as well. And now, because of you, I have a dream. That will keep me going."

———

On the drive back to the farm, Winny was quiet, her mind running over everything Mary had said. She was exhausted by all the emotions they'd just shared, but she breathed more easily. Mary wasn't as strong as she'd once been, but she was still a fighter. A fighter with scars. She would survive this.

"Mistress," Winny said quietly. "I need to thank you for whatever you said to your sister when I first told you what had happened. Mary is so much better now."

Mistress Adams nodded, her eyes straight ahead. "I did it for my sister. Her reputation rests on her husband's. I merely reminded her of that."

"Thank you just the same," Winny said.

"Your friend—" She hesitated, then her voice dropped. "She's just a girl. Of course I knew that, but I suppose I understood better when I saw her today. I am very sorry about what has happened to her. No one deserves that."

They drove without speaking for a while, then Mistress Adams broke the silence. "How did you meet your friend?"

Winny was taken aback by the question. She had lived here for almost a year, and Mistress Adams had never asked her anything about her life before the farm. "We met a long time ago in London. She's like a sister to me."

"Do you have any actual sisters or brothers?"

"I have four brothers, but I've no idea where they are. Or my mum."

"You don't know where your mum is?"

"No, Mistress. She sent me into the street because she couldn't afford to feed me, and her new husband didn't like me. That's when I met Mary."

Mistress Adams glanced at Winny then, her brow knitted with concern. "That must have been difficult for both you and your mother."

"I like to think she didn't have a choice. It was hard to make a living in England."

"That's how it is here, too. The Depression wiped out many of the farms, and there are no jobs in the cities. It has been a terrible challenge to keep afloat, but I can't imagine being so desperate I would have to send my children away."

Winny studied the passing fields, not sure how to respond.

"I suppose you are aware that I have four daughters," Mistress Adams said after a moment. "Things are not always easy between mothers and daughters, but I do miss them now that they're married and living their own lives. I miss my son even more." She hesitated. "He died just over a year ago. I'd give anything to have one more day with him. I'm sure your mother would, too. With you, I mean."

Winny thought hard, forcing the faded image of her mother back into her mind. Could her mistress be right? Was it possible that her mother might actually grieve for her? *Anybody gonna miss you when you're gone?* Jack's words rang in her ears. Maybe someone did. It was nice to think of that.

"That's kind of you to say," Winny said, swallowing the lump in her throat.

The sounds of the road beneath them filled the cabin of the truck as they continued on, and Winny looked through her window, trying to remember her mother's face.

"Your teacher sent me a letter," Mistress Adams said, her voice lighter. "She wrote that you are an excellent student with commendable manners and attitude, and that you are at the top of your class."

A flush of pleasure rose up Winny's neck.

"She has suggested extra lessons—"

"Did I do something wrong?"

"No, it's not that. She would like you to work on more advanced subjects and has asked if you might spend more hours at school and fewer working for me."

Winny's heart sank. "Oh."

"Tell me, Winnifred. What do you see yourself doing when you are no longer living at our farm?"

Winny was surprised by her interest. "Well, I have been thinking that I might like to be a nurse someday."

Mistress Adams smiled, and the expression transformed her face.

"When I was a girl, I considered becoming a nurse as well. In fact, my parents named me Florence after Florence Nightingale. Have you heard of her?"

How strange, to be reminded in this way. "I read a book about her back at the Home in England," Winny replied. "Why didn't you become a nurse?"

"We didn't have the money for school, so I married a farmer. And my daughters have all done the same." She regarded Winny. "I would like you to go to nursing school when you have completed your studies here. I would like to know that at least one girl has left my house with a future in store. If you are able to pass the entrance examination next spring, you may go."

Winny's mouth was suddenly dry. "Nursing school would be a dream come true for me, Mistress, but I am indentured to you until the age of twenty-one."

"I am aware of that. However, I believe it is within my rights to grant you this."

Tears sprang to Winny's eyes and blurred her mistress's face. "Thank you."

But Winny's joy was tinged with sadness. As much as she wanted to follow her dream, she knew in her heart that she couldn't go. Mary was here, and Winny would never leave her behind. Winny was all Mary had left. And Winny had made her a promise. Winny never broke promises.

nineteen
JACK

❦

Weeks passed with no reply from Barnardo's about Mary and Winny. Every day Jack became more convinced that the girls were lost to him forever.

"We gotta believe they're all right," Edward said. "That's all we can do."

Jack knew it hurt Edward, not knowing where Mary was, but at least he still had his brother. More and more, recently, the two of them had begun to talk about the future, and Jack experienced a new and bitter sense of envy. Edward was learning from Dr. Cogan and had decided to attend school in the fall when he turned eighteen. Cecil, strong and sunburned but happy with this new life, had found purpose running the Cogans' farm. He'd decided to stay on after his indenture was over in another year.

Jack had no idea what he wanted to do. As spring melted the snow and began to warm the fields, resentment grew inside him like weeds, rooted in a garden of grief and guilt that kept him up at night. He withdrew from his friends, choosing instead to spend his days walking the length of the fields.

On Jack's eighteenth birthday, a smiling Mrs. Cogan carried a cake to the dining room table and set it before him. It was another first. None of the boys had ever seen a birthday cake before.

"There you go," she said, delighted to have surprised him. "Blow out all the candles!"

When the little flames were extinguished, Mrs. Cogan sliced the dessert and passed portions to everyone. It was a night for celebration, and Jack listened to every note of his friends' laughter, memorizing the sounds of their voices. Tonight his heart twisted with regret, and yet it felt lighter than it had in a long time. He finally knew what he must do.

Later that evening as the boys prepared to turn in for the night, Jack told them he had something to say.

"I gotta leave," he said quietly, watching the flickering lamp on the bedside table. "I feel trapped here."

The brothers exchanged a glance.

"How can you feel trapped in all this space?" Edward asked. "We're finally free."

"Free from what? What am I supposed to do with all this freedom? It's good you've both figured things out for yourselves, but I haven't. I gotta get out of here, figure out who *I* am. And I gotta find Mary. You know that. I promised her."

"Where you gonna go?" Cecil asked.

"I'll find work somewhere," he said. "I'll see what happens. All I know is I can't stay here."

"Won't be the same without you," Cecil said.

"Hasn't been the same for a long time," he replied bitterly.

"You know what I mean."

"Yeah."

Edward was watching, his gaze soft with sympathy. "If they're out there," he finally said, "you'll find them."

In the morning, Jack thanked the Cogans for everything and told them he was leaving. They were sorry, but they didn't stand in his way. Dr. Cogan suggested a sawmill in Goderich, a couple hours' train ride away. He'd heard they were hiring—one of the few places with jobs these days.

With Goderich in mind, Jack loaded up his old trunk, tucking in the food Mrs. Cogan made him for the trip. Before the five of them squeezed into the doctor's car and headed toward the train station, he walked to the local churchyard and said goodbye to Quinn for what he knew would be the last time.

At the station, the Cogans bid Jack farewell then waited in the car for the boys to say their goodbyes. It felt strange, standing there on the platform with his best friends in the world, studying their faces and fearing a time when he'd no longer know them by heart. It hadn't been that long ago that they'd been standing here with Quinn, nervous but excited about the next chapter, unsure of what was to come next. So much and so little had changed since then, and Jack couldn't help questioning everything he was doing. Like right now. He was about to abandon his only friends with the vague hope of finding the others, and the truth was he could end up with no one at all.

"I'm sorry," he said, seeing the pain in their eyes.

Edward shook his head. "No, mate, you do what you have to do. We will too." He paused and held out his hand. "It's been good knowing you, Jack."

"Hey, it don't have to be like that," Cecil said, pushing Edward's hand away. "It's not like we're at a funeral. You know where we are now. We'll see you again."

Jack reached out an arm and held Cecil a moment, then he did the same with Edward. "Then we won't say goodbye."

"That's right," Cecil said gruffly.

Edward wiped his eyes. "Best of luck to you out there, mate," he said. "I hope you find what you're looking for. Give Mary and Winny a hug for us, won't you?"

"You know I will."

He stepped onto the train and found a seat away from other people. Through the window, he watched his friends, their expressions taut with forced smiles, and as the wheels began to turn, he pressed his palm against the glass. The brothers raised their hands in farewell.

Moments later, the train rolled out of the station and Jack was on his way. The fields blurring past his window were like the ones he'd known and worked, but everything looked different now that he was on his own. Canada was a very big place. Where would he go? Who might he become?

———

Hours later he got off the train and followed the signs to the sawmill. At the door to the office, he took a breath for courage, combed his hair back with his fingers, then entered. The man at the desk was leaning over a stack of paperwork, a cigar smoking in one hand, but he looked up when Jack walked in.

"You looking for work?" he asked, studying Jack.

Jack nodded.

The big man's cheeks sucked in as he inhaled the cigar, and smoke puffed back out. "You ever done this kinda work before?"

"No, sir. But I'm a fast learner."

At Jack's response, the man's eyes hardened. "Don't you read?"

Jack glanced around, wondering what he'd missed. "I do. Why?"

The man emerged from behind the desk with surprising speed and jabbed his cigar toward the door. "Take a good look at the sign out there. We got barely enough jobs for our own men. We don't give work to foreign bums. Now get outta here." He took a step towards Jack. "Now."

Jack staggered outside, confused, then he saw it: a large white sign with bold black lettering that said "No Englanders."

Anger flared in his chest and he looked over at the man, who had followed him out. "I have as much right to be here as anyone else," he said.

"Get back on a boat, limey. Go back where you belong."

A few men were gathering, watching the scene unfold, and their hostile expressions were unmistakable. Jack was more than ready for a fight, but he figured it'd be wise to stick to just one opponent at a time. Swallowing his pride, he turned and headed back toward the main street of Goderich.

Maybe this had all been a big mistake. Right now he could be with Edward and Cecil, living in a place where he was wanted. Where he didn't have insults shoved down his throat. But there was no point in thinking about that. He couldn't go back. Not now. So he followed the first railway track he saw and hoped the next town over would be more welcoming.

But it wasn't. When he inquired about the HELP WANTED sign in a shop window, the shopkeeper eyed him suspiciously and said, "We're not hiring anyone who sounds like you."

With no other options, he headed back out along the railway tracks, and with every step his mood plummeted further. When a train rumbled behind him, making the earth vibrate beneath his feet, he wondered, for a split second, what it would be like to just stand there and let it hit him. He'd hold his arms out and close his eyes, and all his troubles would be over in an instant. But then he remembered Mary, and he stepped off the tracks. He'd come too far to give up now.

As the big black engine surged past, he spotted a number of shabbily dressed men sitting inside one of the boxcars. Some even lay on *top* of the cars, their arms draped comfortably over the short rails, and he couldn't help wondering where they were headed. Had they found work? Because if they had, Jack didn't want to miss out. He picked up his pace, hoping to catch up to the train at the next station, but it was farther than he'd thought. By the time he got there, the train had already left again.

It was easy to get defeated out here, he thought. Easy to figure the great big world was against him when he was in the middle of nowhere, all by himself. And now that night had begun to fall, things looked even more bleak. *I chose to leave,* he reminded himself. *I can't give up now.* He kept on walking until it was too dark to see much, then he started searching for some place out of the way to sleep. Eventually he spotted a tree with a wide trunk and low-hanging branches, just far enough off the tracks that he felt safe. He curled up beneath it, using his trunk as a pillow, planning to start again at first light.

He was just drifting off when a shuffling in the long grass nearby shot adrenaline through him. Jack leapt to his feet, fists at the ready.

"Hand over the trunk," a voice growled. He must have followed him from the tracks.

The moonlight reflected off something in the man's hand. He was holding a knife, Jack realized.

"Ain't nothing in there you'd like," Jack said, his eyes on the blade.

"I'll be the judge of that. Hand it over."

The trunk was all Jack had left in the world, and he wasn't about to give it away. "Come and get it."

Narrowed eyes wary, the man sidled closer. He briefly looked away when he reached for the trunk, and Jack seized the moment. He lunged for the knife, knocking it out of the other man's hand and onto the grass by his feet, then he kicked the weapon away and heard it land somewhere in the darkness, out of reach. In the same movement, he picked up his trunk and swung it, slamming the man across the head and sending him staggering back. Trunk securely in hand, Jack sprinted into the darkness, not slowing to a walk until he was sure he wasn't being followed. From there, he navigated his way back to the tracks and kept to them until the sun began to rise.

At the next station, he came upon a group of four young, ragged men putting out a small fire and packing up a few belongings. They looked like they were just getting ready to break camp.

"I ain't here to fight," he said right out, holding his arms up and hoping luck might be on his side for once. He couldn't take on all four of them. "I'm tired and hungry, and all I want is for someone to tell me what a fella's gotta do to get on the next train."

A lanky man who looked to be the leader slicked a hand over his short brown hair then took a long stride toward Jack. "What you got in the trunk?"

"Trousers and a shirt. That's most of it."

"Got food?"

"If I had food, I wouldn't be hungry."

The man crossed his arms. "You gonna open that trunk and prove it?"

Jack hesitated, then he crouched and undid the latches. The man squatted beside him and rifled through the contents of the trunk. "You don't even got a spare pair of shoes?"

"I don't."

"That's a shame. Mine are wearing thin." The man eyed him from top to toes. "If you're out here, you're at the end of your rope. Am I right?"

Jack nodded.

"Most folks out here won't help you, especially when they hear that accent of yours. But I ain't that kinda guy. Someone helped me once, and for his sake, I'll take you along for a ride, show you how it's done. What's your name, son?"

"Jack Miller."

"Well, Jack, I'm Jimmy Salo." He introduced the other three men with him, said they were heading west. Jimmy himself was going northeast to Kitchener, and he said he'd take Jack along if he was so inclined.

"Just tell me what I gotta do," Jack said.

"First thing you wanna do is get rid of that trunk of yours. Nobody carries something that bulky. I saw a couple of shirts in there, didn't I? Take one out, dump everything on it, then wrap it into a bundle." Jimmy jabbed a thumb at his own earthly possessions, hanging in a sack at the end of a long stick he carried over his shoulder. "Much easier."

Jack did as he suggested then looked down at his empty trunk, the last thing he had from Barnardo's. Feeling strangely free, he picked it up and hurled it off into the grass beyond the tracks, a smile growing across his face. This was a whole new life out here. He didn't need to carry that piece of himself anymore.

Jimmy was as good as his word. As they walked, he educated Jack on the way the rails worked, warning him of the dangers and rattling off names of men who hadn't been cautious enough. Jimmy said that once in a while, if he was real careful and it was real late at night, he might catch a freight train in the yard, but most of the time Jack would have to catch it on the run, as it built speed coming out of the station.

"You gotta watch out for the bulls," he said. "Them fellas are the police of the railway, and their job is to make sure not one of us is riding for free. I'll tell ya, I've seen them do some pretty cruel things. You look strong, but that don't matter. You'll want to stay away from them."

A mechanical squeal shrieked over the thunder of an engine, interrupting his lesson, and Jimmy looked down the tracks, past Jack. "All right, Jack. Here we go. If you get it right this first time, I won't worry about you again. If you don't, I won't have to."

Jack followed his gaze, saw the train rolling toward them, a plume of smoke trailing behind.

"When it gets here, you gotta run the same speed as the train's going, you see? Right away, pick a handle you want and grab for it. There's one on either side of the ladder. When you got a good grip, you kind of swing yourself around so you can grab the second handle, but don't jump onto the ladder until you have both hands holding on tight. You hear me?"

"I hear you," Jack said, his heart thundering, his eyes on the approaching beast.

Jimmy slapped him on the back and started to jog. "All right then. See you up top!"

The engine chugged past, going faster and faster, the metal wheels clacking and rumbling while the whistle kept on blowing, and Jack's blood pounded louder than all of it. He began to run, putting all his energy into matching the train's speed, then he wrapped his hand around the cold, hard steel of a handle and held on tight. It felt like the train was tearing his shoulder from its socket, so he pumped his legs as fast as he could and reached for the next handle, then he launched himself onto the ladder just as Jimmy had said. Suddenly he was standing on the side of a train, the wind shoving at him, the tracks rattling beneath, and the thrill of the ride racing through his veins. Rung by rung he climbed to the top, where Jimmy and some of his cohorts cheered his arrival, then they all settled back to enjoy the ride. When they eventually reached Kitchener, Jimmy saluted him before leaping off. Jack had no destination in mind, so he just continued on.

Riding the rails was like nothing Jack could have imagined. The wind in his hair, the rocking, jostling train speeding along to somewhere unknown, and the men who, like him, couldn't find work and had left their families behind—it all became a salve to his miserable soul. Unless the bulls came along, swinging their sticks to force them off, he could just lie back and let himself drift. He wondered what Mary would have thought. She probably wouldn't enjoy the lack of order, but Edward and Cecil would have loved the adventure. And Winny? She would have been all right with it as long as she had her friends around her. And how the five of them would have laughed, just being together up there. *I'd give the world*, he thought, *just to have them all with me right now.*

twenty

WINNY

⌘

The cicada-screeching heat of summer was upon them, and yet Winny smiled as she leaned over the beans, snapping them off their vines and dropping them into her basket. She'd been to visit Mary last Sunday, and she had been overjoyed to see the healthy smile on her friend's face and the meat on her bones. Just as she'd been promised, Master Renfrew had kept his distance, and Mistress Renfrew had even given Mary a new dress.

"She still says she don't know where my baby is," Mary had said. "I was sure she was lying to me before, but I believe she's telling the truth now."

"We'll find him, Mary. Somehow we will."

"We will," Mary agreed. "I know we will. Now tell me what's happening where you live."

Winny told her about the three new Home Boys who had just arrived at the farm. Like her when she'd first arrived, they knew nothing about working on a farm, but David was teaching them, and they were being treated well. Ever since Mistress Adams had suggested nursing school to Winny, no one had raised a hand to any of the Adamses' Home Children. Not even to the new boys.

"Tell me about school," Mary said. "How is Charlotte doing?"

Winny ached to tell her everything about her studies, how excited she was with the lessons she was getting from Miss Burton, even in the summertime. But Winny still hadn't said a word to Mary about nursing school. She had already decided what she needed to do, and the subject could only cause them both pain. Mary could not leave the Renfrew farm for four more years, and Winny would never leave Mary behind. She knew Mary wouldn't allow her to deny herself such an amazing opportunity, but Winny's mind was made up: she just hadn't yet worked up the nerve to tell Mistress Adams her decision.

"School is over for the season," Winny said, "but when I last saw Charlotte she was ever so happy. If you saw her now, you wouldn't recognize her. She's so confident, and it's impossible not to smile when she does. Perhaps next semester I can figure out a way to arrange a visit."

Mary grinned. "I would love that."

Remembering her happy expression, Winny reached for the next vine and let out a slow, satisfied breath. The worst was over. They were both safe, and they could both manage four more years of living out here. Maybe then she would go to nursing school. Maybe Mary would go with her.

"Winny?" David called, breaking her reverie.

He was leaning against the fence, a frown on his face. She was so glad David was still at the farm. He was eighteen now, and Master Adams had decided to hire him on at a better wage. Now he was in charge of the other Home Boys as well as a lot of the farm work, and she knew he was happy about it. Today, though, he looked uneasy.

"Mistress Adams asked me to find you. She said to come to the house right now."

She rose, her basket looped over her arm, and headed to the house. Mistress Adams met her at the door, her face stricken.

"Mistress? Is something wrong?"

"Come inside, Winnifred."

She entered the kitchen, but Mistress Adams continued into the living room. "In here, please."

Nerves wriggled in Winny's chest. She'd never been allowed in that room before, and now her mistress was indicating a chair. She lowered herself carefully onto the seat, apprehension buzzing through her.

"Winnifred, I have to tell you something." She frowned tightly. "It's something terrible."

"Did I do something wrong?"

"No." For the first time, she saw Mistress Adams pick at her own nails. As if she were nervous about something. "It's your friend, Mary." She said her name softly, like a sigh. "She's . . . gone."

"Gone where?"

"She—she died."

All the blood drained from Winny's head, and a great, yawning hole opened in front of her. She teetered on its edge, lights flickering in her vision. *It isn't true.* She had just seen Mary. She was happy. She was healthy. And yet . . . her mistress was staring at her. Her expression hadn't changed.

"It was a shocking thing."

"How?" Winny heard herself whisper. "How did she die?"

Mistress Adams looked at her hands, knotted in her lap.

"Tell me," Winny said, suddenly frantic. "I need to know."

"She hung herself," she said, choking on the words. "My sister's husband went to her room this afternoon and found her there."

Rage coursed through Winny's veins. "What was *he* doing in her room? *He wasn't supposed to be there!*"

Her mistress's face crumpled, and she met Winny's eyes. "I don't know. I don't know! All I know is what my sister told me. She came here earlier, when you were out in the garden. She told the Mounties every-thing and has reported her husband to them." Tears rolled down her cheeks. "I'm so sorry, Winnifred."

Winny stared straight ahead, numb. *Mary. What happened?*

"She wrote you a note."

Winny stared at the small white paper Mistress Adams had drawn from her apron. She was afraid to touch it, but Mistress Adams placed it in her hand.

"You may read it in here," she said, then she left Winny alone in the room.

It took a few seconds before Winny could make herself unfold the paper, and then tears blurred her vision.

Dearest Winny,

I never meant to hurt you, and I know this letter will do that and so much more.

I need you to know that I really was feeling much better lately, and that was because of you. You're the only reason I survived this long. You saved me from the hell I was living in, but I must be hon-est with you. I never trusted my happiness. I lived in fear of the day my master would come back. For a while, I let myself believe he wouldn't. I dreamed of the day when I would be free, and I would be with you and Jack, and we would find my son together.

Winny, I am sorry. That day will never come.

He came back today. And when it was all happening again, I saw his strap in my mind. The one he used to leave hanging on my wall as a reminder of him. For the first time, I imagined that strap around my neck. And I realized that there was a way for me to be free of him. I know you won't believe it, but in that moment, all the fear and anger and hate left me. I don't have to be here any longer. I know it will be difficult for you to understand, but knowing that I can leave this place has filled me with peace. Now, at last, I feel safe.

The only fear I have is that Jack might someday find out what I decided to do. You know how he is, Winny. He'd blame himself for not stopping me, and it would kill him. If you ever find him, please hold him tight for me. Tell him I loved him and missed him, but never, ever tell him what I did.

Dear Winny, I have one last favour to ask of you. I need you to find my son. Please. It is the last thing I will ever ask. Find my baby. Love him, and raise him like your own.

Your loving sister forever,
Mary

Winny blotted her tears off the paper with her thumb and read the letter again, unable to grasp this new truth: a world without Mary. The letters were scrawled hastily, their lines and whorls inconsistent, except for Mary's name. It had been written carefully, the rises and falls of the ink as deliberate as every other decision she had ever made, and Winny traced them with a feather-light touch. The precious, beautiful word swam in her vision, and she saw again the tips of Mary's fingers extended to her that day on the street, so long before. Their warmth and welcome. Their offer of friendship and more. The gentle tail of the final *y* faded smoothly into the paper, disappearing from sight as Mary had lifted her hand and the pen, and to Winny it seemed almost . . . right. It was the last thing Mary had ever written. The last thing she had ever done for anyone but herself.

How deep her sadness must have flowed. An underground torrent, wearing away at the fragile ceiling that had become Mary's foundation. *I thought I knew*, Winny despaired, tears streaming down her cheeks. *But how could I? How could anyone?*

When she awoke the next morning, Winny milked the cows and

collected eggs and weeded the garden and didn't say anything to any-one beyond what she had to. A numb, aching grief had wrapped itself so tightly around her she could barely breathe. The next day, when she was out in the garden, Mistress Adams came to the side of the fence.

"Mary's funeral is this afternoon," she said gently. "We will leave in ten minutes."

She was touched by the fact that Master Adams and David went with them to the Renfrews' farm, and that they offered to ride in the bed of the truck so she could sit inside. But Winny refused, choosing instead to sit alone in the back, the wind whipping her hair. When they arrived, Mistress Renfrew greeted them quietly then led them behind the house to the family cemetery where strands of lazy grass caressed stone markers. A narrow pine coffin had been placed on the ground by a freshly dug grave. Winny could smell the dirt, the cold, the *alone*, and she hated that Mary would soon be a part of it.

Closing her eyes, she brought Mary's face to her mind. Not the bro-ken, sad expression of the last year, but the open, friendly smile she had first known in London. The challenge in Mary's blue eyes whenever anyone dared go after Winny. That's how she needed to remember her. That's how she prayed Mary looked right now, squeezed within the nar-row confines of that coffin.

A breeze tickled Winny's face. It touched her eyelids and her lips like a friend, keeping her company in the midst of strangers. Jack should be here, she thought, standing right here at her side. These people weren't Mary's family no matter where they decided to bury her body. Winny and Jack were. He deserved to be here, to know what had happened to his sister. But Mary was right. Knowing the truth would only tear him apart.

Two of the Renfrews' Home Boys lowered the coffin into the dirt, and Winny started to shake. Her knees wobbled, and it was Mistress Adams who stepped forward and held her upright.

The minister began to speak. He said very little about Mary herself, and Winny knew that was because he considered suicide to be a sin. In

Winny's mind, it was Master Renfrew who had sinned. He was the one responsible for all of it. But how could a man be punished when a girl took her own life? In a way, Winny was glad the minister didn't try to talk about Mary. No one knew who she had been, except for Winny. He would have said the wrong thing. When he was done speaking, he looked toward Mistress Renfrew for guidance.

Mary's mistress stepped to the edge of the hole and looked down. "I should have done more to protect you," Winny heard her whisper. "I'm sorry." Then she turned and walked toward Winny. Her expression was thick with grief, hardened by guilt, and Winny was glad of it. So, so glad. "I'm sorry, Winnifred. I really am."

Winny's jaw was sealed shut. She had no words for this woman.

Mistress Adams put her hand on Winny's arm and squeezed gently. "You may go say goodbye now."

Winny couldn't stand where Mistress Renfrew had stood. Instead, she knelt beside the grave and stared at the top of the plain wooden box. Her mind flew to the laughter they'd shared, to the times they'd huddled together in the dark, to the dreams they'd shared about their future together. Mary had given her so much, including a final task, and Winny felt a wisp of gratitude for something she could hold on to. Something she could take from this place as she left her heart behind.

I will find your son, she promised her friend and herself. *And he will be truly loved, as he should have been all along. Goodbye my dearest, only sister. Goodbye, Mary.*

She heard a rustling behind her as the others left the cemetery. It was time to go. Her knees felt anchored to the earth, but there was nothing more she could do here. She rose stiffly to her feet and forced herself to walk away. The only sound she could hear was the gentle thump of the Home Boys tossing dirt onto Mary's grave.

At the door to her house, Mrs. Renfrew invited Winny to join them for tea. When she'd first come to the Renfrews' farm so many months ago, Winny had badly wanted to go inside this very house. Now that she sat on one of the woman's fine chairs, a china cup rattling in her hand, she found she didn't care for the place at all. And in that moment, it became quite clear what she needed to do. She would go to nursing school with Charlotte, and she would become a nurse. And she would raise Mary's son as her own.

When she placed her teacup on the delicate, carved table beside her, Winny's hand no longer trembled. With new purpose beating in her chest, she got to her feet and turned to Mistress Renfrew.

"Excuse me, please, but I need to know," she said. "Where is Mary's baby?"

twenty-one
JACK

❧

For two years, Jack rode the rails, stopping at small towns where he'd go from door to door, offering to do anything that needed doing. Most of the time he was greeted with the familiar refrain "No jobs here," but sometimes the locals went a little further and mocked his accent before they sent him packing. On occasion, their sneering turned to worse, and Jack ran off with more than a few cuts and bruises.

"Maybe head west," someone suggested, so Jack followed the tracks and threw himself into a boxcar as it chugged slowly past.

But it never really got any easier. When the temperature dropped, he couldn't ride outside the cars, so he had to open the door as he jumped on board then sit close to the other men huddled inside, their arms pressed against each other for warmth. At least with the cold, the men didn't smell quite as bad, though Jack knew he was part of that problem. Food was even more scarce in the winter, and it wasn't uncommon for him to go a couple of days without a bite to eat. What tattered clothes he had hung on his shrunken frame.

It was the loneliness that got to him the most. He wrote Edward and Cecil when he could, and when he met fellows his age, he asked if any of them had ever heard of a girl named Mary Miller, or one called Winnifred Ellis, but the answer was always no. Sometimes he wondered if he'd made the biggest mistake of his life, leaving the farm. What were the brothers up to now? Was Edward at school? And what about Mary? What if she was looking for him? That was a question he preferred not to think about, because despite his promise to find her, here he was, far away from his responsibilities.

When he met Toby, he'd been somewhere outside Regina in a boxcar, dozing off. All at once a stranger had landed in the car, skidding across the slippery floor and grabbing hold of a crate to stabilize himself. The fellow looked older than Jack, his beard thick and black, his temples streaked by lines, but it was hard to tell ages out here. He eyed Jack, gave him the customary nod, then settled down next to him and pulled his wool scarf higher.

"Nitherin' out there, ain't it?" he muttered, grabbing Jack's attention with his English slang about the extreme cold.

"It is," Jack said, cautious. "Where you from?"

The man spat to the side. "Yorkshire to start. Then some wee farm in Ontario. Most recent was the Winnipeg train station where the Mounties wouldn't do me the kindness of locking me up for a night or two. I need to break more laws, seems like."

"Yorkshire? Are you a Home Child?"

"I was." He lifted his chin. "What of it?"

Jack broke into a rare smile and held out his hand. "I am as well. I'm Jack."

"Toby."

"When did you come over?"

"Back in twenty-two. I was nine."

Jack lifted an eyebrow. "I didn't know there were Home Children back then."

Toby chuckled, rummaging through his pack, and Jack saw he was missing an eye tooth. "Aye, lad. They've been sending us over here nigh on a hundred years. From what I've heard, there's thousands of us."

Jack was so stunned by the news he didn't notice the crust of bread Toby was offering. "I haven't seen many."

"Aye, well." He gave Jack a cheeky grin and kept the crust for himself. "We don't go around talking about it, do we? 'Good morning, sir, the name's Toby and I'm a useless piece of garbage. How are you?' I dunno about you, mate, but I'm not fond of the subject."

True enough, Jack thought.

"Where you heading?" Toby asked. "Anywheres in particular?"

"I don't know," Jack admitted. "I want a job, but—"

"Nah. You'll never find one. There's too many of us," Toby said, talking a mile a minute. "They used to have the relief camps, you know. That was during the worst of it. The Depression, right? They stuck the camps out in the bush in the middle of nowhere so's the regular people wouldn't be bothered by the likes of us. Here's the thing. You didn't have to go, but if you didn't, you'd be jailed for being a bum. Someone's got a sense of humour, I reckon. Anyhow, we cleared bush, built roads and bridges, did whatever they told us to." He shook his head, remembering. "So-called room and board and twenty cents in your pocket for a hard day's work."

"Sounds like a grown man's orphanage."

"Not so different. Forty men trying to sleep in a space for half as many. Government was daft for putting us all in there together, though. The relief camp's where I first heard about the unions and all that. We was like a load of dry wood that kept on sparking until we finally caught fire." He grinned. "What a time that was. Couple of years back I hopped a train along with hundreds of others to protest in Regina, and I've been riding the rails ever since." He studied Jack. "You read the manifesto yet?"

Jack was having a hard time following what Toby was saying. "The what?"

"That's a good read for you, mate," he said, digging in his pack. He produced a well-thumbed book and handed it to Jack. "It's a hundred-year-old book with all the answers."

"*The Communist Manifesto* by Karl Marx and Frederick Engels," Jack read. "What's it about?"

"It's brilliant. It's about how the world needs to be. All for one and one for all. No more rich businessmen making thousands of dollars while the rest of us starve." He leaned back against the wall of the train car, tugged his cap down, and settled in for a nap. "Great book, lad. Read it."

It had been a long time since Jack had picked up a book, and he found it slow going at first, but the more he read, the more righteous he felt about his anger. The word *proletariat* was new to him, but the idea of the poor working for the rich was not. He, Mary, Winny, Cecil, Edward, and the others were the proletariat, the lowest level of humanity. They had been born in poverty because the government had ignored the plights of their parents and grandparents. They were fated to suffer while others prospered. When the numbers of the poor soared and chaos took over the streets, the government corralled them into workhouses and orphanages, establishing control and forcing them to work for everyone but themselves.

Thomas Barnardo might have believed he was doing what was best by taking them from the streets and abusive homes and orphanages, but by selling children to Canada by the thousands, he'd made money off them, too. People like him and Warren, Jack realized, were pure capitalists. Warren's farm did all right because it depended on the backs of boys like Jack, boys who stayed on the bottom rung of a greasy ladder.

Toby's words stayed with Jack long after Toby went his own way, somewhere along the line. More and more Jack joined in on conversations in the railcars, talking about unions and solidarity. He became one of them, and he shared their feverish convictions that someday men like him would no longer suffer. Someday he would have what others had.

twenty-two
WINNY

❧

Mary's final request weighed on Winny throughout the summer. Mistress Renfrew had given Winny all she knew, which was the name of the home where Mary had given birth. Beyond that, Winny didn't have anything to go on. But the more she thought about it, the more she hoped Charlotte might be able to help. On her first day back at school, Winny could barely concentrate on her lessons, she was so anxious to speak to her friend at their secret spot.

"What a long summer it was without you!" Charlotte cried, hugging her tight. She pulled back, and her smile vanished at the sight of tears in Winny's eyes. "What's happened?"

In halting sentences, Winny told Charlotte about Mary's death.

Charlotte stood frozen, then she slowly shook her head. "No. Not Mary." Her voice cracked as she said Mary's name, then she began to cry. "I'm so sorry, Winny. It's so unfair. How could Mary end up with someone so cruel? And yet I end up . . . Oh, I wish I could have done something."

How many times had Winny felt the same aching helplessness over these past few months?

"There's nothing you or I could have done," Winny said. "But I think you can help me now."

"Whatever you need, Winny. You know that."

"Before she died, Mary wrote me a letter. She asked me to find her son."

"You mean to keep him?"

She nodded. "If I pass my exams, Mistress Adams has agreed to release me from service so I can attend nursing school. I'm going to become a nurse, just like you. And I'm going to adopt him."

"Oh, Winny, that is good news."

"But I need your help."

Charlotte leaned forward. "Whatever you need."

"You said the Carpenters were thinking of adopting a baby for a long time, right? I mean before you came along."

"Yes. They changed their minds when they heard about Barnardo's children."

"Since they know how the process works, do you think they might know how to find Mary's baby? He was born in the Toronto Maternity Home."

"Leave it with me. I'll find out what I can."

Winny didn't have to wait long. The next day, Charlotte had news. According to Mr. Carpenter, the maternity home was attached to an orphanage. If Mary's baby hadn't been adopted already, that's most likely where he would be. At the word *orphanage*, the ground dropped under Winny's feet. She should have expected it, but still . . . She couldn't let Mary's son live the same life she had lived.

Charlotte agreed. "But have you thought it through, Winny?" she asked tentatively. "I hope you don't mind, but when I asked Mum and

Dad about the orphanage, they pressed me for more information. So I had to tell them about Mary, and about her baby. They were heartbroken. And they want to help."

"How?"

"Well, you'll need a home for starters. When you go to Toronto, I mean."

She went on to say that the Carpenters had suggested that Winny live with Charlotte in Toronto when it came time for school. They had already planned to rent a room for her there, and knowing how much it would mean to Charlotte to have Winny with her, they offered to cover the cost of a two-bedroom apartment instead.

Winny couldn't believe her ears. "That is so kind of them. How can I ever repay them?"

"They know how much you mean to me, Winny. It's the least they can do." Her eyes twinkled unexpectedly. "You'll also need a husband."

"What? What for?"

"It's a requirement of adoption."

Heat surged to Winny's cheeks. "Where am I going to find a husband in time?"

"You're not," Charlotte replied. "Mum telephoned her nephew Jeffrey to ask for his help. I've met him a few times when the Carpenters brought me to Toronto. He lives there. He's twenty, and a brilliant lawyer. And he's ever so handsome. Blind as a bat, but his eyes are still lovely. Anyhow, he has agreed to pose as your husband," she said, pink with joy. "He says he'll come with you for interviews or whatever you need. Don't worry, Winny. He's a really good sort." She wrinkled her nose. "And he knows how I feel about orphanages."

"Charlotte, I don't know what to say. Truly. You've thought of everything."

"I'm just so happy I can be of help. Without you and Mary, I would still be that scared little mouse sitting in the corner in Barkingside." She squeezed Winny's hand. "I'm glad to return the favour."

With Charlotte's help, Winny wrote a heartfelt letter to the orphanage, and a month later she received the adoption paperwork. As she filled it in, her hands shook with a mixture of excitement and apprehension. It was really happening.

————

The school year flew by, and in the spring both she and Charlotte passed their exams and qualified for nursing school. Every day, Winny's future became a little more real.

On the morning she was to board the train to the city, Winny packed up her trunk with her belongings, including what she had brought with her from Barkingside and the new clothes and shoes Mistress Adams had bought for her to wear in Toronto. When everything was packed, Winny snapped the latches closed and set the trunk on its side.

David appeared in the doorway and held out his hand for it. "I'll miss seeing you around," he said. "Do write when you find time, won't you?"

"Of course," she said, giving him a hug. "Do you have any idea how much you helped me out here? I don't know how I would have survived without your friendship, David."

"It goes both ways, Winny." He looked at his shoes briefly, then back at her. "Take care of yourself. You'll be a terrific nurse. And that baby will have the best mother. Lucky fellow."

He put her luggage in the truck, and she slid into the front seat beside Mistress Adams. As they drove away past the fields, Winny stared out the window. *I will never come this way again*, she thought.

They rode in silence until they reached the station, and through the window Winny could see Charlotte was already there, waiting on the platform with the Carpenters. When the truck was parked and the engine shut off, she turned to Mistress Adams to say goodbye, but the woman surprised her by taking her hand.

"I must tell you, Winnifred, that I have grown unexpectedly fond of you," she said, stiff as ever. "I'm sure you are aware that when you first arrived here, I had rather low expectations. But despite my prejudices, you proved me wrong. You're wearing a sweater made from yarn you made. You can milk a cow with your eyes closed and practically juggle eggs. You're no longer the confused little girl I picked up at the train station almost two years ago but a smart, capable young woman on her way to becoming a nurse." She swallowed hard, and Winny felt the woman's fingers tighten around her own. "I know I wasn't easy on you. I know I was unfair—I see that now—and I'm sorry."

She reached into her purse and withdrew an envelope. "This is for you." She pursed her lips. "This money is from both my sister and myself. My share is to help you with your schooling. My sister's share is for the baby: I told her your plan to adopt the child. She said if you do not find him, you may keep the money, because she will always regret not putting a stop to her husband's vile actions. I've already written to Barnardo's and told them to release the money they're holding in trust for you. I'm not sure if they can do that before you are twenty-one, but I hope they will."

Winny stared at the envelope, thinking what a strange thing it was for two women she'd hated for so long to give her their hard-earned money. She would bear scars forever from the things Mistress Adams had said and done to her, and Mary's baby would be a permanent reminder of the torture her sister had allowed to happen. The money, she supposed, was meant to be an apology. A sad, insufficient apology that could never fix what they'd done. But Winny would accept it, and she would leave all this ugliness in the past.

She tucked the envelope inside her coat pocket. "Thank you, Mistress Adams," she said. "For believing me when it mattered most. And for encouraging me to go to nursing school."

"Your mother would be proud of you, Winnifred. And you'll make a wonderful mother yourself." Her eyes glistened with tears, which she swept away when the train whistle hooted. "Now, off you go. You don't want to miss your train."

Winny nodded, swallowing the unexpected lump that had formed in her throat, and she got out of the truck. Clutching her trunk in one hand, she ran toward the platform where Charlotte was embracing the Carpenters and bidding them farewell. Winny did as well, thanking them once more for all their generosity. Then the girls boarded the train, arm in arm, their hearts overflowing with excitement.

PART
— three —

twenty-three
WINNY

❧

— Present Day —

I remember that day so clearly, the way my heart took flight the moment the train chugged out of the station, away from my life on the farm.

"Were you scared?" Jamie asks, looking up from his laptop. He usually does his homework in his room, but tonight he's brought it down to the kitchen table.

"There's no way she'd be scared," Chrissie says. She's wearing one of her mother's old bracelets, another treasure she's uncovered in the last few days. "I bet you couldn't wait to be out of there, Gran."

"I felt like I was starting all over again," I say. "Like I'd turned a page, and this time I would finally get to write my own story."

"Yeah. I can see that. When I'm eighteen—"

"You're gonna leave your terrible mother behind?" Chrissie teases.

He wraps an arm around her shoulder, at once both her growing son and her best friend. "Never. I was just thinking about what a kid does these days when he's that age."

"Are you going to go to college?" I ask.

"Maybe," he says. "I kind of like the idea of learning all those trades, you know? Being handy. That way I could take care of myself no matter what."

"You could be like your great-grandfather and become an automobile mechanic," I suggest.

He tilts his head, considering the idea. "I do love cars."

"Whatever you do, you have to graduate high school first," Chrissie says. "What's your homework?"

"History of Canada," he says wryly. "You know, there's nothing about Home Children in the curriculum. When I asked my teacher about them, he didn't have any idea what I was talking about. He thought I meant the kids sent to Canada from England during the Second World War."

Chrissie snorts and reaches for his laptop. She types for a few seconds then shows us a black-and-white photograph of a pair of well-dressed, though dazed-looking, children. "Those were the 'Guest Children,'" she says. "The ones they sent over here to keep *safe*. I read they were treated like royalty."

"Lucky for them," I say quietly. The mention of war brings memories of another kind to my mind, and I feel a new weight settle on my shoulders. We're almost at that part of the story.

She passes Jamie back his computer. "I imagine those children weren't from the streets or orphanages."

Since I started telling them about my life, Chrissie has developed a keen interest in history. When she's not working at the hospital, she divides most of her time between the kitchen and her mother's boxes in the basement. When she's not busy with everything else, she's been digging up all kinds of information about Canada's British Home Children, and she's filled in a lot of blanks for me. Some of what she's discovered has shocked me. When she told me over 100,000—some even estimate it could be over 120,000—children were sent over here, as well as thousands more to Australia, New Zealand, and South Africa between 1869 and 1948, I had to excuse myself and go to my room. It was too much for me to bear thinking of all those poor little souls.

Now she sets her chin in her hand and looks at me with that expression that says I am about to learn something new. "Have you ever tried going online to trace your ancestry?"

"Sweetheart, I barely know what 'online' means."

"That's not true. I took you to that library course."

"Oh, I've probably forgotten what they taught me by now," I grumble. "Anyway, I don't think I'll get very far with that if I can't even remember my parents' names. If I ever knew them, even."

Of all the things I dislike about being geriatric, it's the absences in my memory I despise the most. It's as if my brain has decided I already know enough, or have seen enough, and it has turned off a switch. On the other hand, there are many things I wish I could forget, but they will never go away.

She taps her fingers on the table. "I bet I could figure that out somehow. The archives have lists where you can look up—"

"I think you have enough on your plate. Don't you worry about it."

She lets out a sigh, and I can tell she's disappointed that I haven't asked her to find out more. It's just that I'm not all that certain I want to know more. She sits taller and offers a tentative smile. "Well, there's something else I want to talk about. I found something online today, and I thought you might be interested in seeing it." She glances at Jamie. "Tomorrow's Saturday, so you could come too, if you want."

"We're going out?" Jamie and I ask at the same time.

"We can go in the morning. After breakfast. It's supposed to be a nice day."

"Where?"

"I'll show you tomorrow. I promise it'll be interesting."

Jamie's pinched expression speaks volumes.

"It won't take all day," his mother assures him. "And afterwards we'll get lunch."

I'm not usually one for surprises, but Chrissie was right: it's a beautiful day, and I do enjoy getting out to see things. It's difficult for me to do that these days, since I grow tired so easily. None of us speak as we drive away from the house, so Chrissie turns on the radio. I watch the summer colours blur past my window then disappear in a rush as we pull onto Highway 401. Chrissie is a good driver, but I look away, intimidated by the cars speeding around us. We drive west, then merge onto Highway 427. After a few minutes, Chrissie takes an exit ramp, and when I realize we are in Etobicoke, I feel nerves dance all over my body. How long has it been since I was here? I wonder if it's still the same. I look over at Chrissie and try to read her expression. Why has she brought us here? What does she know?

"Come on, Mom," Jamie says from the backseat. "You have to tell us now."

"Almost."

I'm not sure if I'm relieved or disappointed when she drives in a completely different direction from the one I was expecting. Instead, she goes east along Bloor Street and slows as we approach the gates to a cemetery.

"Park Lawn Cemetery, Paradise Mausoleum," Jamie reads. "A graveyard? Mom, you haven't been in a graveyard since—"

Since Susan, I think, my heart skipping a beat.

"I know. But this is different." Chrissie places one hand over mine. "I didn't tell you before because I wasn't sure how you'd react, but I really wanted to see this, and I really wanted you both to come with me."

She drives slowly through the entrance and along a little road that winds between gravestones, some of which look to be well over a hundred years old. The cemetery is a massive space of immaculate green, hushed and shadowed beneath watchful trees. This is a place for the dead, but the living are here as well, strolling through the grass, enjoying the peace. A deer stands about twenty feet away from the car, and her soft doe eyes take us in, but she isn't bothered.

"A few years ago," Chrissie says, "a woman named Lori Oschefski discovered something in this cemetery." She pulls to the side and parks. "We can walk from here."

Jamie helps me out of the car then wanders off the path a bit, intrigued by the ancient stones. Chrissie takes my elbow and leads me past wide, granite gravestones etched with names, dates, and fond remembrances, all of which are fading with time. When we stop walking, we are in a quiet, nondescript spot beneath towering maples.

"This is what I wanted to show you," she says, gesturing to one monument that stands taller than the others.

It looks like a rectangle atop two more, like an angular snowman. But something on the top stone looks unusual. I squint as we approach, curious about the circle cut in the middle of the stone, then I see it all at once. The brass orb is a ship's portal, just like one I peered out of when I was fifteen years old, standing on my tiptoes and searching for land. And above the portal is a plaque that reads "British Home Children." My gaze falls to the inscription below it, etched with names, words, and numbers.

STANLEY LESLIE ALLEBONE:
DIED APRIL 8 1915,
AGED 8 YEARS 6 MONTHS

MARGARET PIKE:
DIED APRIL 18 1927,
AGED 10 YEARS 9 MONTHS

BENJAMIN BUTTERWORTH:
DIED NOVEMBER 13 1898,
AGED 15 YEARS 1 MONTH

CHARLOTTE YARD:
DIED JUNE 16 1914,
AGED 12 YEARS 9 MONTHS

The list goes on and on, and I can't find any words.

"These are two mass graves," Chrissie says gently. "Seventy-five British Home Children are buried here."

Seventy-five children, I think, remembering all the little faces crowded on the dock so long ago. I wonder if any of these names belong to children I once knew.

"More specifically, fifty-eight of them are Barnardo's children. Seventeen infants were buried here as well, babies of Barnardo girls." Her finger goes to a specific name. "Like this one."

> EVELYN WRIGHT:
> DIED MAY 4 1918,
> INFANT DAUGHTER OF
> BRITISH HOME CHILD
> MAUD EMILY WRIGHT

"For decades, nobody knew their bodies were even here, then Lori started a GoFundMe page, and between her and other Home Children descendants, they raised enough money to make and erect this monument."

Jamie crouches by the memorial, runs his fingers over the words engraved on its base. "Oh my God, Gran." His heart is in his blue eyes. "This was you." I hear the catch in his voice, and I am nearly undone.

"I didn't bring you here to make you sad," Chrissie says, still looking at the names, "though I know that's unavoidable. I just . . . I don't know. I wanted you to know that you weren't alone all that time. There were so many others. And I wanted you to know that there are people living today who care about what happened, and who are paying tribute to what you all went through as well as they can. There's even an official National British Home Child Day here in Canada, declared by the government. It's on September twenty-eighth."

I stare at her in wonder, then shift my eyes back to the names on the stone. This place. How had I lived so close and never known it existed?

All these children. And now all these other people, knowing about us, caring about us . . . It's confusing, and I muddle through a fog of emotions. For so long, I've been keeping my secrets, ashamed of where I came from and who I was. Today I discover that others have been doing the opposite: working to remember, to acknowledge. And Chrissie, my thoughtful granddaughter, is one of them. My heart is full of love for her.

I swallow and try to find the words trapped in my throat. "Thank you, Chrissie. I'm . . . I'm glad we came," I say, and I mean it.

It is another silent drive back to the house as each of us is lost in our own thoughts, lunch forgotten. When we get home, Jamie disappears into his room while Chrissie works in the kitchen, and I go lie down, weary from the morning's exertions. An hour later, I wake up to the sound of Jamie's voice and I slowly make my way into the kitchen.

"Do you think she'll like it?"

"Oh, Jamie," Chrissie says. "She will love it. I love it. Think of it. From here we can build on it for years."

"It's not very detailed, but . . ."

"Maybe she can fill in some blanks. Maybe I can. There are some fantastic people on the British Home Children Facebook page who are amazing at finding things like this. Maybe if I just ask—" Chrissie notices me in the doorway. "Gran, you have to see what Jamie made."

"What is it?"

Jamie pulls out a chair for me then places a piece of paper at my spot. I sit and study the angular writing carefully, then I realize he's made a family tree. *My* family tree.

"Why, this is wonderful," I say, entranced. I've never seen my family written out on a page like this, and though it is a short tree with very few branches, I am grateful for every name he's written.

"There's you and Pop." He points to the top of the page. "I can't wait to hear the story there."

I chuckle and ignore his comment. I can already see where I should add my little brothers' names. I skim my finger all the way to the bottom.

"There you are, Jamie. And someday you'll add someone here beside you." He blushes and my finger returns to the top. "Oh, there should be a line here," I say.

Jamie frowns. "I missed something? Where?"

"Here. Beside Susan's name."

Now they are both staring at me, and I realize what I've revealed.

"Whose name would go there, Gran?"

I take a deep breath and picture his dear face again. "Billy."

twenty-four
WINNY

❧

— 1938 —

Amid the squealing streetcar noise and the quick tap of so many boots on the sidewalks, hope sprouted in Winny's heart like a seedling. Looking everywhere at once, she and Charlotte wound their way through the busy Toronto streets, searching for the apartment the Carpenters had rented for them. They had said it was set right on top of a grocery store, offering unimagined convenience.

"Over there," Charlotte said suddenly, pointing across the street. "It's a good thing, too. This trunk is heavy."

Winny took in the front of the little shop, with its bright displays of beans and corn, the cardboard signs painted with prices, and the jolly green-and-white-striped awning stretched over it all. Beside the front door was another, and there the girls paused and held up their individual keys. They stood perfectly still for a second, beaming at each other.

"Here we go," Winny said.

"Will you do the honours?" Charlotte asked.

Winny's key slid smoothly into the lock, and the door opened with a little encouragement, revealing a narrow stairway.

"I can hardly believe it," Winny said, heading up the stairs. She opened the second door at the top and stepped into the apartment. "Just the two of us, on our own."

"Oh," Charlotte said, peering into the space behind Winny. "It's . . . sweet."

Winny took in the cracked yellow walls, the worn, floral sofa and armchair, the dining table with its four mismatched chairs. Setting down her trunk, she made her way into the kitchen, a tight space crowded with a boxy white stove and refrigerator. The tap over the sink kept up a steady drip, and the ceiling light was dotted with dead flies.

Charlotte came in behind. "It's not much, is it? I mean, I suppose we can make do—"

"It's wonderful!" Winny cried, hugging her. "This is our very own home, and I cannot think of a better place to live. Please, please thank the Carpenters again. It's perfect." She spun in a circle. "Come on. Let's go see our bedrooms."

They were identical, each with white walls, a dresser, and a small bed.

"My own bed!" Winny exclaimed, flopping onto the mattress. "How will I sleep without hay scratching me all over and sticking in my ears?"

"The landlady told Mum that she just replaced the mattresses," Charlotte said from the other room.

Winny was certain she had died and gone to heaven.

Mrs. Carpenter had sent them with clean sheets and pillows as well as towels, dishes, and cutlery, and the girls quickly got to work putting everything in place. That night after the sun set, a streetlight beamed into their living room and a car honked loudly, but when Charlotte went to close the curtains, Winny stopped her. The last time she remembered walking in this city at night she'd been laughing with Jack, and Edward had finally admitted to Mary that he fancied her. Winny wanted to stay in that memory as long as she could. Back then, they'd known their time together was limited. They'd never imagined it might be cut so short.

"Ever since Mary died," Winny said, "I've been dreaming of coming here and finding her son. I can't believe it's finally happening." Her pulse quickened, and she turned to Charlotte. "What if he's not there? What if he's already been adopted? What if—"

"Don't worry." Charlotte wrapped a comforting arm around Winny's waist. "He'll be there. The Carpenters said it would be unlikely for any baby of a Home Child to be adopted so soon." She lowered her eyes. "Most families are looking for older children to help on their farms. Or new babies."

"You're right," Winny said, picking at her nails. "What if I find him, but I don't know what I'm doing? You know, with a baby."

"You'll know exactly what to do. You were very good with babies in the nursery at Barkingside, if I recall." She winked. "And just in case you've forgotten, you're about to learn how to be a nurse as well."

"Yes, but what if he doesn't like me? What if I—"

"He will love you, Winny. Mary knew that, and so do I." Charlotte smiled. "Now, let's have a bite to eat then go to bed. Tomorrow's a big day. Your dear husband, Jeffrey, will meet us at the café in the morning, and then we'll go straight there."

Winny flushed at the mention of their little ruse. "Your cousin is so nice to do this for me."

"He is, isn't he? He's a tremendous fellow, and ever so smart. He knows how important this is to you, and he knows how important you are to me." She headed to the kitchen. "Also, technically, Jeffrey's not really my cousin. He's Mrs. Carpenter's nephew."

After a quick supper of sandwiches and tea, they went to their bedrooms and Winny slid between the fresh sheets, pulling her blanket up to her chin. The pillow was so soft behind her head she felt as if she were floating. Within seconds, she was asleep.

The next morning, Winny was up hours before the sun, dressing in her best clothes, trying not to worry her nails to the quick. But there was nothing she could do about her nerves, which buzzed with adrenaline, and she paced the little apartment while she waited for Charlotte to get ready. When at last they stepped outside, Winny breathed in the sweet perfumes of oranges and apples coming from the store, overwhelming the less pleasant smells of the city street.

"Now I'm hungry as well as excited," Charlotte said, taking her arm. "Let's go!"

When they reached the café, Charlotte peered around with purpose, but Winny's eyes went everywhere. The tables were crowded with patrons, and though their noses were buried in menus and coffee cups, she felt as if they all watched her.

"There you are! Hello, Jeffrey!" Charlotte exclaimed, pulling Winny toward a young man already seated at a table near the window. He was strikingly handsome, as Charlotte had said, though his eyes were obscured behind very thick glasses.

Following her friend, Winny felt an odd sense of envy. Charlotte moved so effortlessly between the tables, while Winny fought the urge to duck behind the closest coat rack and stay out of sight. Thanks to the Carpenters, no one had ever told Charlotte she was just a gutter rat, that she didn't belong. Winny lifted her chin, challenging herself. If Charlotte could do this, if she could walk through a crowd with her head held high, then so could Winny, she tried to tell herself. She just had to learn how.

Jeffrey jumped to his feet as they approached, and Winny admired his smart grey suit, accented by a light blue tie. "Charlotte!"

"So good to see you." Charlotte hugged him then introduced Winny. "Jeffrey, this is my best friend in the whole world. Winny, this is the sweetest man I know."

Jeffrey gave a little bow. "It's an honour to finally meet you, Winny."

"I'm very glad to meet you." She clenched her hands to her chest, hoping to still the dancing nerves. "I really don't know how to properly thank you for doing this. Our little charade may not work, but—"

"But it might," he said. "And I'm happy to help."

"Look at that." Charlotte beamed. "You're already finishing each other's sentences. A match made in heaven."

His cheeks reddened, and he gestured toward the table. "Would you like some breakfast?" he asked.

"Yes! We're famished," Charlotte said, settling in.

When they were all seated, Jeffrey turned to Winny. "I'm glad we got this opportunity. I thought maybe you and I should talk a little, learn something about each other before we go in there."

"Good idea," Winny replied. "I'll admit, I've been a little nervous about that."

"Of course. But I'm sure it will all be fine. Actually, I found something that should put you entirely at ease. During all my digging, I stumbled across a court ruling that changes everything. Apparently, you do *not* have to be married to adopt a child."

"What? I don't?" She looked at Charlotte, then back at Jeffrey. "Well, then . . . does that mean they will have no objections at all? Is it as good as done?"

"I'm not entirely sure if they'll have hoops for us to leap through or not, so I still think my standing in as a prospective father will be beneficial to your case."

"Oh, yes," Charlotte said earnestly, leaning over the table toward him. "We need you there, Jeffrey. Having a brilliant lawyer with us just makes everything so much more reputable."

He grinned. "Thank you for your unflagging faith in me, Charlotte. Now Winny, let's get to know each other a little. My middle name is Edgar. Yours?"

"Margaret. Winnifred Margaret Ellis," Winny said. "But you should call me Winny."

"Do you have any hobbies?"

She stared at him. "Hobbies?"

"What do you like to do when you're not working?"

"I . . . I don't think I've ever not worked."

"Let's make something up," Charlotte suggested. "Reading. You always like to read."

"That's true," Winny said. "I do like to read. What about you, Jeffrey?"

"I enjoy reading as well. Mostly newspapers, though," he replied. "I also play hockey."

"I love hockey! Which position?" Charlotte asked.

"Defense," Jeffrey replied.

"How exciting!"

Winny studied her friend, surprised. She'd heard of hockey, but when had Charlotte ever seen a game? She was about to ask when she noticed the sparkle in Charlotte's eyes. It reminded her of how Edward had always looked at Mary, and Winny suppressed a smile.

"Do you like hockey?" Jeffrey asked Winny.

"I have no idea. I've never seen a game."

"The three of us will have to go to one sometime," he said. "I'll find out when the Maple Leafs are in town."

They paused as the waitress approached their table. "Coffee? Tea?"

The others ordered coffee and eggs, but Winny hesitated, briefly dazed by the notion. No one had ever served her like this. She quickly recovered and asked for a cup of tea and a piece of toast, unsure if her stomach could handle much more than that this morning.

"So?" Charlotte said cheerfully as the waitress headed off. "What's your story? How long have you two been married?"

Jeffrey and Winny exchanged a glance. "Two years," he decided. "And we would like a son." He frowned. "Will you recognize your friend's child, do you think?"

Mary's tortured words came back to Winny. "*All I could see was a glimpse of black hair sticking out from inside the blanket.*"

She took a deep breath. "I sure hope so. He'd be a year and a half or so. That should help narrow it down, I hope."

He nodded, leaving that to her. "I'd be happy to do the talking in there. Unless, of course, they ask you something directly. It's just that . . ."

It was a kind offer, and while Winny felt unsteady at the thought of a near stranger taking her fate in his hands, she saw the wisdom in his suggestion. Of course, the people there would prefer to deal with a man, not a woman.

"That makes sense, Jeffrey. Thank you."

"We just want it all to work out for you," he said. "My aunt also mentioned you might need a nanny, so I thought I'd suggest my sister, Esther. If the matron asks about family support, we could mention her. You never know what might come up."

"Esther's lovely," Charlotte assured Winny.

Breakfast arrived, and Winny tried to keep calm as Charlotte and Jeffrey caught up, chatting about a dinner party they'd both attended months before. Before she knew it, it was time to go and they followed Jeffrey to his car. When he opened the door, Winny insisted that Charlotte sit up front with him so they could continue their conversation as they drove towards the maternity home. She needed to sit quietly in the back and clench her hands together, do what she could to stop them from shaking.

As they neared the address, all three of them fell quiet.

"This is Farley Avenue," Jeffrey said. "What number?"

"Two fourteen," Winny said quickly.

"There." Charlotte pointed. "That brick building with the black door and white windows. See? With the white fence."

Jeffrey parked in front of the building then opened the doors for the girls. Once they stood on the sidewalk, Charlotte took Winny's hand.

"You can do this."

Winny imagined Mary, her pleading eyes red from crying, and she knew Charlotte was right. She could, and she would. Impulsively, she reached for Jeffrey's hand as well, and he took it, looking slightly surprised but pleased. For a moment, all three were joined, and Winny felt stronger than ever.

"Let's go get my baby."

A dizzying sense of urgency surged through her as they walked through the big black door, their heels clattering on the tile floor and echoing off the walls. Charlotte fell behind Jeffrey and Winny as they approached the front desk, where a solitary woman welcomed them then introduced herself as Matron Douglas.

"I am Jeffrey Hill," Jeffrey said. "I believe you are expecting us."

"Ah yes," she said. "Nice to meet you both."

"And this is my cousin, Charlotte," he offered.

"Excellent. It is always good to have family support in these situations. We wouldn't want just anyone to walk in here and take one of our children." The matron opened a drawer and flipped through folders, frowning with annoyance. "I apologize. I can't seem to find your file at the moment. It may already be in the other room. No matter. I'm sure we can take care of things without it." She rose then gestured for them to follow her. "Not too many little ones here right now. Eight infants, and four others who are over a year. One girl and three boys, one of whom is starting to walk. The older children have already been sent to another orphanage, since they have outgrown this place. I'm sorry, I don't recall the age of the child you are looking for."

"We're looking for a boy, not too young," Jeffrey said as they walked. "Probably around a year and a half."

She nodded. "Let's see what you think. The babies are in this first room."

As they rounded a corner and entered the room, they were enveloped by the sickly sweet smell of diapers and milk.

"Oh," Winny said, moving instinctively toward the tiny, swaddled bodies. Her heart squeezed, aching with the loneliness and rejection the babies were too young to understand. "Where are their mothers?"

Matron Douglas glanced sideways at her. "These babies come from mothers who were unable or unwilling to care for them. It is our Christian duty to take them in and try to find families for them."

Winny fought the urge to contradict the woman. Mary had wanted her little boy more than anything else. That baby might have saved her life, if he hadn't been stolen from her.

"I wish we could take them all home," Charlotte whispered to Winny, then she turned to the matron. "I have a question, and I know you're the right person to ask. Do you recommend that new parents tell the child they're adopted when they're old enough to understand?"

"Actually, we strongly recommend *not* telling children they were adopted," the matron replied. "From years of experience, we've learned that it can be extremely damaging to a child to learn they were not naturally born to their parents, and worse, knowing they had been rejected by their natural mother. Either that, or she had been unsuitable. I'm sure you would agree it would be terrible for a child to learn he was a bastard."

Winny kept quiet. Even though her own parents had been married, she knew how it felt to be judged. She would never let Mary's son feel inferior to anyone.

"I was adopted, and I never thought of it that way," Charlotte said.

Matron Douglas raised an eyebrow. "I hear an English accent. How old were you when you were adopted, if you don't mind my asking?"

"Fifteen. My mother died in England."

"Well, there you are. It's different for an older child. You understood what was happening. A baby cannot be expected to reason through it that way."

"I see," Charlotte said vaguely.

"Right this way," the woman said, ushering them through another door.

Winny held her breath, taking in the four children in the next room. One girl, three boys, just like the matron had said. The tiny girl, who was easily identifiable with the pink ribbon tied around her head, was deep in thought, trying to fit pegs into a box. One of the boys looked up at Winny then returned to the three blocks he was stacking. He was a beautiful little boy, but his wispy hair was fair. A second boy with dark hair took one look at the three of them and darted behind the nurse's chair, muttering "no, no, no, no" the whole way. But it was the third boy who caught Winny's attention. He had been pulling a toy train behind him by a string, and now he stopped short, considering the newcomers. Winny could almost see his thoughts in his head. His hair was jet black. Just like Mary's. Just like Jack's. *Oh God*, she thought.

It took all of Winny's willpower not to rush in and catch him up in her arms.

A woman in a nurse's uniform sat in the corner of the room, her hands busy with knitting. "Good morning," she said, smiling gently.

"This is the couple I told you about," Matron Douglas said to her. "Winnifred and Jeffrey Hill, and Mr. Hill's cousin, Charlotte."

Winny couldn't wait another second. With all eyes on her, she walked to the middle of the room and crouched in front of the black-haired boy. She picked up the train, and he stopped, confused.

"Hi there," she said. "Is this yours?"

He plopped back onto his diapered bottom, clearly annoyed. She saw it in the tight little lips and the hint of a line that worked its way across his soft brow. She saw it in the piercing blue of his eyes, and she couldn't look away. She held out the train and was instantly forgiven.

The nurse set her knitting aside. "That little one is a darling, but he has quite a temper. Smart as a whip. His name is William. We call him Billy."

"Billy," Winny breathed, seeing Mary so clearly in his face. Tears burned in her eyes. "You're so beautiful, Billy."

As if he understood, Billy's face lit up like a sunrise, and his arms stretched toward her. With her heart in her throat, Winny lifted the solid little body and held it against her own.

"I've got you." Her chest swelled with a love she'd never felt before. "I've got you, Billy. You're safe now."

"Well," Jeffrey said. There was a smile in his voice. "It appears we have a winner."

"I'm impressed," said the nurse. "Billy's usually quite guarded with strangers."

"He doesn't feel like a stranger," Winny said, her fingers stroking the soft down of his hair. Then, because she couldn't resist, she asked, "Can you tell me anything about his mother?"

"As a matter of fact, I met the mother. I was there for Billy's birth."

Winny held her breath. Was this the woman who had swaddled Mary's baby then taken him away? Was this the woman who had told her she was an unfit mother?

"And? What was she like?"

"I'm certain she was a good, Christian girl, but she was English—" She hesitated, as if she had just remembered their accents, then rushed in to clarify. "One of those Home Children. I'm sure the pregnancy wasn't her fault technically, but they come to this country knowing nothing, you see. They don't know right from wrong."

Charlotte stood behind Winny, pressing against her as a reminder of how important it was that they stay calm and not upset the matron. This was their one and only chance.

But Winny had to ask. "Why did she leave her baby here?"

"It was better for everyone. I'm sure you understand. She was returned to her master, and the child was given the possibility of living a better life."

"What a sweet, sweet boy," Charlotte cooed, nudging Winny again. "Isn't he perfect, Winny?"

"Yes," Winny said, letting herself be drawn out of the discussion. When her eyes met his, Billy put his cool little fingertips on her lips, making her smile. "He's absolutely perfect."

"Are you sure?" Matron Douglas asked. "You didn't spend much time thinking about it. Keep in mind you cannot simply exchange one for another if you decide he's the wrong one for you."

"No. This is the one. This is my son." Winny kissed Billy's fingers one by one while he watched in fascination. "I'm absolutely sure."

twenty-five
JACK

❧

— 1939 —

October 1939
Shilo, Manitoba

Dear Edward and Cecil,

I know it's been a while since I last wrote to you and I'm sure you wondered where I went. I can't even really tell you that, because I can't remember. I've been hopping from train to train, and after a while I lost count. I guess you could say that I got a little lost. A man don't have to worry about much out here, just staying out from under the wheels and dodging the bulls. But I have had a lot of time to think about things. Promises I've made and not kept.

I've never stopped wondering about the girls, but in all this time I never saw or heard anything about them. If I'm being honest, I asked a lot of fellas at first, but I gave up on finding them a long time ago. There's only so many times a man can be told no before he finally believes it. I don't suppose Mr. Brown ever got back to you, did he? I doubt it.

Anyhow, I'd just about run out of things to ponder when someone handed me a newspaper that said we're at war. I never was one to run from a fight, was I? Well, this seemed like a pretty big one, and I'm ready to get my hands dirty. I reckon maybe this is my chance to do something good. To stand up and make a difference.

So here I am with the Royal Canadian Horse Artillery, which is part of the 1st Canadian Division. Don't ask me why we're called that, since we don't ride horses. At least I haven't had to so far. For now I'm in Shilo, Manitoba, which is some of the prettiest land I've ever seen. Miles and miles of open prairie, but just when you get bored it turns into hills and trees, and even to sand dunes. I reckon they'll be sending us overseas in the next few months, but I can't say when. Maybe back to jolly old England. Guess they'll send us through Halifax again.

You gonna come out and fight with me? I know it ain't the home cooking of Mrs. Cogan, but it is three square meals a day, and you get to sleep in cots just like in the old days. Remember those things? Squeeze us all together in one room so we can hear each other snore and fart all night long. Good times. Well, I'm doing that again, and it would be a hell of a lot more fun if you two were here.

Jack

October 1939
London, Ontario

Dear Jack,

Mr. Brown never got back to us. You aren't surprised, are you?
Edward just went to buy the train tickets. We're on our way.
Save us a couple of cots.
We've missed you.

Cecil

twenty-six
WINNY

❧

— 1942 —

Winny finished stocking the inventory cupboard with bandages and syringes then flinched when she checked her watch. She was running late. As fast as she could, she finished what she was doing and rushed over to sign out at the nurses' station. Her graduation ceremony was in less than an hour, and she still needed to change into a clean uniform before she could head over to the school. Esther would meet her there with Billy. Thank heaven for Esther.

Back in the nurses' room, she pulled her fresh uniform from her locker and got changed, doing up all the little buttons and setting her cap on straight. When she stepped in front of a mirror to check her appearance, it hit her: tomorrow morning when she showed up for her shift, Winny would be a fully fledged nurse at the Toronto General Hospital. And just in time, too.

Nobody could have imagined the war would still be raging three years on. Now there seemed to be no end in sight. The hospitals were overflowing with injured men from the front, and qualified nurses were needed now more than ever. Since the war had begun, Winny had tended the most horrific injuries and seen more pain than she ever could have imagined. The unspeakable damage that had been done to thousands of these men filled her nightmares, but she never complained to a soul. It was her duty to carry on and do what she could to help their bodies and their minds. After all, it was not she lying in a bed without eyes or arms, not she whose hip had been shattered. Winny could go home every night and spend time with the people she loved, but she could not say the same for these men.

She turned from the mirror and quickly left the room. Passing the front desk, she trotted to the main doors and into the fresh air, then she headed toward the school. She checked her watch again and picked up her pace; she should be right on time if she kept moving.

Even out in the brilliant sunshine with thoughts of Billy and graduation flitting through her head, Winny's mind still dwelled on the war. It was so difficult to shut it off, because when she thought of the war and the people she loved, things got complicated. Whenever she saw young men in uniform marching in the streets, she studied their faces, looking for Jack, Edward, Cecil, and David. Even after so many years apart, they were always with her. Had they gone to war? She knew the kind of boys they'd been years ago: always rough and ready to take on the next battle. She imagined as grown men they hadn't thought twice about going to fight. Just as she had reached for her nurse's uniform, they would have reached for a soldier's. And because of that, whenever she pulled back a curtain to tend a new patient, she pushed the faces she loved from her mind. Otherwise it was too difficult to turn to the next bed. At least Jeffrey was safe. Lucky for him, his vision was deemed bad enough that the army didn't want him.

"Winny!" Charlotte stood at the top of the school steps, hopping on her toes. "Come on!"

"I'm here, I'm here," Winny said, running up to her.

"I was worried you weren't going to make it."

"Sorry, sorry, sorry! Where's Billy?"

"Already inside with Esther."

Winny followed Charlotte into the foyer, where the rest of their class had gathered, then Charlotte turned to straighten Winny's little cotton cap. "I can't believe we're graduating," she said. "Are we really ready for this?"

"Of course we are."

The girls fell into lines of two and marched into the auditorium then onto the stage. From there, Winny looked into the audience and spotted Charlotte's adopted parents, the Carpenters, cheering her on. Beside them sat a beaming Jeffrey, a bouquet of red roses on his lap. For Charlotte, no doubt. And beside him, sitting on Esther's lap, was Billy. His lips moved constantly with words Winny wished she could hear.

It felt like just last week that she'd first brought him home to the apartment. She'd watched with delight as his chubby little fingers pointed at everything he saw, and she couldn't help laughing along with him as he took in the noises of the city. Inside their new home, he had wandered behind and around the furniture and lamps, exploring his new surroundings until he tired of it, then he'd held out his arms for Winny. Within seconds, he had fallen asleep, melted contentedly into a warm, lovable lump on her lap. In that moment Winny realized, without a shadow of a doubt, that she would do anything in the world for this little boy.

It hadn't always been easy, of course. Jeffrey's sister, Esther, was a godsend, but even then, most days Winny needed an extra twelve hours on top of the twenty-four. Even today she felt a little like Charlotte's brass wind-up clock, except she kept forgetting to wind herself up. Nursing school had kept Winny and Charlotte busy, and their heads were filled with lessons on practical and surgical nursing as well as complicated classes about anatomy, communicable diseases, physiology, and diseases of the eye, ear, nose, and throat. Because of the war, a whole host of extra lessons on treating wounds and limb loss had been added to their course.

And then there were the nights when Billy put Winny's nursing skills to the test, fighting fevers or incoming teeth, and Winny had felt as if she were hanging on by a thread.

The first time Billy called her "Mama," she broke down and cried, thinking how unfair it was that Mary would never hear those two beautiful syllables. That had unsettled him terribly, so she had turned her tears to happy ones, hugging him and tickling him until he made those wonderful belly laughs that she couldn't resist.

Despite the late nights and the endless worry, Winny wouldn't have changed a thing. She had kept her promise to Mary and given Billy all the love she had. Now she couldn't imagine her life without him. He was such a happy boy. And so smart. The matron at the maternity home had been right about his temper, but Winny knew how to calm him. After all, she'd done it for years with his mother. Billy was everything to Winny, but sometimes his sweet face broke her heart. And it wasn't just that he was Mary's son. The dimple that curled in his soft cheek whenever he gave Winny that saucy, one-sided smile belonged to Jack.

"Doesn't Jeffrey look handsome?" Charlotte whispered beside her.

"He only has eyes for you, Charlotte," Winny replied.

Their romance had finally blossomed last fall. Jeffrey had insisted on accompanying his sister to their apartment almost every day, despite Esther's protests that she walked only during daylight hours and only on safe streets. Winny wasn't fooled, and she loved watching Charlotte primp while she waited for him, pinching her cheeks before he arrived and adding a touch of vivacious red lipstick—which she had to remove before they reached the hospital—to her already beautiful lips. When Jeffrey appeared one evening with a bouquet of fresh flowers and asked her to dinner, Charlotte had floated on air for the rest of the week.

Winny, on the other hand, had no time to think about dating, but when she pushed Billy's stroller through the park on sunny weekends, the fact that she was a woman walking alone with a baby never went unnoticed. Now that her fictitious husband was dating her best friend,

Winny resorted to telling nosy pedestrians that her husband had gone to war.

Settling onto her seat, Winny gazed out at the rest of the audience and caught her breath. There, sitting by herself near the back, was Mistress Adams. She shifted under Winny's scrutiny, clearly uncomfortable, and turned her face to the side. Over the past two years, Winny had sent brief updates to the woman detailing how she was doing. She'd felt obligated, since her mistress's money was helping to finance her schooling. But Winny had never expected her to show up at her graduation, and she wasn't sure how she felt about seeing her there. The sight stirred an uncomfortable rush of emotions that Winny had thought she'd put to rest.

From the podium on the far end of the stage, an aged professor addressed the graduating students, and Winny reminded herself to pay attention. This would be her one and only graduation ceremony, after all.

"You are no longer naïve little children," his wavering voice said into the microphone. "You are important, productive, valuable members of our society. You are the future of Canada. Everything in your past is behind you now, whether it was good or bad, and it all matters. All of those things will contribute to the person you become in the future."

Winny bit her cheek, trying not to cry. The ugliness *was* all behind her, but so were some of the best moments of her life. The people she had loved before were gone, but they had helped make her who she was now. Because of Jack, she ran faster and reached higher. Because of Mary, she knew the meaning of true friendship. Because of Charlotte, she understood the sun would always rise again. Even Mistress Adams had contributed to who Winny had become.

At the end of his address, the professor began calling their names, and applause rose from the crowd as each student went to receive her diploma. Then it was Winny's turn.

"Miss Winnifred Ellis," the professor said, and she got to her feet. Flushing with pride, she walked across the stage toward him, her white leather shoes padding quietly on the floor. As she shook his hand and collected her diploma, she heard her friends in the crowd clap and cheer, and she turned toward them with a smile. One voice rang above the rest, bringing tears of joy to her eyes.

"Mummy!" Billy was jumping up and down, waving his cap at her. "That's my mummy!"

Grinning, Winny waved back at him, her heart full. In that moment everyone in the audience was watching her and applauding her accomplishment. Not one person in the crowd was judging her or sneering at the Home Girl. No one out there truly knew how far she'd come, except maybe Mistress Adams, who was dabbing her eyes with her handkerchief, a warm expression of genuine admiration on her face.

Winny glanced over at Charlotte, meeting her dancing eyes, and was startled by a long-ago memory: the face of a terrified little girl alone in a dark room, fruitlessly awaiting her mother. The illusion passed in a blink, but Winny's sense of unease lingered. Back then, she had thought she was happy. She'd thought she had everything she'd ever need, living with Mary at Barkingside. How little she had understood. How much their lives had changed after that. Her gaze returned to Billy, struggling to loose himself from Esther's caring arms, and she wondered what that said about her life right now. So many things were uncertain. So many things yet to come.

twenty-seven
JACK

⤜∾⤛

— 1943 —

Jack closed his eyes, riding the swell of the ocean, inhaling the open sea air. The wind felt good against his face. It was a different wind from the one that had pushed him from train to train, the one that had reddened his cheeks all winter through iced-over miles, and the one that had drenched him during spring rains. The wind always felt right to him. Cleansing, in a way. As if the grime of the past could fall off and be left behind.

"I feel like all we ever do is wait." Cecil's chin rested on his folded arms. He was bent over the ship's rail, staring glumly at the water. "I just want to get there."

Edward chuckled. "We're always in a hurry to get somewhere, then we can't wait to leave. What's the rush, I say."

"I ain't never liked boats," Cecil said.

Jack felt a little of both. He was eager to get to the war, but he never got tired of being with the brothers. Jack had met them at the Shilo station when they came out to join the 1st Canadian Infantry Division, and it was as if they'd never been apart. Just like him, they joined up ready to fight, but the training had gone on forever. Even after they were shipped back to England to join the British forces, the training continued. Some of the men with whom they shared barracks complained about the cots, the food, and the discipline, but for the Home Boys, almost everything about training camp was a luxury.

Now it was late June and they were finally headed into conflict. During their first week at sea their commander had told them they were part of "Operation Husky," along with several other divisions travelling in the Mediterranean Sea, en route to join a huge armada involving over twenty-five hundred Allied ships. Two miles off the southern tip of Italy was the volcanic island of Sicily, currently held by both Italian and German forces, and the island was in the perfect position for attacking and destroying the shipping routes of the Allied forces. The Allies' mission was to storm the beaches and take the island. The boys were eager to flex some muscle, to make use of their skills. To have a purpose.

In the meantime, they spent as much time as they were allowed on the top deck, breathing in the warm wind rather than the stale air below. With their days full of little but ocean, it was impossible not to think about their original sail out of England. A different ocean, a different lifetime.

"Think it's still the same?" Cecil asked. "If we'd gone back to London for a visit, would we have seen the same people and buildings?"

"Some of it's been destroyed by the Germans," Edward said. "But I imagine some of it's the same."

Jack's mind wandered back to those cold, wet streets, to the jostling marketplace where no one had wanted them. "I wonder if what they said is true," he mused. "If they gave us a better life by sending us away. I mean, England wasn't so different. Just like in Canada, the folks here called us thieves, sneaks, vermin . . . you know."

"Yeah, but in England we deserved it." Edward paused. "I have a question. I know who we're fighting against. But who are we actually fighting *for*? England or Canada?"

"One and the same," Jack replied. "We're the good guys, no matter what."

"Where are you gonna go after the war?" Cecil asked. "We're on our own now, don't owe nobody nothing. No one cares that we're Home Boys anymore."

"Back to Canada," Jack said without hesitation. There he would find meaningful work, like he'd always intended to do, and there he would find Mary and Winny. Seven years ago he'd made the girls a promise, and he'd wasted a lot of time not following through. He'd been wrong to give up before, and when this was all over, he would search for them, even if it took the rest of his life.

⸻

A few nights later, they were again standing by the rail when Jack heard a splash nearby. He knew where the other fifty or so boats in their convoy should be, and this noise seemed out of place. There was just enough moonlight to let various shades of grey play with his vision, so he pressed binoculars to his eyes, scouting the endless void of water. Another splash came from his right, sounding even closer. This time, he clearly saw the source . . . and more.

He grabbed the front of Edward's shirt and shoved the binoculars into his friend's hand. "Look!"

Edward peered through the lens, and his jaw dropped. "Cecil. Get over here."

Cecil laughed out loud when he saw. "Those Nazi bastards won't know what hit 'em!"

The sea, which had seemed so vast hours before, was now crowded with Allied ships, manned by tens of thousands of Canadian, American, and British troops. Everywhere Jack looked there was another immense ship teeming with men. The spray of thousands of steel bows slicing through the surface, the sheer military might that covered the sea around him, filled Jack with an undeniable sense of power.

But doubt returned a week later when their convoy floated slowly through a well-known U-boat hotbed. All at once, torpedoes blasted through the water, and there was nothing he or any of the others could do but stand on deck and watch in horror as three of their freighters blew up, one after another. Almost sixty men lost in the blink of an eye, along with five hundred vehicles and weapons. That night he and the rest of the division lay in their cots, haunted by what they'd seen.

The day before the scheduled invasion, a storm blew in. As if to protect the island, the wind stirred the water to colossal waves that tossed the warships like toys. The men were ordered to keep to their quarters for safety, but the ship rolled so badly that even the hardiest sailor had trouble keeping control of his stomach. It came as a great relief when evening finally arrived and the winds began to die down. Jack, Cecil, and Edward were among the first to escape to the top deck for fresh air. They should have been sleeping, Jack knew—he had a feeling this day would demand more from him than he had to give—but a restless flow of apprehension and excitement ran through his veins like wildfire.

A new roar started up from somewhere behind them, growing louder and louder until it shook the sky, and the boys stared in awe as airplanes soared overhead.

"Paratroopers!" Edward hollered over the noise. "Someone said they'll be dropping behind enemy lines to prevent escape."

"Crazy bastards," Cecil yelled, waving a fist in the air. "Go get 'em, lads!"

Just then a major walked over and ordered them back downstairs. "If you can't sleep, then clean your guns and shine your boots and buttons." He patted Cecil's shoulder on his way by. "But you're gonna wish you'd slept."

Two hours later they were jolted awake by deafening booms as the Allied ships started shelling the shore. The blasts were continuous, shuddering through Jack's chest and pounding in his ears. The men were primed, and they stood shoulder to shoulder as they waited for orders. When it was time, they climbed down the ship's outer stairs, fully loaded with guns, grenades, and ammo, then they stepped aboard a landing craft along with dozens of other men. From the middle of the crowd, Jack could see nothing but the sky and the backs of the men in front of him. Battle was unavoidable now, and Jack fought to contain his rising panic. As the boat cast off, he heard someone whispering prayers.

Ping! Jack jerked sideways out of reflex when something hit the wall of the craft right beside him. Bullets, he realized, heart racing. When the ramp at the front of the craft opened, he and the others would rush out and run straight into those bullets. More and more hit the vehicle as they drew closer to the beach, and suddenly everything was much too real.

Cecil and Edward stood stiffly beside him, and Jack could sense their fear. They'd been through too much together not to know what the others were thinking, and this time they not only faced the unknown, they faced possible death. Jack's mind went to all the times they'd been in trouble, and how they'd stuck together through it. When things got out of hand, Jack had been the one they'd turned to, and they'd been the ones he'd counted on. Today would be no different.

"Hey," he said. The brothers' faces were pale, their eyes large under metal helmets. "What do you say we meet at a nice Italian restaurant after this is all done? Maybe just on the other side of the beach."

They didn't answer, but he saw the softening in their expressions, the moment they'd needed to break through the fear and remember who they were. How far they'd come. And that they weren't alone.

He gave a quick, single nod. "Right then. First one in gets the table. Last one in pays."

Their commander took his position at the front of the boat. "Gentlemen! Remember your objective. Take out the enemy's defenses and head past the beach. Do not stop. Do not assist any fallen men. Do you understand? I don't care who he is, leave him there and keep running."

"Not bloody likely," Edward muttered.

"Ready!" the man yelled. "Five . . . four . . . three . . . two . . . one."

The ramp dropped with a sharp squeal and splashed into the water. Jack pushed forward with the rest of them, and when he leapt off the edge he sank unexpectedly to his chin in warm Mediterranean water. Cecil splashed in at his side, but he couldn't see Edward. Bullets hacked into the surface around them, and though the weapons and ammo weighed him down like an anchor, Jack's mind flew ahead, listing everything he needed to do *right now*. Get out of the water. Get onto the beach. Don't get hit. Head toward the dunes, sprint toward the barbed wire—

A private he'd had breakfast with two days before fell in front of him. Jack yanked the man back to his feet and kept moving. It was getting easier, since his knees were above water now. To his left, another soldier cried out and a plume of blood exploded from his arm. When someone reached to help him, he was hit too. Cecil grunted to his right, and Jack wheeled toward him, eyes wide.

"I'm okay, I'm okay," Cecil said, and Jack saw Edward on his other side, pulling Cecil to his feet. "I tripped."

A bullet landed in the water to Jack's left, another one ahead, and streams of bubbles rose in their wake. He lifted his gun as if it were a part of his arm and fired at the enemy bunkers over and over again, though he had no idea if any of his bullets would hit. When he reached the sand dunes, the brothers went in the same as he, guns blazing over the crest, but the enemy wasn't there. They had expected tens of thousands of Italian forces to be waiting for them, and thousands of Germans behind them, but despite the urgency of everything going on around them, this seemed like a light resistance. Where was the enemy?

The three of them joined others from their battalion, already hunkered down in the sand and awaiting direction. Jack studied the expanse of scrub brush spread before them, but he couldn't see any opposing forces there either. Had the sheer magnitude of the Allied armada intimidated the enemy enough to send them running?

Their commander jumped over the dune, then waved them on through the sweltering heat. "On your feet," he yelled. "Let's see if we can find any of the cowards. Looks like most have fled inland, but a lot are surrendering."

The troops headed toward a dry dirt road, always on the lookout, but they saw no opposition.

"They may not be shooting at us, but it's still gonna be a long day," Edward said.

Jack resigned himself to the unavoidable walk ahead. Thanks to the earlier U-boat attack, most of their jeeps and trucks now lay at the bottom of the Mediterranean, along with hundreds of guns. The army had no choice but to walk the entire way across the barren, rocky hills of Sicily, smothered by the oppressive heat and accompanied by tanks that stirred up clouds of choking dust. Their mud-green uniforms were soon a thick, chalky yellow.

They were at the front of the unit when they eventually reached a small village dotted by little white houses, and Edward clutched his gun out of reflex.

Jack shook his head, put his hand on the barrel. "Look at the white flags. Those aren't soldiers. And they look pretty happy to see us."

———

For the next week, they passed carefully over mine-filled roads and through more villages, receiving mixed but usually harmless welcomes. Still, they could never completely drop their guard, because the enemy occasionally infiltrated the villages and hid within the innocent-looking walls.

The farther inland they marched, the more it became a battle against the land, with its punishing mountains and canyons, its rugged, winding roads. The heat baked their steel helmets and burned their faces. The dust was unrelenting, and Jack's eyes felt like sandpaper. When he reached for his water bottle to soothe his parched throat, the water was hot. As the mountains rose more steeply, they began to run into skirmishes, and they discovered the Germans knew this terrain well. The enemy had learned to dig into a fortified spot on a mountain then swiftly move to the next, using their hidden vantage points to fire onto the weary Canadians.

Jack and the brothers were assigned to a small contingent of men that was frequently ordered to the tops of the hills to scout for Germans. When their commander sent them up again, they went without question. Despite the heat, which Cecil repeatedly declared must rival the temperature of hell, the squad clambered up the steep rise toward the peak, conditioned by three years of hard training. Once they reached the top, they leaned against a rock face, taking a few minutes to recover from the climb. A pearl of sweat rolled down Jack's cheek.

"I've never been this hot," Cecil groaned, leaning against the hill. He took his helmet off and scrubbed his fingers through his hair, which was plastered to his skull.

"Yeah, you have," Edward said. "You recall those good old days working for Warren?"

"I choose Italy," Jack muttered. "Look at that water down there. You ever seen such a beautiful colour?"

"Yeah," Cecil said, his voice wistful. "It's almost worse that we can see it, you know? Feels like it's teasing us."

Suddenly one of the men close to Cecil cried out, clutching his leg, and bullets pelted the rock face.

"Snipers! Take cover!" Jack yelled.

Cecil slid down the dirt, reaching for the fallen man, who was slipping helplessly down the mountainside. "Come on, lad! Get up!"

"Cecil! Get over here!" Edward yelled.

Cecil wasn't giving up on the injured man, so Edward and Jack ran out to help. Edward got there first, grabbing the man's pack strap, and the brothers heaved him out of danger.

"Idiot," Edward said, handing Cecil the helmet he'd left behind. "You forgot—"

Cecil suddenly flew backwards, showering the dirt with blood. Jack and Edward dove down beside him, shielding his body and dragging him behind a shrub, out of harm's way.

"Jesus." Edward pressed hard against his brother's neck, but blood seeped out between his fingers. "His artery. It hit his artery, Jack! I don't know what to do!"

Cecil gasped desperately for air and his body shook unnaturally.

"It's nothing, mate," Jack tried, his voice cracking as he looked in Cecil's eyes. "They can stitch that up quick. You just gotta stay awake."

"Cecil, don't you do this." Tears streamed down Edward's face, cutting through the layers of dust. He touched his nose to his brother's and tried to speak, but he choked on his words. "Breathe, damn you!"

"Don't leave me," Cecil mouthed. "Don't leave me."

"Never," Edward promised.

"We're right here," Jack said, squeezing Cecil's arm hard and hoping he could feel it.

The battle carried on around them. Enemy snipers were firing out of enclaves they'd dug out of the volcanic rock across from them, and the Canadians were shooting back. Bullets pummelled the dirt on both sides and cracked into rocks, men yelled desperately at each other, but all Jack could think about was Cecil.

"No, no, no," Edward sobbed, still pushing on Cecil's neck.

"It's been a laugh," Cecil managed, struggling to keep his eyes open. "My two brothers. Watch out for each other."

"Cecil!" Edward yelled, and his brother's eyes fluttered open. "Don't give up!"

The corners of Cecil's dust-covered lips lifted as his eyes closed for the last time, and Edward collapsed on top of him, weeping. Jack rose, his head throbbing with every pulse, and the ground swayed beneath him.

The Germans would pay for this.

He backed away then dove behind a shrub just as a bullet skimmed past. From his relatively protected position, Jack raised his gun and set his sights on a German, but his hands shook so violently, his first shot missed, cracking off a stone near the sniper. He shot again, and it went wide. Furious at his clumsiness, he took a moment to concentrate before he tried again. This time, everything inside Jack focused on the German across the way. All his hate and grief manifested into a solid strength that he knew would not miss. What he needed was a better angle. Stepping out from behind the bush, he stood up tall, fired the shot, and hit his target straight on.

A searing pain cut through his body, and he staggered backwards, stunned by the blow. As he fell to the ground, he gripped his stomach reflexively, and all he could think was *I hit him! I got him for you, Cecil!* But the burning agony in his gut couldn't be ignored.

"I'm hit!" he yelled, his voice strangled. "I'm hit!"

Edward lifted his head from his brother's body. "Oh God," he breathed. Keeping his head low, he crawled to Jack then dragged his body back toward Cecil.

"Is it bad?" Jack asked, but he thought he already knew.

Edward's blood-covered hands went to Jack's stomach. He ripped Jack's shirt open to see the wound and Jack jerked, gasping with pain.

"Hold on, Jack."

White-hot agony shot through him when Edward rolled him to his side then put him back. Through the growing fog in his mind, he heard Edward yell at another soldier to come and help.

"Push here. Hard," Edward ordered the man, and Jack cried out at the pressure. Then Edward lowered his face to Jack's. "Listen, Jack. We have to stop the bleeding. The bullet went right through, which is good. Means I don't have to go look for it. And I think it missed all the important bits, which is even better."

"The bad news?" Jack asked huskily.

"This is going to hurt like hell."

He gritted his teeth, trying not to howl as Edward packed his wound tightly then wrapped him round and round with a bandage. Stars danced in his vision.

Poor Edward, he thought vaguely, following the stars. *Losing two of us in one day.*

twenty-eight
WINNY

❦

Winny knelt on the sidewalk, pasting a bright smile onto her face as she tucked Billy's shirt into his trousers and adjusted his collar, though it was already fine.

"Well, my big boy," she said, patting his tummy. "Here we are. Your first day at school. You'll have so much fun."

Billy nodded, all business. How she loved that little face. When he laughed, he was Jack all over again, and when he cried, she saw Mary's broken soul. Right now he was the spitting image of his uncle, and she could see stars dancing in his eyes.

"I'm excited."

"I'm sure you are." She flinched when the school bell rang in the yard, then she held on to her smile for dear life. "And you're going to show everyone how smart you are. I'm very proud of you, Billy. Can I have a hug?"

He wrapped his arms around her neck, squeezing hard on purpose so she'd make her funny groan for him.

"Why are you crying, Mummy?"

She wiped the telltale tears away. "Oh, Billy. It's just that I'll miss you."

"Don't worry, Mummy. I'll see you tonight."

"You're right. Remember, when school is over, you wait right by the door and Esther will come for you."

"Okay." He turned toward the school, glancing back over his shoulder one more time. "Bye, Mummy!"

She stayed until he disappeared inside along with all the other children, then she walked determinedly toward the hospital, trying to keep her mind on work instead of the little boy she was leaving behind.

When she walked into the nurses' room, Charlotte was there with two others from the night shift, changing out of their uniforms. She was fastening the buttons of a pretty dress she'd made, its skirt a muted wave of autumn leaves.

"Off to see Jeffrey?"

She nodded, checking her hair in the mirror, then she leaned in to apply the perfect shade of lipstick. "We're having breakfast together. Do you know, if we were married, this would be almost our fourth anniversary?"

"I was just thinking how quickly time passes," Winny replied, doing up her own buttons. Selfishly, she was glad nurses weren't allowed to be married, because she hated to think of losing her roommate, but she did feel sorry for Charlotte. She and Jeffrey were so obviously in love.

"Did Billy get off to his first day of school all right?"

"He could hardly wait to say goodbye."

Charlotte's smile was sympathetic. "Jeffrey says he wants to introduce you to his lawyer friend, Stephen."

"That sounds . . . nice," Winny said. The last time Jeffrey had introduced her to anyone it had been a terrible flop. Not too many men were interested in dating a single mother, she'd found. Even though Billy had been an absolute angel every time she introduced men to her son, and even though she told them she was a war widow, they weren't interested in carrying that kind of added weight.

"I know that tone," Charlotte said, heading to the door. "Well, I'm off. I'll see you at home later. I'll be there to spell off Esther after seven. Have a good shift."

She knew Charlotte was only trying to help, but the truth was Winny didn't mind being single. Her only family in the whole world was Billy, and that was fine with her. Just like Charlotte, he wasn't even with his real mother. But unlike Charlotte, he didn't know that.

Winny checked her face in the mirror, then went right to work, checking on the patients on her floor, starting with poor Private Hinton. Most of the man's lower jaw and tongue had been blown off somewhere in France. She couldn't imagine what he'd gone through before he'd finally arrived here. The hospital's plastic surgeon was in the process of completing some delicate and fragile reconstruction, but healing took time, and poor Private Hinton was wont to tear off his bandages as soon as his latest nurse turned her back. Winny assumed that had something to do with whatever was going on in his mind, which had to be something awful. It was rare to see a man in here who didn't suffer from the types of wounds a bandage could not help. It didn't matter how many times or how tightly she bound him up, Private Hinton eventually tore the covering off and made himself worse. He'd done it again this morning, she saw, reaching into her cart for a fresh wad of bandages.

"Wouldn't you like to get out of here one day?" she said gently as she tended him. "If you'd let it heal, we could take you out of doors in a wheelchair, and you could breathe fresh air again."

He answered with a grunt. Given the state of his face and the condition of his mind, Winny was fairly sure he would never say anything coherent again. She pushed the tragic thought from her mind and moved to the next bed.

"Good afternoon," she said cheerily, pulling back the curtain.

"If you say so," her patient replied.

Private Shuman had come in a day earlier after being hit by a streetcar.

According to reports, he'd been on shore leave and toasting everyone on the street with a mostly empty bottle of whisky at the time. Winny's heart went out to the extremely pale young man. His eyes were filled with far too many memories of war, and now he'd have to cope with a badly mangled leg as well.

"Which hurts worse, your leg or your head?" she teased, slipping a thermometer under his tongue.

He gave her a sheepish shrug. She extracted the thermometer and examined the numbers: 99.3. That was fine.

"With the whisky I didn't feel much of the leg pain."

"I see your point. However, without the whisky you wouldn't have any leg pain at all," she reminded him. "I've brought you some aspirin for now, but the surgeon will be here in about an hour, and he'll have more to tell you."

His expression grew serious. "Do you think I'm gonna lose my leg, Nurse?"

"I'm in no position to offer an opinion," she said, avoiding his eyes. "I'm sorry. But the surgeon will be here soon. He's very good. Oh, and you have a visitor."

"I do?"

"Do you recall giving the nurse a telephone number last night?"

He searched his memory and came up empty.

"Your mother. She's just outside."

He closed his eyes. "She's not gonna be impressed."

"She'll be glad you're still alive to scold. I'll send her in."

From what she'd seen on his chart, Winny feared the young man was indeed facing amputation, but it wasn't up to her to tell him the dreaded truth. What an awful thing—for him to have survived the war intact only to ruin it during his brief sojourn at home.

Major Antonici was propped up at the next bed, dark eyes twinkling, his right leg suspended in a cast. "Good morning, Nurse Beautiful."

"You are looking much better!" she exclaimed. "How's the leg today?"

"Itchy as ever. Think you could get your fingers in there, give it a scratch?"

She laughed. "You are such a charmer, Major Antonici."

"Marco! Please!"

"All right. You are such a charmer, *Marco*. I'll see if I can find a knitting needle you can poke around in there. Here's your aspirin and water. Are you hungry?"

"Could eat a horse."

"Another good sign. If you keep this up, you could be leaving here sooner than I thought."

He feigned a pout. "Maybe I'd better slow down. I'm only just getting to know the prettiest nurse in the hospital."

"Miss Ellis?"

Winny turned toward Miss Applegate, the head nurse. She was an older woman, nearly a head shorter than Winny, with a kind but toad-like face.

"Yes, ma'am?"

"Can you cover a few more patients today, dear? Constance is not feeling particularly well."

Winny nodded dutifully. As tired as she was of the long hours, it was still somewhat of a novelty to be asked politely for anything. "Of course."

"Thank you," she replied, indicating with one hand. "It's these beds here. A fresh batch of wounded soldiers. They arrived yesterday."

Winny nodded. Whether they were wrapped in bandages, hot with fevers, or cold with resignation, it never got any easier to see their misery. She crossed the room to the beds Miss Applegate had pointed out and opened the first curtain. The man in the bed was lying on his side, his back to her, but she could tell he wasn't sleeping.

"Good morning," she said, and he began to roll toward her. She checked the chart. Gunshot through the abdomen, she read, but it was pretty much healed. Just here for observation overnight. "Dr. Andrews will be in to see you in about an hour, and he'll tell you what to expect. Are you in pain, Mr. . . . Miller?"

She glanced up from the chart and met his eyes.

"It's you," he whispered.

At first she just stared. Then the lines under his eyes fell away, his dark whiskers melted into the smooth skin of a boy no more than sixteen years old. A boy she had always loved and never forgotten.

She sucked in her breath. "Jack?"

twenty-nine
JACK

❧

Blood rushed to Jack's head, and he curled his fingers around the sides of the cot, needing to steady himself. *Winny*. He blinked, clearing the daze from his eyes. Was she real? He had so many dreams these days, but none of them were like this. He needed to look her in those big brown eyes, make sure she wasn't a hallucination.

"I . . ." Words stuck in his throat. "I thought . . ."

"Is it really you?" Her voice was almost a whisper. She was clutching his chart tightly against her chest, frozen in place, and a lifetime of emotions flickered through her shining eyes. "I never thought I'd see you again."

"Me neither." He couldn't look away. "Come here, Irish," he said softly, falling easily into the old nickname. He suddenly needed to touch her. Needed proof. He opened his hands for an embrace, but she hesitated, her gaze going to the bandage on his stomach.

"Are you all right?" she asked. "I mean it says on here that you are, but . . ."

"I'd be better with a hug from you."

Setting the chart to the side, she carefully lowered herself to the edge of his bed. "Don't sit up. Your stitches—"

"They're all healed up. Come here, Winny."

He could hardly breathe as her arms wrapped around his neck, and her soft, cool skin touched his. His cheek found a spot behind her nurse's cap where he could nestle among those wild curls of hers, and he felt his heart ease.

It was the first time he'd felt like himself in years.

"I've missed you very much," he whispered.

She leaned slightly back, wiping tears from her eyes. "Oh, Jack. Where did you go?"

His joy turned to sand, jamming in his throat as the memory of his last morning in Toronto returned. How he'd left her behind. How he'd promised to find her then betrayed her instead, running off out west then sailing overseas. He couldn't answer.

She glanced at his bandage. "Am I hurting you?"

"I don't even feel it anymore."

"You look good," she said, touching his cheek with trembling finger-tips. "I had wondered if you went to war."

"Never could resist a fight, could I?" He took her hand from his face and held it in both of his. One question pounded in his chest. "Mary. Do you know where she is?"

She took a breath to speak, then he saw something shift behind her eyes, and a twinge of concern quivered through him. She never used to keep secrets from him.

She shook her head. "They took her away first."

He couldn't picture that. Couldn't imagine the two girls being sepa-rated. "You were alone?" he asked, and his sense of shame deepened. "Did you . . . did you manage all right?"

"It . . . got better over time. After all, here I am."

"Nurse Ellis?" A short, round woman had approached on the other side of Jack's bed. Her mouth was a wide, straight line.

Winny jumped to her feet. "I'm sorry, Miss Applegate. It's just . . . This is Jack. I grew up with him. It's been a very, very long time since I've seen him, and—"

The woman's smile stretched thinly, but not unpleasantly. "Nice to meet you, Private Miller." She turned to Winny. "Private Miller's injury will not keep him here long. You have a lot of patients to see to, especially since you are covering for Constance. Perhaps you could continue your conversation outside of hospital hours." She faced Jack again. "Sorry to cut this short, but Nurse Ellis has work to do."

"Of course," Jack replied, his heart sinking. "I didn't mean to take up her time."

Miss Applegate moved on, and Winny stood back, hugging his chart under her chin again. "I still can't believe you're here. Right here, with me." She touched the back of his hand, and he turned it over so their fingers could link. "I really can't."

"We can see each other after this, can't we?" he asked, his words coming out in a rush. After all this time, he couldn't lose her again.

"Oh Jack. You couldn't chase me away." She smiled, bringing out the sun. "I'll come back later and hear what the doctor has to say. Then we can figure out what to do next."

She turned away reluctantly, and he watched her lean over the other patients, tending to their needs. He listened to her cheerful voice singing with encouragement as she moved from bed to bed. She looked so sure of herself, so grown up, and he wondered what she thought of him.

He was very different from the boy she had waved goodbye to seven years before. Back then, he'd been apprehensive about leaving England, but he'd always harboured a sense of optimism about Canada. Mary hadn't, and now he knew she'd been right. Everything that had happened since then had taught him that life was hard, and he'd become just as hard in order to survive it.

When he'd first woken up in the medic tent before being shipped back to England for treatment, all he could see was Edward crying over

Cecil's lifeless body. Cecil was gone; he'd left his brother behind. And then, so had Jack. He'd abandoned his last friend back in the barren mountains of Sicily, surrounded by Germans. When he had felt well enough, Jack had written to Edward, but he hadn't heard back. He didn't like to wonder why.

Winny drifted past, writing something as she walked. It was so strange seeing her here. Life had torn all of them apart from each other so many times. Losing them, finding them, losing them again was like picking at an open wound. But today offered hope. If he and Winny could find each other, maybe they could find Mary, too. Maybe they could all try to heal together. For the first time in a long while, he reached for the possibility of happiness. When Winny looked up at him from across the room and smiled, warmth flooded his heart, and he felt it filling in the cracks, softening the hard places.

thirty
WINNY

W inny stood at the end of the hall, her hands deep in her coat
pockets. She had to purposefully hold them there because
her nerves were taking over, and she didn't know what else to do with
them.

After examining Jack, Dr. Andrews had told Winny that he was surprisingly healthy considering the gravity of his wound, and he was considering releasing him right away if he could count on Winny's being on
hand. He understood they were old friends, and after all, the hospital was
always short on beds and long on patients.

"Of course, Doctor," she'd replied, then she'd telephoned Jeffrey to
see if Jack could stay with him until he could find a place of his own.

Jeffrey had agreed as she'd known he would. "But if he's anything like
me, he won't take charity. Tell him I have a job for him to do when he's
well enough. To pay for his room."

"What job?"

"I'll think of something. I've been meaning to build a shed in the yard..."

Charlotte had a good man, Winny thought for the hundredth time. "That sounds perfect," she said. "But Jeffrey, I need to ask you another favour, and it's really important. The thing is, I'm not ready to tell Jack about Billy. I need you to keep Billy secret."

"I don't understand. Didn't you say Jack was the boy's uncle?"

"He is, but I haven't told him anything yet. You have to give me time to figure that out."

"Winny, my lips are sealed. It is your secret to keep or share. If the subject ever comes up, I'm deaf and dumb as a doorknob. But if I were you, I wouldn't keep it from him for too long."

When she told Jack she'd found him a place to stay, something in his eyes shifted. "He sounds like a good bloke. I'm glad you have a man like him around."

"Jeffrey's a very good friend," she said lightly. "He has been going steady with my roommate for years."

His brow lifted. "Oh, I see. Well, thanks for doing that, Winny."

She smiled, pleased the unexpected tension was gone. "I'll meet you at the reception desk after you're dressed and ready to go, all right?"

So now she waited, and her thumb covertly picked at her ring fingernail. *It's just Jack. Nothing to be concerned about.* But there was. They couldn't just fall back into how they'd always been, could they? Not when she had to keep such big secrets from him. To Winny, secrets had always felt like lies, and they ate her up inside. But she'd made Mary a promise. She intended to keep that promise, even after all this time.

But what if Jack wanted to come visit her apartment, and he saw Billy? How on earth could she explain her little boy? It wasn't as if she could hide him away: that would only compound the lies. She let out a quick breath, told herself she had time to figure this out. After all, Jack wasn't about to come over to her apartment right away.

Minutes later, he appeared at the end of the hallway. He came toward her with the same long stride she remembered, his uniform coat hanging off one broad shoulder. His hair had been slicked back, but now a thick black fringe hung over his brow.

"Let's go for a walk," he suggested.

They headed outside and turned up University Avenue, walking side by side through the fallen leaves. At first, they both faced straight ahead, not saying anything. Jack lit a cigarette, and Winny glanced sideways at him, wondering how to start the conversation. When she spotted him doing the same to her, they both looked away, and she understood. He was just as nervous as she was.

"I don't think I've gone a day without thinking of you and Mary," he finally said.

"Me neither. In the beginning I used to wake up hoping you'd come and find me," she admitted. "As if you knew where I was. As if you had anything to say about any of it."

He hesitated. "We've come a long way, haven't we?"

"It got better for me eventually," she told him, hoping to lighten the mood, though neither of them was fooled. She would have to talk about her experiences sooner or later. Just like the professor at her graduation had said: good or bad, they were a part of who she was now. "I love what I do here. And I have a nice apartment with Charlotte."

"Do I know Charlotte?"

"Oh, that's right. You never met her." She told him about her friend from Barkingside then about their little place over the shop. She ached to tell him about Billy. About how much she loved the little boy. About how much he resembled his uncle.

"It sounds like a good life."

She didn't like this, walking and not seeing his expressions. "Can we stop in for a coffee somewhere? Do you have time?"

"I think we'll need more than coffee, don't you, Winny?" His eyes locked on hers. "I've got all the time in the world."

They stopped in at the first diner they saw. The place was small and too bright for Winny's liking, but it was close and warm, and Jack found them a table at the back where they could talk. The waitress brought water and menus, but Winny was too nervous to think about what she might eat.

"What's the special?" Jack asked, setting the menu aside.

"Meatloaf and mashed potatoes with peas."

He looked at Winny, and she nodded. "Okay, we'll have two plates of that, please."

Winny watched as he lit another cigarette then leaned forward, and she swallowed her dread. She knew what was coming.

"Winny, I need to know about Mary. What happened after they took us boys away that morning?"

She faced the window, hating herself for what she had to say and even more for what she couldn't say. "We were put on the train a couple of days after you left. We stood on the platform while people came to get us. Was that how it was for you?"

"Yeah." His hand rested on the table between them, a thread of white smoke rising like a ribbon from his cigarette. His eyes were like magnets.

"A woman came for her." She pictured Mistress Renfrew on that day, and her heart ached, just as it had when she'd watched Mary ride away. "I'll never forget the sadness in her eyes when she looked at me from the back of that truck. Like she—"

"There was nothing you could do, Winny."

"I know," she whispered hoarsely. "I know that, but when I look back now, I still wish I could have done something. Anything. I still see her face." She swallowed the lump in her throat. "A few hours later, Mistress Adams came and took me away."

The waitress arrived at that moment and set the meatloaf in front of them. "Anything else?"

"No, thanks," Jack said. He stubbed his cigarette out in a heavy brass ashtray at the side of the table and waited for the waitress to leave before he said anything else. "I thought in the beginning that I'd gotten lucky."

"Did you? How?"

"Because I wasn't alone. I had Cecil and Edward with me. And Quinn. I don't think you knew Quinn. He was quiet. Not that bright, you know? But a good lad. Worked hard, never lost his patience."

She felt an unexpected flare of resentment. "You were all together? At the same place?"

"We shared a bunkhouse," he said, cutting into the meatloaf. "Best part of the day was listening to the lads snore."

She hesitated. "I slept on the floor of a sheep barn." The shame she felt was almost too much, as if she still carried the smell of the animals on her.

He set down his fork. "By yourself? You didn't have a bed?"

"In the winter the sheep came in, and they kept me warm. And I got to go to school after a while, which I liked. That's how I ended up at nursing school."

"We never did get to school before we left the farm."

"You left? You mean when you turned eighteen?"

"No. We didn't make it that long." A frown touched his brow. "I guess you could say we ran away."

The thought baffled Winny. She'd never have found the courage to do that, no matter how many times she'd dreamed of it.

"We didn't have a choice."

He clenched his jaw against something in his memory. Wherever he had been, she could see the experience had scraped the softness away and left scars in its place.

He caught her studying him. "What?"

"Nothing. Go on. Tell me what happened."

He couldn't meet her eyes. "Our master, Warren, he was a bad man. We got beat regularly. Look at him the wrong way and you wouldn't eat for two days." Jack picked at his meatloaf, then he told her about one winter night when the farmer's daughters had come after them, keen on causing trouble. "We told them to get lost, because we knew we was gonna get beat just for them being there. They didn't like that one bit, us telling them what to do. From the moment the one looked at me, I figured it was me that was gonna get it. But I didn't."

He took a sip of his water then set the glass back down.

"Who did?"

"Quinn," he said, his voice cracking. "Warren beat him and beat him, and—" She reached across the table, laying her hand on his arm. "A couple of days later me and the lads, we carried him away in the middle of the night, thinking maybe we could save him. We got to a house where a nice old couple took us in. We buried him a day later."

"Oh, Jack." Winny ached to wrap her arms around him, to tell him it was all right, that it wasn't his fault, that there was nothing he could have done. As hard as it was to believe it, Winny knew that feeling all too well.

"Edward and Cecil stayed there, but I couldn't," he said coldly. "I was restless and angry and needed to get away. I went looking for work, and for a while, everywhere I went I asked about you and Mary. But no one had seen you, and I reckon I gave up after a while. I couldn't get a job either, because nobody wanted an Englishman anywhere near them. So I gave up on that, too. I started riding the rails, with nowhere to go and nothing to do. After losing everything, it seemed like a good place to maybe find myself again."

"Did it work?" she asked softly.

"No. Me and the lads went overseas and got lost all over again."

She put her hand over her mouth, stunned to see the soft vulnerability of Billy's eyes shining in Jack's in that moment—but in a blink it was gone.

"There's nothing like it, you know. Killing men like that . . . it's not human. I don't think you can ever be the same after living through that. It's . . ." He reached in his coat for a cigarette then held the pack out to her, questioning.

"No, thanks," she said, spellbound.

"We didn't mind the army much," he said, striking a match. "Not after everything else we'd lived through, you know? Out there it wasn't us always at the losing end. In the army, I wasn't standing in front of a master, taking whatever he gave out whenever he felt like it. And I wasn't that vile, diseased, pathetic Home Boy everyone loved to hate. I was just one of the battalion. I worked hard, and I needed that work to keep me going."

"And Cecil and Edward?" Winny asked.

He shook his head then blew a stream of smoke out the side of his mouth. "Cecil died over there."

She caught her breath as Cecil, the funny, tough, near-brother rushed into her mind. How she and Mary had chastised him, laughed at his jokes, pretended to be angry with him. She remembered running through the market after him, trying to keep up as he cut around stalls and people. She tried to imagine Cecil dead and failed.

What had happened to their little group?

"Edward's still out there. As far as I know, anyway."

She looked at her plate, but she'd lost her appetite. Even if she was hungry, it would be impossible to eat with so many words jammed in her throat.

"I'm sorry, Winny," he said, and she met his gaze. "I was going to wait to tell you, but it didn't feel right to. It felt like a lie if I didn't say something, and I'd never lie to you."

There it was.

"I lied to you," she said faintly.

"Why?"

"I'm not as brave as you. I don't even know if I can tell you now."

He watched her through the smoke, his blue eyes sharp. "It's Mary, isn't it?"

She closed her eyes. "I did find her, Jack, but she made me promise not to tell you. She said it would hurt you too much to know the truth."

"I need to know."

If she said nothing, she would be lying to him. What if she told him some of it, but not all? Just enough? If she kept the worst part to herself, was she still keeping her promise to Mary?

"She had a terrible master, Jack," she said slowly, thinking through what she could say. She knew he could see her cheeks burning, but she had to hope he thought that was just from being emotional. "It took me a while to find her, but when I did, I could see she was being beaten real bad. She tried to be tough. She talked about finding you all the time, about all of us running away together. I only got to see her a few times, but she was so happy when I did, and we'd sit for an hour, remembering, talking about better days."

"Where is she?"

She looked up at the ceiling, as if Mary was there, and sent up a plea. She saw her bruised neck, her filthy hair, the exhaustion in her red eyes. She saw the desperation. And she saw Master Renfrew's strap hanging by the door. She wished she'd never seen any of it. *Forgive me, Mary.*

"She's dead, Jack."

All the blood drained from his face. "What did they do to her?" His voice was hoarse.

"Jack, it's . . ." How could she tell him? "Do you really want to know?"

"Of course!" he shouted, making her jump.

He had caught everyone's attention, and Winny felt the eyes of the other patrons on them.

"Winny."

The only way she could tell him the facts was to make a direct statement, try to keep her grief out of it. She took a deep breath and, for better or worse, she decided to tell him only as much as he needed to know. That way it wasn't truly a lie. She told herself she could live with the slight deception if it saved Jack the worst of the pain.

"They kept her in a shed," she said flatly. "During the day, she did her chores and took care of children. Her mistress set scraps out for her in the evening, but she never spoke to her. At night, her master went to her shed." She hesitated for a heartbeat, then she said, "He beat her. For months, Jack. I don't think I could have lasted as long as she did."

Jack's stone facade gave way, cracking and crumbling. "Some bastard beat her to death?"

It was a white lie, but it was easier than the truth. She didn't say anything more. She didn't need to.

Jack shot to his feet, and Winny could tell from the look on his face that he didn't see her anymore. Grabbing his coat, he whirled toward the exit and Winny watched helplessly through the window as he burst outside and disappeared into the night. Mary had been right. Telling him even part of the truth had torn him apart. And now Winny wondered if she'd ever see him again.

thirty-one
JACK

❧

Jack cracked his eyes open and shuddered with cold. His head throbbed, and whatever he'd drunk last night after he'd left Winny rolled in his empty stomach. The alley where he had curled into a miserable lump the night before was still dark. Like him, Toronto was only just waking up.

He'd wondered for years where Mary was. Now he knew, and the truth would haunt him forever. Nothing could change the fact that he'd broken his promise to keep her safe, and now that she was gone, there was no way to make it up to her.

He sat up slowly, wincing at the burn of his healing wound, and leaned against the cold brick wall. His stomach rumbled with hunger, and his mind returned to the abandoned meatloaf from last night. Bracing his hand against the wall, he eased onto his feet and set off toward the early morning sounds. Light poured onto the sidewalk from a large deli window, so he wandered in. He ordered a coffee and wrapped his hands around the steaming mug, trying to coax his mind out of the fog.

The waitress arrived, pen and paper at the ready. "Can I get you something else? Bacon and eggs? Pancakes?" she asked. "The cook makes great pancakes."

"Bacon and eggs."

The food warmed him from the inside, and he started to see a little more clearly, but his fork trembled against the plate as he asked himself the same questions over and over. Who had he been, this monster with the brutal power to destroy his sister? Where was he now? Jack's fist closed so tightly around his fork the metal bit into his hand. He barely noticed it. All he felt was the need to wrap his fingers around the man's neck then squeeze without stopping.

The only person who would know who the man was, was Winny. He finished the meal and paid the bill, then he swept out of the deli, headed toward the hospital. The nurse on duty was curt with him, eyeing his rumpled appearance with disdain, but she'd eventually told him Winny was due in an hour. He waited on the grass outside the front door, soaking in the rays of the rising sun, and as he watched people walk past he thought about the last time he'd seen Mary happy. She'd been with Edward, he remembered, her expression bright after he'd told her he liked her. A lifetime ago. He'd have to write to Edward, he thought, tell him what had happened. If he could even find him. If he was even alive. Jack still hadn't heard back from him after his first letter. All he could do was hope his friend was just too busy to write.

"Jack!"

He jumped to his feet, spotting Winny. She was walking quickly toward him in a belted brown coat and gloves, her hair tamed by a ribbon. She looked like an angel.

"Are you all right? Did you . . . where did you sleep?"

He shrugged. It didn't matter where he'd slept. "Listen, I'm sorry I walked out on you last night."

"I understand. You had a lot to think about." She peeked at her wrist-watch then reached for his hand. "Come with me. I have a little time before work."

She led him to a park with brass statues and pigeons, and they sat on a bench. She still held his hand, and he didn't pull away. When he was with Winny, the fog cleared a little.

"Are you all right?" she asked again.

He hesitated. "I don't reckon I'll ever be able to say I'm all right again."

"Give it time."

That reminded him that she'd lived with this awful reality for years, and he was sorry for his tone. "When did it happen?"

"Six years ago. 1937. Mary and I were sixteen."

Where was he in 1937? Somewhere on a train, hundreds of miles away from helping his sister survive.

"Who was her master?"

"It doesn't matter."

He scowled. "Of course it matters. I'm going to kill him."

She believed him. He could see that. "He's in jail."

It felt like a door had slammed in his face. How could he get vengeance for Mary if the man was already locked up? Jack pulled out his cigarettes, offered her one, then lit his own when she declined.

"Will you stay, Jack?" Her voice was soft. The girl he'd taken care of, the woman he was just getting to know. One and the same.

"I got nowhere else to go."

"After last night, I was afraid I'd lost you again."

He dropped his chin. "I should have stayed."

"When I lost you the first time . . ." She let her breath out slowly. "I was left with such a big hole in my heart. And I guess it was there for so long I forgot about it until yesterday. All of a sudden I felt like it was back, and I—"

"I felt it too, Winny." He swallowed. "You're all I have left."

Those captivating eyes creased in their corners, and her smile filled his heart. She was the sunshine after his long, miserable night. He supposed he'd always loved her, but not in the sense that a man loves a woman. When they'd met she'd been a sad little street kid with eyes like a kitten's, and she'd become a sort of second sister. A lot had happened to both of them since then, and he saw so much of it in the woman before him. She could still break hearts with those eyes of hers, but he saw a new intensity in their depths. She was stronger now. Her cheekbones had been sharp with hunger for so many years, but now their lines looked delicate rather than gaunt, and her skin was flushed with health. She was beautiful.

She leaned closer, and he didn't draw away when her gloved hand pressed lightly against his face. "Let me take care of you this time, Jack."

It was the simplest of requests and the greatest of gifts. He brought her fingers to his lips, and they held each other's gaze for a moment.

Then she said, "I have to get to work."

"Right."

They headed back, and he wondered briefly if he should take her hand like she'd taken his, but she was adjusting her handbag, keeping her fingers busy. Maybe he'd read her wrong.

When they reached the main doors of the hospital, he asked if he could take her to dinner after her shift. "What do you say, Irish? Last night didn't really count."

"I would love that."

She agreed to choose the restaurant because he didn't know any, and she promised to pick a different spot from the night before, which was a relief. He'd never go back to that place again.

━━━━

After Winny went to work, Jack set out for the Veterans' Centre. A nurse at the hospital had given him a couple of brochures about job opportunities that the government was creating for soldiers, and talking with

Winny had given him a good feeling about what might be in store for him. One pamphlet in particular, called *To Civvy Street—the Common Sense of Re-establishment*, had caught his eye. If he visited the Veterans' Centre, the brochure said he would receive a one-hundred-dollar clothing allowance plus a "rehabilitation grant" that gave him thirty days' pay. After another month, he could apply for his "war service gratuity." That wasn't all, either. The brochure said he could get paid sixty dollars a month to go to school for a trade. For once, the system was taking care of him. He planned to take full advantage of the offer.

Later that night at the restaurant, Jack told Winny all about it. "I've decided to become an automobile mechanic. It's just about the only trade I haven't learned yet, and I reckon automobiles aren't going to go out of style anytime soon."

"That's brilliant. Good for you, Jack."

"It feels good to start planning for the future." There was an awkward pause, so Jack figured he might as well spit out the question that had been on his mind all afternoon. "What about you? I imagine you're married by now. Who's the lucky fellow?" He'd seen no ring, but that wasn't unusual.

Her cheeks bloomed. "Oh no. You're not allowed to be married if you're a nurse. Besides, it never really came up. No one really interested me that much, I'm afraid."

He nodded, holding his expression steady, but he was amazed. How could a woman this special still be single?

"What about you?" she asked shyly. "There must have been someone. You're far too handsome to be a bachelor."

He chuckled. "Being in the army, I haven't had time. And it's like you said, no one really interested me."

As they caught up, he watched everything she did with new eyes. He'd never noticed that freckle by her right ear before, or that one of her bottom teeth was slightly crooked. When she twisted a finger in one thick curl he noticed the different shades of brown threading through it, from a deep copper to almost black.

After supper, he offered to walk her home, claiming he needed her to give him directions to Jeffrey's. She agreed right away, and they walked slowly. Not once did they run out of things to say.

She stopped outside a grocery store, closed for the night. "This is me," she said, pointing at the windows overhead. "That's our apartment."

He wondered if she'd invite him in, but she looked tired. It was the end of another long day for both of them. "Good night, Winny," he said. "Maybe I'll see you tomorrow."

"Thank you for dinner," she said. "I loved every minute of it."

On impulse, he bent and kissed her on the cheek, catching a whiff of floral perfume, somewhat faded from the day, and a touch of antiseptic from the hospital. When he leaned back, he noticed she hadn't stepped away from him. With her chin lifted this way, she was close enough that he could feel her breath against his lips.

"Sorry," she said, shifting backward, her face flushed. "I don't know what I was thinking."

"I think I might," he said softly, putting his hands on her waist. Did he dare? Would he ruin everything? He held his breath as he drew her in then gently kissed her lips, but she didn't move away. Instead, her eyes opened, wide and warm and full of wonder. She wrapped her arms around his neck and kissed him back, and he was lost all over again. But this time he was just fine with being lost, as long as he was with her.

After a moment, he reluctantly pulled away. "Now, Nurse Ellis, you need to get some sleep so you can save lives tomorrow. And I have school. Can I meet you after?"

She smiled. "Yes, please."

He pressed his forehead against hers, a sense of peace settling over him. "Winny, I want you to know something. Finding you again, finding *this* with you . . . You've made my life worth living again."

She lifted onto her toes and held his face in her hands, then she kissed him lightly on the mouth. "Thank you, Jack. For coming back to me."

After watching her step safely inside, he turned down the street and headed towards Jeffrey's place. That night, he pulled out paper and pen and wrote to Edward. He told him about Mary's abuse and her death, and he told him about finding Winny after all that time. It was a lot of news for one letter.

I still can't believe Mary is gone. When Winny told me how she'd lived on that farm, I didn't know what to do. It was too much. I failed both of them, and I'll have to live with that for the rest of my life.

He put his head in his hand, trying to unravel the knot of emotion jammed in his throat.

I gotta tell you about something else that happened tonight. Between me and Winny. You're the only one left who might understand. I don't know if there was something there all along between us, or if everything that happened over here drew us together, but I know I've never felt anything like it before. She's changed everything for me. I have been so angry for so long, for Quinn, Cecil, and now Mary. I should be shaking with rage. But Winny's turned my anger into something else, and I don't know what I would do if it weren't for her.

I can hear you saying "Slow down, Jack. Go slow," and I thank you for the advice, but I'm going to ignore it. This thing between Winny and me feels so right. It's like we've been waiting for each other all along.

Two weeks later, he made plans to take Winny somewhere special, knowing his first pay from the government would be in. He still had an hour left in class, but he was having trouble concentrating on the engine they were rebuilding. Winny was all he could think about. The other evening they'd talked in the park for hours, and he could have stayed there all night, listening to the ups and downs of her voice. He wondered if she knew she did that, let her voice fade to almost nothing then return again depending on what she was saying.

He'd tried to imagine what life on the Adams farm had been like for her. If those people had been anything like Warren, they'd probably viewed her as less important than they were, and he hated them for that. Because the Winny he knew had always been *more* of everything, and she'd deserved so much more. He still remembered that day when he'd chased her through the market, trying to make her go faster, and how she'd argued with him as soon as they stopped despite the fact that she could hardly breathe. Small, feisty, sweet, and unique, his Winny.

"I feel like I'm home when I'm with you," she'd told him that day.

Turns out she'd been right. He felt the same way.

After picking up his pay, Jack stepped into the cold afternoon on his way to Jeffrey's to get cleaned up and changed. He hadn't yet met Charlotte, but he'd gotten to know Jeffrey pretty well, and he seemed to Jack like a real stand-up guy.

"You look good," Jeffrey said as Jack passed him on his way out. "You know, Charlotte's been telling me how happy Winny is these days. You must be doing something right. Winny's a special gal."

"She sure is."

By the time Jack was on his way to the girls' apartment, the wind was coming in hard and cold, sharp with a threat of icy rain. Jack pulled up the collar of his coat and held onto his hat as he strode through the streets. At the grocery store, he bought Winny a bouquet and it struck him that it was the first time he'd ever bought anyone anything before, other than a meal here or there. He smiled, knocking on Winny's door, thinking about how good life could be.

A stunning creature who could have given Lauren Bacall a run for her money answered his knock. Jack fumbled for something to say.

"You must be Jack," she said. "Gosh. You really do look—" She stopped and shook her head. "Oh, never mind me. It's been a long day. Come on upstairs. Winny has told me about you for . . . oh, I don't know how long. Years."

Jack smiled to himself. "You must be Charlotte."

He followed her up the stairs and into the girls' living room, listening to Charlotte's continuous chatter as they went. "Winny was my favourite person in the world back at Barkingside. She took care of me." She faltered slightly and turned to face him. "Her and Mary. I'm so sorry, Jack. About your sister."

He wasn't sure how to respond. "Thank you."

Her eyes went to the bouquet in his hand. "How lovely! Shall I put them in water?"

"Sure," he said, handing her the flowers. "Winny's not here?"

"She's a little late, but she'll be here," she said from the kitchen. He heard the water running, then she came back out with the flowers in a vase. "She's always covering for someone else. That's our Winny."

Spotting an ashtray on the table, he reached for his cigarettes and offered one to Charlotte.

"Thanks," she said, leaning in when Jack lit a match. "Can I get you something to drink?"

"Who's that?"

Jack looked up, startled by the unexpected sound of a little boy's voice.

Charlotte caught her breath then rushed over to the boy, tossing an apologetic smile Jack's way. "Billy, dear, didn't I tell you to stay in your room?"

He looked about six years old. Dark hair, serious frown. "Yeah, but who's that?"

"This, this is Jack," she said. "And he's a friend of—"

The latch rattled, and Winny entered, sweeping her hair out of her eyes. Billy rushed ahead and wrapped his arms around her waist.

"Mummy!"

Jack felt all the air leave his lungs.

Winny met his gaze, her eyes swimming with regret. "Jack, I—"

She had a *child*? And she'd kept him a secret?

"I have to go," he said, stepping around her.

"Oh please, Jack. Don't go. Can't we—"

He wheeled toward her, shock thick and solid in his throat. "What? Can't we what? Talk? Because, correct me if I'm wrong, but I thought we had everything out in the open by now. I thought you were done lying to me."

"Wait, Jack. Please. We can talk—"

Without another word, he pulled open the door and left her behind, his heart in a thousand pieces.

thirty-two
WINNY

❧

Winny lay curled on her bed, a pillow over her face to muffle her sobs. She'd only just found him, and he was already gone.

After Jack had left, Billy had been all over her, wanting to know everything about the man at the door. All she'd said was that he was an old friend. It wasn't as if she could say, "Oh, that's your Uncle Jack. He's your dead mum's brother and the man I love." No, she thought wryly, that would not have been appropriate.

She heard a soft knock at the door. "Can I get you anything?" Charlotte asked.

"Cyanide," Winny moaned into the pillow.

The mattress dipped as Charlotte sat down. "I brought you water. Shall I pour it through the pillow?"

Winny blinked up at her friend through burning eyes. "Thank you," she said, sitting up.

Charlotte waited while Winny drank the full glass, sympathy in her gaze. "What are you going to do?"

"Maybe I won't have to do anything. He's gone."

"Do you think he's gone for good?"

"He didn't look pleased, and I can't blame him for that."

"No, he didn't." Charlotte stared off into space. "Gosh. I can't get over how much he looks like Mary. They could have been twins. And Billy . . . How could Jack not see it?"

"I reckon he wasn't paying much attention to Billy." She put her hands over her face. "Oh, God. The way he looked at me. I'll never get over that, Charlotte."

They could hear Billy in the other room, singing to himself, interrupted briefly by the buzzing of toy airplanes. The problem of how to tell Jack about Billy—and what to tell him—had always hovered in the background, but Winny had been so busy being happy she hadn't wanted to think about it. Now it was too late. If she told him Billy was her son, he'd want to know who the father was. If she lied about being married, it would be a hard lie to live with if she and Jack ever ended up together, which she had to admit was probably unlikely now.

A part of Winny wondered what would happen if Jack ever found out the awful truth about Billy's origins. If he learned that Billy was his own flesh and blood. He'd understand then that the boy was as much of an orphan as he was. Would that help him get past his anger? Or would he look at Billy and see only the man who had raped his sister?

Mary had been right all along. She couldn't tell him the last part of the story.

"It's better that he's gone," she said.

"He'll come back. He was just surprised."

Winny threw an arm over her eyes. "No, it's all right. I love Billy more than my own life. If Jack isn't here, we can all carry on as if he'd never come back. Maybe it's better that way. At least I know he's alive."

Except, of course, it wasn't that easy. She'd loved Jack before, and now she was *in love* with him. He'd always been a part of her. That hole in her heart was back and deeper than ever.

———————

Winny had the next day off, and she went about her business in a daze, cleaning the apartment, mending a tear in Billy's trousers. When it was close to noon, she and Billy went for their Saturday walk to the park, but she was distracted, hoping for a glimpse of Jack at every street corner.

"Can I have a cookie?" Billy asked as they drew near to the bakery. Such a smart little boy. He knew the area as well as she did.

"Of course," she said. "But only one. We don't want to spoil your supper."

"And one for after supper, too. We'll need four. Two for you and two for me."

"That's very thoughtful of you."

"Is your friend coming back? Should we get one for him, too?"

She swore he could read her thoughts sometimes. "No, he won't be coming back." Then, because she couldn't help herself, "Would you like it if he did?"

"No. He made you cry."

She squeezed his hand gently, wishing he'd never seen any of that.

They carried the cookies to their regular bench in the park and sat to enjoy them. Billy wolfed his down in seconds then sprinted toward the swing set. While he laughed and called for her attention, flying through the air so his hair fluffed in the wind, her eyes drifted over the other children, to the girls with their skipping ropes and the shouting boys on the carousel. Mothers and some fathers sat on the sides of the playground, in ones or twos, their pretty clothes and shiny prams a sign of their comfortable place in the world. She felt the familiar rise and fall of her pulse as she rode a wave of jealousy, but it was short-lived. Billy wouldn't exist in the shadows like she had. She was doing everything she could to give him a life filled with love, just like Mary wanted.

"Mummy! Watch!" He climbed the monkey bars, and she held her breath as he hooked his knees over one then carefully released his hands and hung upside down.

"He's pretty good for such a young boy," a woman said, stopping by Winny. She was immaculate, dressed in a neat new coat and shoes to match. "Did his father teach him how to do that?"

"No," Winny replied, leaving it at that.

"Say, didn't I see you in a nurse's uniform the other day?"

"Yes, I work at the General."

The smile wavered. "And you have a son? You're married?"

As a nurse, she wasn't supposed to be married. As a mother, she was supposed to have a husband. The old lie rolled off her tongue. "I went back to work after his father died overseas."

"Oh no! In the war?" Pity flooded the woman's eyes. "You poor, poor dear. So many good men killed over there, fighting for our freedom, and to think he left you behind with a child to raise on your own. I'm so sorry."

"Why?" Billy had run over on his silent feet. "Why do you feel sorry for my mummy?"

"Because your father—"

Blood rushed to Winny's face, and she grabbed Billy's hand as she pushed past the woman. "Come on, Billy. We need to get home."

"Already?"

"Yes, already." She dragged him behind her for the first few steps, then he trotted to catch up, questions bubbling.

Winny had needed this sharp reminder. She had a place in the world, but that place was not here, with the regular mothers and children. She wasn't married. She wasn't Billy's real mother. She didn't belong in the park, smiling and enjoying Billy's happiness. Her life was a lie and always would be. No wonder Jack didn't want her.

"Slow down, Mummy!"

"Sorry," she said, checking her pace. Now that they were away from the park, she felt safer.

He tugged on her arm, alarmed. "We forgot to get a cookie for Aunt Charlotte!"

"That's all right," she assured him. "She won't mind. She can have mine."

When they reached their front door, she put the key in the lock and let Billy turn it—one of his favourite things to do—then they walked up the stairs to the apartment. The first thing Winny saw was Charlotte's coat, carelessly tossed over the nearest chair. Something must be wrong. Her friend was fastidious about being neat and tidy.

She rushed into Charlotte's room. "What's happened?"

"I got a letter," Charlotte sniffed, her face bright red and wet with tears.

"Who is it from?"

"Barnardo's." She took a shaky breath then held out the paper. It trembled like a blade of grass in the breeze. "Winny, my mother isn't dead."

thirty-three
JACK

❧

It had taken Jack a week to build the floor of Jeffrey's shed. He'd been taking it easy because of his wound, which still oozed with too much effort, and because he'd been spending a lot of time either at school or with Winny. Now, with frustration seething through his veins, most of the walls had gone up in a day, complete with the door and window frames. Jeffrey had come out to watch, bringing him a cold beer and offering conversation, but Jack drank it in three gulps then got back to work. Jeffrey, he assumed, would be well versed in everything going on in the girls' apartment right now, and Jack wasn't sure he wanted to hear it.

Jeffrey took the hint and turned back to the house. "I'll pick up the shingles tomorrow."

Fallen leaves whipped through the unfinished wall and littered the floor, and the icy wind bit at Jack's face. His fingers felt frozen to the hammer, but he kept pounding, finding escape in the task. When it got dark, Jeffrey came out and suggested Jack pick it up again tomorrow.

"You know, you don't have to look after me," Jack snapped.

"If you want to talk about it . . ."

"Nothing to talk about."

"Okay. I left some soup in the kitchen for you, and I brought home bread if you're hungry."

"Do me a favour," Jack said. "Don't worry about me. I've done just fine on my own for a long time."

When he climbed the stairs to his bedroom later that night, he heard the wind buffeting the walls of the house, and he thought of Winny, whirling into his life like a storm, sweeping him off his feet. He'd never felt that way before, never known something with all his heart before, and he didn't entirely understand what was happening. He knew without a doubt that he and Winny were meant to be together. He knew she did too. He *knew* she did. Then why had she kept such a big secret from him?

And it wasn't just that. Who was he kidding? The fact was, Winny had had a baby. He didn't mind that in itself: he could love any child of hers. The trouble was that he couldn't stop thinking about what the presence of the child meant. She had gotten pregnant, and the idea of another man holding her felt like a physical stab to his heart. Who was the father? Jack hadn't really looked at the boy, but at first glance he'd looked like he was about five or six, which meant Winny had still been at the farm when it happened. Had she fallen in love while she was there? Why were she and Charlotte raising that boy alone?

He reached toward his desk and opened the drawer, pulling out pen and paper, and began to write.

Dear Edward,

The thing about writing letters to you is I'm never sure if I'm writing to anyone at all. So write me back, won't you? Tell me you're alive, mate. You don't need to say anything else if you don't want. Just tell me that and I'll leave you alone about it.

> *Whether you're out there or not, I need to write some things down.*
>
> *I told you I found Winny, and I told you we're meant to be together. We're in love. I've never known anything so fully in my life. So all that's great, right? But then I found something out, and I don't know what to do . . .*

He finished the letter, addressed it to the battalion, and mailed it the next day. For so many reasons, he hoped it would eventually reach his friend.

———

Days blended together. Every morning, Jack put in his hours at school, and on his way home he stopped in a local bar and threw back some drinks with strangers. Eventually he was going there often enough that he recognized a few of the regulars. A couple were vets like him, sent home early for some kind of wound. Usually talk turned to the war, and tonight they were toasting Italy.

"You were there, weren't you, Jack?" one of them said, holding up a beer.

"I was. Me and the boys." Jack took a long drink. He still dreamed of Sicily sometimes, still saw Cecil's blood pulsing through his brother's fingers.

"The Italians changed teams today. Did you see the news? Their new premier just declared war on Hitler."

"That's a step in the right direction." He wasn't in the mood tonight. He didn't want to talk about Italy or war or auto mechanics or anything. He'd rather be alone. Except that wasn't true. He'd rather be with Winny. He finished his beer then stepped out into a snowstorm toward Jeffrey's.

"You got a letter," Jeffrey told him as he walked into the kitchen.

Jack nearly tripped over a chair to grab the envelope in Jeffrey's hand. He ripped it open and stared at the top two lines, his heart in his throat.

Jack,

I'm alive. There you go.

Thank God, he kept thinking. *Thank God.* He took a deep breath and read the rest of Edward's words as he climbed the stairs to his room.

You want to know why I didn't write back? A couple of reasons. First, yeah. It's rough out here. Damn Nazis everywhere. I did get your letters, and I meant to write back. But then you wrote to me about Mary. I'll tell you, I had to be held back from running into the field toward the enemy and all their guns. That's God's truth, Jack. How could I write back to you about her? Of course I'm sorry for you, mate, but I needed to deal with my grief on my own. The thing is, if I was back there right now and Mary was still alive, I'd be with her. I know I would.

As for Winny, she's always loved you, Jack. I guess you just didn't see it. Sure, we were kids, but we all saw the way she looked at you. That's where you belong. You had Winny, I had Mary. And all our kids had good old Uncle Cecil. That's how I always thought it would go.

So I'm living with that now. There's nothing I can do about any of it.

Listen. If you don't fix this with Winny, I'll come back and kill you myself. You didn't ask her what happened. You didn't ask who the father is or where he was. She's raising the boy on her own, which is a hell of a lot of work. And she's got a career, too.

You're a good man, Jack, and I've always looked up to you, but I have to say it. What kind of man runs out on a girl in trouble? Especially the girl he loves? Obviously, it's not your kid, but it's Winny. She's always meant something to you. Does she still? Does judging her past matter as much as looking after her future? After all this time, after everything we've survived, shouldn't we keep the ones we love close?

That's my two pence. You asked for it.

I'm working on getting a nice clean belly shot like you did so I can come home. Maybe we can have a drink together soon. Take care of yourself out there in the big city, Jack.

Your brother always,
Edward

"What have I done?" Jack whispered. Even from the other side of the ocean, Edward could see what was happening before Jack's eyes better than he could.

He had no idea what time it was, but Jack pulled on his coat and was out the door in seconds, sprinting through the snow to Winny's apartment. When he reached the grocery store, he saw the girls' curtains were drawn, but the light was still on behind them. No one answered the door when he knocked, so he tried again and waited. Maybe they just hadn't heard. Then the thump of feet came from within, the lock clicked, and Winny peered through a crack in the door. When she saw him, she opened the door fully and stared at him like he was a ghost.

He took off his hat, folded it nervously between his hands. "Winny, I'm sorry to drop in unannounced."

"What are you doing here?"

"I've made an ass of myself."

She nodded slowly. "You have. But what are you doing here?"

"I've come to apologize. To beg for your forgiveness, maybe even ask for a second chance."

The wariness in her expression melted away. "We have a lot to talk about."

"I'm ready when you are."

She glanced behind her then back at him. "I'm ready too, but I'm sorry, Jack. This is a really bad time."

"I can come back later," he suggested.

"No, no." She regarded him a moment. "Come in out of the cold."

He stepped in and stomped the snow off his boots.

"Actually, maybe you can help," she said. "If you'd like."

"Sure." He followed her up the stairs, more than willing to do whatever she asked.

At the top of the stairs, she paused outside the second door. "It's Charlotte," she told him. "I've been thinking in circles trying to figure out what to do. I know it's a strange thing I'm asking, but maybe you're the outside perspective we need right now." The question in her eyes was so familiar. "You were always so good at thinking clearly."

"Lead the way."

She led him into one of the bedrooms where Charlotte sat on her bed, looking distraught. "You remember Charlotte."

"Of course. Good to see you again."

Charlotte flashed him a nervous smile. "I knew you'd come back."

That surprised him, but he let it go. "How can I help?"

"I hope you don't mind," Winny said to her friend. "I thought maybe he could help."

"Of course I don't mind."

Winny turned to Jack. "It's about Barnardo's."

He stiffened. Of all the things she might say, that was one he hadn't expected.

"The thing is," Winny continued, "Charlotte was never supposed to come to Canada. When we were at Barkingside, Barnardo's wanted to send her to a family to be adopted, but she told them she already had a mum. She was just waiting for her to get back on her feet then take her home again." She took a breath. "But all of a sudden, she showed up in my school, right here in Canada. Barnardo's had told her that her mother had died. That's when Charlotte came over and was adopted by the Carpenters. The family was wonderful to her." She held her hands out. "They even got us this apartment."

Jack ran his hand through his hair, wondering how on earth anyone could be unhappy with that kind of story. Then Charlotte held out a piece of paper.

"What's this?" he asked.

"A letter from Barnardo's," Charlotte said, her voice cracking. "I got it a couple of weeks ago. My mother's not dead after all. She has been looking for me ever since I was shipped out. She wants me to go home. Winny and I have been talking about it ever since, and I just can't figure out what to do."

Jack sucked in a breath. Now he understood, but he wasn't particularly surprised that Barnardo's had done something so hurtful, telling a deliberate lie to get the children over here. The whole scheme had been a lie, hadn't it?

"What's happening?" A small voice came from behind Jack.

He turned toward the boy as Winny rushed past and knelt in front of him. "It's all right, Billy. Aunt Charlotte got a letter, and we're just talking about it."

The boy's brow drew tight under the short black fringe of his hair, and for a split second, Jack had the uncanny feeling he could almost hear the thoughts racing behind his blue eyes.

"There's nothing to be sad about, Aunt Charlotte," Billy said. "If you got a letter, that means somebody is thinking about you. You should be happy."

The boy has a heart of gold, Jack thought. He wanted to make everything right even though he had no idea what was wrong. Something about that felt so . . . familiar.

"You're right, Billy," Charlotte said, her eyes brimming with tears. "It's a very nice letter, and I'm ever so happy they decided to mail it to me, even though it is a few years too late."

"You'll go, won't you?" Jack asked her.

Billy spun around, eyes flashing. "Hey! It's you again. Are you going to make my mummy cry again?"

"I will try very hard not to."

"Yes. I'll have to go," Charlotte told Jack, "but travel right now is impossible. This darn war. It's just that my mother—"

"You have a mother!" Billy exclaimed. "Is she coming to meet me?"

"Oh, Billy, I wish she could. But she lives far, far away from here, and she's sick. I shall have to go to her."

"The trouble is," Winny said to Jack, "Charlotte is afraid of how the Carpenters will feel if she tells them. They've been so good to her, and really, they've been wonderful parents."

"My mummy's wonderful too," Billy said, wrapping his arms possessively around Winny's leg and glaring defiantly up at Jack.

Jack was smitten. "Listen, little man, how about you and I go talk about boy stuff in the other room?"

Billy puffed out his chest and considered the invitation. "Okay. I'll go get my trains."

When Jack looked up, both women were watching him intently. "What?"

As one, they blinked and said, "Nothing."

"The Carpenters sound like good people," he said.

"They are," Charlotte said. "And I love them like a mum and dad. But I've never forgotten my real mum."

"Of course not."

"The best way to do things is always the honest way, innit?" he said gently, keeping his gaze averted from Winny. "If you don't tell them about this because you're afraid, there's bound to be a misunderstanding along the way, and that's when people get hurt. I bet if you talk to them about this—rather than going without telling them—that will actually mean a lot to them."

Winny reached for Charlotte's hand. "He's right, you know."

"I just don't want to hurt anyone's feelings."

Billy peered around the door. "I got my trains!"

"If you don't mind, I think someone's waiting for me out there," Jack said to the girls.

Winny looked like she wanted to say something, and he knew it was about Billy. She was finally going to open up to him, but their conversation would have to happen later on. There was a train waiting for him. Again. He nodded. *We can talk later. I'm not going anywhere.*

"You see?" Winny said after a pause. "Jack always knows what to do."

Chuckling to himself at the irony of what she'd said, Jack headed to the living room, but he stopped short in the doorway. Billy stood waiting for him, his hands on his waist, his head cocked to the side just right. And all Jack saw was Mary.

thirty-four
WINNY

⌘

Jack and Billy were bent over a train engine when Winny came into the living room. For a moment, she saw father and son, and her heart ached with love.

"It's way past your bedtime, Billy," she said, tapping him on the head. "Go and put your pyjamas on, and I'll be right there to help you brush your teeth."

"Can I stay up a little longer?"

"Not tonight." She glanced at Jack. "Maybe Jack can come back another time."

"Tomorrow," Jack said.

Charlotte came out of her bedroom. "I'll put him to bed," she offered. "You two need some time together. Give your mummy a hug and kiss, Billy."

Winny hugged her little boy tight, and over his shoulder, she noticed Jack watching. "Would you like to give Jack a hug and kiss?"

When the little boy wrapped his arms around his neck, Jack's eyes closed tight and Winny had to turn away to hide her tears.

"Maybe tomorrow I can show you the airplane Aunt Charlotte gave me for my birthday," Billy said.

"I'd like that," Jack replied.

"Come on," Charlotte said. "You can pick a story for me to read."

Once they were gone, Winny turned to Jack, suddenly nervous. "Would you like some tea?"

"Sure."

"I'll be right back." In the kitchen she set the water to boil. As it heated, she added teacups to the tray then picked furiously at her fingernails. "I'm so glad you came when you did," she said, carrying the full tray into the living room. The china clinked as she placed it on the table. "Charlotte already feels better about talking with the Carpenters."

He was watching her, his expression unreadable. He lifted his chin toward the bedroom. "That boy—"

Panic coursed through her, and she leapt to her feet. "I forgot to turn off the stove. I'll be right back."

In the kitchen, she braced herself against the counter and forced herself to breathe, trying not to give in to the hysteria bubbling in her chest. *He knows. What am I supposed to do, Mary? Lie to him? Tell him something he wouldn't believe just to keep a five-year-old promise, then lose him forever?* Ever since Mary had died, Winny had lived every day of her life keeping that promise, raising Billy as her own, loving him more every minute. But the secret was crumbling, the truth obvious to anyone who cared to look at the growing boy's face.

Jack stood in the doorway. "Winny?"

She swallowed. "I'd just left the water on, and I—"

"Don't lie to me, Winny. No more lies."

"I'm . . . I'm not lying."

"We've all done things we're not proud of," he said, "and we've all had things done to us. We're not to blame for any of it."

He took a step closer, and she gripped the counter's edge.

"Everyone has secrets. But this is you and me. Whatever this one is, it's coming between us. I can't lose you again. Please, Winny. You know you can trust me."

"I made a promise to Mary," she said quietly. "The last time I saw her, she made me swear never to tell you the truth."

He set his jaw. In the silence, they could hear Charlotte's quiet voice reading to Billy.

She was trapped. She could feel it in the nerves pulsing through her. But she was also so close to being free. She took a deep breath and started taking bricks off the top of the dam. Not all of them yet. One at a time.

"I told you that her master beat her, so you assumed that he'd killed her. Like your master when he killed Quinn. But that's not the truth." She met Jack's gaze. "Mary had bruises on her neck and on her face. She had bruises everywhere. She told me her master never left her alone."

He closed his eyes.

"I suspected there might be more going on than she was telling me, but there was nothing I could do." The words came faster and faster, rolling through the crumbling barrier. She told Jack about the conversation David had overheard, how Winny had gone through the blizzard to find Mary, but Mary wasn't there. "I was so scared that I went up to the farmhouse and asked her mistress. She told me she'd sent her away."

"Why?"

"She was pregnant."

Jack took a step back, his lips slightly open.

Winny thought back to that winter and into the spring, how she'd waited for months with no news. "Her mistress called her the most awful names and accused her of being with a Home Boy, but I knew the truth. Jack, the reason I was able to find Mary in the first place was that our mistresses were sisters. I found that out by accident. Once I heard about Mary being pregnant, I ran home and told my mistress what Mary had said about her master. She told her sister." She paused, the memories bittersweet. "In the spring, after the baby was born, my mistress drove me to see Mary. She looked so much better, Jack. She told me that ever since I told my mistress about her master, her own mistress was kinder to her. She even promised her husband would never go near Mary again."

Winny's breath caught in a sob. "The last time I saw Mary, she told me she would be all right, now that she was safe from him. She said she would be fine. And I believed her." She took a shaky breath. "That's when I asked her where her baby was. Oh Jack, the pain in her expression was so different then. So much deeper. She told me that after she had her son, the nurse took him away. They never let her see him, Jack. She never touched her own son."

He dropped his gaze. Maybe he understood now, how hard it had been to keep the secret. Why she hadn't told him.

If only she could shield him from the rest of the story. In her mind, she reached for the bricks again, buckling under the rising tide, but she couldn't protect him forever.

"A few weeks later, my mistress brought me into her house, which she'd never done before. She told me to sit down, then she . . ." She closed her eyes briefly, transported back. "She told me Mary had hung herself."

When she opened her eyes, Jack was staring at her, frozen in place.

"She gave me a letter that Mary had written to me before she died. In it, she asked me to do two things." She stared at him, willing him to understand. To forgive. "The first was to never, ever tell you about what she'd done. She said knowing the truth would kill you, and neither of us could bear to hurt you. So I kept her secret to myself all these years. Just like she'd asked."

A tear trickled down Jack's cheek, but he didn't make a sound.

"The second thing she asked me to do in that letter was to find her son and raise him like my own. If anyone asked, she wanted me to lie about his father, to do whatever it took to keep him from growing up in an orphanage. She couldn't stand to think of him repeating the lives we had lived." She looked at her hands, remembering the night she'd held

Mary's letter to the flame of her lantern. "I destroyed the letter. I didn't want anyone to ever have to see it but me. Especially not you."

"But why?" he asked after a moment. "Why did she . . . do that if everything was better?"

"Because her master came back."

His fists clenched so hard she saw the whites of his knuckles. "And he is . . . ?"

"Locked away, Jack. Like I said before. The Mounties threw him in jail."

His nod was almost imperceptible.

A strange sense of ease filled Winny for the first time in years. She could see clearly that Mary's story had broken Jack's heart, but Winny's burden was so much lighter now that it was shared with him.

"So now you know," she said, suddenly tired. "Everything I did was because she asked me to do it. Billy's not my baby, Jack. He's Mary's. But I'm his mummy, and I love him more than anything in the world."

Jack scrubbed his hands over his face. He looked ten years older than he had before. "He looks just like her," he said hoarsely.

"Yes, but Jack, he looks just like you, too. It's been so hard, not knowing if you were out there, if you were dead or alive or if I'd ever see you again. And every time I looked at Billy, I saw you both. It was the sweetest kind of torture. One I was prepared to suffer for the rest of my life."

thirty-five

JACK

❧

Jack nodded at the bartender then downed the whisky shot in one gulp. He hung on to the burn as it lit up his throat, but it was over too fast, so he lit a cigarette and inhaled slow and deep. He lifted his finger and a fresh glass was set in front of him.

He couldn't remember if he'd thanked Winny for finally telling him the truth. He should have. He knew he'd grabbed his hat and coat then gone to the door. He'd said something about how she needed sleep and he needed a drink.

God. Every time he thought of his sister he wanted to cry, and every time he imagined her life on the farm he tasted bile. When he remembered that Mary's master was already locked up, safe from Jack's reach, he pinched the bridge of his nose until it hurt. He wanted the man let out so he could kill him with his own hands.

They'd been no more than children when they'd been shipped over here as chattel. Trusting, innocent, and vulnerable, just like Billy was now.

They'd been treated as less than human, and Quinn and Mary had died as a result of that. The bitterness Jack felt was a constant edge, scraping at his heart until it hardened to stone.

Winny might just be the one thing in this world that was keeping him human. She was a lifeline for him. And what about Billy? What was Jack going to do about that little boy? Every time he looked into Billy's eyes, he saw Mary, and it was just as Winny had said: a sweet torture. One he was more than willing to live with. Could he step into Billy's life and become a father to him? He didn't remember his own, and he hadn't liked most of the fathers he'd met since then, but life kept throwing him curveballs, and maybe this one he'd be able to catch. Maybe, with Winny and Billy beside him, he could become the father he'd never had.

He paid the tab, strode into the night, and headed to Jeffrey's. Tomorrow, he decided, he would go back to Winny, his one true home.

———

"Hey, Billy," Jack said, after the little boy opened the door. "Is your mummy home?"

Billy regarded him him warily.

"I won't make her cry. I promise. What I want is to make her happy."

Billy thought about it. "All right. You can come in."

Jack tightened his jaw against the swell of pride he felt for the boy. Mary would have loved her son so much. He already did.

He followed Billy into the living room where Winny was sitting, mending something blue. She looked up, her beautiful brown eyes awash with love, and guilt swelled in his chest. She'd opened her heart to him, and he'd run off. Again. He didn't deserve that love.

"I'm sorry, Winny." He moved toward her, unsure. "I'm so sorry."

"Hey!" Billy cut in front of Jack and wrapped his arms protectively around Winny's neck. "He said he wouldn't make you cry, but you're crying already."

She patted his back, still watching Jack. "I'm okay now. These are happy tears. I think everything will be all right now. Why don't you go play in your room so Jack and I can talk?"

Billy gave Jack one more warning glare before leaving them alone, and Jack felt a fresh pang of grief. Mary had looked at him that way so many times.

"Winny," he said, kneeling at her feet. "You've been a rock, staying strong for all of us for so long."

"I'm sorry I didn't tell you before."

"I understand why you didn't, but I'm glad you finally did. Now there are no secrets between us." He took her hand, pressed it to his lips. "Right?"

"Right. Those were all there ever were between you and me."

"I don't want anything to ever come between us again, Winny. Never."

"Never."

"Because the last few weeks, I've been a wreck without you. Life has made me into a hard man, Winny, and I know I'm not a lot of fun to be around anymore. You've seen it, I'm sure, because you see everything. You always have. But when I'm with you, the anger seems to go away. You've always had that effect on me. When I'm not around you it's like I can't get past it." She was watching him through kind, liquid eyes that saw into his soul. "I remember your face so clearly from that morning they ripped us apart the last time, when I was forced to leave you behind. The way you looked at me, Irish, that has never left me. I've been eaten up for years for not finding you sooner."

He looked down at her little fingers, twined in his. "I have always loved you. I was just too young and stupid to know it. Now I can't imagine living without you."

"Oh, Jack. I love you, too. I always have."

"I promise, Winny, that I will never leave you behind again." He hesitated. "That's . . . that's if you want me."

PART
— *four* —

thirty-six
WINNY

∞

— Present Day —

W e got married two months later," I say, reaching across the table
and sliding the trunk toward me. "Jack didn't see any reason to
wait, and neither did I. We were actually going to do it even sooner, but
Jack got a letter from Edward." I frown and dig in the trunk, feeling for
the brittle old envelope. "Wait. I still have it in here."

I pull it out and hand it to Chrissie. She opens it cautiously as if she
fears the yellowed paper might crumble to dust in her hands.

"He'd been wounded and they were shipping him to Toronto."

"'Jerry threw some shrapnel my way a month or so ago,'" Chrissie
reads, then she grins, "'and I caught it with my face. I'm all right now, but
I'll warn you, I'm uglier than ever.'"

A look of wonder comes into Jamie's eyes. "He would have been just
a few years older than I am now. We could have hung out together." He
pauses. "I can't imagine being him. Going to war, I mean. We have nothing like that these days."

"We're pretty lucky," his mother agrees.

Jamie stands then comes around to see the letter for himself. "Did he make it home safely?"

I smile, happy to be telling this part of the story. "Jack wrote right back and asked him to be his best man as soon as he felt up to it, and he made it to the wedding."

"What about Charlotte? Was she still there? Or did she have to get back to England to see her mother?" Chrissie asks.

"By the time all her paperwork was done, she decided to wait until after our wedding to go. In the meantime, Jeffrey proposed."

She beams. "This is all so romantic!"

"The timing worked out well. A few weeks before the wedding, we both quit our jobs at the hospital, but I'll admit that was bittersweet. We'd wanted to be nurses for so long, and we loved our work. Of course when we started, we weren't thinking about getting married."

"That's so silly that you couldn't be married and still be a nurse," Chrissie says.

"It was a different time. Wives and mothers were expected to stay at home. They changed the rules in the fifties when they started running out of nurses. They asked us to come back, so I did."

Jamie chuckles. "Some girls at my school say they want to be nurses, but there's no way they'd choose one or the other."

"No, I can't imagine women these days agreeing to those rules. Things are different now, and in a good way. I guess men finally realized we're just the same as they are," I say, "only prettier."

On the counter behind us, Jamie's phone rings, but he ignores it. "Did you go back to England with Charlotte?"

"We talked about it, but Jack and I didn't want to go back to a place that didn't want us in the first place. Besides, we didn't have much money."

"But you had each other," he says with a wink.

"We did. For over sixty years. It wasn't always perfect, but we loved each other. We knew each other inside and out."

"Tell me about your wedding," Chrissie probes.

"I have some photographs," I say. "Somewhere in here."

My fingers close around the old, black leather album, and I place it on the table. The years have not been kind to it, and I can see it is falling apart. A few photos fall onto the table when I open the cover.

"I could scan those for you, Gran," Jamie says, sorting through the loose ones. "Then we'll always have a copy. We won't have to worry about them getting faded and ruined. I might even be able to add them to the online ancestry registry."

"The what?"

"I put our family tree online in a special website. I can show you later."

"You were so pretty!" Chrissie says, reaching for a picture. It had been taken outside City Hall on my wedding day, but it feels like yesterday.

"I like your suit," Jamie says. "Very dapper, the way your hat is angled over one eye."

"Dapper, eh? Charlotte dressed me that day. I was so excited I could barely tell the difference between gloves and boots." My gaze passes to Charlotte, and though the photo is in black and white, I still remember how stunning she was, dressed all in pink and glowing on Jeffrey's arm. Charlotte died a long time ago, but that dear girl will never truly leave me.

"She's gorgeous," Chrissie says. "So was she already married to Jeffrey in these pictures?"

I nod, studying Charlotte's joyful expression. "It was a lovely day."

"You look so happy," Jamie says, pulling out another photograph. It's me, laughing about something Jack has said.

"That was the happiest day of my life. The sun was out, the flowers were blooming, and I was marrying the most wonderful man in the world."

I take the picture Chrissie's holding, of the four of us standing there—Charlotte and Jeffrey, Jack and me—and my crooked old finger caresses Jack's face. He looks proud as a peacock beside me, tall and handsome, wearing his army dress uniform. That was the only time I ever saw him wear it.

"Gran's right, Jamie. You look just like him." Chrissie leans in for a closer look. "That is your exact expression when you win a soccer game." She picks up a different picture, one where Jack is giving the camera a cocky grin, his arm around my waist. "I totally see you in him."

Jamie studies the photograph, a half smile rising. "I am pretty handsome, aren't I?" He taps the picture, indicating a tall man behind Jack, his face swathed in bandages. "Who's behind him?"

"That's Edward. Remember he'd been hit by shrapnel? He came back from the war forever changed, with a terrible scar covering half his face. We were so lucky to have him with us that day. I had Charlotte, and Jack had Edward. All that was left of our little family."

Only two people had been missing that day, and I recall so clearly the heavy weight of their absence. As we'd listened to the justice of the peace talk about our future, Jack and I were both aware of Mary and Cecil standing with us. Mary's eyes would have sparkled with joy—as Billy's did the day we told him Jack would be his father.

"These are so beautiful," Chrissie says. "I love seeing the faces behind the names." She turns a page. "Look at you two. So in love."

"That's my favourite picture of us. Jeffrey took it. It felt silly to pose so intimately, but he gave strict instructions: 'Just put your arms around each other, and put your foreheads together. Forget we're even here.' As soon as I saw the finished photographs, I had to admit he was right. Jeffrey always had a good eye for beautiful things."

The truth was, no one ever had to force me to stare into Jack's eyes. Looking at the photo now, I'm transported back to that moment, when it was just me and Jack, and no one else. Back then it had felt as if I was losing myself in the most wonderful way. I was so sure I would never be alone again.

Jamie turns the page and spots a photograph hidden behind another one, so he digs it out. It's the only photo of Billy I have from that day. We'd wanted more, but we didn't want him to find them and ask difficult questions. In the picture, he stands at my feet. Jack is behind us both. His right hand is on Billy's shoulder, and his left is on my waist. I can still feel it there.

Jamie cocks his head at me. "So where's Billy now?"

thirty-seven
WINNY

༄

— 1944 —

It was impossible for Winny not to look around the restaurant table and see the missing faces. Then her gaze went to Edward, laughing at something Jeffrey had said, and she was overcome with gratitude that he was there. But Cecil should have been beside him. And Mary should have been beside her. She knew they were all thinking the same thing.

After the meal, the old friends sat and talked of the many lives they had lived, of their joy and grief, marvelling at how far they'd come. How life constantly changed, and how it had changed them. After all the fun and celebration, not to mention the wine that had come with dinner, Winny found herself sinking deeper into her chair and missing bits of the conversation. A little later, she felt Jack's cheek pressing against the side of her head.

"Ready to go home, Mrs. Miller?" he asked softly.

They would be staying at Jeffrey's that night, because everyone had convinced them they needed one evening free of parental obligations.

But as the two of them walked together toward Jeffrey's house, Winny couldn't help thinking about Billy, curled up in his bed with no goodnight hug from his mummy. Then they walked into Jack's room, and Billy became the furthest thing from her mind.

Her husband closed the bedroom door behind him then stepped toward her, and she moved easily into his arms, craving his warmth and the solid proof that he was really there. *He loves me.* His breath was in her ear, his fingers sliding down her back, and Winny felt so dizzy with desire she almost lost her balance. She had felt this kind of need before, when they'd been alone together, kissing, touching, wanting. Tonight she wouldn't have to walk away from it.

His kisses were slow and tender, and she moved with him as he edged toward the bed.

"I think I'll need some help," she suggested breathlessly, then she turned her back to him and closed her eyes. His fingers went to the line of pearly buttons down her spine, and she felt his warm touch as he released them one by one. She shifted her shoulders, helping the soft yellow material slip down her back.

"God, Winny." His hands brushed over her skin, and she closed her eyes to savour the luxurious feeling before realizing what he was tracing. She wondered how terrible the scars looked. She hadn't felt any pain in years, though sometimes she felt the urge to scratch where she couldn't reach.

"We all have scars," she reminded him.

The tips of his fingers drifted over her, and his lips followed. They rose up her spine to the base of her neck like butterfly wings, then travelled up to her ear.

"No one should ever have hurt you, Winny," he said, his voice husky.

She turned to face him, eager to leave the past behind. "Jack, please. I'm all right."

"I'm sorry I wasn't there. I wish I could have saved you, and her, and everyone else."

"So do I, but we couldn't, Jack. We'll make our own happiness from now on." She touched his cheek. "Let me make you happy."

She began unbuttoning his shirt, and when she took it off, her soul bled for the mess his master had made of his body. Faded pink lines crisscrossed over the skin, one on top of the other, like a jagged map detailing the many times he'd been lost. A faded puncture scar drew her eye, a mere two inches from his more recent war wound, and she wondered where it had come from. Would he ever tell her? Her fingers caressed the lines and dimples, raising goosebumps along his skin, and he shivered.

"Come here, Irish," he said gruffly, turning towards her. "I want to make love to you."

She caught her breath, every nerve tingling with longing, but he misinterpreted the sound. "I'll be careful," he said. "I don't want to frighten you."

She reached behind and unhooked her brassiere, then let it slip down. A new light came into his eyes, one that gave her a sense of confidence she'd never felt before, and she reached for him.

"I'm not afraid," she said.

———

The next winter, Susan was born. The moment the nurse laid the swaddled infant in her mother's arms, Winny felt herself reborn as well. *I made you,* she thought. *I created you. I will always take care of you.* When Jack came into the room, she saw in his eyes that tiny Susan would come before her in his heart, but Winny didn't mind. Someone had once told her a father's love was an unbreakable bond, and she knew she would always have a place amid so much love.

"She's so beautiful," he cooed, touching the tip of his daughter's nose with his fingertip.

Winny loved watching him, watching their baby. "So are you."

At first, they worried that Billy would object to having a baby sister seven years his junior, but he put their fears to rest right away. He and Esther were in the living room waiting when Winny and Jack came home from the hospital, Susan sleeping in her mother's arms. With Esther's help, Billy had decorated the apartment with cutout stars and hearts, and he'd even made a card for his little sister, complete with a drawing of himself as a stick man holding a baby-sized lump.

As far as Billy knew, Susan was his true sister, just as Winny and Jack were his true parents. When Winny had first brought him home from the orphanage, she had taken the matron's advice to heart. No good could ever come of telling Billy he wasn't their natural child, and Jack had agreed wholeheartedly with the plan. There was no reason to complicate the boy's life, and since he would never know his natural mother, he wouldn't be missing anything.

It had taken no time at all for Billy to forget that Jack had once been a stranger in their apartment. From the moment the couple returned home as man and wife, Billy followed him everywhere, asking endless questions, copying the man he soon called Dad.

Jack and Billy were devoted to Susan. Winny often woke in the night to find her husband standing over the crib, singing to the baby. He was fiercely protective of his daughter, watching everything she did with such a fascination that Winny started to wonder if it was normal for fathers to feel this strongly. She had very little to base it on. She remembered vaguely that as a child she had loved her own father, and he had done what he could to make her life a good one, but any true memories she had of him were gone.

Billy was a great help to Winny when he wasn't in school. At eight years old, he was strong and confident, and from his dark looks and cheeky grin, she could see he would one day be a real charmer. He took to clearing dishes and folding clothes as if it was something he was proud of, and Winny was sure to give him new tasks whenever he asked. He was smart and eager, and his love was as big as the moon.

He was kneeling on the floor across from Winny one day, holding out his arms and encouraging his baby sister to take her first steps when Jack burst through the front door, a smile lighting his whole being.

"It's over!" he cried, shaking a copy of the *Evening Telegram* in the air. "It's all over!"

Winny hopped up and read the paper, then she whooped with joy. He hugged her tight and spun her around, and all of them cheered the end of the war.

"I gotta go see Edward," Jack said, off to change his shirt. "He's gonna want to celebrate."

She felt a pang of disappointment at not being invited, but she understood. She was needed here.

"Mummy!" Billy cried, and she turned just in time to see Susan grab on to a table and wobble to her feet, then take her first step toward her big brother.

Winny was often sorry Charlotte couldn't see how much their little Billy had grown, and even more that she had never met Susan, but she knew Charlotte was happy. She and Jeffrey had sold his house in Toronto and moved to England to take care of her mother; they'd bought a small house outside London. Winny made sure to send photographs of the children often, and she'd received letters back raving about how beautiful they were. Charlotte and Jeffrey hadn't had any success in starting their own family yet, but neither seemed concerned.

With Susan walking, the apartment grew more and more crowded by the day, and Winny and Jack started to think about getting a real home. It was hard to imagine buying anything on his mechanic's salary, but one day he pulled out a government brochure he'd received in the mail called *A Home on Civvy Street.*

"Remember this?" he said, flipping through. "This is how I got paid to go to school. I hadn't bothered to look at the housing information back then. But now . . . What do you say, Irish? Shall we buy a house?"

They talked late into the night, pillow to pillow, about where to buy or build, drunk on the idea that, after everything, they would soon have a home to call their own. They agreed right off the top that they wouldn't be buying a country home: there would be no more farm work for either of them.

Jack had become indispensable at the garage as an auto mechanic, and with Winny's encouragement, he decided to see what he could do with that status. When he asked the boss if he could give him a deal on a used car, the boss sold him a five-year-old Ford for a hundred dollars and even let him use his shop to fix it up. Once they had a car to get them around, Winny and Jack took advantage of the government offer and put three hundred dollars down on a three-thousand-dollar "Victory House" in Etobicoke. They bid the downstairs grocer farewell and crowded into Jack's car, then they drove out of town and into a neat little community with sidewalks and nicely planted trees.

"Which one is ours?" Billy kept asking.

"Look for number sixty-eight," Jack told him. "It's white with a black roof."

"They're all white with black roofs!"

But Billy had no complaints about his big new yard or his very own bedroom upstairs. "I can see everything from up here!" he yelled, looking out the window. "This is gonna be great."

Even Susan got her own room, right across from Billy's, though at first it was difficult for Winny to tuck her into her crib and leave her there all by herself. Fortunately, Susan quickly let the whole family know that she could be loud enough to wake them up no matter how many rooms there were.

Winny loved the house. Her kitchen was beyond her wildest dreams, with its clean, white stove and oven, refrigerator, even her own Maytag washing machine with a ringer at the top. When the water was squeezed out, she carried the wet clothes outside and hung them on the line, and the sweet songs of birds chattered through the growing trees. Sometimes her neighbours came out to hang theirs as well, and Winny was thrilled when she started to make new friends.

"It almost seems too good to be true," she confided to Jack one night.

"We deserve every bit of it," he replied, and she flinched when she heard the old edge return to his tone. "Every bit of it and more."

Billy entered his new school with the plan of being the smartest one in it, but talk soon turned to soccer and baseball and hockey, and he decided his new goal was to be the best at everything. When Winny received a gracious note from his grade-four teacher saying what a helper he was in the classroom, she revelled quietly in the knowledge that she and Jack had raised a good, happy boy.

"Miss Hanson says we're going to learn about our country's history," Billy told her one day when he came home from school. "She says Canada is seventy-eight years old this year."

"That sounds interesting," Winny said, digging out her recipe book. With rations as tight as they were, she'd decided to make chili. That way she could cut back on the ground beef and add more beans. Maybe Jack wouldn't notice. *Now where did I put that recipe?*

"She says Canada is made up of all different kinds of people from all over the world. We're the youngest country, and everyone left the old places to come here for a better life."

"Mm-hmm," she said. "Oh! There you are." Her finger skimmed down the page as she checked she had everything she needed.

"She said we are going to make a big wall of pictures, and she wants all of us to bring in a special family photograph to share. Can I bring one in?" He waited. "Mummy?"

She turned from the recipe book, distracted. "What is it, Billy?"

"I need a family photograph to bring to class. Do we have any that aren't in frames that I could take?"

"Sure we do," she said. "There's a box at the back of my closet. You can take whichever one you like, as long as you return it when you're done."

An hour later he reappeared. Winny was setting the table, pleased with the comforting smell of chili in the air. She hoped Jack wouldn't stay out too late tonight.

"Is this me?" Billy asked. "I think I remember this."

"What is it, dear?"

He held out the photo and her stomach dropped. What had she been thinking? How could she just let him sort through that box? "Yes, that's you. That's our wedding photo."

"I don't understand. How can I be in your wedding photo?" He eyed her sideways. "Was I born *before* you were married?"

She could feel sweat, slick on her palms, as the lies started up again. "Oh no, Billy. We were married. Of course we were. It's just that we had to have a quick ceremony because your father had to go overseas for the war. We decided to have a more formal ceremony with our friends later on. Look how handsome you were in your little suit."

"But the war started *after* I was born, didn't it?"

"Silly me. I forgot. He had to go away to work for a couple of years before then. Jobs were hard to find, so he had to leave me here."

He was still frowning at the photograph. "But you never put this one in a frame. Why not?"

Her mouth was parched. "Oh, I must have just forgotten. Here, hand it to me. You know, I have a much nicer photograph you could take. I think Miss Hanson would like that much more. It was at Christmas last year, remember? When you got that new baseball mitt from Dad?"

That night she stared at the photograph he'd given her, wondering what to do with it. The thought of destroying that perfect moment in time made her feel sick inside, so she stuffed it away again then hid the box.

———

Their new home in Etobicoke was far from the mechanic shop in downtown Toronto, so Jack had to drive quite a way to get to work in the morning. By the time he came home each night, he was tired and greasy. Sometimes he arrived a little later than usual, the sour-sweet smell of beer clinging to his shirt, and Winny would wash it off along with the grease and not say a word. If it helped him relax, she didn't mind at all. As he said often enough, he'd earned it.

Winny found solace in her vegetable garden, which Jack and Billy had dug at the side of the yard for her. The wide rectangle was in a perfect spot, where the sun eased her seeds into sprouts that grew into a harvest she served on their dinner table. As she seeded and weeded, clearing the lines and rows, a peace descended over her, a reminder of how she had found an unexpected contentment in Mistress Adams's garden.

These days their lives were busy, and sometimes Winny got so caught up she briefly forgot about her past. Then she'd see or hear something and be reminded of before, and if no one was around she'd sink to the ground and let the sadness of times past wash over her. This garden, her very own garden to do with as she pleased, was where she went to heal.

One rainy day, Jack came home early from work and found her there, sitting between the rows as the rain pummelled the ground around her, turning her garden to mud.

"Winny!"

She looked up at him, surprised. She'd been thinking of Mary and hadn't noticed the storm.

Stepping carefully around the young plants, Jack crouched in front of her and slid a finger across her brow, clearing the wet hair from her eyes. His own was straight and dripping, loosened from his Brylcreem. He looked younger, and she preferred it that way. His skin bore proof of his years, but when his hair was messy and unkempt, she saw that fearless boy from the streets.

"Hey there."

She couldn't think of a thing to say.

"You're all right, Irish," he said, then he scooped her up in his arms and carried her toward the house. She clung to his neck, wet cheek against his wet shirt, safe again.

thirty-eight
JACK

❧

— 1952 —

Jack climbed out of the car and was instantly engulfed in the sticky September heat. He glared at the black stain on the driveway that reminded him the old car was leaking oil. He'd have to order a new set of piston rings and try to find time between customers to fix the engine. Not a lot of work, just time, and there never seemed to be enough of that these days. As he headed toward the door, he heard the lawn mower in the backyard, and he was glad that Billy was finally cutting the grass. He looked out over the front lawn and frowned at a strip the boy had missed, the wispy blades standing a full two inches over the rest.

"Daddy!" Susan called, running out the front door, her wild hair in a cloud.

"There's my girl," he said, lifting her warm little body and hugging her against his chest. She was a beam of sunshine, just like her mother. How had he managed to be a part of creating such a beautiful human being?

"How was school today?"

"It was lots of fun. We're doing a play!"

"Oh really? What's it about?" he asked as he walked into the house, Susan still wrapped around him. His annoyance was left in the yard; his little girl could easily clear his mind of every storm cloud.

"I don't know yet, but Miss Grantham says she'll tell us tomorrow."

"You're getting too grown up, Susan." He put her down and gave Winny a kiss. "Something smells real good in here, and I don't just mean dinner."

"Jack!" Winny laughed. "What a flirt you are."

Behind them, the front door opened then slammed shut, and Billy strode in. His hair was plastered to his face by sweat, and his shirt stuck to his narrow chest. He was a strong boy, but he was only fifteen. He had an adolescent, sort of stretched-out look to him. He'd grow into it, Jack could see. He'd been there himself.

"You missed a whole strip of lawn out there, Billy."

Billy sighed and jogged up the stairs. "But I did the rest of it."

Jack shot Winny a look. More and more he was hearing a belligerent tone from the boy, and he didn't like it. "Get down here, young man."

Billy reappeared, looking nonplussed.

"You did the *rest* of it? You think that's good enough?" Jack pointed to the door. "Get out there and do the job right."

"Dad, it's fine like that. No one will notice, and I'll cut it next time. I'm really hot right now."

"You don't know what being really hot is."

Billy rolled his eyes. "Tell me, Dad. When were you this hot?"

The warm, dank water from Warren's well returned to his mind, and he saw Quinn again, bent over a shovel and hacking at the dry earth. That day made today feel like winter, he thought. But the story of Warren's farm was one that he'd never tell his children. He'd only ever told Winny, and neither of them talked about those days anymore.

"Little place called Sicily," he said. "You'll have heard of it if you've studied your history and geography."

"I've heard of it. Must be nice to have lived by the sea."

Jack clenched his jaw. He'd talked about the war before, and he knew Billy didn't want to hear about it. "Go on. Finish the job."

"Fine." Billy stomped past him and out the door, slamming it behind him.

"He's going to break that door one day," Winny muttered.

"Why do you let him get away with it? You're here with him. Make him take responsibility for what he's doing."

"Don't start with me again, Jack. And don't tell me what to do with our children." She sighed. "Go wash up. Dinner's almost ready."

He headed into the bedroom, and in the instant he shut the door behind him, he realized he'd done exactly what Billy had done. He should apologize to Winny, admit that he shouldn't have acted that way. Really, he shouldn't have gone out for a drink with Joey, either. Every time he went out with that guy he ended up frustrated. He was tired. He was hungry. And he owned the doors, dammit. He could slam them if he wanted.

Through the wall, he heard Winny reassuring their daughter. "Daddy's just tired, sweetie. Don't worry about a thing."

When the bitter feelings had washed over Jack before, he'd been able to control them enough that they never completely took over. But these days, he felt himself increasingly overpowered by an angry sense of helplessness. Lately it took something as insignificant as accidentally cutting a finger at work to set him off. Or Billy missing a one-inch-wide strip of grass. After that, everything around him became a cause to lash out. Every time he told himself to snap out of it, he couldn't find the strength to do it. He felt strung tight, his chest burning, his jaw clenched until he started waking in the morning with cramps in his face. Everything loosened for a little while with the help of whisky, but when that wore off, things were even worse than before.

Dinner was subdued. Everyone was reacting to his mood. He sensed it, but he wished they'd just talk about whatever they'd done that day and leave him out of it.

"Billy got an A on his grade ten math test," Winny said, trying to ease the tension.

"That right?" Jack nodded. He'd never been much good at arithmetic unless he could apply it to something real. "Hard works pays off. Good for you, son."

"I'm gonna try out for the football team."

Jack liked that, thinking of Billy as being part of a team, making friends while learning skills. The tension in his chest eased a little. "I bet you'll do well. You're looking stronger every day."

Billy's mouth twitched with pleasure. "Thanks, Dad."

Jack cut the chicken breast on his plate and took a bite. "And thanks for looking after the yard. It looks good."

The family's relief was palpable, and he burned with shame. This wasn't the man he wanted to be. It wasn't just Billy; he was pushing Winny away as well. Since they'd moved here, Winny was always trying to make an effort with their neighbours, but the few dinner parties she'd thrown had seen him sitting quietly to the side, unable to stop judging these people, with their happy lives and easy pasts. He didn't care about the church's potluck supper. He didn't care about their children or relatives or cars or anything. He didn't want them around, and he didn't want to be there either.

After one such dinner, Winny followed him into their bedroom and leaned against the door, her arms crossed.

"I'll thank you not to embarrass me in front of my friends."

"I didn't do anything."

"You're right. You didn't. You didn't talk, you didn't laugh, and you looked hard-pressed to pass the potatoes."

"They're not my friends."

She sighed. "But they could be, Jack. There's no reason for them not to be. Or anyone else in the neighbourhood either. They're nice folks, a lot like us."

"They're not like us."

"They are," she insisted. "And I like them. I want to invite them over again, and I want to accept their invitation for us to go to their house."

"Go ahead," he said sullenly.

After a moment, she sat beside him on the bed, studying him. "What's happening to you?"

"Nothing."

"Jack, this isn't you. I mean, we all get a little blue, but this is worse. I rarely see you smile anymore."

Little Susan popped into his mind. "I still smile." But Winny was right, and he was sorry.

She left the room, and a sickening thought hardened in his stomach. What if she was nearing the end of her patience with him? What if she did the unthinkable and left him? Without Winny, his life would be cold and dark with no hope of light.

The next day he came home with a bouquet of flowers and a bottle of wine, and they sat in the yard together and watched the sun set while Billy tried to teach Susan how to catch a ball. It was the best night he could remember in a long time, and he watched Winny bloom again every time he laughed. He swore to remember how easy it had been for him to create that feeling for all of them. He wanted to do it again whenever he felt the gloom coming for him.

A few nights later, he surprised the family with a television set, then Billy approached him about getting a job at the garage where Jack worked after he finished high school.

"You want to be a mechanic like your old man?"

"Yeah. I think so."

But Billy had Mary's dark, brooding side, and Jack had his own deep resentment. The truces were hard for both of them to keep.

thirty-nine
WINNY

Winny was sitting on the sofa with her head in her hands when Jack came home on the evening of Billy's eighteenth birthday. The sound of the door closing behind him sent nervous butterflies through her chest. She was so tired of feeling unhappy, of walking on eggshells whenever he was around. It was too much like living at Mistress Adams's farm, when she'd had to look over her shoulder all the time.

She had originally planned not to say anything tonight. Not about how she was feeling. A birthday was supposed to be fun, and she wanted to make Billy feel special. She'd thought it might even be a night for mending fences between Jack and Billy. But after this afternoon, she couldn't just pretend everything was all right.

Jack knelt beside her chair, regarding her closely. "Are you crying? What's the matter, Winny?"

"I don't know." She lifted her head, wiped the tears off her face. "What's the matter with *you*?"

He pulled back a little. "Nothing's wrong with me. I've been working all day. You don't see me sitting around, crying."

"No, no, you don't get to say that. I don't see you having any emotions at all other than anger. I used to know you so well, but I have no idea what you're thinking anymore." She studied him. "I know you're mad about something, but you won't tell me, and—" She pressed her hand against her chest. "I remember this feeling."

"What feeling?"

"Like I'm all alone."

He stood and went to the sideboard, poured himself a glass of whisky. It was his regular routine these days. "What are you talking about? You have the children. You have me."

"No, I don't," she said. "Susan is all I have. You won't talk to me, and Billy looked like he'd be happy to murder me when he got home today."

Anger burned in Jack's cheeks. "Where's that boy? I'll teach him—"

"Stop it, Jack. Just stop." He was missing the point. Again. She reached for his hand. "The two of you fight too much these days, and I can't stand it. I don't understand. We have a beautiful life. Why are you tearing it apart? What's happening?"

She saw concern flash in his eyes, and her fingertips went to his warm, stubbled cheek. "Come back to me, Jack," she whispered, a tear rolling down her face. "I need you."

"I don't know how," he admitted quietly. "I love you, Winny. I never meant to hurt you. I will try harder." He wiped her tear away with his thumb. "I really will try."

She paused then set her mouth tight. "I hope so, but the thing is, I can't wait. I need you to start trying tonight. I've . . . I've never seen Billy this way. He says he has something to talk about with us after supper, and that's all he said. He wouldn't even look at me."

As they sat down at the table for their meal, Billy was like a cold, silent boulder. Jack did his best, asking him about his day, about his interests, about the news, but Billy refused to engage. Winny and Susan fluttered around the table and the kitchen, serving roast chicken and potatoes, Billy's favourite. When it was time to light the candles for the cake, Winny's fingers trembled, but she put on a smile and came back to the dining room, singing.

"Happy birthday to you! Happy birthday to you!" Susan and Jack joined in. "Happy birthday, dear Billy. Happy birthday to you!"

Billy's scowl softened briefly, and Winny tried desperately to make everything all right with extra hugs and kisses. Susan followed her, bouncing to her brother's side and presenting him with a picture she'd drawn that day. Billy leaned down and hugged Susan tight.

"Susan, you are the one good thing in this world. I love you so much," he said. "And guess what? I brought you something."

"It's not my birthday," Susan objected, but delight danced in her eyes.

"No, but you are very special, and you deserve it. I put it on your bed, and I'm wondering if you could go play with it in there for a little while. I need to talk to Mum and Dad for a few minutes."

Winny's stomach dropped, and Susan frowned. "Grown-up talk?"

"That's right."

She tilted her head. "I guess you're a grown-up now. But you have to blow out the candles first."

Billy would do anything for his sister, Winny thought, watching him blow out the little flames. Susan giggled, satisfied, then she gave him another hug before skipping off to her room. When she was gone, Billy reached into his pocket and pulled out an envelope.

"I have two things to discuss tonight," he said, sounding much older than eighteen. "First, I am leaving. Now that I'm eighteen, I'm joining the army."

Winny felt her chest tighten. *No.*

Jack's expression was unreadable, but his jaw was clenched.

Billy faced Jack. "You fought for our country, and if the time comes, so will I. I leave in the morning. That's all I have to say about that. Now, in order to join the military, I needed to provide identification, obviously.

That meant I had to produce a birth certificate." He slid a piece of paper out of the envelope. "That's the second thing I want to discuss."

There on the table were his adoption papers. Winny glanced at Jack, who had turned a pale shade of green.

"Who are you people?" Billy asked, matter-of-fact. "You're not my parents."

Winny clamped her mouth shut, feeling like she might be sick. She had tried everything she could think of to prevent this moment from ever happening.

Jack cleared his throat. "All right, Billy. I am your mother's brother," he said evenly. "This is your mother's best friend."

Billy folded his arms. "And where is my mother?"

I'm right here, Winny wanted to say. Jack opened his mouth to respond, but she laid a hand on his forearm and braced herself. It was her turn. "She died just after you were born, Billy. She asked me to find you and raise you as my own. I found you at an orphanage and adopted you when you were a year and a half old."

"Why is Uncle Jeffrey's name on this paper?"

"Back then I wasn't married, and we thought it would be easier for me to adopt you if I was. Uncle Jeffrey stepped in to help. That was before he and Charlotte were even dating."

Billy turned to Jack. "Where were you all this time?"

Jack hesitated, and she knew what he was thinking. Telling Billy he was adopted was one thing. Telling him they'd been Home Children was an entirely different thing.

"That's complicated, but basically I was in the army. All this happened just before the war started."

"So my mother is dead. Who is my father?"

Winny was fighting a losing battle against her tears, and they threatened to overflow. "I don't know. I don't know. I'm so sorry, Billy. I'm sorry I didn't tell you. It's my fault. I thought—"

Billy slammed the table with his hand, sending a jolt through Winny. "You *didn't* think, did you?"

"Listen, kid." Jack held a hand toward Winny. "*This* is your mother. Before my sister died, she begged her to find you. This incredible woman turned her world upside down so she could keep you, and after that she pretty much dedicated every minute of her life to you. Your father, from what I know, was a son of a bitch, and we hope he's dead. But we've given you a great life. You never suffered a day in your life, and you have no idea what that's like."

"So tell me about it."

"No," Winny said, blinking away her tears. "You do not need to know about our past lives. All that matters is we made sure yours was better than ours."

Billy pushed his chair back under the table. "You took great care of me, but you lied to me every single day of my life."

"We never lied!" she cried, jumping to her feet. "We did what we thought was best for you."

"Which was to lie."

"Sit down, Billy," Jack said, rising. "We're not done here."

"No? Why not? You want to finally fill me in on the details of who you really are?"

Winny could see Jack wavering. "Jack."

He closed his eyes briefly, but didn't speak.

"What happened to us makes no difference about who you are, Billy," Winny said. "You're our son, and we love you. We always will."

"That's not enough. Don't you understand? When they asked me for my identification papers, and I realized I had none, I felt like I didn't even exist. You have no idea what it's like not to know who you are."

If he only knew how wrong he was. If he only understood how much he was ripping her apart by saying things like that.

"I know you're mad right now, but someday you'll understand we did it for you. We did it all for you."

Billy took a step away from the table. "I'm not waiting for tomorrow morning. I'm leaving tonight."

"What?" she cried, following him to the base of the stairs. "No! Billy!"

He turned his back and marched upstairs.

"Please, Billy," she called after him, her knees starting to buckle. "Please don't go."

Jack put his arm around her, and she held on to him, hearing the fast thump of his heartbeat against her ear. Moments later, Billy returned, his bag over his shoulder.

"Well. That's it, then. I'm going." His voice caught and he cleared his throat. "I don't want you to think I don't appreciate everything you did for me. But you always taught me not to lie. You said I should never keep secrets from the people I loved." He bit his lower lip so hard his teeth left a white line. "And I just don't know how I could live here any longer, knowing you don't care enough about me to tell me the simple truth of where I came from."

"Billy?" Susan stood at the bottom of the stairs, pale as a ghost.

Billy reached her in three strides and lifted her against him. "I'm sorry, Susan. I'm so sorry, but I have to go."

"But where?"

"I'm going far away. But I promise to write to you."

"Don't go!" She looked at Winny, anguish in her eyes. "Mummy? What's happening?"

"I can't stay here any longer," Billy said, setting her on her feet. "I love you, baby sister. Never forget that."

He turned again, leaving her alone to weep. Then he walked past Winny and Jack, strode out the door, and disappeared into the night.

PART
— *five* —

forty
WINNY

❦

— Present Day —

Silence hangs over the kitchen, then Jamie speaks. "He never came back, did he?"

"No. I haven't seen Billy in sixty-three years." My eyes well up at this realization. "He's been out of my life much longer than he was in it."

Chrissie puts her arm around me. "Oh, Gran. It wasn't your fault."

But she's wrong, and I close my arthritic fingers into fists. "Wasn't it? Billy left because of all the secrets. For years, I've asked myself why I kept everything from him. Was I sparing him the knowledge that his true mother was dead, or had I feared he might leave me if he knew? If I had told him the truth, then what?"

Chrissie sniffs. "Gran, I kind of understand why Billy was so upset. I know it might be a bit harsh of me to mention right now, but he wasn't the only one who was kept in the dark for so many years."

"Mom!" Jamie exclaims. "It's not Gran's fault."

"But why did we have to wait so long to hear this story?" Chrissie asks tentatively. "I never even knew I had an uncle until all this. I have to admit that it hurts, finding out this way."

"I'm sorry, sweetheart. I never meant to hurt you or anyone else."

"I know you didn't. And I'm sorry to mention it. It's just that I've been thinking a lot about Mom lately, and I wonder what she would have said if she'd known all this. It would have been so nice to talk about all this as a family. To learn about you and Pop and all of our pasts when she was still here." She lets out a long breath, sounding sad. "I understand why you wanted to protect us, but I'm sorry you felt like you couldn't share it with us. We love you, and we would have wanted to help you however we could."

I look down. "We were ashamed of who we were. We didn't want the people we loved to see us as we'd been before. If we kept all that history to ourselves, we could just be who we wanted to be. It was easier to forget all the bad and skip ahead to the good, telling everyone a vague story about moving from Ireland as a child, becoming a nurse, marrying the man I loved, and having a beautiful daughter. If a story is dull, no one will ask questions, and that was perfect for me, because I didn't want to answer any."

"Gran," Chrissie says, and I look up. "You had nothing to be ashamed of."

My eyes fill with tears and I blink them away. "After all these years, I can finally see that."

Chrissie wipes her face, and Jamie hands us tissues.

"You know people get therapy for this stuff nowadays, right?" Chrissie says, blowing her nose.

"I'm a little old for therapy, don't you think?"

My granddaughter is picking at her nails just like I did. "I went for therapy."

"Did you? Did it work?"

"I suppose it did."

It's my turn to reach for her. "Chrissie, I'm sorry."

She shakes her head. "You shouldn't have to apologize after all you survived. I just wish things had been different. I wish Mom was here." She looks across the room at Jamie. "At least we know now."

"What happened to Billy?" Jamie asks, his voice low.

I let out a long breath. "I don't know. When we never heard from him, we assumed he'd eventually gone to Vietnam and died there. There were no official Canadian troops there, so he would have had to register with the American army, like a lot of the Canadian men did. I remember writing to the U.S. Government, demanding they let his grieving parents know where his body was, but they never did. The world is a big, ugly, mud-covered place, and I imagine there are so many unnamed corpses rotting under the soil—in other countries as well as here in Canada— that no one will ever know who they all are."

I can tell from Jamie's expression that my answer is not good enough. He wants to know more about his great-uncle. How I wish he could have met him.

"What happened after he left your house that night?"

"Jack went after him the next morning. He went to the Veterans' Centre and demanded information, but they knew nothing. Or they refused to tell him. Either way, we never heard another word about him." I remember the sorrow in Jack's eyes when he'd come home that day.

How ironic that, as a child, I had spent many years hoping never to be forgotten, trying to find my lost friends. My son appeared to have forgotten all about us, and he had never wanted to be found.

"Jack was never quite the same after Billy left, but neither was I. Suddenly a big part of us was gone, and we mourned his loss. He left because of us, and it took a toll."

Chrissie sets her chin in her hand. "The stories about Jack from when Billy was a teenager don't sound anything like the Pop I knew. I remember him as being a quiet but gentle man. When Jamie was born, he couldn't keep his eyes off him."

I nod. "Nowadays, I am fairly sure Jack would have been diagnosed with PTSD. He saw and suffered so much—working under Master Warren, riding the rails, serving during the war, then losing Cecil right in front of him—and he didn't know how to handle all that. None of us did. Drinking helped dull the noise, but it made him a worse husband and an angry father. The drinking stopped the day Billy left. It was like the door slamming behind Billy jolted Jack back to real life, and he fought his demons so he could come back to Susan and me. In his own way, he was happy," I say fondly, thinking of his smile. "And he lived over eighty years, which I imagine would have been cut much shorter had he never left the streets of London."

"It must have been hard for Grandma Susan to lose her big brother so early," Jamie says.

"It was. It was hard for all of us. But maybe because she was so young, she bounced back more easily than we did. She asked after him for a couple of years, less and less as time passed, then she stopped."

Chrissie and Jamie sit in silence, stunned by the end of the story.

Then Jamie says, "I wonder how things would have turned out if Mary had lived."

I manage a smile. "I wonder that every day."

———

The next afternoon, when Jamie is still at school, Chrissie sets a plate of tea and cookies before me. It's always tea and cookies, isn't it? The universal medicine for pain of the heart. She needs to talk about something. I can tell, because she's been scratching at her nails since yesterday.

"I want to talk about Mom," she says, staring at her tea. "Hearing all your stories and finding out where Mom came from has me missing her even more. It kind of breaks my heart to think of her never knowing all this about her own past. She loved you and Pop very much, and she never would have thought less of you."

"I know. She was the light of our lives. I'm sorry I never told her."

"She never even told me about Uncle Billy. She kept your secret for you."

"I suppose it was just one more sad story that didn't need telling. I guess she was a lot like me that way."

Chrissie shifts in her chair. "I think she knew it was important to you. But it must have been very hard, keeping a secret that long."

I take a sip. "It becomes a part of you, I suppose. It did with me."

"Mom had another secret," she says slowly. "I just found out about it last night."

I feel a twinge of apprehension. "Oh?"

"You know that I've been going through Mom's things lately. It's been hard, but I needed to remember a lot. It's one of those steps of grief they talk about. Anyway, after you'd gone to bed last night, I went into the basement to go through more of her boxes." She hesitates. "I think I found something that you'd like to see."

She disappears for a moment then returns with her hands overflowing with neat stacks of envelopes. The little piles are held together with elastic bands, but she's holding them so I can't see what is written on them.

"Don't keep me in suspense," I say. "I'm far too old for that."

She puts the first bundle before me and removes the elastic band. The paper on the top envelope is translucent from age, but I'm still able to see the postmark, dated 1955. It's addressed to Susan. The return address says the letter is from Billy Miller, 25th Canadian Infantry Brigade.

"Oh," I murmur, and my fingers scramble to open the envelope. Chrissie reaches across, helping me when my twisted fingers cannot manage.

Dear Susan,

I promised I would write to you, didn't I? Don't be worried about me. I am having a great time out here. We've been spending most of our time training. They say we're going to ship off soon . . .

"Billy," I sigh.

Halfway down the letter he writes,

I need you to make me a promise. I want to keep writing to you, but you must promise not to tell Mom and Dad. They can't know where I am. Can you keep this secret? If they find out, I will have to stop writing to you. I sure hope you don't, because I miss you already. I want to hear all about your life! How's grade 6?

Poor, poor Susan. I know what it is to be sworn to secrecy and what it demands of you. What a tangled web of secrets to be caught up in.

I reach for the second letter, but Chrissie covers my hand with her own.

"Gran," she says. "Billy did go to Vietnam, but he didn't die there." She spreads the bundles in front of us and her eyes hold mine. "These letters only stopped in 2016, after Mom died."

My mind whirls. What does this mean?

"I haven't read all the letters, Gran, just the first few. It's not really my place—though with your permission, I would love to." She squeezes my hand. "But because of his return address, I know where he was two years ago."

Two years ago.

"If he's still alive, I can find him for you," she whispers.

A tear rolls down my cheek. "Would you please, Chrissie?"

She nods. "Wait here, Gran."

I lose track of time, listening to her voice through the wall, and I wonder if this can be real. Billy's been gone so long. Where has he been? What has he been doing for all these years? How old would he be now, our little Billy? I do the math in my head, my fingers drawing in the air. He would be eighty-one. Old and grey. I've missed so much.

Chrissie comes back in, her cheeks flushed. "I found him, Gran." She sits down, watching me cautiously, as if I'll keel over from a heart attack. I fear she might be right.

"He lives right here in Toronto. I spoke with his son. If you're up for it, he's bringing him over tomorrow morning at ten."

———

The next morning I put on the prettiest dress I own, and Chrissie helps me with my hair. Then there is nothing else to do but wait, and I sit in my armchair by the window.

"You okay, Gran?" Jamie keeps asking.

"What time is it?"

"Nine thirty."

"Ask me again in a half hour," I tell him, then I look at Chrissie. "If he comes, that is."

"Oh, he's coming," she says, beaming. "And I can't wait to meet him."

When the doorbell rings, I am a bundle of nerves. Every inch of me is tingling. Chrissie leaps to her feet but Jamie stays with me and holds my hand. I give it a squeeze.

"You wanna get up?"

I nod. He puts a strong young arm under my elbow and helps me to my feet.

And then I am standing in front of Billy.

"Mum," he says.

I can't speak, I'm shaking so hard. Tears fall off my face.

He stares at me, and I see he is afraid.

"Billy."

"I was a fool," he says, wrapping his arms around me. My fingers hook into the back of his sweater, and I never want to let go. His back jerks slightly, and I know I am not the only one crying. "Such a god-damned fool. I should have come back to you. I should have told Dad how sorry I was. You didn't deserve all those things I said. I never should have left you. I never stopped loving you, Mum. Never stopped missing you."

I loosen my grip and reach up to touch his wet cheek. He is a good foot taller than I am—of course I have done a good amount of shrinking over the past sixty-odd years—and his hair is a dignified grey. But his eyes are the same. They are no longer cushioned by a child's soft, healthy skin, but I know those vivid blue eyes—Mary's eyes, Jack's eyes.

"We thought you were killed in Vietnam."

"I'd hoped you would. I . . . I kind of lost my mind after the war, and when I found it again, I couldn't face what I'd done to you and Dad. I thought it would be easier if you just forgot all about me."

"How could I ever forget you, Billy? You were my heart."

"Oh, Mum. I'm so sorry."

He hugs me again, and by now everyone in the room is sniffling. I hear them all around me.

"Who are all these people?" I ask, looking at the unfamiliar faces.

Billy clears his throat. "This is your family. My lovely wife, Shelly, and our sons and our daughter. We left the ten grandchildren at home."

"Ten grandchildren!" I exclaim.

"Pleased to meet you," Billy's first son says. He's got to be at least fifty. "I'm Jack."

I throw my arms open, feeling like my entire world just blossomed into a million flowers, and I embrace my new grandson, tears now mixing with laughter. Billy's two other sons and daughter step up for a hug, and I see the Miller in each of them.

Look at your boy, Mary. Look what we did, Jack.

———

The others depart after a short visit, but Billy doesn't leave my side all day. He returns the next morning, and his stories are like a balm to my soul. We're both desperate to make up for lost time, and I cannot get enough of the sound of his voice, the love in his eyes. Before he leaves for the day,

Chrissie makes sure Billy and I both understand how to do video calls on her computer.

After two eventful days, I go to bed early. All alone in my bedroom, I marvel at the quiet. My heart still sings for Billy, and I smile as I pull the duvet up to my chin, the soft familiarity of my mattress a far cry from the barn and the sheep. Ninety-seven years old. I never dreamed I might live this long. That's more than enough years for anyone.

Last week I was a childless widow. Now my family has more than doubled, and my son has forgiven me. He has freed me.

It's time. I close my eyes and take a long, deep breath. As I let it out, I see Jack's smile shining through the darkness, and I long for him with my entire being.

There's only one place where I've ever truly felt like I was home.

"I'm coming, Jack," I whisper, my lips curving into a smile just for him. "Wherever you are, I'm coming."

A Note to Readers

I first learned about the British Home Children a few years ago, when I stumbled upon an article about them online. The article said that starting in 1869, more than 120,000 destitute British children between the ages of three and eighteen were taken from England's streets, orphanages, and homes, and then shipped across the ocean to work in other countries, where it was thought they'd have a chance to lead better lives. This went on for nearly eighty years, until 1948. The more I read, the more intrigued I became. The idea of improving their young lives sounded plausible, but then I read on and discovered the alarming truth. Once the children arrived in their new country, there were few to no checks and balances in place. What could go wrong? Some of the children did benefit from the scheme. Those were informally adopted and their lives improved unquestionably. Most of the children, however, did not. The majority became indentured servants, working as farm labourers and domestic servants.

Here's what got to me: Where were all the children shipped? Here, to Canada. I was filled with questions. How could something so significant have happened here without it becoming general knowledge? Why had I never learned about this in school?

How could I *not* write their story?

My initial challenge was finding information. There were a few books and articles, but in general, no one seemed to be talking about it.

British immigrant children from Dr. Barnardo's Homes at landing stage, Saint John, New Brunswick. *(Isaac Erb / Library and Archives Canada / PA-041785)*

When I asked around, I was met with a lot of blank stares. Then I found the website for the Canadian British Home Children, and from there, multiple Facebook pages for British Home Children descendants. Most of the members on those pages have at least one British Home Child in their family tree, and everyone shares a common goal. They are there to learn more about their family history, but most of all they want to raise public awareness about some of Canada's earliest and youngest pioneers, the children who helped make our country what it is today.

As you'll remember from the novel, Winny's granddaughter Chrissie connects with other descendants in a Facebook group just like the real ones. If you believe you have a British Home Child in your family tree and are looking for information, I highly recommend you join one of these groups. Every member is an eager volunteer waiting for people to post questions, and I have seen descendants matched up with their ancestors within hours. It's incredible to watch. They're also passionate about adding the history of the British Home Children to the Canadian school curriculum—something that Winny's great-grandson, Jamie, alludes to in the book.

When I mentioned to the groups that I was writing a novel based on the British Home Children, I was welcomed with open arms and immediately invited to the Nova Scotia British Home Children Descendants' reunion to speak about my book. Here in Nova Scotia, most of the children had been brought over by Middlemore Homes, an organization based in Birmingham, England. In fact, more than fifty organizations were involved in the child migrant scheme. I focused on Dr. Barnardo's in this book because they brought in the largest number of children by far.

When I went to the reunion, I already had a sense of the larger history and a basic plotline in mind, but that wasn't enough. I needed to understand the children's experiences more deeply. I handed out surveys, mixing generalized questions about their ancestors with more personal ones, and within a week, I had more than two hundred responses. Many of them broke my heart. When I asked the descendants what kind of people their ancestors were (based on what they either remembered or had been told), the answers were mixed, but the adjective that kept showing up was *bitter*. Almost every one of them said their relative's greatest pain came from never knowing what had become of their families. Their

The carpentry shop at Dr. Barnardo's Boys' Home Stepney Causeway, in 1905. *(Mary Evans / Peter Higginbottom Collection)*

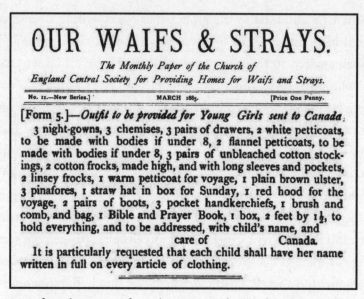

OUR WAIFS & STRAYS.

The Monthly Paper of the Church of England Central Society for Providing Homes for Waifs and Strays.

No. 11.—New Series.]   MARCH 1885.   [Price One Penny.

[Form 5.]—*Outfit to be provided for Young Girls sent to Canada*: 3 night-gowns, 3 chemises, 3 pairs of drawers, 2 white petticoats, to be made with bodies if under 8, 2 flannel petticoats, to be made with bodies if under 8, 3 pairs of unbleached cotton stockings, 2 cotton frocks, made high, and with long sleeves and pockets, 2 linsey frocks, 1 warm petticoat for voyage, 1 plain brown ulster, 3 pinafores, 1 straw hat in box for Sunday, 1 red hood for the voyage, 2 pairs of boots, 3 pocket handkerchiefs, 1 brush and comb, and bag, 1 Bible and Prayer Book, 1 box, 2 feet by 1½, to hold everything, and to be addressed, with child's name, and care of   Canada. It is particularly requested that each child shall have her name written in full on every article of clothing.

List of trunk contents for girls at Homes for Waifs and Strays from *Our Waifs and Strays*, March 1885.

responses shaped the core characters of Winny, Mary, Jack, Edward, Cecil, Quinn, and Charlotte.

Everything you read about in *The Forgotten Home Child* happened to the actual Home Children. The trunk Winny built and carried with her was real, as was the list of contents. Ill-fitting shoes like the ones she wore were not uncommon. Some children were forced to work in the snow in bare feet. The children's exhaustion and hunger were all well-documented. One descendant wrote to me about her grandmother falling asleep in a haystack in the barn and being whipped for it. The granddaughter said, "When I grew up, she lived with us and she would take my school books to learn. When I would go to retrieve them, she would jump up and state, 'I am not sleeping!'" The poignancy of that story, and the fact that decades later it still impacted that woman so deeply, wouldn't let me go, so I wove it into Winny's tale.

There were many other, even more difficult stories to accept. A large percentage of the girls, like Mary, suffered sexual abuse and rape. Many boys were beaten to death, like Quinn, and other children committed suicide. In 1905, fourteen-year-old Arnold Walsh arrived in Canada and was sent to work for a wealthy farmer in Quebec, where he lived in the barn. After seven months, he froze to death. Authorities discovered his undersized coffin buried in a pile of manure. A later autopsy showed he was undernourished, poorly clad, had severely frostbitten hands and feet, a fractured skull, and his body was full of pitchfork holes.

Those children who did survive their indenture were deeply affected by the experience, and many chose to keep their stories to themselves as Winny and Jack did. Many carried with them a lifetime of trauma, and that anguish reverberated as they married and started families of their own. One descendant described their father as loving, but said that he had a lifelong feeling of inferiority. Another said their grandfather was an angry man with no love to give. As I wrote about Winny and Jack in their later years, these were the emotions I kept in mind.

Despite being rejected by both England and Canada, more than thirty thousand British Home Boys fought in the World Wars. The incident with Jack, Edward, and Cecil in the Italian countryside in 1943 is lifted from the pages of history. The 1st Canadian Infantry Division and the 1st Canadian Armoured Brigade were both involved in Operation Husky, the seaborne invasion of the island of Sicily. Though the role of Canadians has been marginalized—some might even suggest forgotten—*The Canadian Encyclopedia* includes a sweet tribute to our boys:

> On 18 July, the Canadians met their heaviest resistance to date at Valguarnera. Fighting before the town and on adjacent ridges resulted in 145 casualties, including 40 killed. But the Germans lost 250 men captured and an estimated 180 to 240 killed or wounded. Field marshal Albert Kesselring reported that his men were fighting highly-trained mountain troops. "They are called 'Mountain Boys,'"

he said, "and probably belong to the 1st Canadian Division." German respect for the Canadian soldier was beginning.

But that respect was nonexistent on the farms where they'd been as children. Throughout the writing of the book, I couldn't stop wondering how anyone could possibly treat children that way. Master Warren, of course, was the epitome of the baseness of human nature, but what about the Renfrews and the Adamses? Perhaps the hardest part of writing this story was trying to put myself in their place and understand where their callousness and cruelty came from. To do that, I looked more deeply at the harsh and unforgiving life in rural Canada in the nineteenth and early twentieth centuries. While there is no excuse for what they did, I came to understand how it could have happened. Canadian farms were rural, isolated, and failing. The growing season was short, soil and water were unreliable, and the Great Depression was grinding the country into the dirt. Families already struggling with extreme poverty tried to have large families in order to work the farms, but in such terrible, remote conditions and without proper medical care, the child mortality rate was alarmingly high. So when these struggling farmers saw advertisements for British Home Children and realized they could pay so little to get help on their farms, they quickly sent in applications. They weren't thinking about children, they were thinking of workers. That's all they wanted, and they wanted them desperately. The sending agencies couldn't keep up with all the requests—at one point Dr. Barnardo said there were seven applications for each child.

The children, meanwhile, were told that going to Canada was the chance of a lifetime. As Winny's story illustrates, many of them came from poverty-stricken families that could no longer support their children. In the mid-1800s, the child mortality rate in the UK was 26 percent (compared to the 0.5 percent of today). Children started working very young, toiling in terribly dangerous jobs underground, in chimneys, in factories, as matchmakers, as beggars, and worse. The streets were crowded with small, filthy urchins, their faces drawn with hunger. The

An unidentified British Home Boy ploughing a field at Barnardo's Training Farm in Russell, Manitoba, 1900. The 8,960 acre (or fourteen square miles) industrial farm started in 1887 with accommodations for one hundred boys and closed twenty years later. *(Library and Archives Canada / PA-117285)*

workhouses were filled to bursting. Imagine *Oliver Twist, David Copperfield*, and *Annie*—but without the singing and dancing, as Jamie says. There was no future for them in England. Canada was supposed to be something completely different: a land of opportunity, offering adventure, income, and hope, not to mention clean air to breathe. The reality was quite the opposite for most. About 75 percent of the children who came here experienced abuse and neglect.

Which means that 25 percent did not, and that was also apparent in the survey responses I received. Plenty of descendants acknowledged that while many did suffer, their relatives viewed the emigration plan as an escape from a life that was not unlike those described in Dickens's novels. Because their ancestors came to Canada, their children, and *their* children, were given a better future. I chose to tell these happier stories through sweet Charlotte. However, despite the economic opportunities she enjoyed and the love she received from the Carpenters, her character highlights one of the great myths about this chapter of history: That these children were mostly orphans. In fact, only about 2 percent did not have parents. The majority were surrendered to shelters like Dr. Barnardo's Barkingside Home for Girls—often temporarily, while their parent(s) got back on their feet—or they were forcibly removed from families deemed unable to properly care for them. Just like with Charlotte, the children were deceived into believing they were unwanted or that their parents had died. Many of them never knew that their mothers and fathers were still very much alive and continued to search for their children for the rest of their lives.

While rare, reunions did happen, as they did in Charlotte's case. And while these children, now adults, at last had some of their most urgent questions answered, it was far too late. I've read heartbreaking newspaper stories of siblings reuniting after forty, fifty, even sixty years, all across Canada. Sisters Mary and Marjory Johnson were finally reunited after sixty years, but by then, Marjory had Alzheimer's and didn't remember Mary. Brothers Joe and Dennis Waterer met again after more than half a century of separation, only to discover they had lived ten minutes from each other for years. In Montreal, Daisy Bance and her younger brother Albert were reunited after eighty years when they were eighty-five and eighty-four, respectively.

Because of stories like these and the unflagging determination of the children's descendants, awareness is growing. The monument Chrissie shows to Winny and Jamie in Park Lawn Cemetery in Etobicoke was erected in 2017, and it is one of quite a few British Home Children monuments across the country. Lori Oschefski, CEO of the British Home Children Advocacy and Research Association (BHCARA), discovered the two mass graves of seventy-five British Home Children. After raising $16,000, Lori and other BHCARA volunteers identified the remains of every one of those children using archival records, death certificates, and cemetery plot cards. These children have been traced back to their

Lori Oschefski, CEO of the British Home Children Advocacy and Research Association, unveiling the monument for two mass graves of British Home Children discovered in Park Lawn Cemetery, in Etobicoke, just outside of Toronto. (*Judy Preston*)

families and connected to their family trees on Ancestry.ca. The following year, in 2018, September 28 was decreed National British Home Children Day in Canada. In 2019, more than two hundred major landmarks across Canada were voluntarily lit up for one special night to mark the 150th anniversary of the first shipload of children to arrive in Canada.

Thanks to the growing accessibility and popularity of genealogy, we now know that approximately 12 percent of Canada's population—more than *four million Canadians*—are descended from British Home Children. Whether they chose to come to Canada or not, those children were integral in building our nation, which has now become what it was supposed to be then: a vast, welcoming land of opportunity. Because children like Winny chose to keep what they considered to be their shameful past lives to themselves, their contributions and sacrifices have been forgotten. It is their ancestors who are shining light on those dark times and by doing so, showing their respect and love. Now it is up to the people of Canada to remember these children and make sure they are never forgotten again.

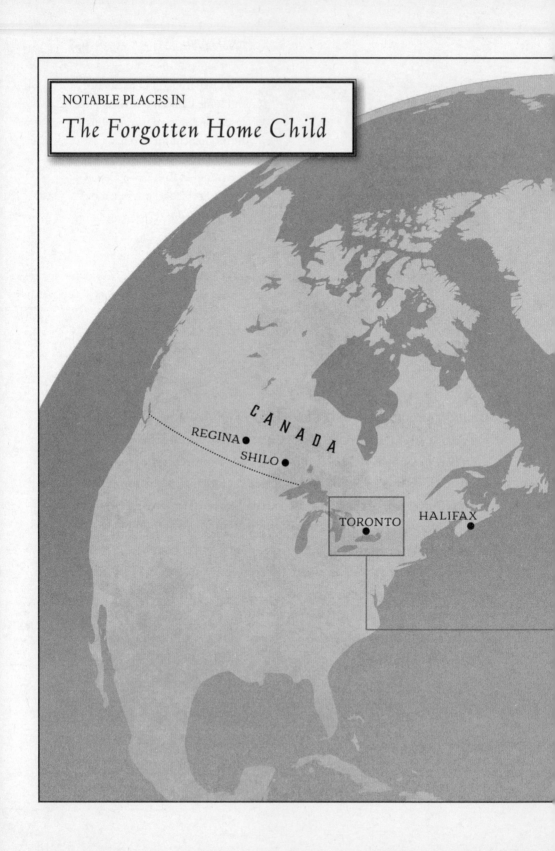

NOTABLE PLACES IN

The Forgotten Home Child

CANADA

REGINA

SHILO

TORONTO

HALIFAX

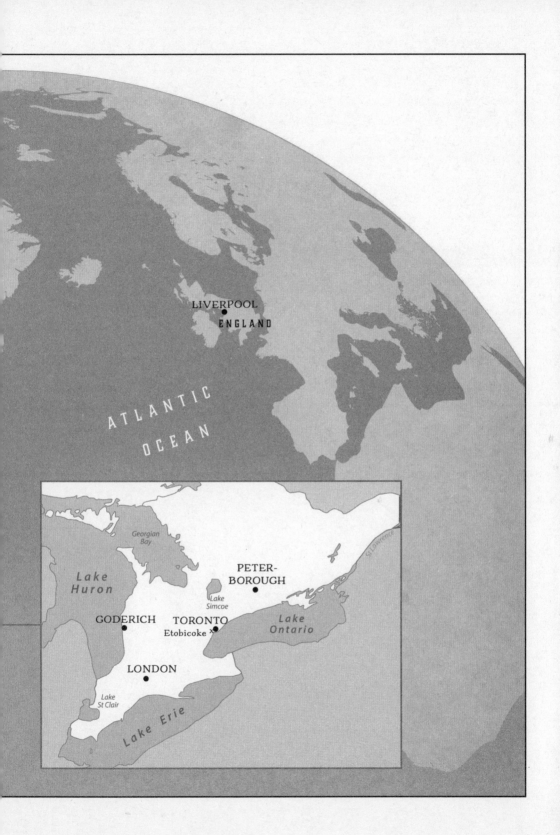

The Forgotten Home Child

GENEVIEVE GRAHAM

A READING GROUP GUIDE

TOPICS & QUESTIONS FOR DISCUSSION

1. Did you know who the British Home Children were before reading this book? How does this chapter in history shape your understanding of Canada as a British colony and as its own nation?

2. Winny's family moves from Ireland to England for a better life, but they experience tragedy, poverty, and hunger. Compare and contrast her early life with Mary and Jack's, and discuss the different events that drove them to the streets along with so many other children. What might this say about the economic reality of England at this time?

3. In the present-day storyline, Winny says that Dr. Barnardo "was a well-intentioned man with a good heart." After reading this book, what do you think of Dr. Barnardo and his Homes, and later, his plan to send children to Canada? Was there any merit to his actions? Where did his plan go wrong? And why?

4. Winny and her friends were told that Canada was a land of opportunity and that there were families waiting to take them in as their own, but in most cases, this was far from the truth. Why do you think there was so much hostility toward the Home Children? Do you think Canada is more welcoming to newcomers now? What prejudices still exist today?

5. Canada was a country struggling through the Great Depression and on the brink of another world war. Did knowing this historical backdrop change how you saw the actions of Mistress Adams and Mistress Renfrew? In what other ways does the author complicate our view of these families and even elicit our sympathies?

6. When Winny arrives on the Adams farm, she finds solace in picturing the faces of her friends. Discuss the importance of remembrance in the novel. What are some other key scenes where Winny or Jack remember their friends? How does this act evolve throughout the novel? For instance, when is it healing? And when is it too painful?

7. Mary and Winny are closer than friends; they see each other as sisters, and Winny goes on to adopt Mary's son, Billy, as her own. Consider the theme of family in the novel. What other close ties beyond blood relations do we see? What do these portrayals say about the value of family and belonging?

8. Both Mary and Quinn die as a result of their mistreatment. In the author's note to readers, she shares that Mary's and Quinn's experiences were not uncommon. How did learning this change your understanding of this history?

9. The Home Children make their own trunks at Barnardo's Homes to bring to Canada. Winny keeps hers for her entire life, but Jack abandons his. Beyond being luggage, what is the role of the trunks in the novel? What do they come to symbolize?

10. Why does Jack connect with the messages in *The Communist Manifesto*? How does this reference contextualize Jack's personal story within a larger socioeconomic lens?

11. Winny often says that the loneliness was the worst part of her experience. How does her past continue to isolate her from those she loves in her later years? How does seeing the British Home Children memorial in the Park Lawn Cemetery change that?

What might this tell us about the importance of historical commemoration?

12. When Winny goes to adopt Billy at the maternity home, the matron recommends not telling Billy that he is adopted. Discuss the portrayal of adoption by comparing and contrasting Charlotte's and Billy's experiences.

13. At their graduation from nursing school, Winny and Charlotte are called "the future of Canada." When war breaks out, Jack, Edward, and Cecil enlist to fight for Canada. How were the Home Children fundamental to Canada's growth and nationhood? How does their mistreatment complicate their sense of identity?

14. In what ways did the war change Jack's life when he returned to Canada? Consider the novel's references to communism. Do you think Jack achieved the equal and fair treatment that he sought while reading *The Communist Manifesto*? Why was Jack still unhappy?

15. Winny tells Jack that she feels like home when she's with him. Discuss the meaning of home in the novel. What does the word come to symbolize?

16. Winny and Jack carry the shame of being a Home Child for their entire life. How did their experiences affect their ability to love, trust, develop relationships, and lead normal lives? How did their trauma affect them differently? Discuss the lingering effects on their own family.

17. Why does Winny open up about her past after so long? How does sharing her experiences help Chrissie work through her own grief and bring Winny, Chrissie, and Jamie closer together?

18. Throughout the novel, many characters wish to know more about their family history, including Billy, Chrissie, and Jamie. How are their motivations the same? How are they different? Why is knowing their personal history so important to their sense of self and family?

19. Discuss the theme of forgiveness in the novel. In your opinion, do Mistress Adams and Mistress Renfrew do enough to atone for their actions? Should Winny's family forgive her for keeping secrets? Do you think it's possible to forgive a wrong even if it is never forgotten?

20. Consider the dual timeline structure of the novel. How does this reflect the experience of the Home Children?

21. Discuss the significance of the title *The Forgotten Home Child*.

ENHANCE YOUR BOOK CLUB

1. Have you ever looked up your own ancestry? Are you wondering if you are one of the 12 percent of Canadians descended from Home Children? Visit the British Home Children website here: **https://www.britishhomechildren.com/**.

   Or dig deeper in their Registry, where they have catalogued more than 70,000 of the children: **http://www.britishhomechildrenregistry.com**.

   And check out the Government of Canada immigration records: **https://www.bac-lac.gc.ca/eng/discover/immigration/immigration-records/home-children-1869-1930/immigration-records/Pages/search.aspx**.

2. Read the poem "Forgotten Children" by Walter Richard Williams. How does this novel overlap with and differ from the poem's summary of the Home Children's experiences? In what ways is this book also a testament to the lives of the Home Children?

3. Though the Home Children are not well-known, Guest Children, or "the lucky ones," were equally little known. Read more about them here: **https://ingeniumcanada.org/channel/articles/digital-archives-canadas-guest-children-during-second-world-war**.

   How did their situations differ from Home Children? Why do you think they were treated much better?

Acknowledgements

In order to write a story based on more than a hundred thousand -children's lives, I had to rely on a lot of people. It doesn't matter if those people were "online" contacts or if I met them in real life: every one of them had an effect on *The Forgotten Home Child*.

First of all, I would like to thank Ms. Lori Oschefski, genealogical researcher and tireless advocate whose work is recognized worldwide. In 2008, Lori discovered that her mother had been adopted. The news was shared somewhat reluctantly by her mother, and when Lori looked into the reason for the adoption, she realized her mother was, in fact, a Child Migrant of the Salvation Army, brought to Canada from Britain as part of the Child emigration scheme in 1924. From there, Lori found fifteen other British Home Children in her family tree. Moved by years of research, she founded the first national organization in Canada for the British Home Children in 2012: the British Home Children Advocacy and Research Association. Since then, the group's army of volunteers has registered more than seventy thousand British Home Children's names and histories on their extensive website. After filling her email and messenger inbox with my questions, I finally met Lori at the site of their award-winning "Breaking the Silence" exhibit in Black Creek Pioneer Village in Toronto, and she took the time to show me individual children's trunks, books, photographs, and letters. She was passionate, patient, and determined that I should be armed with everything I needed to tell this story.

She also directed me to the British Home Children Descendants' Facebook pages, of which there are a few both in Canada and in the UK. Those pages were full of more people wanting to help me. Since I live in Nova Scotia, I reached out to that group in particular, and they immediately invited me to their annual reunion. They showed me the posters made in a school competition intended to create awareness for British Home Children, and they walked me to the dedicated park bench they'd recently had installed. They even asked me to cut their ceremonial reunion cake! Thanks go to Chairperson Gail Bennett, Vice-Chair Catherine West, Secretary/Treasurer Betty Blaauwendraat, and Directors Carolyn MacIsaac, Charlene Ellis, Edith Selwyn-Smith, Jeanette McNutt, Cecil Verge, Bill Hill, and Susan Mosher. While I was there, I handed out copies of a survey I had put together in advance, wanting to ask deeper questions about their ancestors and bring more authenticity to my characters' lives. By the end of that reunion, I had about thirty completed surveys. I gave the group extras to hand out, and I shared the survey online, and within a week I had more than two hundred responses. In addition, other British Home Children Facebook groups contacted me, offering whatever help I needed. Without the generous input from all these generous people, I couldn't have truly understood as much as I did, and I'm grateful to every one of them.

From the beginning, my editor at Simon & Schuster Canada, Sarah St. Pierre—with whom I am extremely honoured to be working—saw something special in this manuscript, and she and Assistant Editor Siobhan Doody put their hearts into helping it take shape. I knew right away that I wanted to write a past and present timeline because it was critical to the message of the story, but I had never written anything like that before and was somewhat at a loss about how to handle it adeptly. Together, I think we achieved everything we'd set out to do and more. I couldn't be prouder of this book. I am truly grateful to the entire team at

Simon & Schuster Canada for supporting me along this journey. Thank you to President Kevin Hanson, VP Editorial Director Nita Pronovost, Marketing Associate Alexandra Boelsterli, Publicity Assistant Michelle Skelsey, Director of Sales Shara Alexa, Sales Rep Sherry Lee, Manager of Library and Special Sales Lorraine Kelly, Editorial Intern Aneeka Sihra, and everyone who believed in this story. Thanks also to Elizabeth Whitehead for designing the stunning cover.

To my agent, Jacques de Spoelberch, thank you for your tireless efforts on my behalf. I am so honoured to be represented by you.

My family is always, and will always be, my biggest support, and I hope they all know how much that means to me. Writing is a solitary sport, and to attain the clarity I need, I often withdraw. It may sometimes be slightly alarming for them to walk into a dark room, lit only by the pale glow of my computer screen, but I love that they know to leave the lights off for me.

If you've read my acknowledgements before, you know this is where I thank the love of my life, Dwayne, just for being him. For taking care of me in every way, for doing his best to fill in plot holes when I panic, for my nightly reminder that the day is done when he gently slides a glass of wine beside my elbow, for keeping me fed and balanced, for asking me how my day went, for just sitting with me and providing that perfect sense of quiet calm we all need and deserve. Back in 2007, he was the first person to tell me that if I wanted to be a writer, I should be a writer. Even when I didn't know if anyone would ever want to read what I wrote, he knew what his encouragement meant to me. So if you enjoy my books, you can thank him!

And if you are reading this, then thank you. Thank you for choosing to pick up this book and spend your valuable time reading it. I hope it provided you entertainment; I hope it taught you something that matters to you. I hope that when you close the back cover you wander off with a hunger for more. Because that's what happens to me. Know that when you write a review online or if you recommend my books to a friend, I am truly grateful. If you invite me to your book club either online or in person, I am thrilled. Personal notes, emails, and messages can and have made me cry because it's an amazing feeling to know I am touching people I've never met through these stories. Please keep those coming—and I promise to keep the books coming as well.

Also by
GENEVIEVE GRAHAM

National Bestsellers

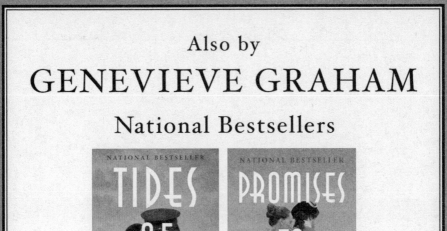

"Time and time again, Genevieve Graham
shows us just how fascinating our past is."

JENNIFER ROBSON,
bestselling author of *The Gown*

SIMON &
SCHUSTER